Human Rights

Pennsylvania Studies in Human Rights

Bert B. Lockwood, Jr., Series Editor

A complete list of books in the series is available from the publisher.

Human Rights

A Political and Cultural Critique

Makau Mutua

PENN

University of Pennsylvania Press

Philadelphia

10 9 8 7 6 5 4 3 2 1

Published by
University of Pennsylvania Press
Philadelphia, Pennsylvania 19104-4011

Library of Congress Cataloging-in-Publication Data

Mutua, Makau.
    Human rights : a political and cultural critique / Makau Mutua.
      p. cm.—(Pennsylvania studies in human rights)
    Includes bibliographical references and index.
    ISBN: 978-0-8122-2049-0
    1. Human rights. 2. Human rights—Africa. 3. Human rights—South Africa. I. Title.
II. Series.

JC571 .M95 2002
323—dc21   2001050750

For

Lumumba, Amani, and Mwalimu

To Whom the Future Belongs

Contents

Preface

I have always found human suffering unacceptable. But I did not name my struggles against deprivation, dehumanization, and oppression a fight for human rights. For me it was the injunction for persons and groups with a conscience. As human beings we are—in a manner of speaking—called on the one hand to resist human degradation in all its forms and manifestations. On the other hand, we are symbiotically required to fight to advance the frontiers of human dignity. The scope of human dignity has for me always been as broad as the human condition. It is not just about humans as political and economic beings. These dimensions are, of course, foundational and basic, but I have always believed that we are much more than the total sum of economic denominations and political calculations. Histories, cultures, and traditions constitute spiritual cosmologies for every people, and every individual who is a member of that people.

It is true that no culture is monolithic but that all are dynamic and internally discontinuous. Internal *desensus* is a hallmark of all cultures. But that truth does not diminish the distinctive nature of each individual culture or negate the fact that each culture represents the accumulated wisdom of a people and its individual members. Nor does it do away with the description of culture as an ethnographic fingerprint. What these truths evidence is the difficulty of making cross-cultural judgments about norms of social, political, economic, cultural, and spiritual behavior for individuals and societies. Attempts to construct universalist creeds and doctrines—or to present a particular creed or doctrine as universal—run the risk of destroying or decimating dissimilar universes. The claim of a universalist warrant is an extremely tricky proposition, if not altogether impossible. That is why attempts at creating an international consensus on what constitutes human dignity must be approached with nuance, open-mindedness, and the complexity that it deserves.

That is why I wrote this book. I wanted to explain why I believe that the human rights corpus should be treated as an experimental paradigm, a work in progress, and not a final inflexible truth. It is important that the human rights movement be fully exposed so that its underbelly can be critically examined. I know that many in the human rights movement mistakenly claim to have seen a glimpse of eternity, and think of the human rights corpus as a summit of human civilization, a sort of an end to human history. This view is so self-righteous and lacking in humility that it of necessity must invite probing critiques from scholars of all stripes.

I know that many movement activists and scholars will be disturbed by the book and some will even question why I would hold the views expressed in these pages. Many of these activists and scholars are my colleagues, acquaintances, and close friends. I have worked with them on many a human rights project. Whether it was on a rule of law project in Ethiopia, a human rights meeting or workshop in Brazil, France or Japan—or even in my work as co-founder and chair of the Nairobi-based Kenya Human Rights Commission—the road that we have traveled together has been long. Yet we must now diverge so that we can converge. I now ask them to join me in this dialogue about the re-thinking of the entire human rights project so that we can reconstruct it. If our—theirs and mine—commitment is to the construction of a higher human intelligence from which human dignity can better be defined and safeguarded, then we must engage these difficult questions and talk with each other across our bridges. We must seek to include each other in this conversation. Exclusion, name-calling, or stigmatizing will only be counterproductive.

But I also wrote the book for another reason. That reason is personal although it is also deeply political. I was born in a part of colonial Africa that the British had named Kenya. My people and society were in the throes of both destruction and reconstruction. The African pre-colonial universe was completely under attack, being directly dismantled and rejected—almost in entirety—by the colonial state and its attendant apparatuses. In its place, a new Eurocentric political, cultural, economic, and spiritual dispensation was being forced upon society. As a young African, I was being forced to abandon and reject the Africa of my ancestors and embrace the Europe I had never seen. That moment—of disconnecting me from my past—was so violent and profound that it is difficult to describe in any language. Just imagine what the rejection of my past meant. The colonial dispensation had created images of my past. Barbaric, primitive, tribal, savage, satanic, uncultured, uneducated. It was a past without a history.

I recall in particular one event that served as a metaphor for the entire colonial experience. My parents were converts to mission Catholicism. But my grandparents—maternal and paternal—had successfully rejected conversion. At my baptism as a Catholic, I was required to take a "Christian" name. The list the Irish priest gave me included Peter, Robert, Richard, James, and others which I now cannot recall. I asked him if I could just keep my African name, and failing that, whether I could take another African name. His response was unequivocal. I had to take a "Christian" name because my entry into the Church required it. I had to take a European name, which the Church presented as "Christian." Case closed. What I took from that experience was that I could not go to Jesus as an African. Jesus did not accept Africans. Period.

At least one more thing is important about this *de-naming* story. Note that neither I nor my parents had the opportunity to interrogate the claims of Christianity and its truthfulness as opposed to the African spirituality of my grandparents. There was a basic assumption that Christianity was *superior* to, and better than, any African spirituality. It was presented as a cultural package. What is interesting are the parallels between Christianity's violent conquest of Africa and the modern human rights crusade. The same methods are at work and similar cultural dispossessions are taking place, without dialogue or conversation. The official human corpus, which issues from European predicates, seeks to supplant all other traditions, while rejecting them. It claims to be the only genius of the good society. It is this view that I challenge in this book and call for the multi-culturalization of the human rights corpus.

I see myself as an insider-outsider. There are aspects of the official human rights corpus that I think are universal. Prohibitions against genocide, slavery, and other basic abominations violate humanity at the core. But beyond these obvious points of agreement, the ground becomes tricky. What typology of political society should the human rights corpus sanction, if any? What types of economic philosophies should the human rights corpus develop or endorse? Should it sanction free market capitalism, as it currently seems to do? Should famine and other dire economic deprivations be treated as an abomination equal in scale to genocide or slavery? What understanding of the human being in relationship to society should the corpus develop?

I am deeply vexed by all these issues. But I believe that the current human rights corpus has no answers to these questions. It does not have the tools to deal with these deeply embedded questions. That will only be possible, I believe, if we re-open debate on the entire normative scheme of the human rights corpus and reconstruct it from the ground up. The participation of all societies and cultural milieus must be required if the corpus is to claim genuine universality. It may be that agreement is only possible on a limited number of questions. If that is the case, so be it. This book will have served its purpose if it provokes us to think more openly about these questions.

Introduction

In 1998, amid much fanfare and pageantry, many important personalities and institutions, including numerous governments, celebrated the fiftieth anniversary of the Universal Declaration of Human Rights. That seminal document launched human rights internationally, an idea that has arguably given expression to one of the most important development of our times. But largely lost in those celebrations were the voices that problematize the idea of human rights and point to its difficulties from normative, institutional, and multicultural perspectives. Perhaps there should have been wrenching, soul-searching, and probing inquiries into the phenomenon known as the human rights movement. But it was not to be. Was it because the human rights movement is an unqualified good, or were critical voices muffled and silenced? What could have accounted for the universally near-total approval and unbridled joy that marked the moment of the UDHR milestone?

It is a virtual certainty that the human rights corpus, if fully implemented, would alter the fundamental character of any state, its cultures, and society. On that basis alone, without even judging its appropriateness, the doctrine of human rights bears close scrutiny. It is true that there are emergent debates and disagreements between scholars, policy-makers, and advocates about the character and purposes to which the human rights corpus should be put. Some of these debates focus on questions of normativity, the need for a cultural consensus and legitimacy, and the problems of effective and consistent enforcement. Others suggest a radical reformulation of human rights. It is these vexing problems that led me to write this book.

Since the human rights corpus has profound implications for all human societies, particularly those that are non-Western, there is a need to openly discuss the political agenda of the human rights movement. The movement's apoliticization obscures its true character and the cultural identity of the norms it seeks to universalize. While many cultures and peoples of all political and historical traditions around the world have accepted the idea of human rights, many have wanted to couple their embrace with a degree of originality. This ranges from marginal contributions, on the one hand, to radical reformulations on the other. Thinkers who are non-Western resist the idea that the official UN-sanctioned human rights movement is the "final" answer and should not be subject to attack or scrutiny. I reject this assertion of a final truth and will demonstrate in this book its limitations.

In the decade, my research and scholarship have opened huge vistas of doubt about blind faith in the officially constructed human rights movement. While my work has focused on the relationship between the state and the language of rights as an avenue for protecting human dignity, it questions the "official" formulations of the corpus and the purposes they serve. It is a view that constitutes a philosophy that seeks the expansion of the scope of human rights and pleads for alternative understandings of the human rights movement. There is a paucity of scholarship by non-Westerners like myself in this idiom, although there is a dire need to speak across cultures and identities in human rights. My work fits in this category and will hopefully serve the purpose of enriching dialogue in human rights. The outcome is a book that advances critical approaches to human rights.

This book presents a view of human rights that questions the assumptions of the major actors in the human rights movement. It attempts to make an explicit link between human rights norms and the fundamental characteristics of liberal democracy as practiced in the West, and to question the mythical elevation of the human rights corpus beyond politics and political ideology. It questions the deployment of human rights to advance or protect norms and practices that may be detrimental to societies in the Third World. In other words, the book presents a series of critical lenses and approaches through which human rights should be viewed.

The main authors of the human rights discourse have thus far been reluctant to be critical of the human rights movement. There are several reasons for this trepidation of critical analysis. First, I suspect that many of the movement's authors sincerely do not believe that an honest inquiry could pin the human rights movement down to a specific political structure or deconstruct it in a way that bares its biases and politics. The cold war, which pitted the capitalist West against the socialist and communist bloc, deeply perverted the philosophies of states toward human rights. The West purported to champion civil and political rights, whereas the Soviet bloc posed as the sole guarantors of economic, social, and cultural rights. In addition, it would have been an admission against interest in the context of the cold war, amid states only too eager to exploit cultural and political excuses to justify or continue repressive policies and practices, to engage in such critiques. Whatever the case, it now seems imperative that probing inquiries about the philosophical and political raison d'etre of the human rights regime can no longer be avoided; in fact, they must be encouraged and welcomed.

While I do not think that the human rights movement is a Western conspiracy to deepen its cultural stranglehold over the globe, I do believe that its abstraction and apoliticization obscure the political character of the norms it seeks to universalize. As I see it, that universe is at its core, and in many of its details, liberal and European. The continued reluctance to identify liberal democracy with human rights delays the reformation, reconstruction, and multiculturization of human rights. Defining those who seek to reopen or continue the debate about the cultural nature and the raw political purposes of the human rights regime as "outsiders" or even as "enemies" of the movement is the greatest obstacle to the movement to bring about true universalization.

Just over a half century after the Universal Declaration of Human Rights laid the foundation for the human rights movement, those ideas have been embraced by diverse peoples across the earth. That fact is undeniable. But it is only part of the story. Those same people who have embraced that corpus also seek to contribute to it, at some times by radically reformulating it, at others by tinkering at the margins. The human rights movement must not be closed to the idea of change or believe that it is the "final" answer. It is not. This belief, which is religious in the evangelical sense, invites "end of history" conclusions and leaves humanity stuck at the doors of liberalism, unable to go forward or imagine a postliberal society. It is an assertion of a final truth. It must be rejected.

From the perspective of this author, the human rights corpus as a philosophy that seeks the diffusion of liberalism and its primacy around the globe can ironically be seen as favorable to political and cultural homogenization and hostile to difference and diversity, the two variables that are at the heart of the vitality of the world today. Yet, strangely, many human rights instruments explicitly encourage diversity through the norm of equal protection, which Henry Steiner, for instance, sees as the cardinal human rights norm.[1] As he correctly notes:

> Other rights declared in basic human rights instruments complement the ideal of equal respect and confirm the value placed on diversity. Everyone has a right to adopt "a religion or belief of his choice" and has freedom "either individually or in community with others and in public or private" to manifest belief or religion in practice and teaching. Rights to "peaceful assembly" and "freedom of association with others," in each case qualified by typical grounds for limitation like public order or national security, further commit the human rights movement to the protection of people's ongoing capacity to form, develop, and preserve different types of groups.

The paradox of the corpus is that it seeks to foster diversity and difference but does so only under the rubric of Western political democracy. In other words, it says that diversity is good so long as it is exercised within the liberal paradigm, a construct that for the purposes of the corpus is not ne-gotiable. The doors of difference appear open while in reality they are shut. This inelasticity and cultural parochialism of the human rights cor-pus needs urgent revision so that the ideals of difference and diversity can realize their true meaning. The long-term interests of the human rights movement are not likely to be served by the pious and righteous advocacy of human rights norms as frozen and fixed principles whose content and cultural relevance is unquestionable.

Based on this premise, the human rights movement needs to alter its orientation, which has been an orientation of moral, political, and legal certitude. There needs to be a realization that the movement is young and that its youth gives it an experimental status, not a final truth. The major authors of human rights discourse seem to believe that all the most impor-tant human rights standards and norms have been set and that what re-mains of the project is elaboration and implementation. This attitude is at the heart of the push to prematurely cut off debate about the political and philosophical roots, nature, and relevance of the human rights corpus.

Debates about the universality of the corpus between the industrialized West and the South should not be viewed with alarm or as necessarily symptomatic of a lack of commitment to human rights by those in the Third World. Attempts to question the normative framework of human rights, their cultural relevance, and the need for a cross-cultural re-cre-ation of norms will not be silenced or wished away by universalists who are unwilling to engage in the debate. As Francis M. Deng and Abdullahi Ahmed An-Na'im argue in a volume exploring these issues, the debate is just beginning:

Whatever the reason for the controversy surrounding cross-cultural perspectives on human rights, the essays in this volume clearly demonstrate that the debate has just begun and that its parameters are still to be defined and its course is still to be charted. The central issue in this debate is whether looking at human rights from the various cultural perspectives that now coexist and interact in the world com-munity promotes or undermines international standards.[2]

There is little doubt that certain states and governments will hide be-hind the veil of culture to perpetuate practices that are harmful to their populations. That cynicism, however, must not be confused with genuine attempts to bequeath cross-cultural legitimacy to a universal human rights corpus. Deng and An-Na'im ask a series of biting questions that leave little doubt about the indispensability of cross-culturalism.[3] Richard Schwartz af-firms this point of view: he sees the necessity of a cross-fertilization of cul-tures if a universal human rights corpus is to emerge. According to him,

Every culture will have its distinctive ways of formulating and supporting human rights. Every society can learn from other societies more effective ways to implement human rights. While honoring the diversity of cultures, we can also build toward common principles that all can support. As agreement is reached on the substance, we may begin to trust international law to provide a salutary and acceptable safeguard to ensure that all people can count on a minimum standard of human rights.[4]

The failure of most universalists, particularly their most conventional thinkers and activists, to engage positively in this debate unnecessarily antagonizes Third World cultural pluralists and lends itself to legitimate charges of cultural imperialism. This is particularly the case if the human rights corpus is seen purely as a liberal project whose overriding goal, though not explicitly stated, is the imposition of Western-style liberal democracy, complete with its condiments. The forceful rejection of dialogue also leads to the inevitable conclusion that there is a hierarchy of cultures, an assumption that not only is detrimental to the human rights project but is also inconsistent with the human rights corpus' commitment to equality, diversity, and difference. Ultimately, the unrelenting universalist push seeks to destroy difference by creating the rationale for various forms of intervention and penetration of other cultures with the intent of transforming them into the liberal model. This view legitimizes intervention and leaves open only the mode of that intervention, that is, whether it is military, through sanctions systems, bilateral or multilateral, as a cultural package bound in one or another form of exchange, or through trade and aid.

What should not be at stake when conversations about human rights are held is the singular obsession with the universalization of one or another cultural model. Rather, the imagination of norms and political models whose experimental purpose is the reduction if not the elimination of conditions that foster human indignity, violence, poverty, and powerlessness ought to be the overriding objective of actors in this discourse. For that to be possible, and to resonate in different corners of the earth, societies at their grassroots have to participate in the construction of principles and structures that enhance the human dignity of all, big and small, male and female, believer and unbeliever, this race and that community. But those norms and structures must be grown at home, and must utilize the cultural tools familiar to the people at the grassroots. Even if they turn out to resemble the ideas and institutions of political democracy, or to borrow from it, they will belong to the people. What the human rights movement must not do is to close all doors, turn away other cultures, and impose itself in its current form and structure on the world. A postliberal society, however that will look, cannot be constructed by freezing liberalism in time.

The promise of human rights to the Third World is that problems of cruel conditions of life, state instability, and other social crises can be contained, if not substantially eliminated, through the rule of law, grants of individual rights, and a state based on constitutionalism. The Third World is asked to follow a particular script of history for this promise to mature. That script places hope for the future of the international community in liberal nationalism and democratic internal self-determination. The impression given is that a unitary international community is possible within this template if only the Third World follows suit by climbing up the civilizational ladder. It is the argument of this book, however, that this historical model, as now diffused through human rights, cannot respond to the needs of the Third World absent some radical rethinking and restructuring of the international order.

Today the presence of the United States—which has succeeded France and the United Kingdom as the major global cultural, military, and political power—is ubiquitous. This became especially true after the collapse of the Soviet Union and communism. There is virtually no conflict or issue of importance today in which the United States does not seek, and often play, the crucial role whether by omission or commission. From the conflicts in central Africa to the crises of the former Yugoslavia to the corridors of the United Nations, the United States is the single most important actor in the world today. In a sense the United States chief executive sits atop a global empire. It is an empire governed by the cultures, traditions, and norms of the European West. The European colonial powers of yesteryear have, as it were, passed the torch to the United States. The United States has renewed and revitalized the Age of Europe. The domination of the globe exercised by European powers for the last several centuries has been assumed by the United States. The U.S. is now the major determinant for "international peace and security" and the spokesperson for the "welfare" of humanity. Never before has one state wielded so much power and influence over so vast a population. A global policeman, the United States now plays the central "civilizing" role through the export of markets, culture, and human rights.

Increasingly, the human rights movement has come to openly be identified with the United States, whose chief executive now invokes human rights virtually every time he addresses a non-European nation.[5] In fact, former President William Jefferson Clinton's international speeches had come to resemble lectures and sermons, very much in the savior mode.[6] This is the wrong course. The human rights movement, and its "ally" the American state, must abandon the pathology of the savior mentality if there is going to be real hope in a genuine international discourse on rights. The relentless efforts to universalize an essentially European corpus of human rights through Western crusades cannot succeed. Nor will demonizing those who resist it. The critiques of the corpus from Africans, Asians, Muslims, Hindus, and a host of critical thinkers from around the world are the avenues through which human rights can be redeemed and truly universalized. This multiculturalization of the corpus could be attempted in a number of areas: balancing between individual and group rights, giving more substance to social and economic rights, relating rights to duties, and addressing the relationship between the corpus and economic systems. This book does not develop those substantive critiques. That calls for another project. Further work must done on these questions, and on the corrupting influences of the individualism of the human rights corpus, to chart out how such a vision affects or distorts non-European societies.

Ultimately, a new theory of internationalism and human rights, one that responds to diverse cultures, must confront the inequities of the international order. In this respect, human rights must break from the historical continuum expressed in the grand narrative of human rights that keeps intact the hierarchical relationships between European and non-European populations. Nathaniel Berman is right in his prognosis of what has to be done:

The contradictions between commitments to sovereign equality, stunning political and economic imbalances, and paternalistic humanitarianism cannot be definitively resolved logically, doctrinally, or institutionally; rather, they must be confronted in ongoing struggle in all legal, political, economic, and cultural arenas. Projections of a unitary international community, even in the guise of the inclusive U.N., or a unified civilizational consensus, even in the guise of human rights discourse, may be provisionally useful and important but cannot indefinitely defer the need to confront these contradictions.[7]

The approach in this book views the human rights text and its discourse as requiring the typology of state based on the ethos of constitutionalism and political democracy.[8] The logic of the human rights text is that political democracy is the only political system that can guarantee or realize the fundamental rights it encodes.[9] As Henry Steiner points out, the basic human rights texts, such as the International Covenant on Civil and Political Rights (ICCPR), "should be understood not as imposing a universal blueprint of the myriad details of democratic government but rather as creating a minimum framework for popular participation, individual security, and non-violent change."[10] Fair enough. The point then is that, if this were a game or sport, its essence would have been decided, leaving those who adopt it only the option of tweaking or revising the rules governing it without transforming its purpose. In other words, genuine universality is not possible if the core content of the human rights corpus is exclusively decided, leaving non-European cultures with only the possibility of making minor contributions at the margins and only in its form.

Using political democracy as one medium through which the human rights culture is conveyed, it is possible to capture the imperial project at work. First, the choice of a political ideology that is necessary for human rights is an exclusionary act. Thus cultures that fall outside that ideological box, no matter how large, immediately wear the label of the savage. To be redeemed from their culture and history, which may be thousands of years old, a people must then deny themselves or continue to churn out victims. The savior in this case becomes the norms of democratic government, however those are transmitted or imposed on the offending cultures. Institutions and other media—some like the United Nations purport to have a universalist warrant, while others like the United States Agency for International Development are the obvious instruments of a particular nation's foreign policy and its interests—are critical to the realization of the grand script of human rights explored in this book. It has, however, been my argument that the imposition of the current dogma of human rights on non-European societies flies in the face of conceptions of human dignity, and rejects the contributions of other cultures in efforts to create a universal corpus of human rights. Proponents of human rights should accept the limitations of working within this official script. Then they must reject it and seek a truly universal platform.

Stepping back from the current official human rights rhetoric would create a new basis for calculating human dignity and identifying ways and societal structures through which such dignity could be protected or enhanced. Such an approach would not assume ab initio that a particular cultural practice was offensive to human rights. It would respect cultural pluralism as a basis for finding common universality on some issues. With regard to the practice labeled female genital mutilation in the West, for instance, such an approach would first excavate the social meaning and purposes of the practice as well as its effects, and then investigate the conflicting positions over the practice in that society. Rather than being subjected to demonizing and finger-pointing, under the tutelage of outsiders and their local ilk, the contending positions would be carefully examined and compared to find ways of either modifying or discarding the practice without making its practitioners hateful of their culture and of themselves. The zealotry of the current rhetoric gives no room for such a considered intracultural, or intercultural, dialogue and introspection.

The purpose of this work is not to raise or validate the idea of an original, pure, or superior Third World society or culture. Nor is it to provide a normative blueprint for another human rights corpus, although that project must be pursued with urgency. It did not set out to provide a substantive critique of the Eurocentric human rights corpus, although doing so is necessary and must be part of making a complete case against the dominant Western human rights project. It is rather a plea for genuine cross-contamination of cultures to create a new multicultural human rights corpus. What is advocated here is the need for the human rights movement to rethink and reorient its hierarchized, binary view of the world in which the European West leads the way and the rest of the globe follows in a structure that resembles a child-parent relationship. Nor does the book mean to suggest that all human rights communities in the West believe and work to ratify that hierarchy. Human rights can play a big role in changing the unjust international order, and particularly the imbalances between the West and the Third World. But it will not do so unless it stops working within its rigid script. Ultimately, the quest must be one for the construction of a human rights movement that wins.

Chapter 1
Human Rights as a Metaphor

The Metaphor of Human Rights

The human rights movement is marked by a damning metaphor.[1] The grand narrative of human rights contains a subtext which depicts an epochal contest pitting savages, on the one hand, against victims and saviors, on the other.[2] The savages-victims-saviors (SVS)[3] construction is a three-dimensional compound metaphor in which each dimension is a metaphor in itself.[4] The main authors of the human rights discourse, including the United Nations, Western states, international nongovernmental organizations (INGOs),[5] and senior Western academics, constructed this three-dimensional prism. This rendering of the human rights corpus and its discourse is unidirectional and predictable, a black-and-white construction that pits good against evil.

This chapter elicits from the proponents of the human rights movement several admissions, some of them deeply unsettling. It asks that human rights advocates be more self-critical and come to terms with the troubling rhetoric and history that shape, in part, the human rights movement. At the same time, it not only addresses the biased and arrogant rhetoric and history of the human rights enterprise, but also grapples with the contradictions in the basic nobility and majesty that drive the human rights project—the drive from the unflinching belief that human beings and the political societies they construct can be governed by a higher morality.

This first section briefly introduces the three dimensions of the SVS metaphor and how the metaphor exposes the theoretical flaws of the current human rights corpus. The first dimension of the prism depicts a savage and evokes images of barbarism. The abominations of the savage are presented as so cruel and unimaginable as to represent their state as a negation of humanity. The human rights story presents the state as the classic savage, an ogre forever bent on the consumption of humans. Although savagery in human rights discourse connotes much more than the state, the state is depicted as the operational instrument of savagery. States become savage when they choke off and oust civil society.[6] The "good" state controls its demonic proclivities by cleansing itself with, and internalizing, human rights. The "evil" state, on the other hand, expresses itself through an illiberal, antidemocratic, or other authoritarian culture. The redemption or salvation of the state is solely dependent on its submission to human rights norms. The state is the guarantor of human rights; it is also the target and raison d'être of human rights law.

But the reality is far more complex. While the metaphor may suggest otherwise, it is not the state per se that is barbaric but the cultural foundation of the state. The state only becomes a vampire when "bad" culture overcomes or disallows the development of "good" culture. The real savage, though, is not the state but a cultural deviation from human rights. That savagery inheres in the theory and practice of the one-party state, military junta, controlled or closed state, theocracy, or even cultural practices such as the one popularly known in the West as female genital mutilation (FGM),[7] not in the state per se. The state itself is a neutral, passive instrumentality—a receptacle or an empty vessel—that conveys savagery by implementing the project of the savage culture.

The second dimension of the prism depicts the face and the fact of a victim as well as the essence and the idea of victimhood. A human being whose "dignity and worth" have been violated by the savage is the victim. The victim figure is a powerless, helpless innocent whose naturalist attributes have been negated by the primitive and offensive actions of the state or the cultural foundation of the state. The entire human rights structure is both anti-catastrophic and reconstructive. It is anti-catastrophic because it is designed to prevent more calamities through the creation of more victims. It is reconstructive because it seeks to reengineer the state and the society to reduce the number of victims, as it defines them, and prevent conditions that give rise to victims. The classic human rights document—the human rights report—embodies these two mutually reinforcing strategies. An INGO human rights report is usually a catalogue of horrible catastrophes visited on individuals. As a rule, each report also carries a diagnostic epilogue and recommended therapies and remedies.[8]

The third dimension of the prism is the savior or the redeemer, the good angel who protects, vindicates, civilizes, restrains, and safeguards. The savior is the victim's bulwark against tyranny. The simple yet complex promise of the savior is freedom: freedom from the tyrannies of the state, tradition, and culture. But it is also the freedom to create a better society based on particular values. In the human rights story, the savior is the human rights corpus itself, with the United Nations, Western governments, INGOs, and Western charities as the actual rescuers, redeemers of a benighted world.[9] In reality, however, these institutions are merely fronts. The savior is ultimately a set of culturally based norms and practices that inhere in liberal thought and philosophy.

The human rights corpus, though well meaning, is fundamentally Eurocentric,[10] and suffers from several basic and interdependent flaws captured in the SVS metaphor. First, the corpus falls within the historical continuum of the Eurocentric colonial project, in which actors are cast into superior and subordinate positions. Precisely because of this cultural and historical context, the human rights movement's basic claim of universality is undermined. Instead, a historical understanding of the struggle for human dignity should locate the impetus of a universal conception of human rights in those societies *subjected* to European tyranny and imperialism. Unfortunately, this is not part of the official human rights narrative. Some of the most important events preceding the post-1945, UN-led human rights movement include the antislavery campaigns in both Africa and the United States, the anticolonial struggles in Africa, Asia, and Latin America, and the struggles for women's suffrage and equal rights throughout the world.[11] But the pioneering work of many non-Western activists and other human rights heroes are not acknowledged by the contemporary human rights movement.[12] These historically important struggles, together with the norms anchored in non-Western cultures and societies, have been either overlooked or rejected in the construction of the current understanding of human rights.

Second, the SVS metaphor and narrative rejects the cross-contamination of cultures and instead promotes a Eurocentric ideal.[13] The metaphor is premised on the transformation by Western cultures of non-Western cultures into a Eurocentric prototype and not the fashioning of a multicultural mosaic.[14] The SVS metaphor results in an "othering" process that imagines the creation of inferior clones, in effect dumb copies of the original. For example, Western political democracy is in effect an organic element of human rights. "Savage" cultures and peoples are seen as lying outside the human rights orbit and by implication, outside the regime of political democracy. It is this distance from human rights that allows certain cultures to create victims. Political democracy is then viewed as a panacea. Other textual examples anchored in the treatment of cultural phenomena, such as "traditional" practices that appear to negate the equal protection for women also illustrate the gulf between human rights and nonliberal, non-European cultures.

Third, the language and rhetoric of the human rights corpus present significant theoretical problems. The arrogant and biased rhetoric of the human rights movement prevents the movement from gaining cross-cultural legitimacy.[15] This curse of the SVS rhetoric has no bearing on the substance of the normative judgment being rendered. A particular leader, for example, could be labeled a war criminal, but such a label may carry no validity locally because of the curse of the SVS rhetoric.[16] In other words, the SVS rhetoric may undermine the universalist warrant that it claims and thus engender resistance to the apprehension and punishment of real violators.

The subtext of human rights is a grand narrative hidden in the seemingly neutral and universal language of the corpus. For example, the UN Charter describes its mandate to "reaffirm faith in fundamental human rights, in the dignity and worth of the human person, in the equal rights of men and women and of nations large and small."[17] This is certainly a noble ideal. But what exactly does that terminology mean here? This phraseology conceals more than it reveals. What, for example, are fundamental human rights, and how are they determined? Do such rights have a cultural, religious, ethical, moral, political, or other bias? What exactly is meant by the "dignity and worth" of the human person? Is there an essentialized human being that the corpus imagines? Is the individual found in the streets of Nairobi, the slums of Boston, the deserts of Iraq, or the rainforests of Brazil? In addition to the herculean task of defining the prototypical human being, the UN Charter puts forward another pretense—that all nations "large and small" enjoy some equality. Even as it ratified power imbalances between the Third World and the dominant American and European powers,[18] the United Nations gave the latter the primary power to define and determine "world peace" and "stability."[19] These fictions of neutrality and universality, like so much else in a lopsided world, undergird the human rights corpus and belie its true identity and purposes. This international rhetoric of goodwill reveals, just beneath the surface, intentions and reality that stand in great tension and contradiction with it.

This chapter is not merely about the language of human rights or the manner in which the human rights movement describes its goals, subjects, and intended outcomes. It is not a plea for the human rights movement to be more sensitive to non-Western cultures. Nor is it a wholesale rejection of the idea of human rights. Instead, the chapter is fundamentally an attempt at locating—philosophically, culturally, and historically—the normative edifice of the human rights corpus. If the human rights movement is driven by a totalitarian or totalizing impulse, that is, the mission to require that all human societies transform themselves to fit a particular blueprint, then there is an acute shortage of deep reflection and a troubling abundance of zealotry in the human rights community. This vision of the "good society" must be vigorously questioned and contested.

Fourth, the issue of power is largely ignored in the human rights corpus. There is an urgent need for a human rights movement that is multicultural, inclusive, and deeply political. Thus, while it is essential that a new human rights movement overcome Eurocentrism, it is equally important that it also address deeply lopsided power relations among and within cultures, national economies, states, genders, religions, races and ethnic groups, and other societal cleavages. Such a movement cannot treat Eurocentrism as the starting point and other cultures as peripheral. The point of departure for the movement must be a basic assumption about the moral equivalency of all cultures.

The fifth flaw concerns the role of race in the development of the human rights narrative. The SVS metaphor of human rights carries racial connotations in which the international hierarchy of race and color is retrenched and revitalized. The metaphor is in fact necessary for the continuation of the global racial hierarchy. In the human rights narrative, savages and victims are generally nonwhite and non-Western, while the saviors are white. This old truism has found new life in the metaphor of human rights. But there is also a sense in which human rights can be seen as a project for the redemption of the redeemers, in which whites who are privileged globally as a people—who have historically visited untold suffering and savage atrocities against nonwhites—redeem themselves by "defending" and "civilizing" "lower," "unfortunate," and "inferior" peoples. The metaphor is thus laced with the pathology of self-redemption.

As currently constituted and deployed, the human rights movement will ultimately fail because it is perceived as an alien ideology in non-Western societies. The movement does not deeply resonate in the cultural fabrics of non-Western states, except among hypocritical elites steeped in Western ideas. In order ultimately to prevail, the human rights movement must be moored in the cultures of all peoples.[20]

Human rights renew the meaning and scope of rights in a radical way. Human rights bestow naturalness, transhistoricity, and universality to rights. But this chapter lodges a counterclaim against such a leap. It is certainly informed by the works of critical legal scholars,[21] feminist critics of rights discourse,[22] and critical race theorists.[23] Still, the approach here differs from all three because it seeks to address an international phenomenon and not a municipal, distinctly American question. The critique of human rights should be based not just on American or European legal traditions but also on other cultural milieus. The indigenous, non-European traditions of Asia, Africa, the Pacific, and the Americas must be central to this critique. The idea of human rights—the quest to craft a universal bundle of attributes with which all societies must endow all human beings—is a noble one. The problem with the current bundle of attributes lies in their inadequacy, incompleteness, and wrongheadedness. There is little doubt that there is much to celebrate in the present human rights corpus just as there is much to quarrel with. In this exercise, a sober evaluation of the current human rights corpus and its language is not an option—it is required.[24]

The chapter continues to build on this theoretical background. It relates human rights to the emergence of European and American senses of global predestination and the mission to civilize by universalizing Eurocentric norms. It then focuses on the metaphors of the savage, victim, and savior, and looks at human rights norms, work, and scholarship to underscore the theme of the SVS metaphor.

The Grand Narrative of Human Rights

The Charter of the United Nations, which is the constitutional basis for all UN human rights texts, captures the before-and-after, backward-progressive view of history. It declares human rights an indispensable element for the survival of humankind. It does so by undertaking as one of its principal aims the promotion of "universal respect for, and observance of, human rights and fundamental freedoms for all without distinction as to race, sex, language, or religion."[25] This self representation of human rights requires moral and historical certainty and a belief in particular inflexible truths. The Universal Declaration of Human Rights (UDHR), the grandest of all human rights documents, endows the struggle between good and evil with historicity in which the defeat of the latter is only possible through human rights.[26] This is now popularly accepted as the normal script of human rights.[27] In fact, there is today an orgy of celebration of this script by prominent scholars who see in it the key to the redemption of humanity.[28] But this grand script of human rights raises a multitude of normative and cultural questions and problems, especially in light of the historical roots of the human rights movement.

Any valid critique must first acknowledge that the human rights movement, like earlier crusades, is a bundle of contradictions. It does not have, therefore, a monopoly on virtue that its most vociferous advocates claim. I argue here that human rights, and the relentless campaign to universalize them, present a historical continuum in an unbroken chain of Western conceptual and cultural dominance over the past several centuries. At the heart of this continuum is a seemingly incurable virus: the impulse to universalize Eurocentric norms and values by repudiating, demonizing, and "othering" that which is different and non-European. By this argument, I do not mean to suggest that human rights are bad per se or that the human rights corpus is irredeemable. Rather, I suggest that the globalization of human rights fits a historical pattern in which all high morality comes from the West as a civilizing agent against lower forms of civilization in the rest of the world.

Although the human rights movement is located within the historical continuum of Eurocentrism as a civilizing mission, and therefore as an attack on non-European cultures, it is critical to note that it was European, and not non-European, atrocities that gave rise to it. While the movement has today constructed the savage and the victim as non-European, Adolf Hitler was the quintessential savage. The abominations and demise of his regime ignited the human rights movement.[29] Hitler, a white European, was the personification of evil. The Nazi regime, a white European government, was the embodiment of barbarism. The combination of Hitler's gross deviation from the evolving European constitutional law precepts and the entombment of his imperial designs by the West and the Soviet Union started the avalanche of norms known as the human rights corpus.

Nuremberg, the German town where some twenty-two major Nazi war criminals were tried—resulting in nineteen convictions—stands as the birthplace of the human rights movement, with the London Agreement[30] and the Nuremberg Charter[31] its birth certificates. Originally, the West did not create the human rights movement in order to save or civilize non-Europeans, although these humanist impulses drove the antislavery abolitionist efforts of the nineteenth century.[32] Neither the enslavement of Africans, with its barbaric consequences and genocidal dimensions, nor the classic colonization of Asians, Africans, and Latin Americans by Europeans, with its bone-chilling atrocities, was sufficient to move the West to create the human rights movement. It took the genocidal extermination of Jews in Europe—a white people—to start the process of the codification and universalization of human rights norms. Thus, although the Nuremberg Tribunal has been argued by some to be in a sense hypocritical,[33] it is its promise that is significant. For the first time, the major powers drew a line demarcating impermissible conduct by states toward their own people and created the concept of collective responsibility for human rights. But no one should miss the irony of brutalizing colonial powers pushing for the Nuremberg trials and the adoption of the UDHR.

Perhaps more important, two of the oldest and most prestigious international human rights NGOs—the International Commission of Jurists (ICJ) and Amnesty International (AI)—were established to deal with human rights violations in Europe, not the Third World. The ICJ was formed as a tool for the West in the Cold War.[34] According to A. J. M. van Dal of the Netherlands, one of its original officials, the mission of the ICJ was to "mobilize the forces—in particular the juridical forces—of the free world for the defense of our fundamental legal principles, and in so doing to organize the fight against all forms of systematic injustice in the Communist countries."[35] AI was launched in 1961 by Peter Benenson, a British lawyer, to protest the imprisonment, torture, or execution of prisoners held in Romania, Hungary, Greece, Portugal, and the United States because of their political opinions or religious beliefs.[36] In all these cases, the targets of AI were European or American, and not the Third World.

Thus the human rights movement originated in Europe to curb European savageries such as the Holocaust, the abuses of Soviet bloc communism, and the denials of speech and other expressive rights in a number of Western countries. The movement grew initially out of the horrors of the West, constructing the image of a European savage. The European human rights system, which is now a central attribute of European legal and political identity, is designed to hold member states to particular standards of conduct in their treatment of individuals.[37] It is, as it were, the bulwark against the reemergence of the unbridled European savage—the phenomenon that gave rise to and fueled the Third Reich.

The human rights corpus, only put into effect following the atrocities of the Second World War, had its theoretical underpinnings in Western colonial attitudes. It is rooted in a deep-seated sense of European and Western global predestination.[38] As put by Slater, European "belief in the necessity of an imperial mission to civilize the other and to convert other societies into inferior versions of the same" took hold in the nineteenth century. This impulse to possess and transform that which was different found a ready mask and benign cover in messianic faiths, in the spread of Christianity and Islam. By the nineteenth century, the discourse of white over black superiority had gained popularity and acceptance in Europe:

The advocates of this discourse—[German philosopher Georg] Hegel most typically, but duly followed by a host of "justifiers"—declared that Africa had no history prior to direct contact with Europe. Therefore the Africans, having made no history of their own, had clearly made no development of their own. Therefore they were not properly human, and could not be left to themselves, but must be "led" towards civilization by other peoples: that is, by the peoples of Europe, especially of Western Europe, and most particularly of Britain and France.[39]

As if by intuition, the missionary fused religion with civilization, a process that was meant to remove the native from the damnation of prehistory and to deliver him to the gates of history. In this idiom, human development was defined as a linear and vertical progression of the dark or backward races from the savage to the civilized, the premodern to the modern, from the child to the adult, and the inferior to the superior.[40] Slater has captured this worldview in a powerful passage:

the geological power over other societies, legitimated and codified under the signs of manifest destiny and civilizing missions, has been a rather salient feature of earlier Western projects of constructing new world orders. These projects or domains of truth, as they emanated from Europe or the United States, attempted to impose their hegemony by defining normalcy with reference to a particular vision of their own cultures, while designating that which was different as other than truth and in need of tutelage.[41]

The United States, whose history is simply a continuation of the Age of Europe,[42] suffers from this worldview just like its Western predecessors. American predestination, as embodied in the Monroe Doctrine, is almost as old as the country itself. President Theodore Roosevelt expressed this sense of predestination when he referred to peoples and countries south of the United States as the "weak, and chaotic people south of us" and declared that it was "our duty, when it becomes absolutely inevitable, to police these countries in the interest of order and civilization."[43] The treatment of Portuguese- and Spanish-speaking Latin America as the United States backyard was instrumental in consolidating the psyche of the United States as an empire.

In the last several hundred years, the globe has witnessed the universalization of Eurocentric norms and cultural forms through the creation of the colonial state and the predominance of certain economic, social, and political models. International law itself was founded on the preeminence of four specific European biases: geographic Europe as the center, and Christianity, mercantile economics, and political imperialism as superior paradigms.[44] Both the League of Nations and its successor, the United Nations, revitalized and confirmed European-American domination of international affairs. In the postwar period, non-European states were trusted or mandated to European powers or became client states of one or other European state.[45]

Since 1945, the United Nations has played a key role in preserving the global order that the West dominates. A critically important agenda item of the United Nations has been the universalization of principles and norms that are European in identity. Principal among these has been the spread of human rights which grow out of Western liberalism and jurisprudence.[46] The West was able to impose its philosophy of human rights on the rest of the world because it dominated the United Nations at its inception.[47] The fallacy of the UDHR, which refers to itself as the "common standard of achievement for all peoples and all nations,"[48] is now underscored by the identification of human rights norms with political democracy. The principal focus of human rights law has been on those rights that strengthen, legitimize, and export the liberal democratic state to non-Western societies.

Some scholars have argued that democratic governance has evolved from a moral prescription to an international legal obligation.[49] According to Thomas Franck, the right to democratic governance is supported by a large normative human rights canon. He asserts that people almost everywhere, including Africa and Asia, "now demand that government be validated by a Western-style parliamentary, multiparty democratic process." He concludes, rather triumphantly, that

This almost-complete triumph of the democratic notions of Hume, Locke, Jefferson and Madison—in Latin America, Africa, Eastern Europe and, to a lesser extent, Asia—may well prove to be the most profound event of the twentieth century and, in all likelihood, the fulcrum on which the future development of global society will turn. It is the unanswerable response to those who have said that free, open, multiparty, electoral parliamentary democracy is neither desired nor desirable outside a small enclave of Western industrial states.[50]

Franck presents the apparent triumph of liberal democratic nationalism as the free, uncoerced choice of non-Western peoples.

Although the corpus springs from Europe, Third World states have also participated in its legitimation, particularly at the United Nations, the institution most responsible for the creation and universalization of human rights norms. Although some academics point to the increasing role played by non-Western states and cultures in the development of human rights norms, too much should not be made of Third World participation in the making of human rights law. Mary Ann Glendon, in her impressive and well researched book, has argued, for instance, that non-Western scholars and diplomats were key players in the construction of the UDHR.[51] But the levers of power at the United Nations and other international lawmaking forums have traditionally been out of the reach of the Third World. And even if they were within reach, it is doubtful that most Third World states represent their peoples and cultures. In other words, a claim about the universality or democratization of human rights norm-making at the United Nations cannot be made simply by looking at the numerical domination of that body by Third World states.

Although the human rights movement arose in Europe, with the express purpose of containing European savagery, it is today a civilizing crusade aimed primarily at the Third World. It is one thing for Europeans and North Americans, whose states share a common philosophical and legal ancestry, to create a common political and cultural template to govern their societies. It is quite another to insist that their particular vision of society is the only permissible civilization which must now be imposed on all human societies, particularly those outside Europe. The merits of the European and American civilization of human rights notwithstanding, all missionary work is suspect, and might easily seem a part of the colonial project. Once again, the allegedly superior Europeans and North Americans descend on supposedly backward natives in the Third World with the human rights mission to free them from the claws of despotic governments and benighted cultures.

But the human rights project is no longer just a critique of the Third World by the West. Individual states of all cultural and political traditions, including those in the Third World, have taken coercive measures against other states in the name of human rights. Many non-governmental organizations in the Third World openly oppose human rights violations committed by their own states and societies based on imported Western norms and definitions. Non-Europeans now confront each other within the confines of their states over the enforcement of human rights. The observance or denial of human rights now pits African against African, Arab against Arab, and Asian against Asian.

Today, most of the activities of the ICJ, AI, the other Western-based INGOs such as Human Rights Watch and the Lawyers Committee for Human Rights, both based in New York, and the Washington-based International Human Rights Law Group are focused on the Third World. As a consequence, the predominant image of the savage in the human rights discourse today is that of a Third World, non-European person, cultural practice, or state.

At first blush, there appear to be sufficient grounds for the INGOs' unrelenting emphasis on Third World states as the foci for their work. As a general rule, INGOs concentrate their work on the violations of civil and political rights—the species of legal protections associated with a functioning political democracy. Admittedly, there are more undemocratic states in the Third World than in the developed West. Third World despots have acted with impunity. Violations of civil and political rights and the plunder of Third World economies by their leaders are common and flagrant. The spotlight by INGOs here is appropriate, necessary, and welcome, particularly where local advocacy groups and the press have been muzzled or suffocated by the state. There is no doubt that mechanisms for the protections of human rights are more fragile in many Third World states, if they exist at all.

But while this explains the work of INGOs in the Third World, it does not excuse their relative inactivity on human rights violations in the West. Western countries, like the United States, are notorious for their violations of the civil rights of racial minorities and the poor. Although both Human Rights Watch and AI have haltingly started to breach the publicity and advocacy barriers in these areas,[52] such reports have been sparse and episodic, and have given the impression of a public relations exercise, designed to mute critics who charge INGOs with a lopsided Third World focus. The ravages of globalization notwithstanding, INGOs have largely remained deaf to calls for advocacy on social and economic rights.[53] There certainly is no sufficient defense for their failure to address the violations of economic and social rights by Western states. It is true, of course, that dominant public discourse in the West generally opposed the mainstreaming of an agenda for economic and social rights, and instead characterized them as inimical to free enterprise. But in reality, most countries—socialist, capitalist, and Third World—have never seriously sought to fulfill economic, social, and cultural rights, even those which rhetorically championed them, such as the Soviet Union.

The historical pattern is undeniable. It forms a long queue of the colonial administrator, the Bible-wielding Christian missionary, the merchant of free enterprise, the exporter of political democracy, and now the human rights zealot. In each case the European culture has pushed the "native" culture to transform. The local must be replaced with the universal—that is, the European. Are the connections between human rights and particular attributes of European-American culture, such as hedonism, excess individualism, free markets, and now globalization contingent and not organic? Is, in fact, the text of human rights so open that it is up for grabs, allowing different interests to make whatever claims they wish on it? In other words, are non-European cultures better advised to adopt the human rights text to their specific contexts, but to leave its core in place, if they seek redemption from their own backwardness? Can they segregate the "good" from the "bad" in human rights and reject the baggage of the West, while building a culture that is free from the evils that deny human potential?

Although the purpose here is not to address particularized national settings, it is sufficient to note that the savage-victim-savior metaphor has deep historical parallels in the national histories of states where nonwhites, and especially persons of African ancestry, have been subjected to oppression, abuse, exploitation, and domination by whites. The history of South Africa, as told by Nelson Mandela, is not just a testament to the cooperation of black and white South Africans against apartheid, the system of official segregation.[54] There is in that history a strong undercurrent of white benefactors, sometimes pejoratively referred to as "do-gooders," a species of humans cut from the abolitionist cloth.[55] During the darkest days of apartheid, many individual white lawyers, white law firms, and white human rights organizations spoke for and defended black South Africans.[56] Many whites became key leaders in what was essentially a black liberation struggle.[57] In the United States, from the earliest days of the enslavement of Africans by whites up to the civil rights movement, whites often played important roles in the struggle for equality by blacks. As in South Africa, many American whites held key positions in the fight for civil rights.[58] It seems politically incorrect to consign white participation in these noble causes to the SVS metaphor. But it is an unavoidable conclusion that the metaphor largely describes their involvement. It would also be a tragic historical error not to recognize the importance of those struggles to the liberal project and its centrality to democracy and the freedom of whites as a people themselves.

My purpose here is not to assign ignoble intentions or motivations on the individual proponents, leaders, or participants in the human rights movement. Without a doubt many of the leaders and foot soldiers of the human rights movement are driven by a burning desire to end human suffering, as they see it from their vantage point. The white American suburban high school or college student who joins the local chapter of AI and protests FGM in faraway lands or writes letters to political or military leaders whose names do not easily roll off the English tongue are no doubt drawing partly from a well of noblesse oblige. The zeal to see all humanity as related and the impulse to help those defined as in need is noble and is not the problem addressed here. A certain degree of human universality is inevitable and desirable. But what that universality is, what historical and cultural stew it is made of, and how it is accomplished make all the difference. What the high school or college student ought to realize is that his or her zeal to save others—even from themselves—is steeped in Western and

European history. If one culture is allowed the prerogative of imperialism, the right to define and impose on others what it deems good for humanity, the very meaning of freedom itself will have been abrogated. That is why a human rights movement that pivots on the savage-victim-savior metaphor violates the very idea of the sanctity of humanity that purportedly inspires it.

The Metaphor of the Savage

Human rights law frames the state as its primary target. Although voluntarily entered into, human rights treaties are binding on the state. The state is both the guarantor and subject of human rights. Underlying the development of human rights is the belief that the state is a predator that must be contained. Otherwise it will devour and imperil human freedom. From this conventional international human rights law perspective, the state is the classic savage.

But it is not the state per se that is predatory, for the state in itself is simply a construct that describes a repository for public power, a disinterested instrumentality ready to execute public will, whatever that maybe. There is a high degree of fluidity in the nature of that power and how it is exercised. For instance, a state's constitutional structure could in its configuration require a particular form of democratic government. Or a state's constitution could locate public power in religious bodies and clerics, as has been the case in the Islamic Republic of Iran.[59] However, a state could, through revolution or some other device, be Islamic today and secular tomorrow. Since the state in this construction appears to be an empty vessel, the savage must be located beyond the state.

The state should be unmasked as being a mere proxy for the real savage. That leaves the historically accumulated wisdom, the culture of a society, as the only other plausible place to locate the savage. Culture represents the accumulation of a people's wisdom and thus their identity; it is real and without it a people is without a name, rudderless, and torn from its moorings. In this sense, culture is a set of local truths which serve as a guide for life's many pursuits in a society. The validity of a cultural norm is a local truth, and judgment or evaluation of that truth by a norm from an external culture is extremely problematic, if not altogether an invalid exercise.[60] But culture itself is a dynamic and alchemical mix of many variables, including religion, philosophy, history, mythology, politics, environmental factors, language, and economics. The interaction of these variables— both within the culture and through influence by other cultures—produces competing social visions and values in any given society. The dominant class or political interests that capture the state make it the public expression of their particular cultural vision. That is to say, the state is more a conveyor belt than an embodiment of particular cultural norms. The state is but the scaffolding underneath which the real savage resides. Thus, when human rights norms target a deviant state, they are really attacking the normative cultural fabric or variant expressed by that state. The culture, and not the state, is the actual savage. From this perspective, human rights violations represent a clash between the culture of human rights and the savage culture.

The view that human rights is an ideology with deep roots in liberalism and democratic forms of government is now supported by senior human rights academics in the West.[61] The cultural biases of the human rights corpus can only be properly understood if it is contextualized within liberal theory and philosophy. Understood from this position, human rights become an ideology with a specific cultural and ethnographic fingerprint.[62] The human rights corpus expresses a cultural bias, and its chastening of a state is therefore a cultural project. If culture is not defined as some discrete, exotic, and peculiar practice which is frozen in time but rather as the dynamic totality of ideas, forms, practices, and structures of any given society, then human rights, as it is currently conceived, is an expression of a particular European-American culture. The advocacy of human rights across cultural borders is then an attempt to displace the local culture with the "universal" culture of human rights. Human rights, therefore, become the universal culture. It is in this sense that the "other" culture, that which is non-European, is the savage in the human rights corpus and its discourse.

In major international human rights instruments, the "other" culture is quite often depicted as the evil that must be overcome by human rights themselves. An example is the Convention on the Elimination of all Forms of Discrimination against Women (CEDAW), which is based on equality and antidiscrimination, the two basic and preeminent norms of the human rights corpus. The most transformatively radical human rights treaty, CEDAW refers to offending "social and cultural patterns,"[63] and demands that the state take all appropriate measures to transform attitudes and practices that are inimical to women. The treaty explicitly requires that states seek the "elimination of prejudices and customary and all other practices" that are based on the ideas of the inequality of the sexes.[64]

While there are no cultures that are innocent of discriminatory practices against women, human rights discourse treats non-Western cultures as particularly problematic in this regard. For example, in its first report, the Women's Rights Project of Human Rights Watch focused on wife-murder, domestic battery, and rape in Brazil.[65] Significant here is the fact that HRW's first report on violations of women's human rights did not focus on the wife-murder, domestic battery, and rape commonplace in the United States or a European country but rather on Brazil, a Third World state. Other reports by the Women's Rights Project have concentrated on violations in Botswana, Haiti, and Turkey, which is Muslim and on the periphery of Europe.[66]

The impression left by the reports and the activities of powerful INGOs is unmistakable. While the West is presented as the cradle of the feminist movement, countries in the South have been constructed as steeped in traditions and practices which are harmful to women. In one of her first reports, Radhika Coomaraswamy, the UN Special Rapporteur on Violence Against Women, confirmed this impression when she noted that "certain customary practices and some aspects of tradition are often the cause of violence against women." She noted that "besides female genital mutilation, a whole host of practices violate female dignity. Foot binding, male preference, early marriage, virginity tests, dowry deaths, sati, female infanticide, and malnutrition are among the many practices that violate a woman's human rights."[67] All these practices are found in non- Western cultures. Images of practices such as "female genital mutilation," dowry burnings, and honor killings have come to frame the discourse, and in that vein stigmatize non-Western cultures.

Elsewhere, non-European political traditions that lie outside the liberal tradition and do not yield political democratic structures are demonized in the text of human rights and its discourse. Take, for example, the view expressed by human rights documents in the area of political participation. Here, the human rights corpus expects all societies to support a pluralist, democratic society. Both the UDHR and the ICCPR, the two key documents in the area of civil and political rights, are explicit about the primacy of rights of expression and association. They both give citizens the right to political participation through elections and the guarantee of the right to assemble, associate, and disseminate their ideas.[68] This scheme of rights coupled with equal protection and due process rights implies a political democracy or a political society with a regularly elected government, genuine competition for political office, and separation of powers with judicial independence. While it is true that the human rights regime does not dictate the particular permutation or strain of political democracy, it suggests a Western-style liberal democracy nevertheless. Systems of government such as monarchies, theocracies, dictatorships, and one-party states would violate rights of association and run afoul of the human rights corpus.[69] When it rejects non-Western political cultures as undemocratic, the human rights corpus raises the specter of political savagery.

In scholarship by many Western academics, the same sharp contrast is drawn between human rights supporters and the cultural or political savage who must be civilized by human rights. Industrial democracies in the last two decades have worked to link human rights to aspects of foreign policy such as development assistance, aid, and trade with non-Western states.[70] Such linkage requires the recipient, usually a non-Western state, to conform aspects of its domestic laws, policies, or programs to human rights or democratic norms. The coercive maneuver is intended to civilize the offending state. In this sense, Western states frequently use human rights as a tool of foreign policy against non-Western states.[71]

Some writers have depicted certain practices as part of a savage culture. In the gruesome conflict following the collapse of Yugoslavia, genocide and other war crimes were perpetrated with chilling callousness. In particular, one of the most horrifying war crimes was the massive rape by Serbs of Muslim Bosnian women, with some reports estimating as many as 20,000 victims.[72] Todd Salzman characterizes these offenses as "an assault against the female gender, violating her body and its reproductive capabilities as a 'weapon of war.'"[73] He traces these atrocities to a savage Serbian patriarchal culture that usurps the female body and reduces the female to "her reproductive capacities in order to fulfill the overall objective of Serbian nationalism by producing more citizens to populate the nation." According to Salzman, this view of the female body is deeply rooted in Serbian culture, the Serbian Orthodox Church, and Serbian official policies. The savage here is located in religion, politics, and culture which the state supports and implements for the purpose of creating "Greater Serbia."

The image of the savage is also painted impressively by INGOs in their work through reporting and other forms of public advocacy. The focus here is not on domestic human rights NGOs in the Third World because many simply imitate the practices of their predecessors in the North. Typically, INGOs perform three basic functions: investigation, reporting, and advocacy.[74] The focus of human rights INGOs is usually human rights violations in a Third World country, where the "investigation" normally takes place. Generally, a Western-based INGO—typically based in the political and cultural capitals of the most powerful countries in the West[75]—sends a team of investigators called a human rights mission to a country in the South. The mission lasts anywhere from several days to a few weeks and collects data and other information on human rights questions from victims, local NGOs, lawyers, local journalists, human rights defenders, and government officials. Information from these local sources is usually crosschecked with other, supposedly more objective sources—meaning Western embassies, locally based Western reporters, and other Western interests such as foundations. Upon returning to the West, the mission systematizes the information and releases it in the form of a report.

The human rights report is a catalog of abuses committed by the state against liberal values.[76] It criticizes the state for departing from the civil and political rights obligations provided for in the major instruments. Its purpose is to shame the Third World state by pointing out the gulf between the state's conduct and internationally sanctioned civilized behavior. This departure from good behavior is stigmatized and used to paint the state either as a pariah or out-of-step with the rest of the civilized world. Reports normally contain corrective measures and recommendations to the offending state. In many instances, however, the audience of these reports is the West or some other Western institution, such as the European Union. The pleas of the INGO report here pit a First World state or institution against a Third World state or culture. The report asks that the West cut off aid, condition assistance, impose sanctions, and/or publicly denounce the unacceptable conduct of the Third World state.[77] INGOs thus ask First World states and institutions to play a significant role in "taming" and "civilizing" Third World states, even though such a role relies on the power and economic imbalances of the international order which favors the North over the South.

The human rights report also tells another, more interesting story about the target of the human rights corpus. In this story, the report describes several images of the savage, including the Third World state, the quintessential savage. Human rights literature is replete with images of bloodthirsty Third World despots and trigger-happy police and security forces.

Perhaps in no other area than in the advocacy over "female genital mutilation" is the image of culture as the savage more poignant. The word "mutilation" itself implies the willful, sadistic infliction of pain on a hapless victim, and stigmatizes the practitioners and their cultures as barbaric savages. Descriptions of the practice are so searing and revolting that they evoke images of a barbarism that defies civilization.[78] Although the practice has dissipated over the last several decades, it is still carried out in parts of Africa and the Middle East. Given Western stereotypes of barbaric natives in the "dark" continent,[79] Western advocacy over FGM has evoked images of machete-wielding natives only too eager to inflict pain on women in their societies. The speed, for example, with which the 1994 mass killings in Rwanda took place, and the weapons used, have come to symbolize in the Western mind the barbarism of Africans. Philip Gourevitch, an American journalist, was one of the instrumental voices in the creation of this portrayal:

Decimation means the killing of every tenth person in a population, and in the spring and early summer of 1994 a program of massacres decimated the Republic of Rwanda. *Although the killing was low-tech—performed largely by machete—it was carried out at dazzling speed: of an original population of about seven and a half million, at least eight hundred thousand people were killed in just a hundred days.* Rwandans often speak of a million deaths, and they may be right. The dead of Rwanda accumulated at nearly three times the rate of Jewish dead during the Holocaust. It was the most efficient mass killing since the atomic bombings of Hiroshima and Nagasaki.[80]

These images are critical in the construction of the savage. Human rights opposition and campaigns against FGM, which have relied heavily on demonization, have picked up where European colonial missionaries left off.[81] Savagery in this circumstance acquires a race—the black, dark, or non-Western race. The Association of African Women for Research and

Development (AAWORD), by contrast, opposed female circumcision but sharply denounced the racism inherent in Western-led, anti-FGM campaigns:

This new crusade of the West has been led out of the moral and cultural prejudices of Judaeo-Christian Western society: aggressiveness, ignorance or even contempt, paternalism and activism are the elements which have infuriated and then shocked many people of good will. In trying to reach their own public, the new crusaders have fallen back on sensationalism, and have become insensitive to the dignity of the very women they want to "save."[82]

AAWORD vigorously questioned the motives of Western activists and suggested that they were twice victimizing African women. It stopped just short of asking Western activists to drop the crusade, yet openly denounced the use of the savage-victim-savior metaphor:

[Western crusaders] are totally unconscious of the latent racism which such a campaign evokes in countries where ethnocentric prejudice is so deep-rooted. And in their conviction that this is a "just cause," they have forgotten that these women from a different race and a different culture are also *human beings*, and that solidarity can only exist alongside self-affirmation and mutual respect."[83]

As illustrated by the debate over FGM, advocacy across cultural barriers is an extremely complex matter. Making judgments across the cultural divide is a risky business because the dice are always heavily loaded. Not even the black-white pretense of human rights can erase those risks. But since that is precisely what the human rights movement does—make judgments across cultures—there is an obligation to create truly universal standards. Otherwise, the human rights enterprise will continue to present itself as a struggle between the cultures of non-Western peoples and the "universal" culture of the West.

The Metaphor of the Victim

The metaphor of the victim is the giant engine that drives the human rights movement. Without the victim there is no savage or savior, and the entire human rights enterprise collapses. This section examines the victim from the perspective of the United Nations, human rights treaties, human rights law, and, especially, human rights literature. Also, intertwined in the victim identity are questions of race and the legacy of colonialism.

The basic purpose of the human rights corpus is to contain the state, transform society, and eliminate both the victim and victimhood as conditions of human existence. In fact, the human rights regime was designed to respond to both the potential and actual victim, and to create legal, political, social, and cultural arrangements to defang the state. The human rights text and its discourse present political democracy, and its institutions of governance, as the sine qua non for a victimless society.

On the international level, the United Nations pursues civilizing campaigns that ostensibly seek to prevent conditions that create human victims, to "save succeeding generations from the scourge of war," to "establish conditions under which justice" can be maintained, and to "reaffirm faith in fundamental human rights."[84] Human rights treaties are therefore a series of obligations assumed by states to prevent the creation of victims. To accomplish this, the state obligates itself to three basic duties for every basic human right: to avoid depriving, to protect from deprivation, and to aid the deprived.[85] The first duty, being negative, may be the least costly and mainly requires self-restraint; the latter two are positive and demand the expenditure of more resources and the implementation of programs.

Human rights law protects against the invasion of the inherent dignity and worth of the potential victim. Regardless of whether an individual is guilty of some offense, the state is not permitted to violate his fundamental rights without abiding by certain state-created norms. The state's culpability extends to individuals and entities within its jurisdiction, whether or not the violation can be traced directly to it. Thus, for example, the state's failure to prevent or punish domestic violence can be seen as a human rights violation.

In human rights literature, the victim is usually presented as a helpless innocent who has been abused directly by the state, its agents, or pursuant to an offensive cultural or political practice.[86] The most visible human rights victims, those that have come to define the term, are subjected to the now numbingly familiar set of abuses: arbitrary arrest and detention; denials of the rights to speech, assembly, and association; involuntary exile; mass slaughters and genocide; discriminations based on race, ethnicity, religion, gender, and political opinion; and denials of due process.[87]

Consider this descriptive report of an incident where Iraqi government soldiers randomly selected Kurdish male villagers and executed them within earshot of their wives, children, and relatives:

The soldiers opened fire at the line of thirty three squatting men from a distance of about 5–10 meters. . . . Some men were killed immediately by rifle fire. Others were wounded, and a few were missed altogether. . . .[S]everal soldiers approached the line of slumped bodies on orders of the lieutenant and fired additional individual rounds as a coup de grace. The soldiers then left the execution site, without burying the bodies or otherwise touching them, according to survivors who lay among the corpses.[88]

A basic characteristic of the victim is powerlessness, an inability for self-defense against the state or the culture in question. The usual human rights narrative generally describes victims as hordes of nameless, despairing, and dispirited masses. To the extent they have a face, it is desolate and pitiful. Many are uneducated, destitute, old and infirm, too young, poorly clad, and hungry: peasants, the rural and urban poor, marginalized ethnic groups and nationalities, and lower castes. Their very being is a state of divorce from civilization and a large distance from modernity. Many are women and children twice victimized because of their gender and age,[89] and sometimes the victim of the savage culture is the female gender itself.[90]

Another example of the images of helplessness and utter degradation of victims comes from a report by AI, detailing the torture and abuse, including rape, of women in detention in many states around the globe. An account from an Israeli detention center, while not unique, is particularly disturbing:

> Dozens of Palestinian women and children detained in the Israeli-Occupied Territories have reportedly been sexually abused or threatened in sexually explicit language during interrogation. Fatimah Salameh was arrested in Nablus in July 1990. Her interrogators allegedly threatened to rape her with a chair leg and told her they would photograph her naked and show the pictures to her family. "They called me a whore and said that a million men had slept with me," she said. Fatimah Salameh agreed to confess to membership in an illegal organization and was sentenced to 14 months' imprisonment.[91]

The language of the human rights reports suggests the need for help— most likely outside intervention—to overcome the conditions of victimization. In many instances, the victims themselves deeply believe in and openly declare their helplessness and plead for outside help. A classic example was the case of the Kosovars who sought Western support in their conflict with the Serbian government of Slobodan Milosevic.[92] Individual victims serve as more vivid illustrations of this particular victim syndrome. Tong Yi, a Chinese dissident who was jailed and freed in 1997 partly due to the pressure exerted by Human Rights Watch and the U.S. government, was profusely grateful to Robert Bernstein, the human rights patriarch and founder of HRW, whom she credited with her release. Despite her torturous time in prison, Yi noted that "If there's a smile on my face, it's because of Bob Bernstein."[93]

The victim must also be constructed as sympathetic and innocent. Otherwise it is difficult to mobilize public outrage against the victimizer. Moral clarity about the evil of the perpetrator and the innocence of the victim is an essential distinction for Western public opinion, for it is virtually impossible to evoke sympathy for a victim who appears villainous, roguish, or unreceptive to a liberal reconstructionist project.[94]

In the case of the Kosovo Albanians, the demon was Milosevic, the hated autocrat who has refused to join the democratic-privatization dance currently in vogue in the former Soviet bloc. The NATO intervention may have been more intended to oust him and replace him with a "good

Serb"[95] than to save the Kosovars. The Kosovars and their ragtag band of fighters were painted as defenders of an innocent population against the cruel repression of Milosevic. Although Kosovars are Muslims, the press did not employ the stigma of Islamic fundamentalism to discredit their victim status. In stark contrast to this depiction, Chechen fighters have been portrayed as Islamic zealots and dangerous terrorists responsible for bombings and fundamentalist atrocities in both Chechnya and Russia.[96]

The face of the prototypical victim is nonwhite. With the exception of the wars and atrocities committed in the former Yugoslavia and in Northern Ireland, the most enduring faces of human rights victims have been black, brown, or yellow. But even in Bosnia and Kosovo the victims were Muslims, not Christians or "typically" white Westerners. The images of the most serious suffering seem to be those of Africans, Asians, Arabs, or Latin Americans. Thus, since the Second World War, the major focus of human rights advocacy by both the United Nations and INGOs has been in the Third World in Latin America, Africa, and Asia.

Rarely is the victim conceived as white.[97] Due to sensationalistic reporting by dominant Western media organizations and the instantaneous availability of these stories worldwide,[98] the human rights crises afflicting the nonwhite world seem to be overwhelming and without number. As a result, many affluent Westerners have in the past decade spoken of what Susan Moeller terms "compassion fatigue,"[99] a euphemism for lack of interest in the suffering of people who are seemingly remote, benighted, look different, speak another language, and do not have any discernibly immediate impact on the lives of people in the West. Yet it is precisely these dire, seemingly catastrophic situations that the human rights movement is relentlessly committed to change.

While many victims in Latin American countries are white, the popular perception of Latin Americans in the West is that of nonwhite, underdeveloped victims of crude despotism. Latin American whites, who form the ruling elites of the region, are not perceived in the West as "typical" whites, with the attendant benefits of modern affluence, presumed intelligence, global power, and influence. At best, they have been constructed as "second class" whites, lower in the racial pecking order than whites in Australia, New Zealand, and even South Africa, the three other countries outside Europe and North America with substantial white populations. In any case, the typical Latin American victim is presumed to be indigenous.

The representations of the victim in human rights literature spring from a messianic ethos in both the INGO and the United Nations. There is a colonial texture to the relationship between the human rights victim and the West. In the colonial project, for example, the colonizer justified his mission by drawing a distinction between the "native" and the "civilized" mind. In one case, which was typical of the encounter between Africa and the West, a European missionary compared what he called the "Bantu mind" to that of a "civilized man":

It is suggested that the mere possession on the part of the Bantu of nothing but an oral tradition of culture creates a chasm of difference between the Native "mind" and that of civilized man, and of itself would account for a lack of balance and proportion in the triple psychological function of feeling, thinking and acting, implying that thinking is the weakest of the three and that feeling is the most dominant. The Native seeks not truth nor works, but power—the dynamical mood.[100]

The view that the "native" is weak, powerless, prone to laziness, and unable on his own to create the conditions for his development was a recurrent theme in Western representations of the "other." Early in the life of the organization, an International Labour Organization report concluded, for example, that indigenous peoples could not by themselves overcome their "backwardness." It noted: "it is now almost universally recognized that, left to their own resources, indigenous peoples would have difficulty in overcoming their inferior economic and social situation which inevitably leaves them open for exploitation."[101] In the culture of the human rights movement, whose center is in the West, there is a belief that human rights problems afflict people "over there" and not people "like us." The missionary zeal to help those who cannot help themselves is one of the logical conclusions of this attitude.

The idea that the human rights corpus is concerned with ordering the lives of non-European peoples has a long history in international law itself. More recent scholarship explores this link between international law and the imposition of European norms, values, ideas, and culture on non-European societies and cultures.[102] Since the inception of the current international legal order some five centuries ago, there have been outright challenges by non-European cultures to the logic, substance, and purpose of international law.[103] The development of human rights has only blunted, but not eliminated, some of those challenges.

The Metaphor of the Savior

The metaphor of the savior is constructed through two intertwining characteristics—Eurocentric universalism and Christianity's missionary zeal. This section examines these characteristics and the institutional, international actors who promote liberal democracy as the antidote to human rights abuses.

First, the savior metaphor is deeply embedded in the Enlightenment's universalist pretensions, which constructed Europe as superior and as center of the universe.[104] International law itself is founded on these assumptions and premises.[105] International law has succeeded in governing "states of all civilizations, European and non-European."[106] International law has become "universal" although some have argued that it bears an ethnocentric fingerprint.[107]

In addition to the Eurocentric focus of human rights, the metaphor of the savior is also located in the missionary's Christian religion. Inherent to any universalizing creed is an unyielding faith in the superiority of at least the beliefs of the proselytizer over those of the potential convert, if not over the person of the convert. The project of universality or proselytism seeks to remake the "other" in the image of the converter. Christianity has a long history of such zealotry. Both empire-building and the spread of Christendom justified the means.

Crusades, inquisitions, witch burnings—which invariably meant the . . . burnings of heretics and gay people, of fellow Christians and of infidels—all in the name of the cross. It is almost as if Constantine, upon his and his empire's conversion to Christianity in the fourth century, uttered a well-fulfilled prophecy when he declared: "In the name of this cross we shall conquer." The cross has played the role of weapon time and time again in Christian history and empire building.[108]

In fact, the political-cultural push to universalize one's beliefs can be so obsessive that it has been identified frequently with martyrdom in history:

the supreme sacrifice was to die fighting under the Christian emperor. The supreme self-immolation was to fall in battle under the standard of the Cross. . . . But by the time Christianity was ready to meet Asia and the New World, the Cross and the sword were so identified with one another that the sword itself was a cross. It was the only kind of cross some conquistadores understood.[109]

There is a historical continuum in this impulse to universalize Eurocentrism and its norms and to ratify them under the umbrella of "universalism." Whether it is in the push for free markets, liberal systems of government, "civilized" forms of dress, or in the ubiquity of the English language itself, at least the last five centuries can appropriately be called the Age of Europe. These Eurocentric models have not been content to remain at home. They intrinsically define themselves as eternal truths. Universalization is an essential attribute of their validity. This validation comes partly from the conquest of the "primitive" and his introduction and delivery to "civilization."[110] For international law, Antony Anghie has captured this impulse clearly:

the extension and universalization of the European experience, which is achieved by transmuting it into the major theoretical problem of the discipline [international law], has the effect of suppressing and subordinating other histories of international law and the people to whom it has applied. Within the axiomatic framework of positivism, which decrees that European states are sovereign while non-European states are not, there is only one means of relating the history of the non-European world, and this the positivists proceed to do: it is a history of the civilizing mission, the process by which peoples of Africa, Asia, the Americas, and the Pacific were finally assimilated into a European international law.[111]

The impulses to conquer, colonize, save, exploit, and civilize non-European peoples met at the intersection of commerce, politics, law, and Christianity and evolved into the Age of Empire. As put by John Norton Pomeroy, lands occupied by "persons who are not recognized as belonging to the great family of states to whom international law applies" or by "savage, barbarous tribes" belonged as of right upon discovery to the "civilized and Christian nation."[112]

The savior-colonizer psyche reflects an intriguing interplay of both European superiority and manifest destiny over the subject. The "othering" project degrades although it also seeks to save. One example is the manipulative manner in which the British took over large chunks of Africa. Lord Lugard, the British colonialist, described in denigrating language a "treaty-making" ceremony in which an African ruler "agreed" to "British protection." He described himself and the African ruler "seated cross-legged on a mat opposite to each other on the ground, you should picture a savage chief in his best turn-out which consists probably of his weapons of war, different chalk colorings on his face, a piece of skin of a leopard, a wild cat, sheep, ox."[113] As put by a European missionary, the "Mission to Africa" was "the least that we [Europeans] can do . . . to strive to raise him [the African] in the scale of mankind."[114] Anghie notes that the deployment of denigrating, demeaning language is essential to the psyche of the savior. He writes:

The violence of positivist language in relation to non-European peoples is hard to overlook. Positivists developed an elaborate vocabulary for denigrating these peoples, presenting them as suitable objects for conquest, and legitimizing the most extreme violence against them, all in the furtherance of the civilizing mission—the discharge of the white man's burden.[115]

Human rights law continues this tradition of universalizing Eurocentric norms by intervening in Third World cultures and societies to save them from the traditions and beliefs that it frames as permitting or promoting despotism and disrespect for human rights.

While it is incorrect to equate colonialism with the human rights movement, at least in terms of the methods of the two phenomena, it is not unreasonable to draw parallels between them with respect to some of their motivations and purposes. Colonialism was driven by ignoble motives while the human rights movement was inspired by the noblest of human ideals. However, both streams of historical moment are part of a Western push to transform non-European peoples. Henkin celebrates the embrace of human rights by diverse states across the globe as the triumph of the post-1945 era. He refers to this era as the "age of rights.[116]

Henkin is so quick to celebrate universality that he fails to problematize the human rights project. Why does he not express more suspicion about the contrasting diversity of states that have ratified human rights instruments? Might that not mean that they are simply bowing to a false international consensus because in some sense their statehood and belonging to the "international community" is dependent on paying homage to international law, to human rights? Do non-European states really have a choice of rejecting in any sustained manner any doctrine of international law, particularly human rights, which represent the ultimate civilizing project of international law? Why should credence be given to states here when many, if not the majority, do not even speak for their peoples or cultures? Might states not just be acting cynically because they want to be seen to belong among the ranks of the "civilized?" After all, how much does the ratification of international law instruments mean to Third World states when they live under a patently unjust international order in which they are the subordinates? Yet Henkin rejects this debate and argues that "cultural relativists" who question the human rights corpus on ideological or cultural grounds desire a vague, broad, and ambiguous text of human rights.[117] He ignores these questions because they may be fatal to the project of universality, which is essential for the human rights project.

Proponents of human rights universality claim that the antidote to illiberal, authoritarian, and closed societies is constitutionalism and political democracy. The corpus proceeds from the premise that the world should be a marketplace of ideas. The expressive rights in the basic human rights instruments are based on this assumption although they are subject to some limitations.[118] But this assumption imposes on other cultures the obligation and the requirement to compete against human rights, even though those cultures may not be universalistic and may be ill-equipped to compete in the marketplace of ideas.

Human rights are part of the cultural package of the West, complete with an idiom of expression, a system of government, and certain basic assumptions about the individual and his relationship to society.[119] The spread of the liberal constitution—with its normative assumptions and the political structures it implies—makes human rights an integral part of the Western conception of modern society and its ubiquitous domination of the globe.

Institutionally, saviors constitute a broad range of actors and interests which are driven by a belief in the redemption of nonliberal, usually non-European, societies and cultures from human rights abominations.

At the intergovernmental level, the United Nations' vertical enforcement processes and machineries act as the official guardians of the human rights corpus, and its location at the heart of UN activities and purposes gives it the imprimatur of objectivity and neutral internationalism.[120] A maze of human rights bodies—committees and commissions—is responsible for developing, overseeing, monitoring, and enforcing human rights.[121] Most UN work in human rights focuses on Third World states and societies, complete with technical assistance programs and other "handholding" projects to ensure the incorporation, dissemination, and enforcement of human rights norms, as well as the creation and nurturing of institutions to perform these tasks.[122] The United Nations is, in a sense, the grand "neutral" savior, and Western liberal democracies treat it as such.

Although the United Nations is an institution composed of states, and therefore is bound in theory to respect the sovereignty of all states, it has recently taken a more active posture in human rights matters. United Nations failures in Rwanda and Somalia as well as the atrocities in the former Yugoslavia have embarrassed the world body and have made an urgent case for more effective intervention.[123] The creation of the International Criminal Tribunal for the Former Yugoslavia,[124] the International Criminal Tribunal for Rwanda,[125] and the 1998 adoption in Rome of the Statute of the International Criminal Court are just several recent examples of this renewed urgency in the area of human rights.[126] But these actions came after long periods of resistance by major Western powers, including the United States, and only after intense public scrutiny and media exposures of atrocities.[127] Following the Yugoslav and Rwanda crises, Human Rights Watch lamented the "moral vacuum in the halls of the United Nations."[128] It decried the UN "posture of neutrality between murderer and victim" and argued that the "failure of leadership, eagerly abetted by the Security Council's permanent members, led to a squandering of the United Nations' unique capacity on the global stage to articulate fundamental human rights values and to legitimize their enforcement." The weight of responsibility placed on the United Nations in the area of human rights is undeniable.

After the UN, the second powerful tier of saviors is constituted by Western states and Western or Western-controlled institutions, including, recently, the World Bank, which is not primarily concerned with human rights.[129] Western states usually employ a horizontal state-to-state enforcement of human rights in which their foreign policies become the conveyer belts of "civilization." Through foreign ministries, diplomatic missions, and special agencies, such as the United States Agency for International Development (USAID) and the Canadian International Development Agency (CIDA), Western governments use a carrot-and-stick approach to force certain policy choices on recipient states, frequently but only selectively using human rights to achieve specific policy objectives.

Human rights have featured prominently, if inconsistently, in the calculus of U.S. foreign policy. The U.S. Congress mandated in 1976 that a human rights bureau be established in the State Department and instructed that the office report annually on the human rights conditions of all countries in the world.[130] President Jimmy Carter gave human rights unprecedented rhetorical significance in foreign policy, though President Ronald Reagan dropped this emphasis. In 1994, the head of the human rights bureau was renamed the Assistant Secretary of State for Democracy, Human Rights, and Labor from the Assistant Secretary of State for Human Rights and Humanitarian Affairs. This change seems to acknowledge the broad civilizational sweep of human rights and their inseparability from free markets and political democracy. In other words, the United States sees itself as promoting this cultural package when it advocates human rights abroad.

Increasingly, the human rights movement has come to be identified openly with the United States, whose chief executive frequently invokes human rights when he addresses a non-European nation.[131] In fact, President Bill Clinton's speeches on human rights have come to resemble lectures and sermons, very much in the savior mode.[132] Today the presence of the United States—which has succeeded France and Britain as the major global cultural, military, and political power—is ubiquitous. There is virtually no conflict or issue of importance today in which the United States does not seek, and often play, the crucial role whether by omission or commission. The domination of the globe exercised by European powers for the last several centuries has been assumed by the United States. The United States is now the major determinant of "international peace and security" and the spokesperson for the "welfare" of humanity. Never before has one state wielded so much power and influence over so vast a population. A global policeman, the United States now plays the central civilizing role through the export of markets, culture, and human rights.

European states have similar approaches in their relationships with the Third World. Former communist states in Eastern Europe and the former Soviet Union, whose political cultures the West deems inferior, are treated as being in need of "civilizing."[133] Turkey, the only Muslim member of NATO, has been denied entry into the European Union on human rights grounds.[134] Western European liberal democracies leave little doubt that human rights covenants are meant for the Third World, which needs "improving."

Finally, INGOs constitute perhaps the most important element of the savior metaphor. Conventionally doctrinal, INGOs are the human rights movement's foot soldiers, missionaries, and proselytizers. Their crusade is framed in moral certainty in which "evil" and "good" are as separate as night and day. They claim to practice law, not politics.[135] Although they promote paradigmatic liberal values and norms, they present themselves as neutral, universal, and unbiased. Based in the capitals of the powerful Western states, their staffs are mostly well educated, usually trained in the law, middle class, and white. They are very different from the people they seek to save. They are modern-day abolitionists who see themselves as cleansers, singlehandedly rooting out evil in Third World countries and cultures by shining light where darkness reigns.

INGOs have also been instrumental in the creation of national NGOs in the Third World. Mandates of many national NGOs initially mirrored those of INGOs. However, in the last decade, many Third World NGOs have started to broaden their areas of concentration and go beyond the INGOs' civil and political rights constraints. In particular, domestic Third World NGOs are now paying more attention to economic and social rights, development, women's rights, and the relationships between transnational corporations and human rights conditions. In spite of this incipient conceptual independence on the part of NGOs, many remain voiceless in the corridors of power at the United Nations, the European Union, the World Bank, and in the dominant media organizations in the West.

INGOs occupy such a high moral plane in public policy discourse that they are rarely the subject of probing critiques. Morally righteous, they are supported by an almost universal consensus that they are the "good guys." Even academia has been slow to reflect seriously on INGOs. INGOs and their supporters see those who question them as naive, at best, and apologists for repressive governments and cultures, at worst. This climate of intolerance has a chilling effect on human rights speech, particularly of young, probing scholars and activists. It also encourages a herd mentality and compliance with official or knee-jerk human rights strategies, positions, or responses. It certainly does not encourage innovation on the part of the movement.

INGOs also play the role of gatekeepers to powerbrokers in the West, including powerful Western states. Significantly, national NGOs have virtually no financial independence. They rely almost exclusively on funding from Western states, foundations, charities, development agencies, and intergovernmental institutions such as the European Union. In spite of these criticisms of INGOs, many non-Western NGOs expressed appreciation for the work of INGOs at a retreat which discussed the roles of NGOs in the human rights movement. In fact, many sought a more involved approach by INGOs.

The critics sought a more expanded role of INGOs and not an abandonment of their traditional work. No one at the retreat doubted INGOs' contributions to the growth of the human rights movement as a whole and to heightening consciousness about rights in general, thereby influencing the directions and pace of change. No one doubted the vital importance of INGOs' activities: monitoring, investigative reports, publicity, education, and lobbying or interventions before national and intergovernmental bodies.[136]

The lack of a more vigorous and fundamental disagreement between national NGOs and Western INGOs may speak volumes about the leadership of Third World human rights actors. This complacency also does not take into account locally grown, indigenous, "non-human rights" efforts to oppose repression and fight for political and social change. While it is true that INGOs often spoke and agitated for those who were politically voiceless, especially during the Cold War, it would be a mistake to see local human rights activists as separate from the entire human rights project. Opposing that project would be tantamount to self-repudiation. These so-called human rights activists, local collaborators in the civilizing mission, are drawn primarily from the elite in their own societies and aspire generally to the political, social, and economic models of the West. Many of these activists and their organizations are financially dependent on the West and rely on connections with Western institutions, including the diplomatic missions in their countries, for their social status.

In the last decade in Africa, however, a more politically educated activist and thinker, one who questions the human rights project more seriously and who seeks a culturally grounded program for social change, has started to emerge. This activist and thinker understands the connections among power relations, human rights, economic domination, and the historical relationships between the West and the rest of the world. Such a thinker is aware of the deep contradictions that mark the human rights enterprise and seeks the construction of a different human rights movement. While this new actor is still being defined, and constitutes but a small fraction of the human rights movement on the African continent, he is now increasingly at the center of innovative thinking and action. At the core of this new activism and thinking is the push for intellectual originality and self-reliance, local and not Western foundation support, and a commitment to challenge all sources of violations, be they local or foreign. This development represents the cultivation of a truly local human rights culture in terms of the definition of rights and their enforcement.

Chapter 2
Human Rights as an Ideology

The Authors of Human Rights

Over the last fifty years the international law of human rights has steadily achieved a moral plateau rarely associated with the law of nations.[1] A diverse and eclectic assortment of individuals and entities now invoke human rights norms and the attendant phraseology with the intent of cloaking themselves and their causes in the paradigm's perceived power and righteousness. What is interesting is the failure of this universal reliance on the language of human rights to create agreement on the scope, content, and philosophical bases of the human rights corpus. Intellectual and policy battles have focused on its cultural relevance, ideological and political orientation, and thematic incompleteness. Notwithstanding these questions, the seduction of human rights discourse has been so great that it has, in fact, delayed the development of a critique of rights.[2]

This chapter focuses upon what these polar impulses and positions—the fight over the content of human rights, on the one hand, and their captivating allure, on the other—have obscured: that although it seems implausible to openly deny that the human rights corpus is the construction of a political ideology, the discourse's major authors present it as nonideological. They use a vocabulary that paints the movement as both impartial and the quintessence of human goodness. They portray it as divorced from base materialism, self-interest, and "ideology." Perhaps they do so because "ideology" has a negative connotation: it is the instrument that the "other," the adversary, the opponent, uses to challenge and seek the marginalization of the forces of "good." In reality, however, the human rights corpus is not a creed or a set of normative principles suspended in outer space; the matters that it affects are earthly and concern immediate routine politics. The larger political agenda of the human rights regime has, however, been blurred by its veneration and by attempts to clean it of the taint of partisanship.

The following section discusses the theoretical and practical works of the major authors of human rights discourse are analyzed and discussed.[3] It concludes that human rights and Western liberal democracy are virtually tautological. Although the two concepts seem different from a distance, one is in fact the universalized version of the other; human rights represent the attempted diffusion and further development at the international level of the liberal political tradition. These processes have contributed to the reexamination and reconstruction of liberalism and have in some respects refined and added to the liberal tradition. It seems to be true historically that for political movements and ideologies, from nationalism to free enterprise and beyond, totems or myths are necessary to remove them from their earthly moorings. For liberal democracy that totem appears today to be the human rights corpus, the moralized expression of a political ideology. Although the concept of human rights is not unique to European societies, it seems undeniable that the specific philosophy upon which the current "universal" and "official"[4] human rights corpus is based is essentially European.[5] This exclusivity and cultural specificity necessarily deny the concept universality. The fact that human rights are violated in liberal democracies is of little consequence to this argument and does not distinguish the human rights corpus from the ideology of Western liberalism; rather, it emphasizes the contradictions and imperfections of liberalism. In other words, the elusive state of perfection in which human rights are fully respected and realized tells us, among other things, that both human rights and democracy are works in progress. They are projects that are essentially infinite, open-ended, and highly experimental in nature.

Since World War II, the United Nations, nongovernmental organizations, and scholarly writers have created a thicket of norms, processes, and institutions that purport to promote and protect human rights. Working with the so-called International Bill of Rights as their basis,[6] the key but diverse collection of organizations and scholars has tended to agree on an irreducible human rights core.[7] This core, although stated in human rights terms, is now being formulated into the emergent norm of democratic governance in international law.[8] The routes different authors of human rights have taken to arrive at these conclusions are, of course, varied. Nevertheless, I have identified the four defining approaches or schools of thought into which I believe all the paramount voices writing and acting in the human rights discourse fall.[9] I believe that these voices express the synonymity and close fit of the human rights corpus with its parent, Western liberalism.

The proponents of and adherents to the four dominant schools of thought may be classified as (1) conventional doctrinalists, (2) constitutionalists or conceptualizers, (3) cultural pluralists or multiculturalists, and (4) political strategists or instrumentalists. Although most of these voices differ—in some instances radically—on the content of the human rights corpus and whether or how the contents should be ranked, they are nevertheless united by the belief that there are basic human rights. They also believe that these human rights should be promoted and where possible protected by the state, the basic obligor of human rights law.[10] These different schools disagree, however, on the political orientation of human rights, the weight accorded to certain rights, and strategies and tactics for the enforcement of the human rights movement's norms. These disagreements reflect the different visions and trajectories of liberalism, the types of societies intended by advocates of human rights, and the purposes to which they feel the human rights discourse should be directed.

The human rights corpus, taken as a whole, as a document of ideals and values, particularly the positive law of human rights, requires the reconstruction of states to reflect the structures and values of governance that derive from Western liberalism, especially the contemporary variations of liberal democracy practiced in Western democracies. While these democracies differ in the content of the rights they guarantee and the organizational structures they take, they are nevertheless based on the idea of constitutionalism.

Viewed from this perspective, the human rights regime has serious and dramatic implications for questions of cultural diversity, the sovereignty of states, and ultimately the "universality" of human rights. The purpose here, however, is not to mediate these conflicts, but rather to expose them and to allow diverse stakeholders to reflect on their meaning and the policy issues they raise. The four schools of thought serve as a starting point to explore the divergent pathways that each school's proponents take to converge on the concept of human rights in international law.

The first two approaches, which are espoused by conventional doctrinalists and conceptualizers or constitutionalists, are closest in ideological orientation and share an unequivocal belief in the redemptive quality and power of human rights law. Admittedly, there is a wide and contrasting diversity of attitudes toward the human rights corpus within the two schools. While the doctrinalists tend to be statisticians of violence, conceptualizers are at their core systematizers of the human rights corpus. For the latter, human rights norms arise out of the liberal tradition, and their application should achieve a type of a constitutional system broadly referred to as constitutionalism. Such a system generally has the following characteristics, although the weight accorded to each differs from one state to the next: (1) political society is based on the concept of popular sovereignty; (2) the government of the state is constitutionally required to be accountable to the populace through various processes such as periodic, genuine, multiparty elections; (3) government is limited in its powers through checks and balances and the separation of powers, a central tenet of the liberal tradition; (4) the judiciary is independent and safeguards legality and the rule of law; and (5) the formal declaration of individual civil and political rights is an indispensable facet of the state.[11]

While conceptualizers are more critical of the corpus, many of the conventional doctrinalists see it in almost religious dimensions. Nevertheless, many of the voices in the two schools see themselves in a variety of guises:

as inheritors of the Western historical tradition pitting individual rights against the state, as guardians of human rights law, or as founders, conceptualizers, and elaborators of the human rights corpus. The two schools constitute what I call the human rights "orchestra" in which their proponents are the composers and conductors of the discourse; they control the content and map the margins of the discourse. Conventional doctrinalists are marked by their heavy and virtually exclusive reliance on positive law in treaties, custom, and other sources of international law as the basis for their activist advocacy or scholarly inquiry. The vast majority of doctrinalists "who matter" operate in the context of international nongovernmental human rights organizations (INGOs) in the West, although a number of academics also write in this mold.[12] In contrast, constitutionalists are usually found in the realm of theory.

Both schools enjoy a spirited supporting cast in the non-Western world. In the last several decades, the number of national human rights NGOs and human rights academics has mushroomed in the South. In virtually all cases, they reproduce intellectual patterns and strategies of advocacy similar to those in the West. Although there are some significant differences on the emphasis placed on certain rights, there has been little originality as the corpus has conquered new territory outside the West.

Substantively, doctrinalists stress the primacy of civil and political rights over all other classes of rights.[13] Thus, only a small number of "traditional" civil and political rights comprise the heart of the human rights regime. In addition, doctrinalists seek immediate and "blind" application of these rights without regard to historical, cultural, or developmental differences among states and societies. Many constitutionalists, on the other hand, recognize the supremacy of these "core" rights but point out that the list could or should be expanded. They see the difficulties of "immediate" implementation and prefer a more nuanced approach, staggered to take into account variables of culture, history, and other cleavages. Although many who adopt this approach are positivist, some are critical thinkers who subject the human rights regime to a probing critique. I call them constitutionalists because they believe that, as a whole, human rights law is or should be a constitutional regime and a philosophy that is constitutive of a liberal democratic society, along a spectrum that stretches from a bare republican state to the social democratic state. In the republican "minimum" state, the archetypal nineteenth century liberal state, the government protects the privileges of the few against the poor masses, as well as ethnic, racial, religious, and sexual minorities. Starting in the twentieth century, however, the liberal tradition was developed and constructed the social welfare state in which the government progressively and affirmatively strove to give substance to formal equality.

Cultural pluralists are generally outsiders who see the universality or convergence of some human rights norms with certain non-Western norms and as a result partially embrace the human rights corpus. Many are scholars and policymakers of multicultural heritage or orientation who, though familiar and sometimes even comfortable with the West, see cross-cultural referencing as the most critical variable in the creation of a universal corpus of human rights. They critique the existing human rights corpus as culturally exclusive in some respects and therefore view parts of it as illegitimate or, at the very least, irrelevant in non-Western societies. They are in a sense cultural agnostics because they do not believe that a genuine universal human rights truth can be constructed from any one single culture. They have called for a multicultural approach to reform the human rights regime so as to make it more universal. Many proponents of the first two schools who regard themselves as universalists have labeled many cultural pluralists "cultural relativists," a form of typecasting or human rights name-calling that has generally had the effect of stigmatizing those who resist the Eurocentric formulation of human rights.[14] Were this book confined to this dichotomous view, it would be fair to label the universalists cultural relativists, as well, because universalists operate in a specific cultural space and distinct historical tradition. The perspective reflected here is not, however, sympathetic to cynical elites who purposely manipulate cultural images to justify despotic rule and discriminatory or harmful cultural practices.[15] Rather, by cultural pluralists I refer to academics and policymakers who see the potential dynamism of the human rights corpus as an opportunity for the creation of a multicultural conception of human rights.

The last school, that of political strategists or instrumentalists, abounds with governments and institutions that selectively and inconsistently deploy human rights discourse for strategic and political ends.[16] While all states—socialist or capitalist, developed or underdeveloped—are generally cynical in their deployment of human rights norms, the focus here is not on all states. If that were the case, one would discuss the hypocrisies of the Zairian state under Mobutu Sese Seko, those of the former Soviet Union, and of many other states across the political spectrum that professed allegiance to human rights but violated them as official policy. The concern here is not with claims of states about their internal application of human rights norms. Rather, I am only interested in Western democracies and their institutions which primarily rhetorically champion the universalization of human rights. Such institutions include the World Bank and the North Atlantic Treaty Organization (NATO), whose primary purposes are related to the preservation or the enhancement of liberalism and free markets. Increasingly, they have invoked human rights when dangers to these two goals have been deemed unacceptably high. Examples of such unacceptable dangers include civil war or regional conflicts that threaten "vital" Western interests, such as access to strategic resources. In the view of international financial institutions, donor agencies, and donor countries, such a risk could involve autocratic forms of governance that encourage intolerable levels of corruption and economic mismanagement and negatively affect the growth or functioning of markets and international trade. Responses to such risks, including military ones, have in the past often been couched in human rights terminology.[17]

Obviously human rights issues are not, nor have they ever been, the only factors that determine foreign policy choices of Western states. Other "vital" interests such as trade have often trumped human rights because in the calculus of geopolitics states have "many fish to fry." Yet it is precisely this "necessity" to balance competing objectives that makes states unreliable, unprincipled, and manipulative proponents of the human rights corpus.

By grouping the authors of human rights discourse into these four schools, I do not mean to suggest that the typologies or categories delineated are finite, completely separate and irreconcilable, or that one could not understand the "creators" of the discourse differently. I also do not mean to imply that the proponents of various typologies are one-dimensional; one author could fall into several categories depending upon the circumstances. Any number of critiques—from the feminist to the postmodern—would yield interesting results. This chapter, however, is concerned with correlating the recent and "lofty" mantra of human rights to liberalism, arguably the most dominant political ideology of our time.

This chapter analyzes each of the four schools of thought and action to determine how they may be traced back to liberal democracy. It attempts to respond to the challenges and questions raised for the human rights corpus by these typologies. In particular, it revisits questions of the universality and legitimacy of the human rights corpus and raises the possibility of a new internationality in human rights including its potential implications for the postliberal society.

A Holy Trinity: Liberalism, Democracy, and Human Rights

Liberalism is distinguished from other traditions by its commitment to formal autonomy and abstract equality. It is a tradition that in its contemporary expression requires a constitutional state with limited powers, a state that is moreover accountable to the broad public. These aspirations are the basis for the development and elaboration of liberal democracy and, as I contend, the construction and universalization of the jurisprudence of human rights. In the historical continuum, therefore, liberalism gave birth to democracy, which, in turn, now seeks to present itself internationally as the ideology of human rights. It is therefore useful to briefly explore the relationships that exist between and among these concepts of liberalism, political democracy, and human rights.

While definitions of Western liberal democracy abound, the most dominant cast it in other than substantive terms. Samuel Huntington, for example, emphasizes the Schumpeterian tradition,[18] defining democracy in
purely procedural language.[19] For Huntington, the democratic method involves two basic dimensions: contestation and participation, where the
"most powerful collective decision makers are selected through fair, honest, and periodic elections in which candidates freely compete for votes
and in which virtually all the adult population is eligible to vote." Participation and contestation, according to Huntington, also imply certain civil
and political freedoms which are necessary to free and fair elections,
namely, the right to speak, publish, assemble, and organize.[20]

Significantly, Huntington does not believe that a system is democratic
to the extent that it denies "voting participation" to segments of its population on the basis, for instance, of race or gender.[21] By this logic, the
United States of America was not a democracy until it allowed its population of African ancestry the right to vote.[22] Likewise, South Africa was undemocratic until it granted its black African majority the right to vote in
1994. Many European countries, such as Switzerland, were undemocratic
until they granted women the right to vote, and the same was true for the
United States until 1920.[23] The norm of nondiscrimination is here extended to political participation. The formal right to vote is clearly in itself
an insufficient measure of democracy because quite often it has masked
other hindrances to political participation such as institutional biases and
barriers based on race, gender, religion, social status, and wealth. Nevertheless, the political scientist Robert Dahl has argued that elections are the
critical element in the definition of democracy and the central device for
ordinary citizens to exert a high degree of control over their leaders.[24]

The minimalist definition of democracy does not betray traditional or
conventional conceptions of liberalism; rather, it responds to liberalism's
basic commitment to guarantee citizens their formal autonomy and political and legal equality. Thus, as Henry Steiner puts it, the traditional liberal
understanding of the state requires that it "protect citizens in their political organizations and activities,"[25] guaranteeing autonomy and legal equality, but does not require that it remove impediments to actual equality
which may result from lack of resources and status. Steiner says it clearly:

Choices about types and degrees of [political] participation may depend on citizens' economic resources and social status. But it is not the government's responsibility to alleviate that dependence, to open paths to political participation which
lack of funds or education or status would otherwise block.[26]

In reality, of course, participation in the political process requires more
than the state's permission and protection. Increasingly, states not only
provide these two services but also expend enormous resources construct-

ing the electoral machinery for participation; legislative reforms in many democracies now attempt to address not only the historical, socioeconomic, but the ethnic, racial, and gender-related barriers to participation as well.[27] Such interpretations of political democracy have attempted to build into their frameworks notions of social or economic democracy. In human rights law, the International Covenant on Economic, Social and Cultural Rights (ICESCR) most closely resembles this aspiration.

The main focus of human rights law, however, has been on those rights and programs that seek to strengthen, legitimize, and export political or liberal democracy.[28] Inversely, most of the human rights regime is derived from bodies of domestic jurisprudence developed over several centuries in the West. The emphasis, by academics and practitioners, in the development of human rights law has been on civil and political rights.[29] In fact, the currency of civil and political rights has been so strong that they have become synonymous with the human rights movement, even as the so-called second and third generation rights have attempted to make inroads into the mainstream of the discourse.[30]

There is virtual agreement that the early formulation and codification of human rights standards was dominated by Western cultural and political norms.[31] This was particularly true with the formulation and adoption of the Universal Declaration of Human Rights, the "spiritual parent of and inspiration for many human rights treaties."[32] As one author has remarked, the West was able to "impose" its philosophy of human rights on the rest of the world because in 1948 it dominated the United Nations.[33] The minority socialist bloc abstained after it put up ineffectual resistance on grounds that economic, social, and cultural rights were downgraded. More important, non-Western views were largely unrepresented because the Third World at the United Nations was mainly composed of Latin American countries whose dominant worldview was European. In 1948, most African and Asian states were absent from the United Nations because they were European colonies.[34] On account of this exclusivity of major cultural blocs, it was presumptuous and shamelessly ethnocentric for the UDHR to refer to itself as the "common standard of achievement for all peoples and all nations."[35]

A closer examination of the rights listed in both the UDHR and the International Covenant on Civil and Political Rights leaves no doubt that both documents—which are regarded as the two most important human rights instruments[36]—are attempts to universalize those civil and political rights which are accepted or aspired to in Western liberal democracies. Many articles in the Universal Declaration echo or reproduce provisions of the U.S. Constitution and the jurisprudence of Western European states such as France and the United Kingdom. The UDHR prohibits "cruel, inhuman or degrading treatment or punishment";[37] the U.S. Constitution prohibits the infliction of "cruel and unusual punishments."[38] Other parallels include due process protections,[39] speech rights,[40] and privacy.[41] During the drafting of the ICCPR and the ICESCR, both of which were opened for signature in 1966, there was some discernible influence from the newly independent states of Africa and Asia, though the ICCPR retained its distinctly Western character.[42] Although non-Western perspectives on human rights, such as the African conceptions of peoples' rights and duties and the more celebrated right to development,[43] have acquired some notoriety in human rights debates, they remain marginal to the mainstream practice of human rights.[44] The same has been true of economic, social, and cultural rights since their relegation to the "other" human rights treaty.[45]

The purpose of this segment was to track some of the historical roots of the human rights corpus and to establish its evolution from liberal thought and political democracy. This connection leads to the conclusion that the postwar elaboration and codification of human rights norms has been the process of the universalization of liberalism and its outgrowth, Western political democracy. Seen in this light, the human rights movement is a proxy for a political ideology, a fact that would shear it of the pretense of nonpartisanship. Although the movement's authors present it as nonideological, and as universal and noncontentious, the human rights regime does not transcend or stand removed from politics. The human rights movement is not post-ideological, although its mantra of universal morality and timeless righteousness attempts to mask its deeply political character.

The Conventional Doctrinalists

Perhaps no other school in the human rights movement has been more influential in the promotion of the "universalization" of human rights norms than that of the conventional doctrinalists, even though the formal creation of human rights law is carried out by collections of states—the so-called international community—acting in concert and separately within and outside the ambit of the United Nations. It is generally accepted that the full-court press for the universalization of human rights ideals was not applied until after the Hitler atrocities half a century ago, although the development of human rights norms and ideals preceded the Holocaust. Prior to 1945, the antecedents to the human rights corpus included the 1926 Slavery Convention, the work of the International Labour Organization, and some opinions of the Permanent Court of International Justice. After Hitler, the United Nations set out on a crusade to codify "universal" human rights norms.

The most active element in the internationalization of the human rights movement has been the so-called international nongovernmental organization (INGO),[46] the movement's prime engine of growth. The most prominent INGOs in this regard are based in the West and seek to enforce the application of human rights norms internationally, particularly toward repressive states in the South. They are ideological analogues, both in theory and in method, of the traditional civil rights organizations which preceded them in the West. The American Civil Liberties Union (ACLU), one of the most influential civil rights organizations in the United States, is the classic example of the Western civil rights organization.[47] Two other equally important domestic civil rights organizations in the United States are the National Association for the Advancement of Colored People (NAACP)[48] and the NAACP Legal Defense and Educational Fund (LDF).[49] Although these organizations are called civil rights groups by Americans, they are in reality human rights organizations. The historical origin of the distinction between a "civil rights" group and a "human rights" group in the United States remains unclear. The primary difference is that "international" Western human rights groups focus on abusive practices and traditions in what they see as relatively repressive, "backward" foreign countries and cultures, while the agenda of domestic civil rights groups has a focus on primarily domestic issues. Thus, although groups such as Human Rights Watch publish reports on human rights abuses in the U.S., the focus of their activity is the human rights "problems" or "abuses" in other, "foreign" countries.

In American popular culture, several assumptions are implicit in this thinking: "human rights problems" do not apply to "people like us," but rather to "backward" peoples or those who are "exotic"; these "problems" arise where the political and legal systems do not work or cannot correct themselves; and "we are lucky" and should "help those less fortunate" overcome their history of despotism. Unfortunately, this dichotomy has calcified in academic institutions where civil rights questions are taught and explored under the rubric of "American" courses while human rights offerings and activities are treated under the umbrella of "foreign," "area studies," or "international" disciplines and classifications. For example, American law school graduates who have taken courses on race, gender, employment law, sexuality, housing, or the criminal justice system probably associate those fields with civil rights, not human rights. This organizational format could lead to a sense of cultural superiority and may exacerbate problems of nationalism. In turn, this development could adversely affect attempts at an international consensus on human rights, as non-Western cultures see crusading human rights activists from the West as the "civilizers" that many of the activists cast themselves as.

At any rate, the half-dozen leading human rights organizations, the prototypical conventional doctrinalists, have arisen in the West over the last half-century with the express intent of promoting certain basic Western liberal values—now dubbed human rights—throughout the world, especially the non-Western world. These INGOs were the brainchildren of prominent Western civil rights advocates, lawyers, and private citizens. The International League for the Rights of Man, now the International League for Human Rights (ILHR), is the oldest such organization, founded in New York in 1942.[50] At various times it has focused on victims of torture, religious intolerance, the rights of human rights monitors at its affiliates abroad, the reunification of Eastern Europeans with relatives in the West during the cold war, and the human rights treaty state reporting system within the United Nations. Roger Baldwin, the founder of the ACLU, also founded the ILHR.[51]

The ILHR itself was responsible for establishing in New York in 1975 the Lawyers Committee for International Human Rights, now known as the Lawyers Committee for Human Rights (LCHR), another of the more important Western INGOs. The LCHR claims to promote the human rights standards contained in the International Bill of Rights. The New York-based Human Rights Watch (HRW)[52] was founded in 1978 and has developed into the most dominant American INGO working to expose violations of basic liberal freedoms. The founder of HRW was Aryeh Neier, a former national executive director of the ACLU.[53]

The last significant American INGO is the Washington D.C.-based International Human Rights Law Group, which was established by the Procedural Aspects of International Law Institute (PAIL), a private American organization that explores issues in international law.[54] Some American domestic civil rights NGOs are acutely aware of their pioneering role in the creation of similar organizations abroad.[55] Until recently, and to a large extent even today, none of these American INGOs focused on human rights issues in the United States, except to seek the reform of U.S. foreign policy and American compliance with aspects of refugee law.

The two other leading INGOs are located in Europe, in the United Kingdom and Switzerland. The Geneva-based International Commission of Jurists (ICJ) was "founded in 1952 to promote the 'rule of law' throughout the world."[56] The ICJ has been accused of being a tool of the West in the Cold War, spending considerable resources exposing the failures of Soviet bloc and one-party states.[57] Today, however, it is regarded as a bona fide INGO, concerned with rule of law questions in the global South.

Last, the London-based Amnesty International (AI), the most powerful human rights INGO, is today synonymous with the human rights movement and has inspired the creation of many similar human rights groups around the world. It was launched by Peter Benenson, a British lawyer, writing in the May 28, 1961, issues of the *London Observer* and *Le Monde*.[58] Benenson's article, "Forgotten Prisoners," urged moral outrage and appeals for amnesty for individuals who were imprisoned, tortured, or executed because of their political opinions or religion.[59] The recipient of the 1977 Nobel Peace Prize, AI claims that its object is "to contribute to the observance throughout the world of human rights as set out in the Universal Declaration of Human Rights" through campaigns to free prisoners of

conscience; to ensure fair trials within a reasonable time for political prisoners; to abolish the death penalty, torture, and other cruel treatment of
prisoners; and to end extrajudicial executions and disappearances.[60]

Some structural factors provide further evidence of the ideological orientation of INGOs. They concern the sources of their moral, financial, and
social support. The founding fathers of major INGOs—they have all been
white males—were Westerners who either worked on or had an interest in
domestic civil and political rights issues; they sought the reform of governmental laws, policies, and processes to bring about compliance with American and European conceptions of liberal democracy and equal
protection. Although the founders of the INGOs did not explicitly state
their "mission" as a crusade for the globalization of these values, they nevertheless crafted organizational mandates that promoted liberal ideals and
norms. In any case, the key international human rights instruments such as
the UDHR and the ICCPR pierced the sovereign veil for the purposes of
protecting and promoting human rights. The mandates of INGOs are
lifted, almost verbatim, from such instruments. AI also deploys jurisprudential arguments developed in the context of Western liberal democracy
to cast the death penalty as the "ultimate form of cruel, inhuman and degrading punishment."[61]

The pool for the social support of INGOs has therefore come from the
private, nongovernmental, and civil society segments of the industrial
democracies: prominent lawyers, academics at leading universities, the
business and entertainment elite, and other professionals. In the United
States, these circles are drawn from the liberal establishment; the overwhelming majority vote for and support the Democratic Party and its politics and are opposed to the Republican Party. The boards of directors of
American-based INGOs are predominantly white and male and almost
completely American; some, such as those of the Lawyers Committee or
HRW, typically have one or several African Americans or a member of another nonwhite minority.

The boards of directors of the European-based INGOs, the ICJ and AI,
tend to differ, somewhat, from American INGOs, although they too are
dominated by Westerners, Western-trained academics, professionals, and
policymakers, or non-Westerners whose worldview is predominantly Western. Thus, even these Asians and Africans—who, though nonwhite, nevertheless "think white" or "European"—champion, usually uncritically, the
universalization of the human rights corpus and liberal democracy. The
non-Westerners on this board are usually prominent legal professionals
steeped in either the common law or the civil law traditions. AI's International Executive Committee, its principal policymaking organ, is arguably
"more global looking"—it includes a number of members from the
South—although it too has historically been dominated by Westerners.[62]
The staffs of all the major INGOs, including AI's headquarters in London,

are similarly dominated by Westerners, although both AI and ICJ broke the color barrier in this one respect by hiring African heads in the 1990s.[63] The selection of the boards and staffs of INGOs seems designed to guard against individuals, even if they are Westerners, who may question the utility or appropriateness of the conventional doctrinalist approach. This vetting perpetuates their narrow mandates and contradicts the implied and stated norms of diversity and equality, the raison d'être for the existence of these organizations.[64]

The relationship between social, financial, and other material support provides further evidence of the political character of INGOs. Except for AI, which relies heavily on membership dues, most INGOs are funded by a combination of foundation grants, private donations, corporations, businesses, and governments.[65] While most do not accept government funds, some, among them the ICJ and the International Human Rights Law Group, have accepted financial support from governmental sources such as the United States Agency for International Development (USAID) and its Canadian and Nordic counterparts.[66] Those who reject government funds cite concerns for their independence of action and thought. It seems fair to conclude that to be considered for acceptance financial support must come from an industrial democracy with a commitment to promoting human rights abroad; presumably, support from Saudi Arabia or the People's Republic of China, two states which have been vigorously criticized in the West for their human rights records, would be unacceptable.

The value of the board of directors is critical for groups that rely on private funding. Those networks and associations signify an INGO's reputation and acceptability by political, cultural, intellectual, and business elites. In the past decade, some INGOs, especially those based in the United States, have devised a fund-raising gimmick. At an annual dinner they present an award to a noted activist from a repressive country in the South or to a Westerner with superstar quality, such as Senator Edward Kennedy or George Soros, the philanthropist, and invite well-to-do, if not wealthy, citizens, corporations, law firms, and foundations to "buy a table"—by which is meant an invitee purchases the right to the dinner by reserving a table for a certain number of guests for a substantial donation. This tapestry of social and business ties, drawn from leading Americans who believe in liberal values and their internationalization through the human rights regime, underlines the agenda of INGOs.[67]

Substantively, conventional doctrinalists stress a narrow range of civil and political rights, as is reflected by the mandates of leading INGOs like Amnesty International and Human Rights Watch. Throughout the Cold War period, INGOs concentrated their attention on the exposure of violations of what they deemed "core" rights in Soviet bloc countries, Africa, Asia, and Latin America. In a reflection of this ideological bias, INGOs mirrored the position of the industrial democracies and generally assumed an unsympathetic and at times hostile posture toward calls for the expansion of their mandates to include economic and social rights.[68]

In the latter part of the 1990s, especially after the collapse of the Soviet bloc, several INGOs started to talk about the "indivisibility" of rights; some even talked about their belief in the equality of the ICESCR and the ICCPR, although their rhetoric has not been matched by action or practice.[69] Many, in particular Human Rights Watch, for a long time remained hostile, however, to the recognition of economic and social rights as "rights." HRW, which considered such rights "equities," instead advanced its own nebulous interpretation of "indivisible human rights" which related civil and political rights to survival, subsistence, and poverty, "assertions" of good that it did not explicitly call rights.[70] It argued that subsistence and survival are dependent on civil and political rights, especially those related to democratic accountability.[71] According to this view, civil and political rights belong to the first rank because the realization of other sets of concerns or rights, however they are termed, depend on them.[72]

In September 1996, however, Human Rights Watch abandoned its long-standing opposition to the advocacy of economic and social rights. It passed a highly restrictive and qualified policy—effective January 1997—to investigate, document, and promote compliance with the ICESCR. Under the terms of the new policy, HRW's work on the ICESCR would be limited to two situations: where protection of the ICESCR right is "necessary to remedy a substantial violation of an ICCPR right," and where "the violation of an ICESCR right is the direct and immediate product of a substantial violation of an ICCPR right." Furthermore, HRW would only intervene to protect ICESCR rights where the violation was a "direct product of state action, whether by commission or omission"; where the "principle applied in articulating an ICESCR right is one of general applicability"; and where "there is a clear, reasonable and practical remedy that HRW can advocate to address the ICESCR violation."[73]

While an important step by HRW, this policy statement was a continuation of the history of skepticism toward economic and social rights HRW has long demonstrated; it saw economic and social rights only as an appendage of civil and political rights. Its construction conditioned ICESCR rights on ICCPR rights—in other words, economic and social rights do not exist outside the realm of civil and political rights. Thus, one interpretation of the HRW policy could be that civil and political rights are the fundamental, primary rights without which other rights are less meaningful and unattainable. The policy also continued HRW's stress on state-related violations, an orientation that overlooks other important violators, such as businesses and international corporations. What was important about the policy, however, was the commitment by the largest and most influential American INGO to begin advocacy of economic and social rights. No other major INGO has gone that far in its practical work.[74] Henry Steiner has put the character of INGOs succinctly:

the term "First World" NGOs both signifies an organization's geographical base and typifies certain kinds of mandates, functions, and ideological orientations. It describes such related characteristics as a concentration on civil and political rights, a commitment to fair (due) process, an individualistic rather than group or community orientation in rights advocacy, and a belief in a pluralist society functioning within a framework of rules impartially applied to protect individuals against state interference. In a nutshell, "First World" NGOs means those committed to traditional Western liberal values associated with the origins of the human rights movement. Many of these NGOs work exclusively within their home countries, but the "First World" category also includes most of the powerful international NGOs that investigate events primarily in the Third World.[75]

Traditionally, the work of INGOs has typically involved investigation,[76] reporting,[77] and advocacy.[78] Investigation usually takes place in a "Third World" country while reporting and advocacy aim at reforming policies of industrial democracies and intergovernmental agencies to trigger bilateral and multilateral action against the repressive state. Some INGOs now go beyond this denunciatory framework and work to foster and strengthen processes and institutions—rule of law, laws and constitutions, judiciaries, legislatures, and electoral machineries—that ensure the protection of civil and political rights.[79] Although the ideological commitment of these INGOs seems clear through their mandates and work, they nevertheless cast themselves as nonideological. They perceive themselves as politically neutral modern-day abolitionists whose only purpose is to identify "evil" and root it out. Steiner again notes that:

Although committed to civil-political rights and in this sense taking clear moral and political positions, First World NGOs prefer to characterize themselves as above the play of partisan politics and political parties, and in this sense as apolitical. . . . Their primary self-image is that of monitors, objective investigators applying the consensual norms of the human rights movement to the facts found. They are defenders of legality.[80]

Thus, although INGOs are "political" organizations that work to vindicate political and moral principles that shape the basic characteristics of a state, they consciously present themselves as disinterested in the political character of a state. When HRW asserts that it "addresses the human rights practices of governments of all political stripes, of all geopolitical alignments, and of all ethnic and religious persuasions"[81], it is anticipating charges that it is pro-Western, pro-capitalist, and unsympathetic to Islamic and other non-Western religious and political traditions. The first two charges could have been fatal to a group's credibility at the height of the cold war. In reality, however, INGOs have been highly partial: their work has historically concentrated on those countries that have not attained the stable and functioning democracies of the West, the standard for liberal democracy. Target states have included the Soviet bloc and virtually the entire South, where undemocratic or repressive one-party state and military dictatorships have thrived.

The content of the work of INGOs reveals their partiality as well. The typical INGO report is a catalog of abuses committed by a government against liberal values. As Steiner notes:

Given the ideological commitments of these NGOs, their investigative work naturally concentrates on matters such as governmental abuses of rights to personal security, discrimination, and basic political rights. By habit or established practice, NGOs' reports stress the nature and number of violations, rather than explore the socioeconomic and other factors that underlie them.[82]

Reports further document the abridgment of the freedoms of speech and association, violations of due process, and various forms of discrimination. Many INGOs fear that explaining why abuses occur may justify them or give credence to the claims of some governments that civil and political rights violations take place because of underdevelopment. Such an argument, if accepted, would destroy the abolitionists' mission by delaying, perhaps indefinitely, the urgency of complying with human rights standards. Abolitionists fear that this argument would allow governments to continue repressive policies while escaping their obligations under human rights law. INGOs thus demand the immediate protection and respect of civil and political rights regardless of the level of development of the offending state. By taking cover behind the international human rights instruments, INGOs are able to fight for liberal values without appearing "partisan," "biased," or "ideological."

Conventional doctrinalists also perpetuate the appearance of objectivity by explicitly distinguishing themselves from agencies, communities, and government programs that promote democracy and democratization. The "democracy" and "human rights" communities see themselves in different lights.[83] The first is made up of individuals and institutions devoted to "democracy assistance programs" abroad,[84] while the second is primarily composed of INGOs.[85] The human rights community has created a law-versus-politics dichotomy through which it presents itself as the guardian of international law, in this case human rights law, as opposed to the promoter of the more elusive concept of democracy, which it sees as a political ideology.[86] A complex web of reasons, motivations, and contradictions permeate this distinction.

The seeds of the dichotomy are related to the attempt by the human rights community not to "side" with the two protagonists of the Cold War, and in particular Ronald Reagan's crusade against communism and his efforts to pave the way for democracy and free markets across the globe. The human rights community, whose activists and leaders are mostly Democrats or sympathetic to the Democratic Party, in the case of the United States, or Social Democrats and Labour Party sympathizers in Europe—liberals or those to the left-of-center in Western political jargon—viewed with alarm Reagan's and Margaret Thatcher's push for free markets and support for any pro-Western government, notwithstanding its human rights record. This hostility was exacerbated by the Reagan administration's attempts to reverse the rhetorical prominence that the Carter administration had given to human rights in American foreign policy.[87] Although INGOs delighted in Reagan's opposition to communist rule within the Soviet bloc—their own human rights reports on Soviet bloc countries were scathing—they sought "impartiality" and a "principled" use by the administration of human rights as a tool of foreign policy.[88] INGOs also feared that "democracy programs" would focus only on elections without entrenching basic civil and political rights. In addition, INGOs believed that the focus on democracy blurred the focus on violators and dulled the clarity of physical violations of rights.

The differentiation between democratic and free market crusades and human rights had another advantage: Western governments and human rights groups could play "good cop, bad cop" roles in the spread of Western liberal values. While the West in bilateral agreements and projects opened up previously closed or repressive, one-party societies to markets and "encouraged" democratization, human rights groups would be unrelenting in their assault on the same government for violating civil and political rights. Ordinarily, staffs of INGOs consulted extensively with the State Department or relevant foreign ministry, Western diplomats in the "repressive" state,[89] and elements of the United Nations charged with human rights oversight, such as the Commission on Human Rights, the Committee Against Torture, and the Human Rights Committee.

Other factors indicate the commitment of INGOs to liberal democracy as a political project. At least one American NGO, the Lawyers Committee for Civil Rights Under Law, a domestic NGO which used to have an INGO dimension, expressly linked the survival of its international operations to the "attainment" of democracy by, for example, shutting down its Southern Africa Project after the 1994 South African elections. Some INGO reports explicitly lament the failure of democratic reform. They defend and seek to immortalize pro-democracy activists in repressive states.[90] At least one former leader of an INGO recognizes that the distinction made between democracy and human rights is a facade:

This determination to establish impartiality in the face of human rights violations under different political systems led Amnesty International to shun the rhetorical identification of human rights with democracy. But in fact the struggle against violations, committed mostly by undemocratic authoritarian governments, was closely bound up with the struggle for democracy. Thousands of prisoners of conscience for whom Amnesty International worked in its first three decades were political activists challenging the denial of their rights to freedom of expression and association.[91]

In the last decade, some INGOs have started seeking the deployment of the resources of other institutions, in addition to those of the United Nations, in their advocacy for liberal values. The Lawyers Committee for Human Rights, for example, instituted a project that explores ways of encouraging international financial institutions such as the World Bank to build human rights concerns into their policies.[92] INGOs should openly acknowledge the inescapable and intrinsic linkage between human rights and democracy.

The Conceptualizers

Constitutionalists, as the label suggests, see, or would like to see, the human rights corpus as a constitutional framework: a set of norms, ideals, and principles—moral, philosophical, legal, even cultural—that cohere to determine the fundamental character of a state and its society. They do not openly distinguish or distance themselves from doctrinalists whom they see as the human rights movement's critical core, its foot soldiers, those on whom the practical advocacy, proselytization, and universalization of its creed depend. Rather, constitutionalists are the "thinking" corps of the movement; as its ideologues they provide intellectual direction and rigor. They explore and explain issues relating to the movement's origin, its philosophical and historical bases, its normative content, and the connections among social, political, and cultural structures and values, as well as the questions that arise from the norms' enforcement and internationalization. When constitutionalists critique the human rights corpus and its movement, it is in language that is internal and "friendly" to the discourse, that is, conversations which are meant to sharpen the movement's focus, expand its influence, and bare dilemmas for resolution. Such critiques explore moral and political dilemmas, normative conflicts within the corpus, the scope of the movement, and differences in the strategies deployed in the vindication of the movement's values. Constitutionalists were among the founders of INGOs and many serve on their boards.[93]

In this section I explore the works of a number of leading constitutionalists in order to extract and underline the basic messages and themes they advance to create and crystallize what I call the "defining" character of the human rights movement. Principal among the constitutionalists has been Professor Louis Henkin. Perhaps more than any other proponent in this school, Henkin has combined extensive and authoritative scholarship with active association with the "nerve center" of the American human rights community in New York. Among others in this school, I will also briefly explore the work of Philip Alston, Henry Steiner, and Thomas Franck. I contend here that while these thinkers do not completely agree on the content or even the normative importance of different human rights, they nevertheless are generally united in their vision of the approximate political society intended by the human rights corpus.

In the preface to The Age of Rights, a collection of essays that crystallizes his ideas on human rights, Henkin underlines his belief in the omnipotence of human rights by elevating them to a near-mythical, almost biblical plateau. To him, the universality of the acceptance of the idea of human rights sets it apart from all other ideas and puts it in a most distinctive place in modern times. He boldly states:

Ours is the age of rights. Human rights is the idea of our time, the only political-moral idea that has received universal acceptance. The Universal Declaration of Human Rights, adopted by the United Nations General Assembly in 1948, has been approved by virtually all governments representing all societies. Human rights are enshrined in the constitutions of virtually every one of today's 170 states—old states and new; religious, secular, and atheist; Western and Eastern; democratic, authoritarian, and totalitarian; market economy, socialist, and mixed; rich and poor, developed, developing, and less developed. Human rights is the subject of numerous international agreements, the daily grist of the mills of international politics, and a bone of continuing contention among superpowers.[94]

This celebratory and triumphant passage uses a quantitative approach—the idea's dissemination and diffusion to most corners of the earth—as the standard for determining the superiority of human rights over other ideas.[95] But the quantitative approach, while persuasive, has its own problems. One could plausibly argue, based on this criterion, for example, that ideas about free markets as the engine of economic development, among others, are equally if not more universally accepted than human rights. Furthermore, depending on how universal acceptance is calibrated, and who the participants in that construction are, might it not have been possible to argue at the close of the nineteenth century that colonialism enjoyed a similarly elevated status?

In any case, it seems highly doubtful that many of the states which constitute the international community are representative of its societies and cultures. It is certainly questionable whether the homage such states pay to human rights is part of a cynically manipulative strategy to be seen to "belong" among the "civilized" members of the international community. Universality obtained at the expense of genuine understanding and commitment cheapens and devalues the idea of human rights. Ultimately, such universality is of little normative value in the reconstruction of societies.

Like other Western pioneers of the concept of human rights, Henkin rejects claims of "cultural relativism" or a multicultural approach to the construction of human rights. He accuses those who advocate cultural and ideological diversity in the creation of the human rights corpus of desiring a vague, broad, ambiguous, and general text of human rights.[96] He sees such an approach as fatal because it would allow different societies to read into human rights texts what they will. Instead, he turns to the Universal Declaration of Human Rights, which he sees as the bedrock, the constitution of human rights.[97] Although Henkin insists that human rights are universal, he does not offer any non-Western political or moral underpinnings for them. Rather, he emphasizes that human rights are derived from "natural rights theories and systems, harking back through English, American, and French constitutionalism to John Locke."[98] The truth is that human rights instruments did not articulate the Western philosophical basis for the corpus because of the need to present the image of universality; it was not, as Henkin suggests, because the framers were politicians and citizens as opposed to philosophers.[99]

Henkin draws many parallels between human rights and American or Western constitutionalism but concludes, surprisingly, that the human rights corpus does not require a particular political ideology. This conclusion, with which this book disagrees, has been popular among the pioneers of the human rights movement for a number reasons, including their basic assertion that human rights are distinct from politics—defined here as a particular ideology—and can be achieved in different political traditions such as socialist, religious, or free market systems. A further examination of the views of Henkin and other constitutionalists indicates just the opposite: that taken as a whole, their philosophy of human rights leads to the construction of liberal democratic states.

Henkin outlines and uses the basic precepts of American constitutionalism to argue that they are not required by the human rights corpus. He identifies these as: "original individual autonomy translated into popular sovereignty," a social contract requiring self-government "through accountable representatives . . . limited government for limited purposes," and basic individual rights.[100] He argues that in contrast the human rights regime "reflect[s] no comprehensive political theory" about how the individual should relate to the state and vice versa;[101] that a state's failure to respect individual rights does not trigger the right of revolution, although the corpus gives a "nod to popular sovereignty"; and that it requires the state to be more active because of the ideas of socialism and the welfare state.[102] Henkin concedes that human rights instruments point to particular principles, but quickly denies that such principles imply a particular political theory:

Necessarily, however, the idea of rights reflected in the instruments, the particular rights recognized, and the consequent responsibilities for political societies, imply particular political ideas and moral principles. International human rights does not hint at any theory of social contract, but it is committed to popular sovereignty. "The will of the people shall be the basis of the authority of government" and is to "be expressed in periodic elections which shall be by universal and equal suffrage." It is not required that government based on the will of the people take any particular form.[103]

In addition to the UDHR, the ICCPR gives citizens the right to political participation through elections and the guarantee of the right to assemble, associate, and disseminate their ideas. These and the rights to equality and a fair trial imply a society with the following structure: a regularly elected government, real competition for political office, and the separation and independence of powers among the branches of government. The protection of the individual, his autonomy, and property are among the key goals of such a society. The human rights regime does not dictate the particular variant of liberal society or the color of democracy it envisions; but the rights it guarantees, the ones that Henkin champions as the cornerstone of the human rights regime, seem to require a Western liberal democracy.

Although Steiner seems to agree with Henkin—that association and participation rights do not impose a particular government or political ideology—he identifies liberal democratic systems such as parliamentary or presidential systems, unicameral or bicameral legislatures, proportional representation, or "first past the post" system, as permissible under human rights standards.[104] Steiner notes, however, that dictatorships, inherited leadership, and many forms of one-party states would likely violate associational rights.

Henkin seeks to distinguish human rights from American constitutionalism on the bases for which government is instituted. He argues that while "American rights" originally required a government for limited purposes, human rights, born after socialism and the welfare state, "imply a government that is activist, intervening, [and] committed to economic-social planning" to meet the needs of the individual.[105] This distinction, which relies on the traditional bifurcation of the responsibilities of government—either as the hands-off, negative instrumentality or the regulating, positive interventionist—is more fictitious than real.[106] The social democratic strand of liberalism, which Jack Donnelly credits with the welfare state, has deep roots in liberalism and has historically challenged the individualist formulations of American constitutionalism. As Henkin himself acknowledges, the United States is not a welfare state by constitutional compulsion; but it is a welfare state nevertheless.[107] The political struggles of working Americans and in particular historically excluded groups, such as African Americans and women, have transformed "original American rights" and explicitly imposed interventionist commitments on the American state to alleviate economic and social disparities. Thus the distance Henkin creates between "American rights" and human rights is somewhat exaggerated.

Henry Steiner, another constitutionalist whose writing has concentrated on the content of human rights norms and the structure of the human rights regime, is more inclined to the view that human rights norms are best accomplished, and in most cases only accomplished, within liberal democracy. There is no suggestion that a theocracy or a military regime could accomplish human rights. Although he does not state it explicitly, a number of his writings suggest this conclusion.[108] In his first major article on human rights, for example, Steiner chose to explore the question of political participation, a foundational norm in liberal democracies, from a human rights perspective.[109] The article, which was published in the inaugural issue of the *Harvard Human Rights Journal* (then called the *Harvard Human Rights Yearbook*), explores the different understandings of the right to political participation in various political contexts, from liberal democracies to communist states. Drawing primarily on the UDHR and the ICCPR, which Steiner terms the "two most significant" human rights instruments,[110] the article sidesteps any discussion about the philosophical and historical origins or justifications for human rights.[111]

Steiner categorizes the rights enumerated in the ICCPR in five sets which slide on a spectrum of universal acceptability and normative clarity. These are traditional "negative" rights "which lie at the heart of the liberal tradition's commitment to individual autonomy and choice" (these are the physical integrity rights); rights that assure procedural fairness when a state seeks restrictions on individual liberty; rights that involve antidiscrimination norms (involving an individual's right to fair treatment within the criminal justice system); so-called expressive rights, which include free speech, association, and assembly; and finally, the right to political participation.[112] While there is at least formal, near-universal consensus on the normative content of the rights in the first category—the negative rights—there has been no such unanimity on the meaning of the last category, the right to political participation. However, respect for the first four categories of rights is unlikely to materialize in any systemic manner unless the right to political participation is understood and exercised from a particular ideological perspective. Steiner argues that an abusive regime can terminate some of the rights without altering the existing patterns of economic and political power under that regime. However, the "termination" of, say, one-party or military rule and its replacement by a participatory electoral system most likely would be "fatal to those in power."[113] This is particularly the case since such participation involves the exercise of expressive and other rights.

Debates during the drafting sessions of the relevant provisions of the UDHR and the ICCPR revealed divisions among different states about the content of the right to political participation. Although there is almost a twenty-year gap between the UDHR and the ICCPR, with non-Western states achieving a numerical majority in the UN in the interim, it is significant to note that the political participation articles—21 of the UDHR and 25 of the ICCPR—are nearly identical.[114] Divisions on the content of these provisions were strictly ideological. The West and its philosophical allies in Latin America sought language to guarantee competitive multiparty elections through the secret ballot while Soviet bloc countries wanted open-textured provisions that would meet their more closed electoral systems.[115] Article 25 is deliberately vague enough to accommodate differing views. Both the "elections" and "take part" clauses do not spell out a liberal pluralist theory, although that seems to have been their original intention.

The International Covenant does not, then, offer the explicit guidance for the interpretation of article 25 that a reference to Western pluralist theory would have provided. Its provision for elections fails to resolve some basic issues. Countries of radically different political systems which included some form of electoral process ratified it, without considering themselves to be in instant violation of Article 25 and without expressing their willingness to conform to any one political tradition's prescription of basic political processes.[116]

Steiner realizes the complex character of the norm of political participation and even argues that different political systems could meet it as formulated in article 25. He nevertheless pushes for an understanding of it that comes closer to a liberal pluralist formulation. Such an understanding would reject as inadequate hereditary, noncompetitive, one-party, or ritualistic "yes-or-no" electoral systems where the citizenry votes to evaluate only a single candidate. Seen as part of the gamut of the other four categories of rights that Steiner identifies, an interpretation of article 25 brings it closer to liberal political democracy. Steiner seems to echo this view when he concludes that:

Fresh understandings and different institutionalizations of the right in different cultural and political contexts may reveal what an increasing number of states believe to be a necessary minimum of political participation for all states. That minimum should never require less of a government than provision for meaningful exercise of choice by citizens in some form of electoral process permitting active debate on a broad if not unlimited range of issues. But it could require much more.[117]

Elsewhere, Steiner is more explicit about the association of human rights norms with liberalism and the political structures of liberal democracy. In an article on autonomy regimes for minorities, Steiner imagines the application of norms and ideals which are essential to liberalism.[118] He argues for a political regime that recognizes the rights of ethnic, racial, or religious minorities to cultural survival and freedom from violence and repression by the majority. He notes that repressive and authoritarian governments preclude an effective voice for minorities, as would majoritarian democracies where the political structures give the "minority no effective electoral power or political leverage."[119] He further notes that minorities can use the ICCPR to argue for the "kind of fair or equitable political participation that [ICCPR] Article 25 should be interpreted to require." He finds the basis for the protection of the rights of minorities in the human rights regime's insistence and promotion of difference and diversity:

The Universal Declaration and the Civil-Political Rights Covenant accept and, indeed, encourage many forms of diversity. They insist on respect for difference. . . . The value placed on the survival (and creation) of diversity in cultural, religious, political, and other terms permeates human rights law, which evidences throughout its hostility to imposed uniformity.

Steiner emphasizes that the norm of equal protection—"perhaps the preeminent human rights norm"—plays a key role in the protection and encouragement of diversity.[120] He cites the freedoms of association, assembly, and expression as the vital complement to the project of equal protection. In my view, the following passage sums up Steiner's "philosophy" of human rights and reveals his biases, although in most of his writings he seems to studiously avoid identifying human rights law with any one ideological orientation. He states that:

the aspirations of the human rights movement reach beyond the goal of preventing disasters. The movement also has a "utopian" dimension that envisions a vibrant and broadly based political community. Such a vision underscores the potential of the human rights movement for conflict with regimes all over the world. A society honoring the full range of contemporary human rights would be hospitable to many types of pluralism and skeptical about any one final truth, at least to the point of allowing and protecting difference. It would not stop at the protection of negative rights but would encourage citizens to exercise their right to political participation, one path toward enabling peoples to realize the right to self-determination. It would ensure room for dissent and alternative visions of social and political life by keeping open and protecting access to the roads toward change.[121]

Steiner differs from the conceptualizers explored here in that he views the right to political participation as a work in progress while the others tend to see it as a completed norm. For him, political participation is a programmatic right. It is not enough to carry out periodic elections; the "take part" clause is fertile ground for the development of the norm.

Among the constitutionalists, few have had the rare combination of high-level practical and scholarly experience that has characterized the work of Philip Alston.[122] A leading advocate of a broader conception of human rights, one that treats economic, social, and cultural rights as an integral part of the corpus, Alston has stated with approval that "the characterization of a specific goal as a human right elevates it above the rank and file of competing societal goals, gives it a degree of immunity from challenge and generally endows it with an aura of timelessness, absoluteness and universal validity."[123]

In a statement to the 1993 World Conference on Human Rights, Alston's Committee on Economic, Social and Cultural Rights lamented that the massive violations of economic and social rights would have provoked "horror and outrage" if they had occurred to civil and political rights.[124] The Committee noted that it was "inhumane, distorted and incompatible with international standards" to exclude the one-fifth of the global population which suffered from poverty, hunger, disease, illiteracy, and insecurity from human rights concerns. It noted that although "political freedom, free markets and pluralism" had been chosen by a large percentage of the global population in recent years because they were seen as the best routes for attaining economic, social and cultural rights, democracy will inevitably fail and societies will revert to authoritarianism unless those rights are respected. The Statement, which underlines Alston's central goal, seeks the globalization of more humane economic and social structures— a social democracy—to complement the open political society of liberal democracy.

Thomas Franck is the first prominent conceptualizer to argue that democratic governance has evolved from moral prescription to an international legal obligation.[125] Franck sees three occurrences in the last decade of the twentieth century as the unmistakable signs of the emergent right to governance: first, the failure of the August 1991 coup in the Soviet Union; second, the unanimous October 1991 resolution by the UN General Assembly to restore to power Jean-Bertrand Aristide, the then-ousted Haitian president; and third, the proliferation of states committed to competitive elections.[126] In celebratory fashion, Franck highlights the rejection of the "dictatorship of the proletariat," "people's democracy," and the dictatorships of Africa and Asia by "people almost everywhere" who "now demand that government be validated by western-style parliamentary, multiparty democratic process." He emphasizes that "Only a few, usually military or theocratic, regimes still resist the trend." With great optimism he concludes that:

This almost-complete triumph of the democratic notions of Hume, Locke, Jefferson and Madison—in Latin America, Africa, Eastern Europe and, to a lesser extent, Asia—may well prove to be the most profound event of the twentieth century and, in all likelihood, the fulcrum on which the future development of global society will turn. It is the unanswerable response to those who have said that free, open, multiparty, electoral parliamentary democracy is neither desired nor desirable outside a small enclave of western industrial states.

After exploring the involvement of regional and international organizations and governments in activities that enhance the right to democratic governance—such as sanctions systems and election monitoring—Franck lists the human rights instruments that constitute "the large normative canon" which promotes right to democratic entitlement.[127] These instruments recognize individual rights and require equal protection. Franck here deploys human rights law to underpin the right to democratic governance.

While the majority of constitutionalists are reluctant to make explicit connections between the human rights corpus and political democracy, they generally use typically Western conceptions of rights to explain the content and implications of human rights law. Although many make references to the influence of the different types of socialism on the fashion of human rights, such references are spotty and carry minor significance in these analyses. In virtually no instances do constitutionalists explore in an inclusive manner non-Western ideals and notions of rights or duties. There is no paucity of references, however, to non-Western ideas, practices, and political and social structures that contradict human rights norms.

The Cultural Pluralists

One of the most probing critiques of the human rights corpus has come from non-Western thinkers who, though educated in the West or in Western-oriented educational systems in the Third World, have philosophical, moral, and cultural questions about the distinctly Eurocentric formulation of human rights discourse. They have difficulties accepting the specific cultural and historical experiences of the West as the standard for all humanity. As outsider-insiders,[128] cultural pluralists or multiculturalists understand and accept certain contributions of Western (largely European) civilization to the human rights movement but reject the wholesale adoption or imposition of Western ideas and concepts of human rights. Instead, they present external critiques to human rights discourse, while generally applying language internal to that discourse. By pluralists, I do not refer to external critiquers who think that as a Western project the human rights system is irredeemable and cannot rearrange its priorities or be transformed by other cultural milieus to reflect a genuinely universal character and consensus. Rather, I mean those who advocate a multicultural approach in the reconstruction of the entire edifice of human rights.

There is no dispute about the European origins of the philosophy of the human rights movement; even Westerners who advocate its universality accept this basic fact. Refuge from this disturbing reality is taken in the large number of states, from all cultural blocs, which have indicated their acceptance of the regime by becoming parties to the principal human rights instruments. Others argue that as more non-Western states have become significant members of the international community, their influence on international lawmaking has corrected the initial lopsidedness of the enterprise and allowed other historical heritages to exert themselves.

This positivistic approach has some value, but it does not answer the Third World cultural pluralist challenge or endow the human rights corpus with multicultural universality. There are fundamental defects in presenting the state as the reservoir of cultural heritage. Many states have been alien to their populations and it is questionable whether they represent those populations or whether they are little more than internationally recognized cartels organized for the sake of keeping power and access to resources.[129] It is difficult to identify the motivations, for example, that led the abusive Zairian state of Mobutu Sese Seko to ratify the major human rights instruments;[130] what is clear however is that respect for international standards could not have been high among them. Many states seem to ratify human rights instruments to blunt criticism, and because as a general rule the cost to their sovereignty is nominal.

Pluralists look beyond the positive law and explore the historical and cultural imperatives that are essential for the creation of a legitimate corpus. Some point, for instance, to the celebration of the individual egoist in human rights law as a demonstration of its limited application. Some African scholars have been particularly uncomfortable with this emphasis, resisting the unremitting emphasis on the individual. B. Obinna Okere notes, for instance, that "The African conception of man is not that of an isolated and abstract individual, but an integral member of a group animated by a spirit of solidarity."[131] Individuals are not atomistic units "locked in a constant struggle against society for the redemption of their rights."[132] The concept of the group-centered individual in Africa delicately entwines rights and duties and harmonizes the individual with the society. Such a conception does not necessarily see society—organized either as the community or the state—as the individual's primary antagonist. Nor does it permit the over-indulgence of the individual at the expense of the society.[133] This conception resists casting the individual as the center of the moral universe; instead, both the community and the individual occupy an equally hallowed plane.

In the context of Asia, a number of writers have also cast doubt on the individualist conception of rights and its emphasis on negative rights.[134] Although many of these commentators are connected to governments in the region, and therefore have an interest in defending certain policy and development approaches, it would be sloppy to dismiss them out of hand. Such dismissals, which the Western INGO community issues with haste and without much thought about the cultural character of the human rights corpus, have aggravated differences between the West and certain Asian countries over the interpretation of human rights.[135] The University of Hong Kong's Professor Yash Ghai powerfully critiques the cynical distortion of Asian conceptions of community, culture and religion, as well as the use of state apparatuses to crush dissent. He argues that political elites manipulate cultural imagery to further economic development and retain power.[136] That critique, while essential, does not, however, elaborate on the cultural and philosophical differences between different Asian traditions and Western ones and on how those differences might manifest themselves in the construction of human rights norms.

Pluralists or cultural agnostics do not reject the Western conception of human rights in toto; nor do they even deny that a universal corpus may ultimately yield societal typologies and structures similar to those imagined by the present human rights regime. At stake for them is the availability of the opportunity for all major cultural blocs of the world to negotiate the normative content of human rights law and the purposes for which the discourse should be legitimately deployed. Many African critics of human rights discourse and some Africanists, for example, have demonstrated the similarity of human rights norms in Western states to precolonial African states and societies. These included due (fair) process protections,[137] the right to political participation,[138] and the rights to welfare, limited government, free speech, conscience, and association.[139] These rights, however, were not enjoyed as an end in themselves or with the sole intent of fulfilling just the individual. Among the major human rights instruments, only the African Charter on Human and Peoples' Rights attempts the comprehensive unification of these conflicting notions of community, individual rights, and duties to the family, the community, and the state.

Multiculturalists agree that many of the human rights in the current corpus are valid as human rights, their Western origin notwithstanding. The difficulty lies in the emphasis placed on certain rights, their ranking within that universe, and ultimately the political character of the state required or implied by that conception of rights. Although African pluralists, for example, bitterly oppose the violations of civil and political rights by the postcolonial state, they see little redemption in a campaign or worldview that seeks merely to transplant Western notions of political democracy and "negative" rights to African states. The contrived nature of the African state and its inability to claim the loyalties of its citizenry have been compounded by the delegitimization of cultural and philosophical identities by European values and practices. Africa appears to have lost its precolonial moral compass and fallen prey to the machinations of bands of elites who exist in cultural suspension, neither African nor foreign.

Some pluralists call for reconnection with certain human rights ideals from Africa's precolonial past to address social problems in order to arrest political disintegration. The reconstruction of the ancient duty-rights dialectic, which was essential to the vitality of Africa's social and political fabric, is one critical starting point in the redefinition of the relationship between individual and community, and individual and state.

The human rights corpus's over-emphasis on the individual runs counter to this African worldview; it would most likely delay or arrest Africa's reconstruction if applied without the restraint of balance, the tempering of the ego with the fuller understanding of rights that sees them in all their political, economic, and social dimensions. Pluralists feel that while ultimately the state that emerges from this conception may resemble a Western-style democracy in certain respects, such an outcome need not be predetermined or required by the human rights corpus. Asian pluralists accept that changes in the political character of the state are inevitable as their societies become more prosperous economically, but they are reluctant to conclude that this evolutionary process will automatically lead to a Western-type democracy.[140]

The dilemma of the pluralist, therefore, is not that he sees an "evil" in the Eurocentric formulation of the human rights corpus; although he sees much good in it, he does not agree with its zealous Western construction and its close identification with liberal democracy. Ultimately, of course, the major bone of contention is the cultural legitimacy of the corpus in non-Western settings.

Political Strategists and Instrumentalists

The school of political strategists, of all the four typologies explored here, is the least principled and the most open-textured in the manner and the purposes for which it deploys human rights discourse. Apart from the United Nations, whose Office of the High Commissioner for Human Rights (formerly the Center for Human Rights) is responsible for human rights matters, Western governments, and particularly the United States, have been the principal advocates for the use of human rights as a tool of policy against other states. In this respect, human rights standards have been viewed as norms with which non-Western, nondemocratic states must comply. The United States, from the birth of the movement half a century ago, viewed human rights "as designed to improve the condition of human rights in countries other than the United States (and a very few like-minded liberal states)."[141] Louis Henkin believes that, because individual rights "dominate [America's] constitutional jurisprudence, and are the pride of its people, their banner to the world,"[142] such a view is natural. Western European industrial democracies hold similar viewpoints, as evidenced by their trade and aid policies toward each other, as well as toward non-Western states.[143] Western international financial institutions such as the World Bank and the International Monetary Fund (IMF) have followed the lead of these major powers and have started to link some of their activities to human rights concerns.[144]

The United States was a principal player in the drafting of the major international human rights instruments, although it has been reluctant to become a party to most of them.[145] It was not until the 1970s that the United States started institutionalizing human rights within its foreign policy bureaucracy.[146] Policy upheavals triggered by the conflict in Vietnam, American support for repressive regimes in Latin America, and the crises of the Nixon presidency precipitated a more systematic evaluation of human rights concerns in American foreign policy.[147] As a result, laws were amended to restrict assistance to countries with particular levels of human rights abuses.[148] In 1977, President Jimmy Carter elevated the head of the Human Rights Bureau[149] within the Department of State to the rank of Assistant Secretary of State for Human Rights and Humanitarian Affairs.[150] Perhaps Carter's lasting achievement will be the rhetorical prominence that his administration gave human rights in American foreign policy.

The Carter legacy has not resulted in continued support for consistency in the application of human rights to foreign policy. There have always been glaring gaps between declared U.S. policy and actual practice toward foreign countries. Under Carter, inconsistent attempts were made to link support for particular countries to their human rights records, a task made all the more difficult by the logic of the cold war. As a general rule, pro-Western but despotic states such as the Shah's Iran, Zaire, South Korea, and Indonesia continued to receive U.S. military assistance.[151] This fact was understated by the Carter administration official responsible for human rights in the National Security Council in 1979–80:

When it came to specifics, whether the aid was military or nonmilitary, complex interests had to be balanced in reaching decisions on individual cases. Inescapably, there were numerous cases in which the administration was exposed to the charge of inconsistency. Human rights performance became a dominant factor in conventional arms transfers to Latin America; but such considerations were clearly subordinate in weighing military aid to Egypt, Israel, North Yemen and Saudi Arabia.[152]

While Carter was inconsistent and continued American support for abusive client states, the Reagan administration found the "perfect" use for human rights in American foreign policy. Rather than push for the unlikely repeal of human rights concerns from American policy, which many human rights advocates feared, the administration quickly enlisted human rights as a key ally in the greater struggle against communism, which many officials saw as the prime evil of the day. Thus, as Henkin noted,

For the Reagan administration, the struggle between good and evil was itself a struggle for the values commonly associated with human rights. The overriding concern for the United States was to resist, contain, and defeat Communist expansion. That was not only seen as in the United States [sic] interest generally, but it furthered human rights since Communism was the epitome of disrespect for human rights, and where Communism was, or came, human rights were lost irretrievably. Opposition to Communism, including criticism of any new and particular human rights violations by Communist states (as when military rule came to Poland, or Sakharov was confined and mistreated), should be strong and loud and clear.[153]

This reasoning eventually led the administration to solidify its human rights policy around the promotion of democracy. This policy was outlined as the promotion of "democratic processes in order to help build a world environment more favorable to respect for human rights."[154] It was billed as a dual policy that opposed human rights violations while strengthening democracy. The policy aimed singularly at the promotion of democracy "as the human right, rejecting in principle not only military 'juntas' but the many one-party states of Africa and Asia."[155] In reality, of course, the administration coddled right-wing dictatorships and oppressive pro-Western regimes, including apartheid South Africa.[156] With the end of the Cold War, however, political conditionality was frequently used to push one-party states toward the creation of more open, democratic political structures.[157]

The Bush I administration did not dramatically depart from the substance of the Reagan policy, although it countenanced the withdrawal of knee-jerk U.S. support for some pro-Western regimes primarily because of the collapse of Communism.[158] Despite its rhetorical defense of human rights, the Clinton administration has been more concerned with the promotion of democratic initiatives and trade opportunities than with the principled application of human rights norms.[159] The United States has frequently used human rights as a weapon of its foreign policy, but that use has rarely been principled. The invocation of human rights has variously been used to justify access to markets or resources vital to the United States, as was the case with the U.S.-led military defeat of Iraq in 1991. The support and the promotion of popularly elected regimes has, however, been privileged by the Clinton administration as the more effective method for advancing what it sees as the three inseparable goals of democracy, human rights, and, most important, free markets.[160] The Bush II administration, a Republican government, which took office on January 20, 2001, will in all probability pay little attention to either the promotion of human rights or democracy abroad. If past Republican administrations are any guide, Bush II will primarily concern itself with "hard" and "vital" American interests in trade, economic, military, and security matters.

International financial institutions and donor agencies also constitute an increasingly important component of the political strategy approach. World Bank-led groups of donors that keep many states in the South from total economic collapse have used human rights conditionalities to force economic liberalization, a measure of public accountability, and political pluralism. But the World Bank's concern with "good governance" has not been altruistic. That attitudinal change came after the Bank's utter failure to reverse economic decline in Africa. Overlooking its own role in exacerbating Africa's underdevelopment, the Bank concluded in 1989 that "underlying the litany of Africa's development problems is a crisis of governance."[161] In what amounted to a prescription for liberal democracy, it defined governance in the following familiar language:

By governance is meant the exercise of political power to manage a nation's affairs. Because countervailing power has been lacking, state officials in many countries have served their own interests without fear of being called to account. . . . The leadership assumes broad discretionary authority and loses its legitimacy. Information is controlled, and many voluntary organizations are co-opted or disbanded. This environment cannot readily support a dynamic economy. At worst the state becomes coercive and arbitrary. These trends, however, can be resisted. . . . It requires a systematic effort to build a pluralistic institutional structure, a determination to respect the rule of law, and vigorous protection of the freedom of the press and human rights.[162]

The World Bank has used its forbidding political and economic muscle to stare a few states down and push for political reform. Through its consultative groups (CGs)—the collection of donors—it pressed for political change in Kenya and Malawi in the early 1990s, although it did not heed its own message in continuing support for China, Zaire, Morocco, and Indonesia, to name just a few undemocratic states with serious human rights problems.[163] INGOs have seized this opening to seek a more systematic application of human rights norms by multilateral donors.[164] The significance of the Bank's general attitude lies in its conclusions: economic liberalization and free markets are less likely in undemocratic regimes that abuse basic liberal freedoms.[165] Authoritarian but economically prosperous Asian states, such as Singapore, Malaysia, China (PRC), and Indonesia have in the past attacked the linkage of human rights to aid and trade as an abuse of human rights and a new form of imperialism by the West.[166] The trademark of political strategists is their unabashed deployment of human rights and democracy interchangeably for the advancement of a variety of interests: strategic, tactical, geopolitical, security, "vital," economic, and political. The political strategists are the least reliable, and the most manipulative of all the schools discussed here. They are driven by short-term interest, and deploy human rights language for their own convenience. To them, human rights are only a principle when used or abused to advance particular foreign or domestic policy goals, otherwise they are disposable. None of the preceding three schools of thought equals the cynicism and callousness with which the political strategists view human rights.

Chapter 3
Human Rights and the African Fingerprint

Africa in a Rights Universe

The African Charter on Human and Peoples' Rights,[1] the basis of Africa's continental human rights system, entered into force on October 21, 1986, upon ratification by a simple majority of member states of the Organization of African Unity (OAU).[2] The African Charter has attracted criticism because it departs from the narrow formulations of other regional and international human rights instruments.[3] In particular, it codifies the three generations of rights, including the controversial concept of peoples' rights, and imposes duties on individual members of African societies.[4] While a number of scholars have focused attention on apparent tensions between human and peoples' rights, there has been little discussion of the notion of individual duties in the context of the African Charter.[5] Yet a thorough understanding of the meaning of human rights, and the complicated processes through which they are protected and realized, would seem to link inextricably the concepts of human rights, peoples' rights, and duties of individuals. Individual rights cannot make sense in a social and political vacuum, devoid of the duties assumed by individuals.[6] This appears to be more true of Africa than any other place. The individualist, narrow formulation of human rights is ill-suited for the African political and cultural universe.

The argument by political reformers that Africa merely needs a liberal democratic, rule-of-law state to be freed from despotism is mistaken. The transplantation of the narrow formulation of Western liberalism cannot adequately respond to the historical reality and the political and social needs of Africa. The sacralization of the individual and the supremacy of the jurisprudence of individual rights in organized political and social society is not a natural, "transhistorical," or universal phenomenon, applicable to all societies, without regard to time and place. The ascendancy of the language of individual rights has a specific historical context in the Western world. The rise of the modern nation-state in Europe and its monopoly of violence and instruments of coercion gave birth to a culture of rights to counterbalance the invasive and abusive state.[7] John Locke reduced this thinking to a philosophy in his *Two Treatises of Government*.[8]

He argued that each individual, together with his compatriots, contractually transfers to a public authority his individual right to implement the law of nature. But this power is conditional and limited to the state's duty to "protect individual rights and freedoms from invasion and to secure their more effective guarantee."[9] According to Locke, a government that systematically breaches these duties becomes illegitimate. While Locke's conception is the floor—the modern state is more intrusive and pervasive than he imagined—it remains the basic justification for the existence of the state in the West.

The development of the state in Africa is so radically different from its European equivalent that the traditional liberal conception of the relationship between the state and the individual is of limited utility in imagining a viable regime of human rights. The modern African state was imposed on ethnopolitical communities by European imperialists and did not result from the natural progression or evolution of those societies.[10] Only a handful of modern African states bear any territorial resemblance to the political formations which existed prior to their penetration and subjugation by European states.[11] The majority of states were contrived overnight, often dismantling existing ethnopolitical communities and their organizational structures. Communities that lived independently of each other were coerced to live together under the newly created colonial state. Most of these newly minted citizens lacked any instinctual or nationalistic bond to the colonial state.

The failure of the successor postcolonial state points to the continued inability of the "unnatural" and forced state to inspire loyalty and a distinct national identity. This disconnection, between the people and the modern African state, is not merely a function of the loss of independence or selfgovernance over precolonial political and social structures and the radical imposition of new territorial bounds with unfamiliar citizenry. It is above all a crisis of cultural and philosophical identity: the delegitimation of values, notions, and philosophies about the individual, society, politics, and nature developed over centuries. Severe as these problems are, the crisis of the African state is not insoluble.

The purpose of this chapter is to imagine and reconfigure a rights regime that could achieve legitimacy in Africa, especially among the majority rural populace, and become the basis for social and political reconstruction. The reconstruction proposed here is not merely that of human rights norms. In order for the proposal to make sense, a reconfiguration of the African state must also be simultaneously attempted. The imposed colonial state, and its successor, the postcolonial state, stand as moral and legal nullities, entities whose salvation partially lies in new constitutionalism and map-making in the context of self-determination for Africa's many nationalities, democratization, and, most importantly, historical reconnection with certain precolonial ideals. However, the purpose of this chapter is not to explore the creation of a new political map, but rather to reconstruct the human rights corpus. This choice does not imply a hierarchy or ranking. In practice, both paradigms must be simultaneously addressed for the formulation to bear fruit.

For the present purposes, the current human rights movement must be understood as only a piece of the whole. Its roots in the Western liberal thought and tradition necessarily deny it completeness, though not the universality of many of its ideals and norms. To paraphrase the famous metaphor, the gourd is only partially filled by the Western tradition: it falls on other traditions fully to fill it. On this premise, this chapter makes several interrelated arguments. It stresses the African notions of human rights which existed prior to colonization and how those notions differed from the contemporary Eurocentric articulation of human rights. In particular, these notions saw the individual social being as the bearer of both rights and duties. Therefore, it argues that the precolonial concept of duty remains a valid means of conceptualizing human rights and, thus, should be the basis for the construction of a unitary, integrated rights regime capable of achieving legitimacy in Africa.

But this chapter also presents a vision that strikes a balance between duties and rights. Not only does this vision restrain the runaway individualism of the West, but it also has strong roots in the continent and indeed may be Africa's last hope for reversing societal collapse. The present attempt is not meant to deny the validity of the Western liberal tradition to the human rights corpus, but only to inform it with an African contribution that entwines duties and rights in a society consumed by the socialization of the individual, a concept articulated by the African Charter.

It is not necessary to find parallel rights in African conceptions of human rights in order to show the equality of African cultures to European ones. Although that is one incidental by-product, this chapter did not set out to clothe these parallel rights in the language of rights. In fact, the vindication of rights in Africa had a very different dimension. In the West, the language of rights primarily developed along the trajectory of claims against the state; entitlements which imply the right to seek an individual remedy for a wrong. The African language of duty, however, offers a different meaning for individual/state-society relations: while people had rights, they also bore duties. The resolution of a claim was not necessarily directed at satisfying or remedying an individual wrong. It was an opportunity for society to contemplate the complex web of individual and community duties and rights to seek a balance between the competing claims of the individual and society.

This view is not relativist. It does not advance or advocate the concept of apartheid in human rights or the notion that each cultural tradition has generated its own distinctive and irreconcilable concept of human rights.[12] It proceeds from the position that each culture has a valuable contribution to make in the construction of a truly global human rights corpus. Although different cultures may appear to be radically distinctive and irreconcilable, they possess ideals from which universally-shared norms can be excavated. Terms such as "cultural relativists," which demonize Third World scholars, simply act as barriers to the construction of a multicultural human rights corpus. Most critiques of "cultural relativism" are ethnocentric and symptomatic of the moral imperialism of the West.[13] It is an extreme that only serves to detain the development of a universal jurisprudence of human rights.[14]

The construction and definition of human rights norms are dynamic and continuous processes. Human rights are not the monopoly or the sole prerogative of any one culture or people, although claims to that end are not in short supply.[15] In one culture, the individual may be venerated as the primary bearer of rights; while, in another, individual rights may be more harmonized with the corporate body. Rather than assert the primacy of one over the other, or argue that only one cultural expression and historical experience constitutes human rights, each experience should be viewed as a contributor to the whole. The process of the construction of universal human rights is analogous to the proverbial description of the elephant by blind people: each, based on their sense of feeling, offers a differing account. However, all the accounts paint a complete picture when put together. As a dynamic process, the creation of a valid conception of human rights must be universal. That is, the cultures and traditions of the world must, in effect, compare notes, negotiate positions, and come to agreement over what constitutes human rights. Even after agreement, the doors must remain open for further inquiry, reformulation, and revision.

Human Rights in Precolonial Africa

It is important to explore the validity of both the argument made often by Africans, and the controversy it engenders, that the concept of human rights was not alien to precolonial societies and that such notions were the foundation of social and political society. Recent debates, which are primarily interpretive, have focused attention on this divisive theme. They agree on basic behavioral, political, and social characteristics but disagree as to their meaning.[16] There are no easy answers for a number of reasons. In particular, methodological pitfalls exist for any analysis that attempts to address the length and width of sub-Saharan Africa. The sheer size of the continent, and the diversity of African peoples and their societies, defy easy categorization or generalization. Secondly, with regard to human rights, there are very few extant sources of precolonial societies. The oral tradition common to most of Africa had its own imprecision even before its interruption by the forces of colonialism.

Nevertheless, several broad themes are discernible from the past. It is now generally accepted that the African precolonial past was neither idyllic nor free of the abuses of power and authority common to all human societies. However, the despotic and far-reaching control of the individual by the omnipotent state, first perfected in Europe, was unknown.[17] Instead, precolonial Africa consisted of two categories of societies: those with centralized authority, administrative machinery, and standing judicial institutions, such as the Zulu and the Ashanti, and those with more communal and less intrusive governmental paraphernalia, such as the Akamba and Kikuyu of Kenya.[18] But a feature generally common to almost all precolonial African societies was their ethnic, cultural, and linguistic homogeneity—a trait that gave them fundamental cohesion.[19]

Had these political societies developed the concept of human rights? Proponents of the concept of human rights in precolonial African societies are accused by their opponents of confusing human dignity with human rights.[20] This view holds that the "African concept of justice," unlike human rights, "is rooted not in individual claims against the state, but in the physical and psychic security of group membership. " While it is probably correct to argue that African societies did not emphasize individual rights in the same way that European societies did, it is not a correct presumption to claim that they did not know the conception of individual rights at all.

According to Ronald Cohen, a right is an entitlement:

At its most basic level, a human right is a safeguarded prerogative granted because a person is alive. This means that any human being granted personhood has rights by virtue of species membership. And a right is a claim to something (by the right-holder) that can be exercised and enforced under a set of grounds or justifications without interference from others. The subject of the right can be an individual or a group and the object is that which is being laid claim to as a right.[21]

Moreover, a brief examination of the norms governing legal, political, and social structures in precolonial societies demonstrates that the concept of rights, like that articulated by Cohen, informed the notion of justice and supported a measure of individualism. Two societies which are representative of the two basic organizational paradigms prevalent in precolonial Africa illustrate the point. The Akamba of East Africa were symptomatic of the less rigidly organized societies, whereas the Akans of West Africa were characteristic of the more centralized state systems. In Akan thought, the individual had both descriptive and normative characteristics.[22] Both endowed the person with individual rights as well as obligations. Similarly, the Akamba believed that "all members were born equal and were supposed to be treated as such beyond sex and age."[23] The belief prevailed in both societies that, as an inherently valuable being, the individual was naturally endowed with certain basic rights.

Akan political society was organized according to the principle of kinships. A lineage of those who were descended from the same ancestress formed the basic political unit. Adults in each lineage elected an elder. All lineage heads, in turn, formed the town council which was chaired by a chief who, though chosen according to descent, was in part elected.[24] The chief, however, could not rule by fiat, because decisions of the council were taken by consensus. Moreover, council decisions could be criticized publicly by constituents who found them unacceptable. As Kwasi Wiredu explains, there was no "doubt about the right of the people, including the elders, to dismiss a chief who tried to be oppressive."[25]

Among the Akamba, individuals joined the elders council, the most senior rank in Akamba society, after demonstrating commitment to the community and responsibility in personal matters. Maintaining a stable household, which included a spouse or spouses and children, was a necessary precondition. The council was a public forum which made decisions by consensus. Although the Akamba resented any social organization with a central authority, the council's services included the legislation of public norms and customs.[26] These two examples demonstrate that individuals in precolonial society had a right to political participation in determining by whom and through what policies to be ruled.

Much of the discussion about whether precolonial societies knew of and enforced individual human rights has taken place in the absence of considered studies of, and references to, judicial processes in those societies. A preliminary examination of both the Akan and Akamba societies strongly indicates individual-conscious systems of justice. With respect to the Akamba, a party to a complaint appeared before the council of elders in the company of his jury, a selection of individuals who enjoyed the party's confidence. Unlike Western-style jurors, the Akamba jurors did not hand down a verdict, but advised the party on how to plead and what arguments to put forth to win the case. They had to be steeped in Kamba law, customs, and traditions. The threat of the administration of Kithitu, the Kamba oath, which was believed to bring harm to those who lied, encouraged truthfulness.[27]

After presentations by parties, the elders would render judgment or give counsel on the appropriate settlement. Each offense carried a punishment: murder was compensated by the payment of over ten head of cattle; rapists were charged goats; assaults, depending on their seriousness, could cost over ten head of cattle; adultery was punishable by the payment of at least a goat and bull; and an arsonist was required to build his victim a new house or replace the lost property. Individual rights to cultivated land were also recognized and protected.[28] These elaborate punishments present just one indication of the seriousness with which Akamba society took individual rights to personal security, property, marriage, and the dignity and integrity of the family.

In Akan society, the presumption of innocence was deeply embedded in social consciousness. According to Wiredu, "it was an absolute principle of Akan justice that no human being could be punished without trial."[29] The Akans, like the Akamba, also recognized a wide range of individual rights: murder, assault, and theft were punished as violations of the person.[30]

For those who deny the recognition of human rights in precolonial societies, it must come as a strange irony that the human rights corpus shares with precolonial Africa the importance of personal security rights. The right to life, for example, was so valued that the power over life and death was reserved for a few elders and was exercised "only after elaborate judicial procedure, with appeals from one court to another, and often only in cases of murder and manslaughter."[31] This respect for human life was not an aberration. Timothy Fernyhough notes that much of Africa is characterized by a "preoccupation with law, customary and written, and with legal procedure."[32] He adds that the Amhara of Ethiopia, for example, have historically relished litigation and the lengthy cross-examination of witnesses. Whether a society was highly centralized or not, "there existed elaborate rules of procedure intended to protect the accused and provide fair trials."[33] The protection of individual rights was of preeminent importance to precolonial societies.

Many of the Akamba and Akan sociopolitical norms and structures were common to other precolonial ethnopolitical entities or cultural-nations. I refer to these shared basic values as the index of the African cultural fingerprint, that is, a set of institutional and normative values governing the relationship between individuals, the society, and nature. To be sure, the fingerprint belongs to Africa although it is also human and, thus, aspects of it reveal universal characteristics. In the search for the definition of the continent, for what sets it apart from Asia and Europe or the Americas, some writers have labeled the cultural and social patterns distinctive to the continent as the "African personality."[34] Léopold Sédar Senghor, for one, called it negritude or "the manner of self-expression of the black character, the black world, black civilization," while Aimé Césaire described it simply as "recognition of the fact of being black, and the acceptance of that fact, of our destiny of black, of our history and our culture."[35] Julius Nyerere named it *ujamaa*, the Kiswahili term for African socialism.[36] The principles and ideals common to all these conceptions are the protection of the individual and individuality within the family and the greater sociopolitical unit; deference to age because a long life is generally wise and knowledgeable; commitment and responsibility to other individuals, family, and community; solidarity with fellow human beings, especially in times of need; tolerance for difference in political views and personal ability; reciprocity in labor issues and for generosity; and consultation in matters of governance.[37] As aptly put by Ronald Cohen,

Many African cultures value the group—one should never die alone, live alone, remain outside social networks unless one is a pariah, insane, or the carrier of a feared contagious disease. Corporate kinship in which individuals are responsible for the behavior of their group members is a widespread tradition. But in addition, the individual person and his or her dignity and autonomy are carefully protected in African traditions, as are individual rights to land, individual competition for public office, and personal success.[38]

Both Nyerere and Dunstan Wai have argued, separately, that precolonial societies supported individual welfare and dignity and did not allow gross inequalities between members.[39] To buttress his claim that African societies "supported and practiced human rights," Wai argues that the rulers were bound by traditional checks and balances to limit their power and guarantee a "modicum of social justice and values concerned with individual and collective rights."[40] Asmaron Legesse emphasizes the importance of distributive justice in "formally egalitarian," as well as hierarchical, societies to ensure that "individuals do not deviate so far from the norm that they overwhelm society."[41] Wiredu likewise tabulates a list of rights and responsibilities borne by the Akans in the precolonial era. These included rights to political participation, land, and religion, as well as the duty to defend the nation.[42] Fernyhough though not subscribing to a unique African concept of human rights, has outlined many of the rights protected in precolonial societies, including the rights to life, personal freedom, welfare, limited government, free speech, conscience, and association.[43] Many of these rights were protected in complex processes of interaction between the individual and the community.

Thus far, this chapter has identified and elaborated human rights ideals which existed in precolonial societies. However, as in other cultures, notions or practices that contradict concepts of human dignity and human rights also existed, some particularly severe. Among the Akamba, for example, a suspect in a serious crime could be tried by a fire or water ordeal if he did not admit guilt.[44] When a chief died in Akan society, a common citizen's life would be taken so that he could "accompany" the chief and "attend" to him on his "journey to the land of the dead."[45] This practice of human sacrifice was a clear abrogation of the right to life, even by Akan norms, which attached an intrinsic value to every individual. Speech and dissent rights of non-adults or minors were also severely restricted.[46] The discriminatory treatment of women—by exclusion from decision-making processes and the imposition of certain forms of labor based on gender— in the home and outside it flew in the face of the concept of gender equality.[47] However, these practices which were inimical to human rights are not peculiar to Africa; all cultures suffer from this duality of the good and the bad.

A number of Western academics have attacked the index of the African cultural fingerprint and the concept it represents—the African contribution to the human rights corpus—as false and erroneous. In an impassioned critique of scholars she regards as African cultural relativists, Rhoda Howard notes that although "relatively homogeneous, undifferentiated simple societies of pre-colonial Africa" had "effective means for guaranteeing what is now known as human rights,"[48] there was nothing specifically African about them. Such a model, which she calls the communitarian ideal, "represents typical agrarian, precapitalist social relations in non-state societies."[49] Elsewhere, Howard argues that industrialization has dismantled what she refers to as the peasant worldview, or communitarian ideal, and replaced it with "values of secularism, personal privacy, and individualism."[50]

Jack Donnelly, in many respects Howard's ideological soulmate, concedes that while societies based on the communitarian ideal existed at one point in Africa, they are now the exception. He dismisses the notion that precolonial societies knew the concept of human rights; an argument he thinks moot because the communitarian ideal has been destroyed and corrupted by the "teeming slums" of non-Western states, the money economy, and "Western" values, products, and practices.[51] In effect, both Donnelly and Howard believe that human rights are only possible in a post-feudal state, and that the concept was alien to specific precapitalist traditions and ideals such as Buddhism, Islam, or precolonial African societies. In other words, these traditions can make no normative contribution to the human rights corpus. But the other implausible suggestion derived from these positions is that societies—governed under a centralized modern state—necessarily Westernize through industrialization and urbanization. Moreover, such societies become fertile ground for the germination of human rights.

Donnelly and Howard dismiss with too much haste the argument that many Africans are still influenced by precolonial norms and notions. They assume, apparently without adequate research, that the old ways have been completely eroded by modernization. The examples that Howard gives, those of Kenya and Nigeria, two of the "more developed" economies on the continent, in fact point in the opposite direction: that in spite of the ubiquity of the centralized modernizing state, kinship ties and group-centered forms of consciousness still influence growing urban populations. Matters concerning marriage, birth, and death are still supported by extensive family and kinship networks. This is evident even among the peoples of South Africa and Zambia, some of Africa's most urbanized countries. Fernyhough correctly finds "Howard's assessment of the new culture of modernity, like her new 'modern' African, strangely unsophisticated and lacking in sensitivity."[52] It is difficult if not impossible, he adds, to "measure individuation or judge changing world views by counting radios and cinemas." Without a doubt, the coherent scheme of precolonial values has been undermined and deeply traumatized by the forces of change. But it is difficult to believe that this process has completely invalidated them, just as it is unlikely that the modernization of Japan, China, and Saudi Arabia will completely destroy the cultural norms and forms of consciousness evolved through Buddhism and Islam.

Donnelly and Howard face other problems as well. The first difficulty, and perhaps the most troublesome, is the implication in their works that only European liberalism—a philosophy they seem to think inevitable under modernization—can be the foundation for the concept of human rights. Although Donnelly and Howard would deny it, this argument in effect destroys any claim of universality because it places the concept of human rights exclusively within a specific culture. Unless they believe that the ideals of liberalism are inherently universal, it is impossible to reconcile their assertion that the concept of human rights is universal, while at the same time assigning to it uniqueness and cultural specificity.

The second difficulty, which is an extension of the first, is the implied duty on Westerners to impose the concept of human rights on non-European cultures and societies because it is a universal concept that all societies must accept for their own good. Seen from other cultural perspectives, such a view barely masks the historical pattern by the West—first realized through colonialism—to dominate the world by remaking it for the benefit, and in the image, of Europe.

This conflict between Howard and Donnelly, on the one hand, and their opponents, on the other, is summed up beautifully by Fernyhough who illustrates how politicized the debate about the origin of the concept and content of human rights has become:

From one perspective the human rights tradition was quite foreign to Africa until Western, "modernizing" intrusions dislocated community and denied newly isolated individuals access to customary ways of protecting their lives and human dignity. Human rights were alien to Africa precisely because it was precapitalist, preindustrial, decentralized, and characterized by communal forms of social organization. From the opposing viewpoint there is a fundamental rejection of this as a new, if rather subtle, imperialism, an explicit denial that human rights evolved only in Western political theory and practice, especially during the American and French revolutions, and not in Africa.[53]

Fernyhough adds, and I agree, that the protest of those who reject the chauvinistic view of the West articulate the "very plausible claim that human rights are not founded in Western values alone but may also have emerged from very different and distinctive African cultural milieus."[54] It is impossible to sustain the argument made by Donnelly and Howard because of its internal inconsistency and ethnocentric, moral arrogance. Conversely, African writers who claim a distinctively African concept of human rights exaggerate its uniqueness. By implication they make the point that such a concept could not have any universal application, a position which fails to recognize that concepts of human dignity—the basis of a concept of human rights—are inherent in all human societies. As Fernyhough notes:

Thus Donnelly and Howard contend that in precolonial Africa, as in most non-Western and preindustrial societies, forms of social and political organization rendered the means to attain human dignity primarily through duties and obligations, often expressed in a communally oriented social idiom and realized within a redistributive economy. Yet both reject with unwarranted emphasis the notion that in the search for guarantees to uphold human life and dignity precolonial Africans formulated or correlated such claims to protection in terms of human rights.[55]

It is indeed the notion, common to all societies, that human beings are special and worthy of protection that distinguishes humans from animals. The dogged insistence, even in the face of evidence to the contrary, on the exclusive or distinctive "possession" of human rights has no real place in serious scholarship; the only purpose of such a claim could only lie in the desire either to assert cultural superiority or to deny it. It would be more fruitful to vigorously study other cultures and seek to understand how they protect—and also abuse—human rights.

Above all else, the view of the ethnocentric universalist is at best counterproductive. It serves only to alienate state authorities who would purposefully manipulate concepts in order to continue their repressive practices. How are human rights to be realized universally if cultural chauvinists insist that only their version is valid? Through coercion of other societies or modern civilizing crusades? The only hope for those who care about the adherence by all communities to human rights is the painstaking study of each culture to identify norms and ideals that are in consonance with universal standards. Only by locating the basis for the cultural legitimacy of certain human rights and mobilizing social forces on that score can respect for universal standards be forged. It would be ridiculous, for example, for an African state to claim that, on the basis of African culture, it could detain its own citizens without trial. As Abdullahi An-Na'im succinctly explains:

Enhancing the cultural legitimacy for a given human right should mobilize political forces within a community, inducing those in power to accept accountability for the implementation or enforcement of that right. With internal cultural legitimacy, those in power could no longer argue that national sovereignty is demeaned through compliance with standards set for the particular human right as an external value. Compliance with human rights standards would be seen as a legitimate exercise of national sovereignty and not as an external limitation.[56]

The Dialectic of Rights and Duties

Except for the African Charter's clawback clauses and provisions concerning peoples' rights,[57] much of the criticism of the Charter has been directed at its inclusion of duties on individuals.[58] This criticism, which I shared at one point, appears to be driven primarily by the gross and persistent violations of human rights in postcolonial African states and the fear that vesting more power in the states can only result in more abuses.[59] This fear aside, this criticism should examine the concept of duty in precolonial African societies and demonstrate its validity in conceptualizing a unitary, integrated conception of human rights in which the extreme individualism of current human rights norms is tempered by the individual's obligation to the society.

Capturing the view of many Africans, B. Obinna Okere has written that the "African conception of man is not that of an isolated and abstract individual, but an integral member of a group animated by a spirit of solidarity."[60] Keba Mbaye, the renowned African jurist, has stated that in Africa "laws and duties are regarded as being two facets of the same reality: two inseparable realities."[61] This philosophy has been summed up by John Mbiti as well: "I am because we are, and because we are therefore I am."[62] According to this view, individuals are not atomistic units "locked in a constant struggle against society for the redemption of their rights."[63] The Dinka concept of *cieng*, for example, "places emphasis on such human values as dignity, integrity, honor, and respect for self and others, loyalty and piety, compassion and generosity, and unity and harmony."[64] But *cieng* not only attunes "individual interests to the interests of others; it requires positive assistance to one's fellow human beings."[65] Among the Bantu peoples of eastern and southern Africa, the concept of a person, *mundu* in Kikamba or *mtu* in Kiswahili, is not merely descriptive; it is also normative and refers to an individual who lives in peace and is helpful to his or her community.[66] Léopold Senghor, then president of Senegal, captured this view at a meeting of African legal experts in 1979:

Room should be made for this African tradition in our Charter on Human and Peoples' Rights, while bathing in our philosophy, which consists in not alienating the subordination of the individual to the community, in co-existence, in giving everyone a certain number of rights and duties.[67]

In practical terms, this philosophy of the group-centered individual evolves through a series of carefully taught rights and responsibilities. At the root were structures of social and political organization, informed by gender and age, which served to enhance solidarity and ensure the existence of the community into perpetuity. The Kikuyu of Kenya, for example, achieved a two-tiered form of community organization. At the base was the family group composed of blood relatives, namely a husband and his wife or wives, their children, grandchildren, and often great-grandchildren; the second tier consisted of the clan, a combination of several family groups bearing the same name and believed to have descended from one ancestor.[68] Social status and prestige were based on the execution of duties within a third tier: the age-group. Marriage conferred eligibility for the elders council, the governing body.[69] The Akamba were organized in similar lineages and age-groups, culminating in the elders council, the supreme community organ.[70] The Akan organizational chart also was similar.[71]

Relationships, rights, and obligations flowed from these organizational structures, giving the community cohesion and viability. Certain obligations, such as the duty to defend the community and its territory, attached by virtue of birth and group membership. In the age-grading system of the Akamba, for example, each able-bodied male had to join the *anake* grade, which defended the community and made war.[72] In return for their services, the warriors were allowed to graduate into a more prestigious bracket, whereby others would defend them and their property thereafter. The expectations were similar among the Akans:

But if every Akan was thus obligated by birth to contribute to defense in one way or another, there was also the complementary fact that he had a right to the protection of his person, property, and dignity, not only in his own state but also outside it. And states were known to go to war to secure the freedom of their citizens abroad or avenge their mistreatment.[73]

Defense of the community, a state-type right exacted on those who came under its protection, was probably the most serious positive public obligation borne by young men. The commission of certain offenses, such as murder, treason, and cowardice, were also regarded as public offenses or crimes against the public dimension of the community or state, imposing negative public duties on the individual. But most individual duties attached at the family and kinship levels and were usually identifiable through naming: an aunt was expected to act like a mother, an uncle like a father.[74] This is the basis of the saying, found in many African cultures, that it takes a whole village to raise a child.[75] As Josiah Cobbah correctly explains, the naming of individuals within the kinship structure "defines and institutionalizes" the family member's required social role. These roles, which to the Western outsider may appear to be only of morally persuasive value, are "essentially rights which each kinship member customarily possesses, and duties which each kinship member has toward his kin."[76] Expressed differently, "the right of one kinship member is the duty of the other and the duty of the other kinship member is the right of another."[77] Niara Sudarkasa and Cobbah thematically group the principles tying the kinship system together around respect, restraint, responsibility, and reciprocity.[78] In a very real sense, "entitlements and obligations form the very basis of the kinship system."[79]

The consciousness of rights and correlative duties is ingrained in community members from birth. Through every age-grade, the harmonization of individual interests with those of the grade is instilled unremittingly. As Jomo Kenyatta remarked, the age-group is a "powerful instrument for securing conformity" with the community's values; the "selfish or reckless youth is taught by the opinion of his gang that it does not pay to incur displeasure."[80] Through age-groups and the "strength and numbers of the social ties,"[81] community solidarity is easily transmitted and becomes the basis for cohesion and stability. Furthermore, initiation ceremonies—for both girls and boys—taught gender roles and sexual morality.[82] Among the Kikuyu, a series of ceremonies culminating in clitoridectomy for girls and circumcision for boys, marked passage into adulthood. Clitoridectomy, which was brought under sharp attack first by Christian missionaries and now by Western or Western-inspired human rights advocates, was a critical departure point in socialization.

This conception, that of the individual as a moral being endowed with rights but also bounded by duties, proactively uniting his needs with the needs of others, was the quintessence of the formulation of rights in precolonial societies. It radically differs from the liberal conception of the individual as the state's primary antagonist. Moreover, it provides those concerned with the universal conception of human rights with a basis for imagining another dialectic: the harmonization of duties and rights. Many of those who dismiss the relevance of the African conception of man by pejoratively referring to it as a "peasant" and "preindustrial" notion fail to recognize that all major cultures and traditions—the Chinese, European, African, and the Arab, to mention a few—have a basic character distinctive to them. While it is true that no culture is static, and that normative cultural values are forever evolving, it is naive to think that a worldview can be completely eroded in a matter of decades, even centuries. Why should the concession be made that the individualist rights perspective is "superior" to more community-oriented notion? As Cobbah has noted, "in the same way that people in other cultures are brought up to assert their independence from their community, the average African's worldview is one that places the individual within his community."[83] This African worldview, he writes, "is for all intents and purposes as valid as the European theories of individualism and the social contract." Any concept of human rights with pretensions of universality cannot avoid mediating between these two seemingly contradictory notions.

The Duty/Rights Conception

The idea of combining individual rights and duties in a human rights document is not completely without precedent. No less a document than the

Universal Declaration of Human Rights (UDHR) blazed the trail in this regard when it provided, in a rare departure from its individualist focus, that "Everyone has the duties to the community in which alone the free and full development of his personality is possible."[84] However, the African Charter is the first human rights document to articulate the concept in any meaningful way. It is assumed, with undue haste, by human rights advocates and scholars that the inclusion of duties in the African Charter is nothing but "an invitation to the imposition of unlimited restrictions on the enjoyment of rights."[85] This view is simplistic because it is not based on a careful assessment of the difficulties experienced by African countries in their miserable attempts to mimic wholesale Western notions of government and the role of the state. Such critics are transfixed by the allure of models of democracy prevalent in the industrial democracies of the West, models which promise an opportunity for the redemption of a troubled continent.

Unfortunately, such a view is shortsighted. Perhaps at no other time in the history of the continent have Africans needed each other more than they do today. Although there is halting progress toward democratization in some African countries, the continent is generally on a steady track to political and economic collapse. Now in the fifth decade of postcolonialism, African states have largely failed to forge viable, free, and prosperous countries. The persistence of this problem highlights the dismal failures of the postcolonial states on several accounts. The new African states have failed to inspire loyalty in the citizenry; to produce a political class with integrity and a national interest; to inculcate in the military, the police, and the security forces their proper roles in society; to build a nation from different linguistic and cultural groups; and to fashion economically viable policies. These realities are driving a dagger into the heart of the continent. There are many causes of the problem, and, while it is beyond the scope of this chapter to address them all, it will discuss one: namely, the human rights dimensions of the relationship between the individual, the community, and the state.

Colonialism profoundly transformed and mangled the political landscape of the continent through the imposition of the modern state.[86] Each precolonial African "nation," and there were thousands of them to be sure, had several characteristics: one ethnic community inhabited a "common territory; its members shared a tradition, real or fictitious, of common descent; and they were held together by a common language and a common culture."[87] Few African nations were also states in the modern or European sense, although they were certainly political societies. In contrast, the states created by European imperialists, comprising the overwhelming majority of the continent, ordinarily contained more than one nation: "Each one of the new states contains more than one nation. In their border areas, many new states contain parts of nations because of the European-inspired borders cut across existing national territories."[88]

The new state contained a population from many cultural groups co-erced to live together. It did not reflect a "nation," a people with the consciousness of a common destiny and shared history and culture.[89] The colonialists were concerned with the exploitation of Africa's human and natural resources, and not with the maintenance of the integrity of African societies. For purposes of this expediency, grouping many nations in one territory was the most profitable administrative option. To compound the problem, the new rulers employed divide-and-conquer strategies, pitting nations against each other, further polarizing interethnic tensions and creating a climate of mutual fear, suspicion, and hatred. In many cases, the Europeans would openly favor one group or cluster of nations over others, a practice that only served to intensify tensions. For example, in Rwanda, a country rife with some of the worst intercommunal violence since decolonization, the Belgians heightened Hutu-Tutsi rivalry through preferential treatment toward the Tutsi.[90]

Ironically, colonialism, though a divisive factor, created a sense of brotherhood or unity among different African nations within the same colonial state, because they saw themselves as common victims of an alien, racist, and oppressive structure.[91] Nevertheless, as the fissures of the modern African state amply demonstrate, the unity born out of anticolonialism has not sufficed to create an enduring identity of nationhood in the context of the postcolonial state. Since in the precolonial era the primary allegiances were centered on lineage and the community,[92] one of the most difficult challenges facing the postcolonial political class was the creation of new nations. This challenge, referred to as "creating a national consciousness . . . was misleading," as there was "no nation to become conscious of; the nation had to be created concurrently with a consciousness."[93]

This difficult social and political transformation from self-governing ethnocultural units to the multilingual, multicultural modern state—the disconnection between the two Africas: one precolonial, the other postcolonial—lies at the root of the current crisis. The postcolonial state has not altered the imposed European forms of social and political organization even though there is mounting evidence that they have failed to work in Africa.[94] Part of the problem lies in the domination of the continent's political and social processes by Eurocentric norms and values. As correctly put by Art Hansen,

African leaders have adopted and continued to use political forms and precedents that grew from, and were organically related to, the European experience. Formal declarations of independence from direct European rule do not mean actual independence from European conceptual dominance. African leaders and peoples have gone through tremendous political changes in the past hundred years. These profound changes have included the transformation of African societies and polities. They are still composed of indigenous African units, such as the lineage, village, tribe, and chieftainship, but they have been transformed around European units, such as the colony, district, political party, and state.[95]

This serious and uniquely African crisis lacks the benefit of any historical guide or formula for its resolution. While acknowledging that it is impossible to recapture and reinstitute precolonial forms of social and political organization, this chapter nonetheless asserts that Africa must partially look inward, to its precolonial past, for possible solutions. Certain ideals in precolonial African philosophy, particularly the conception of humanity, and the interface of rights and duties in a communal context as provided for in the African Charter, should form part of that process of reconstruction. The European domination of Africa has wrought social changes which have disabled old institutions by complicating social and political processes. Precolonial and postcolonial societies now differ fundamentally. In particular, there are differences of scale; states now have large and varied populations. Moreover, states possess enormous instruments of control and coercion, and their tasks are now without number. While this is true, Africa cannot move forward by completely abandoning its past.

The duty/rights conception of the African Charter could provide a new basis for individual identification with compatriots, the community, and the state. It could forge and instill a national consciousness and act as the glue to reunite individuals and different nations within the modern state, and at the same time set the proper limits of conduct by state officials. The motivation and purpose behind the concept of duty in precolonial societies was to strengthen community ties and social cohesiveness, creating a shared fate and common destiny. This is the consciousness that the impersonal modern state has been unable to foster.[96] It has failed to shift loyalties from the lineage and the community to the modern state, with its mixture of different nations.

The series of explicit duties spelled out in articles 27 through 29 of the African Charter could be read as intended to recreate the bonds of the precolonial era among individuals and between individuals and the state.[97] They represent a rejection of the individual "who is utterly free and utterly irresponsible and opposed to society."[98] In a proper reflection of the nuanced nature of societal obligations in the precolonial era, the African Charter explicitly provides for two types of duties: direct and indirect. A direct duty is contained, for example, in article 29(4) of the Charter which requires the individual to "preserve and strengthen social and national solidarity, particularly when the latter is threatened."[99] There is nothing inherently sinister about this provision; it merely repeats a duty formerly imposed on members of precolonial communities. If anything, there exists a heightened need today, more than at any other time in recent history, to fortify communal relations and defend national solidarity. The threat of the collapse of the postcolonial state, as has been the case in Liberia, Somalia, Sierra Leone, the Democratic Republic of the Congo, and Rwanda, is only too real. Political elites as well as the common citizenry, each in equal measure, bear the primary responsibility for avoiding societal collapse and its devastating consequences.

The African Charter provides an example of an indirect duty in article 27(2), which states that "The rights and freedoms of each individual shall be exercised with due regard to the rights of others, collective security, morality and common interest."[100] This duty is in fact a limitation on the enjoyment of certain individual rights. It merely recognizes the practical reality that in African societies, as elsewhere in the world, individual rights are not absolute. Individuals are asked to reflect on how the exercise of their rights in certain circumstances might adversely affect other individuals or the community. The duty is based on the presumption that the full development of the individual is only possible where individuals care about how their actions would impact on others. By rejecting the egotistical individual whose only concern is fulfilling self, article 27(2) raises the level of care owed to neighbors and the community.

Duties are also grouped according to whether they are owed to individuals or to larger units such as the family, society, or the state. Parents, for example, are owed a duty of respect and maintenance by their children.[101] Crippling economic problems do not allow African states to contemplate some of the programs of the welfare state. The care of the aged and needy falls squarely on family and community members. This requirement—a necessity today—has its roots in the past: it was unthinkable to abandon a parent or relative in need.[102] The family guilty of such an omission would be held in disgrace and contempt pending the intervention of lineage or clan members. Such problems explain why the family is considered sacred and why it would be simply impracticable and suicidal for Africans to adopt wholesale the individualist conception of rights. Duty to the family is emphasized elsewhere in the Charter because of its crucial and indispensable economic utility.[103] Economic difficulties and the dislocations created by the transformation of rural life by the cash economy make the homestead a place of refuge.

Some duties are owed by the individual to the state. These are not distinctive to African states; many of them are standard obligations that any modern state places on its citizens. In the African context, however, these obligations have a basis in the past, and many seem relevant because of the fragility and the domination of Africa by external agents. Such duties are rights that the community or the state, defined as all persons within it, holds against the individual. They include the duties to "preserve and strengthen social and national solidarity";[104] not to "compromise the security of the State"; to serve the "national community by placing his physical and intellectual abilities at its service"; to "pay taxes imposed by law in the interest of the society"; and to "preserve and strengthen the national independence and the territorial integrity of his country and to contribute to its defense in accordance with the law."

The duties that require the individual to strengthen and defend national independence, security, and the territorial integrity of the state are inspired by the continent's history of domination and occupation by outside powers over the centuries.[105] The duties represent an extension of the principle of self-determination, used in the external sense, as a shield against foreign occupation. Even in countries where this history is lacking, the right of the state to be defended by its citizens can trump certain individual rights, such as the draft of younger people for a war effort. Likewise, the duty to place one's intellectual abilities at the service of the state is a legitimate state interest, for the "brain drain" has robbed Africa of massive intellect.[106] In recognition of the need for the strength of diversity, rather than its power to divide, the Charter asks individuals to promote African unity, an especially critical role given arbitrary balkanization by the colonial powers and the ethnic animosities fostered within and between the imposed states.[107]

In addition to the duties placed on the state to secure for the people within its borders economic, social, and cultural rights, the Charter also requires the state to protect the family, which it terms "the natural unit and basis of society," and the "custodian of morals and traditional values."[108] There is an enormous potential for advocates of equality rights to be concerned that these provisions could be used to support the patriarchy and other repressive practices of precolonial social ordering. It is now generally accepted that one of the strikes against the precolonial regime was its strict separation of gender roles and, in many cases, the limitation on, or exclusion of, women from political participation. The discriminatory treatment of women on the basis of gender in marriage, property ownership, and inheritance, and the disproportionately heavy labor and reproduction burdens were violations of their rights.

However, these are not the practices that the Charter condones when it requires states to assist families as the "custodians of morals and traditional values." Such an interpretation would be a cynical misreading of the Charter.[109] The reference is to those traditional values which enhanced the dignity of the individual and emphasized the dignity of motherhood and the importance of the female as the central link in the reproductive chain; women were highly valued as equals in the process of the regeneration of life. The Charter guarantees, unambiguously and without equivocation, the equal rights of women in its gender equality provision by requiring states to "eliminate every discrimination against women" and to protect women's rights in international human rights instruments.[110] Read in conjunction with other provisions, the Charter leaves no room for discriminatory treatment against women.

The articulation of the duty conception in the Charter has been subjected to severe criticism. Some of the criticism, however, has confused the African conception of duty with socialist or Marxist formulations.[111] Such confusion is unfortunate. In socialist ideology, states—not individuals—are subjects of international law.[112] Thus the state assumes obligations under international law, through the International Covenant on Civil and Political Rights (ICCPR) for example, to provide human rights. Under socialism, the state secures economic, cultural, and social benefits for the individual. Hence, the state, as the guardian of public interest, retains primacy in the event of conflict with the individual.[113] Human rights, therefore, are conditioned on the interest of the state and the goals of communist development.[114] There is an organic unity between rights and duties to the state.[115] In this collectivist conception, duties are only owed to the state. In contrast, in the precolonial era, and in the African Charter, duties are primarily owed to the family—nuclear and extended—and to the community, not to the state.[116] In effect, the primacy attached to the family in the Charter places the family above state, which is not the case under communism.[117] In precolonial Africa, unlike the former Soviet Union or Eastern Europe, duties owed to the family or community were rarely misused or cynically manipulated to derogate from human rights obligations.[118]

The most damaging criticism of the language of duties in Africa sees them as "little more than the formulation, entrenchment, and legitimation of state rights and privileges against individuals and peoples."[119] However, critics who question the value of including duties in the Charter point only to the theoretical danger that states might capitalize on the duty concept to violate other guaranteed rights.[120] The fear is frequently expressed that emphasis on duties may lead to the "trumping" of individual rights if the two are in opposition.[121] It is argued that:

If the state has a collective right and obligation to develop the society, economy, and polity (Article 29), then as an instrument it can be used to defend coercive state actions against both individuals and constituent groups to achieve state policies rationalized as social and economic improvement.

While the human rights records of African states are distressingly appalling, facts do not indicate that the zeal to promote certain economic and political programs is the root cause of human rights abuses. Since 1978, the regime of Daniel arap Moi in Kenya, for example, has not engaged in the widespread suppression of civil and political rights because of adherence to policies it deems in the national interest; instead, abuses have been triggered by an insecure and narrow political class which will stop at nothing, including political murder, to retain power.[122] Similarly, Mobutu Sese Seko of Zaire (now the Democratic Republic of the Congo) drove the country into the ground because he could not contemplate relinquishing power.[123] Alienated and corrupt elites, quite often devoid of a national consciousness, plunder the state and brutalize society to maintain their personal privileges and retain power.[124] The use of the state to implement particular state policies is almost never the reason, although such a rationale is frequently used as the pretext.

Hastings Okoth-Ogendo persuasively argues that the attack on the duty conception is not meritorious because the "state is the villain against which human rights law is the effective weapon" and toward which "individuals should not be called upon to discharge any duties."[125] Valid criticism would question the "precise boundaries, content, and conditions of compliance" contemplated by the Charter.[126] It should be the duty of the African Commission in its jurisprudence to clarify which, if any, of these duties are moral or legal obligations, and what the scope of their application ought to be.[127] The Commission could lead the way in suggesting how some of the duties—on the individual as well as the state—might be implemented. The concept of national service, for example, could utilize traditional notions in addressing famine, public works, and community self-help projects.[128] The care of parents and the needy could be formalized in family/state burden-sharing. The Commission should also indicate how, and in what forum, the state would respond to the breach of individual duties. It might suggest the establishment of community arbitration centers to work out certain types of disputes. As suggested by Oji Umozurike, a former chairman to the Commission, state responsibility for these duties implies a "minimum obligation to inculcate the underlying principles and ideals in their subjects."[129]

The duty/rights formulation is also inextricably tied to the concept, articulated in the African Charter, of peoples' rights. Although a long discussion about the concept itself and the controversy it has attracted will not be made here, a brief outline of the concept to the notion of duty would be useful. Like the duty concept, the idea of peoples' rights is embodied in the African philosophy which sees men and women primarily as social beings embraced in the body of the community.[130] It was pointed out during the drafting of the African Charter that individual rights could only be justified in the context of the rights of the community; consequently the drafters made room in the Charter for peoples' rights.[131]

The concept was not new in a human rights document. For example, common article 1 of the two basic international human rights covenants makes peoples the subject of rights, a departure from Western notions that human rights only attach to individuals.[132] There is recognition of the fact that individual rights cannot be realized unless groups hold collective rights. As clearly noted by Louis Sohn,

One of the main characteristics of humanity is that human beings are social creatures. Consequently, most individuals belong to various units, groups, and communities; they are simultaneously members of such units as a family, religious community, social club, trade union, professional association, racial group, people, nation, and state. It is not surprising, therefore, that international law not only recognizes inalienable rights of individuals, but also recognizes certain collective rights that are exercised jointly by individuals grouped into larger communities, including peoples and nations. These rights are still human rights; the effective exercise of collective rights is a precondition to the exercise of other rights, political or economic or both. If a community is not free, most of its members are also deprived of many important rights.[133]

The African Charter distinguishes human rights from peoples' or collective rights, but sees them in cooperation, not competition or conflict. The Charter's preambular paragraph notes this relationship and recognizes "on the one hand, that fundamental human rights stem from the attributes of human beings, which justifies their national and international protection and on the other hand, that the reality and respect for peoples rights should necessarily guarantee human rights."[134] This unambiguous statement, notes Theo van Boven, is conclusive proof of the Charter's view: human rights are inalienable and intrinsic to individuals and are not in conflict with peoples' rights, which they complement.[135] The exercise of sovereignty rights by a "people" or "peoples" as contemplated by the Charter is a necessary precondition for the enjoyment of individual rights.[136] This dialectic between individual and peoples' rights is one of the bases for the Charter's imposition of duties on individuals. Solidarity between the individual and the greater society safeguards collective rights, without which individual rights would be unattainable.

Whither Africa?

Today Africa is at a crossroads. Since colonization, when Europe restructured its political map, Africa has lunged from one crisis to another. Whether it was famine consuming millions, the Sierra Leonean rebels waging a savage war against innocents, semi-illiterate rulers dispatching political opponents and innocents with impunity, senseless coups by soldiers, the Rwandese and Burundian catastrophes, the wars in the Democratic Republic of the Congo and Angola, ethnic tensions turned deadly, or corrupt political elites, the list of abominations is simply unbearable. The failure of the postcolonial state is so pervasive that it has become the rule, not the exception. Needless to say, there are numerous causes for this crisis, perhaps the most important of which is the disfiguration of the continent's political identity by the imposition of European forms and values of government and society. Narrow political elites who barely comprehend the Western notions they eagerly mimic—and who have lost the anchor in their past— remain in power, but without a rudder.[137] This crisis of cultural identity is Africa's most serious enemy. But with the end of colonization and the cold war—the two driving reasons for past European and American interest in Africa—Africans should reexamine the assumptions underlying the role and purpose of the state and its organization. It seems more likely, however, that the negative forces of globalization will further dim any hopes for relief from this past of unthinkable tragedies.

This chapter was not intended to dismiss concerns about the potential for the misuse of the duty/rights conception by political elites to achieve narrow, personal ends. However, any notions are subject to abuse by power-hungry elites. There is no basis for concluding that the duty/rights conception is unique in this respect. While it is true that the precolonial context in which the conception originally worked was small in scale and relatively uncomplicated, the argument made here is not about magnitudes. Instead, the ideals that can be distilled from the past are the central thrust of this argument. Is it possible to introduce in the modern African state grassroots democracy, deepening it in neighborhood communities and villages in the tradition of the precolonial council of elders? Can the family reclaim its status as the basic organizational political unit in this re-democratization process? Is it possible to create a state of laws—where elected officials are bound by checks and balances—as in the days of old, where rulers were held accountable, at times through destooling?

Can the state and the family devise a "social security" system in which the burden of caring for the aged and the needy can be shared? Is it possible to require individuals to take responsibility for their actions in matters relating to sexuality, community security, and self-help projects in the construction of community schools and health centers, utilizing concepts such as *harambee*,[138] the Kenyan slogan for pulling together? Child care and rearing, including lighter forms of discipline such as a reprimand, for example, have always been community affairs in Africa.[139] Could community-based programs be devised and encouraged to promote the "village-raising" of children? These are the typical questions that the new formulation of human rights must ask in the context of recreating the African state to legitimize human rights on the continent.

This chapter represents a preliminary attempt to begin rethinking Africa's precolonial articulation of human rights and propose how some of the ideals imbedded in the past could be woven into conceptions of man, society, and the state in a way that would make the human rights corpus more relevant to Africa today. Part of the reason for the failure of the post-colonial state to respect human rights lies in the alien character of that corpus. The African Charter's duty/rights conception is an excellent point of departure in the reconstruction of a new ethos and the restoration of confidence in the continent's cultural identity. It reintroduces values that Africa needs most at this time: commitment, solidarity, respect, and responsibility. Moreover, it also represents a recognition of another reality. Individual rights are collective in their dimension. "[T]heir recognition, their mode of exercise and their means of protection" is a collective process requiring the intervention of other individuals, groups, and communities.[140] The past, as the Africans of the old used to say, is part of the living. It ought to be used to construct a better tomorrow.

Chapter 4
Human Rights, Religion, and Proselytism

The Problem of Religious Rights

This chapter is not just about the limitations, if any, that should or could be placed on religious rights per se. But it further explores the complex project of universalism in the spiritual world and the torment that results from legal protection to particular cosmologies in their efforts to remake other traditions. At the heart of this crisis is the belief by some spiritual traditions in their own superiority and their view of the "other" as inferior. This chapter is an exploration of the historical experience of religious penetration and advocacy in a very specific context and a quest to demonstrate the possibilities of conflict between certain forms of evangelistic advocacy and certain human rights norms. With the African theater as the basic laboratory, I intend to unpack the meaning of religious freedom at the point of contact between the messianic faiths and African religions and illustrate how that meeting resulted in a phenomenon akin to cultural genocide. The main purpose here is not merely to defend forms of religion or belief but rather to problematize the concept of the right to the free exercise of messianic faiths, which includes the right to proselytize in the marketplace of religions. In societies such as those in Africa where religion is woven into virtually every aspect of life, its delegitimization can eventually lead to the collapse of social norms and cultural identities. The result, as has been the case in most of sub-Saharan Africa, is a culturally disconnected people, neither themselves nor the outsiders in Europe, North America, and the Arab world that they seek to imitate. In other words, I argue that imperial religions have necessarily violated the individual conscience and the communal expressions of Africans and their communities by subverting African religions. In so doing, they have robbed Africans of essential elements of their humanity. Inasmuch as this chapter is a protest, it is also a plea for the better understanding of African religions, their freedom from imperial religions, and the necessity for the rights regime to devise norms and mechanisms for protecting them. I base this argument on several premises.

Since the right to religious freedom includes the right to be left alone—to choose freely whether to believe and what to believe in—the rights regime by requiring that African religions compete in the marketplace of ideas incorrectly assumes a level playing field. The rights corpus not only forcibly imposes on African religions the obligation to compete—a task for which as nonproselytizing, noncompetitive creeds they are not historically fashioned—but also protects evangelizing religions in their march toward universalization. In the context of religious freedom, the privileging by the rights regime of the competition of ideas over the right against cultural invasion, in a skewed contest, amounts to condoning the dismantling of African religions.

I also argue that the playing field, the one crucial and necessary ingredient in a fair fight, is heavily weighted against Africans. Messianic religions have been forcibly imposed or their introduction was accomplished as part of the cultural package borne by colonialism. Missionaries did not simply offer Jesus Christ as the savior of benighted souls, his salvation was frequently a precondition for services in education and health, which were quite often the exclusive domain of the Church and the colonial state.[1] It makes little sense to argue that Africans could avoid acculturation by opting out of the colonial order; in most cases, the embrace of indigenous societies by the European imperial powers was so violent and total that conformity was the only immediate option. In making this argument, I also rely on notions of human rights law which, as I seek to show, suggest that indigenous beliefs have a right to be respected and left alone by more dominant external traditions.

This reasoning poses serious questions that go to the root of the rights regime. Some difficulties are obvious. A key ideal of the human rights movement, and indeed of liberalism, is the unwavering commitment to the open society in which the freedom to advance, receive, and disseminate ideas is assumed necessary for the greater social good. Though not absolute—permissible limitations can be placed on what ideas and under what circumstances advocacy is allowed by the law—this commitment creates a rights regime conundrum in conversations about the universality of human rights norms. Questions arise about the validity of the advocacy of certain norms beyond the borders of their origin. The right of advocacy itself and its centrality in the human rights corpus becomes an issue. Is it possible, for instance, to question advocacy in connection with other creeds, ideologies, and institutions? Should advocacy by the industrial West to spread free markets and democracy to nondemocratic, non-Western cultures, complete with their power to transform and fundamentally change economic, social, and political systems, be protected under the human rights regime? Could theocratic states, for example, seek protection for their political orders and social systems under the rights corpus? Other examples come to mind. Should human rights law invade cultures that subordinate women and seek to eradicate gender bias through advocacy? Are these acceptable forms of advocacy which the human rights movement should protect? Ultimately, one must ask, who decides what is good for the universe and what should be advocated transnationally?

I mention these problems only to indicate the scope of the dilemma posed by this chapter; it would require another exercise altogether to address them properly. My particular concern here is with a certain historical experience and the results of that experience. I shall address the nature and forms of religious advocacy employed by the two major messianic religions—Christianity and Islam—in Africa and the tension between those forms of advocacy and certain norms and ideals of the human rights movement.

I briefly sketch the history of the human rights movement and outline those ideals within it that are relevant for my purposes. Then I will discuss the view of the messianic religions toward human rights and other religious traditions, particularly indigenous religions. My goal here is to indicate some of the bases for demonizing the "other" and draw attention to possible contradictions between the human rights corpus and some of the positions taken by messianic religions. A brief review of the human rights, constitutional, and other legal bases for religious freedom and the protection of indigenous religions in Africa illustrates the difficulties of proselytism. I then explore the forms of proselytization preferred by both Islam and Christianity in Africa and the use of coercion, both physical and cultural, as a tool in that process. The last segment addresses the tension inherent in the rights regime and the dilemmas posed to the human rights movement by the practical and historical experience of evangelization in Africa.

A discussion about limitations on religious rights at first blush appears to frustrate some of the major ideals of the human rights movement. It raises the question about the tension between the restriction of the right to evangelize or advocate a point of view and one of the central ideals of the human rights movement, the promotion of diversity and the right to advocate ideas or creeds.[2] An exploration of the manner in which the human rights corpus ought to view religious rights—whether to further limit or to expand the protections they currently enjoy—raises a fundamental tension: how does a body of principles that promotes diversity and difference protect the establishment and manifestation of religious orders that seek to destroy difference and forcibly impose an orthodoxy in Africa—as both Christianity and Islam, the two major proselytizing religions, attempted, and in many cases successfully did? Precisely because of the ethos of universalization common to both, the messianic faiths sought to eradicate, with the help of the state, all other forms of religious expression and belief and close off any avenues through which other competing faiths could be introduced or sustained. This coerced imposition of a religious orthodoxy implies a desire and a social philosophy to seek the forcible destruction of that which is different. Yet, it seems inconceivable that the human rights movement would have intended to protect the "right" of certain religions to "destroy" others. In this chapter, I explore this tension—between protecting the right to proselytize in Africa and limiting the circumstances in which that right can be exercised within—the confines of the human rights corpus.

It is my argument that the free exercise of religion and belief should find protection within the human rights universe in the context of respect for diversity without giving license to the destruction of other religions and cultures. While I explore the nature, context, and purposes of proselytization in Africa from a rights perspective, I also seek to see whether proselytization in that context constituted a human rights violation and, if so, what the response of the human rights regime should be.

There is a growing realization internationally that the struggle for human rights is a quest for the reduction of conditions that engender weakness; in effect, it is a push against the denial of certain fundamental rights by any individual or institution regardless of its relationship to the state. Certain institutions, such as the family, which traditionally has been part of the private realm, are now coming under increasing scrutiny to comply with international human rights standards. The state—the political instrument that gives legal personality and protection to private institutions—is being pressed to intervene to secure basic rights for individuals under the control or influence of entities in the private realm. Advocates base their claims on the influence or control that the state ought to exercise over such entities.

The challenge for the human rights movement is to move beyond the singular obsession with wrongs committed directly by the state—although it remains the most important obligee of the discourse—and confront nonstate actors in order to contain and control human rights violations in the private sphere. To do so, the movement has to take on powerful private institutions in the private realm, including established religion. It is my argument that although religious human rights must be defined, secured, and protected, there is a correlative duty on the part of religions to respect the human rights of nonbelievers and adherents of other religions or faiths and not to seek their coerced conversion either directly or through the manipulation and destruction of other cultures.

It is true that article 18 of the ICCPR guarantees the "right to freedom of thought, conscience and religion," and provides for certain limitations. But it does not spell out the duties that must be borne by proselytizing religions. This chapter attempts to balance the interests of these religions with those of African societies, both individual and collective, and to explore ways, if possible, in which the respectful coexistence between these radically different spiritualities could be imagined and worked out.

Demonizing the "Other"

The two most geographically diverse religions—Christianity and Islam—
are also the most imperial: they are proselytizing and universalist in their
attempts to convert into their faith the entire human race.[3] Although these
religions are not spread through physical violence today, they have historically been forcibly introduced. They have also been negatively competitive
against each other as well as other creeds as they have fought over the souls
of both different religious groups and individuals.[4] But central to them is
the belief in the racial superiority of the proselytizers; the "other" is quite
often depicted as inferior. Arab Muslims, for example, have historically
viewed black Africans as racially inferior; Islamized Africans are regarded
as having taken an important step toward overcoming that inferiority. The
capture and enslavement of millions of Africans by Arab Muslims over the
centuries bore the trademarks of this theological and racial justification. It
does not require a profound knowledge of history to prove that both Arab
and European perceptions of Africa have been decidedly racist over the
centuries. Asserting that the "Bantu mind" was inferior to that of the "civilized man," a leading European missionary described Africans thus:

> It is suggested that the mere possession on the part of the Bantu of nothing but an
> oral tradition and culture creates a chasm of difference between the Native "mind"
> and that of civilized man, and of itself would account for a lack of balance and pro-
> portion in the triple psychological function of feeling, thinking and acting, imply-
> ing that thinking is the weakest of the three and that feeling is the most dominant.
> The Native seeks not truth nor works, but power—the dynamical tool.[5]

Writing about the importance of evangelization in Africa, another European missionary asserted that the "Mission to Africa was the least that we
[Europeans] can do to strive to raise him [the African] in the scale of
mankind."[6] The catalog of writing by pioneer missionaries in Africa is in-
exhaustible and uniquely similar. Paternalistic at best, African missionaries
left no doubt of their belief in the superiority of their race, religion, and
culture, and the necessity of "freeing" the African from his heathen and
subhuman beliefs and status.

Such attempts, often quite successful, at the universalization of the messianic faiths have resulted in untold suffering throughout history. The religious crusades and jihads waged by both Christians and Muslims, in which
millions were killed and enslaved, are just one example of the destruction
that accompanied or was the excuse for proselytization. In strange symbolism, the cross, with its linear structure, becomes a sword once turned on its
side.[7] The causal link, historically, between evangelization and war appears
to be indisputable.[8] The philosophy and practice of remaking the "other"
appears therefore to be based on the contempt for that which is different
and belief in the superiority of the aggressive creed.

Major bodies of both Christian and Islamic jurisprudence directly assert the inferiority of, and disrespect for, nonbelievers. Although some scholars argue that Shari'a, for example, is just one particular interpretation of the Qur'an, the definitive word of God and Muhammad, his Prophet, it is the only coherent, unified body of law for the world's Muslims.[9] Other, more liberal interpretations of Islam have been of little consequence to the lives of Muslims. Yet Shari'a itself contradicts basic human rights standards by discriminating against non-Muslims. Abdullahi An-Na'im, a leading advocate for reform of Islamic jurisprudence to bring it into conformity with international human rights standards, has written:

The claim that Shari'a is fully consistent with and has always protected human rights is problematic both as a theoretical and a practical matter. As a theoretical matter, the concept of human rights as rights to which every human being is entitled by virtue of being human was unknown to Islamic jurisprudence or social philosophy until the last few decades and does not exist in Shari'a. Many rights are given under Shari'a in accordance with a strict classification based on faith and gender and are not given to human beings as such. As a practical matter, fundamental inconsistencies exist between Shari'a as practiced in Muslim countries and current standards of human rights.[10]

A number of theoretical and scriptural examples illustrate this point. Unbelievers, defined by Shari'a as non-Muslims except Jews and Christians, or those who do not believe in the "revealed heavenly" scriptures,[11] are not regarded as fully human and could be legally enslaved. Shari'a only discusses the manner in which slaves ought to be treated; it does not prohibit the enslavement of nonbelievers.[12] In addition, according to Shari'a, only Muslims can fully enjoy the benefits of citizenship in an Islamic state. Even members of other "revealed" faiths such as Jews or Christians are only entitled to the lesser status of *dhimma*, under which their security of person and property is guaranteed with some freedom to practice their own religion. In return, they have to pay taxes and submit to Islamic rules in all public matters.[13] Shari'a also punishes by execution Muslims who repudiate their faith.[14] The assumption of the "right" to Islamize and then prevent others from converting—or counter-penetrating—is at the very least a manifestation of intolerance for difference and diversity.

Bigoted clergy and their followers, from South Africa to the United States, have continuously mined the scriptures for references to the subhumanity of Africans to justify apartheid, slavery, and other violations of basic freedoms based solely on race and skin color. In the United States and the European colonies and possessions in Africa, law and religion were often synthesized to create an oppressive social philosophy in order to justify the institutionalization of slavery, colonialism, and the ubiquity of white or European power over people of African descent. Many settled on the story of the curse of Noah's son, Ham, in Genesis 9 as the divine curse on all people of African descent. Religion and pseudoscience were often hand-woven to "prove" the bestial, subhuman characteristics of Africans. These philosophies and practices allowed "good" Christians to brutally subjugate, or acquiesce with a clear conscience in the subjugation of, Africans, their cultures, and religious traditions.

Proselytization in Africa

In this segment, I explore the views of the evangelizer and the processes of evangelization in black Africa and raise some of the human rights issues implied by their penetration of the continent. I attempt to highlight the tension between proselytization, coupled with force and power, and respect for difference and cultural identity. Islam was introduced to Africa through military conquest by the Muslim Arabs. Thereafter, the processes of Arabization (in North Africa and the Nile Delta) and Islamization (in East and West Africa) proceeded simultaneously through force, the slave trade, and general commerce. The entry of Christianity into the continent was no less violent, coming as it did in partnership with the colonial imperial powers.[15] Most European missionaries saw their duty in the image painted by Rudyard Kipling in 1899: "Take up the White Man's burden— / Send forth the best ye breed— / Go bind your sons to exile — / To serve your captives' need; / To wait in heavy harness / On fluttered folk and wild— / Your new-caught, sullen peoples / Half devil and half child."[16] A missionary who worked among Zimbabweans early in the twentieth century exemplified these beliefs; to him, "unlettered" natives were in "the technically barbaric and pre-literacy stage of cultural and social development." In a book written for those "responsible for the development of a primitive people or are concerned for their progress—missionary and administrator, government official and teacher, employer and civilian," the missionary stated starkly:

Indeed, primitive people all over the world who have not yet acknowledged a sovereignty of reason arm themselves with similar weapons against their physical and spiritual foes and have the same elemental passions, emotions and instincts. Institutions and beliefs such as initiation ceremonies, the medicine-man, witchcraft, and all the magico-religious assumptions are part and parcel of the lives of such peoples.[17]

In contrast, Christianity, which has undergone "centuries of theological learning," "labour of intellect, and subtlety of reasoning throughout its whole history, stands for a literary type of religion giving prominence to beliefs that can be put into ideas as dogma and doctrine."[18] That is why, according to the missionary, he was "amazed at my own impertinence in desiring to impose a new and strange religion and culture upon a primitive people with whose cultural inheritance I was quite unacquainted." Hence he advises, "Before sowing, know your ground." He emphasizes that the purpose of the evangelist is not "merely to civilize but to Christianize, not merely to convey the Gifts of Civilization."[19]

European missionaries, sociologists, and anthropologists have historically treated African religions as bizarre and primitive phenomena completely different from and inferior to the messianic faiths. Part of this process of demonization betrays the prejudice, ignorance, and cultural vantage point of the outsider. Hence the description of Africans as heathens and pagans. Many of the writers and missionaries describe African religions as superstitious, unscientific, and without reason.[20] Missionaries therefore sought to discredit and dismantle those African religions and cultural expressions that they deemed un-Christian or resistant to Christianization and Westernization. Some missionaries, however, did not advocate the full destruction of "false religions" but rather a process of "assimilation":

It is becoming increasingly clear, and governors and missionaries alike are coming to realize, that the method of the destruction of religion and culture of primitive races, as happened in the cases of the Tasmanians, Australians . . . and American Indians is both scandalous and futile. For such a method destroys all the values that give meaning and zest to their lives, rendering them impotent and ill-equipped to face the future, cutting them loose from all their moorings on a vast and uncharted sea where they drift to despair and finally destruction.[21]

This paternalistic approach, which sought to "secure, at whatever cost, the fullness of the development of the personality of the African," would not simply target African religions but would be a "concerted attempt" in the "spheres of religion, law, medicine, politics and economics for the simple reason that the life of those we are seeking to transform is all of a piece."[22] In this process of reeducation missionaries ended up denouncing as satanic African ceremonies and events of worship for the spirit world. African dances, marriage ceremonies, female circumcision, and polygamy were deemed pagan or heathen practices incompatible with Christianity. Among the Kikuyu and Akamba of Kenya, for example, parents who permitted female circumcision were not allowed access to churches and schools, although the practice was deeply bound up with other cultural norms.[23] As one writer has mildly put it, "The missionaries, as even devout Christians will admit, were extremely narrow in outlook. They taught that Christianity was the only right religion and that all other religions and practices must stop. Such teaching confused the Africans, who believed that all religions were good."[24]

The deliberate destruction of African values was epitomized by the introduction of a "white" god and Jesus Christ and a "black" devil or Satan. The visual images displayed and popularized by missionaries to date—

drawings and other impressions of Jesus Christ, the Virgin Mary, and God—are those of whites with blue eyes and long, usually blond, hair. Verbal and written descriptions of these figures also gave the impression that they were European. Growing up in Africa as a young boy—and my experience was typical—I thought that God was a silver haired white sage resident somewhere in the deep blue sky. The system of formal education introduced by the missionaries and the colonial authorities emphasized the superiority of Europe over the rest of the world. This educational and religious orientation was meant to disembowel, and did so, African traditional outlooks and replace them with Western, Judeo-Christian conceptions of life.

The alliance between, and in many cases the practical fusion of the Church and the colonial flag, even where naked force was not applied, served to quash African values. As a reaction to the Eurocentric and racist curricula of the mission schools, together with their opposition to African cultural and religious practices such as female circumcision, Africans in Kenya started in the late 1920s to establish independent schools under the leadership of Jomo Kenyatta, later the first president of Kenya. This frontal attack on religious values and practices and ethnic and racial identities developed over hundreds of years was particularly damaging because religion was an integral part of being African.[25] African religious beliefs centered individual and group existence; their subversion overthrew ethnic identities. The devaluation of their culture dehumanized Africans and created a self-hatred that continues to devour the continent today.

Predictably, different denominations of Christianity, primarily the Protestant and Roman Catholic, introduced bitter rivalries between African communities. The rivalry engendered by the competition for converts created deep political antagonisms between ethnic groups and introduced one more cleavage in societies already destabilized by colonization. In countries like Uganda, these sectarian rivalries have periodically erupted into ethnopolitical violence. In countries such as Sudan or Nigeria, the primary source of violence has been interreligious: between Muslims and Christians.[26]

It was not the purpose of this segment to document the destruction of African religions and cultural values through the agencies of the messianic religions and colonialism. My purpose was to explore the views of the missionaries and the methods employed in their work. There is little doubt that the coupling of Islam with force and Christianity with the colonial state—with a technologically superior base—virtually assured the decimation of indigenous religions or, at the very least, the imposition of alien religions. The material and military resources available to the colonial administrators enabled them to crush resistance and establish political hegemony. From their privileged vantage points, the missionaries utilizing equally sophisticated means of pacification and communication were able to force and pressure whole communities into abandoning their indigenous faiths if they hoped to benefit from the new order. In all probability, the dismantling of African religions and cultures—even under colonialism—would have been much more difficult without the combination of proselytization and racism. According to Basil Davidson, the Africanist, none of this was an accident or a mistake:

By racism I mean the conscious and systematic weapon of domination, of exploitation, which first saw its demonic rise with the onset of the trans-Atlantic trade in African captives sold into slavery, and which, later, led on to the imperialist colonialism of our yesterdays.

This racism was not a "mistake," a "misunderstanding" or a "grievous deviation from the proper norms of behavior." It was not an accident of human error. It was not an unthinking reversion to barbarism. On the contrary, this racism was conceived as the moral justification—the necessary justification, as it was seen by those in the white man's world who were neither thieves or moral monsters— for doing to black people what church and state no longer thought it permissible to do to white people: the justification for enslaving black people.[27]

The Legal Invisibility of Indigenous Religions

The subject of indigenous religions is one of the most underdeveloped areas of inquiry in human rights. Indeed, it remains a question whether the view adopted by the human rights corpus on the freedom of religion, belief, and conscience—in article 18 of both the UDHR and ICCPR—took into account indigenous religions and their historical relationship with messianic faiths. In this segment, I shall briefly examine what protections, if any, are afforded indigenous religions in the human rights regime and in several African countries. For the purposes of my argument, I shall not attempt to define the complex and contentious term "indigenous peoples." Instead, I shall focus my attention on "indigenous religions" which I define as nonmessianic faiths but excluding dominant and politically established religions such as Judaism, Buddhism, and Hinduism. The key to the inclusion of a religion as indigenous is its history of attack and domination by the imperial faiths and colonialism and its status as the cultural inheritance and spiritual expression of the original, nonwhite, non-Arabic peoples of Africa.[28] But I also examine United Nations documents regarding the cultural rights of indigenous peoples to indicate how the human rights regime might consider thinking about the protection of indigenous religions.

The UDHR and the ICCPR do not specially recognize indigenous religions in relation to dominant faiths or cultures; they do not even refer to them. Article 18 simply provides the right of everyone "to freedom of thought, conscience and religion" and prohibits the use of coercion to "impair" the freedom of others to have or to adopt a religion or a belief of their choice. The freedom to "manifest one's religion or beliefs may be subject to such limitations as are prescribed by law" or limited to protect public "morals or the fundamental rights and freedoms of others."[29] This provision prohibits the use of force to make converts as was the case in early European crusades in Africa and the conquest of parts of the continent by Arab Muslims. It would also appear to disallow using state resources—such as educational, health, and other services—to disadvantage particular faiths. Missionaries who worked against other religions with the help of colonial regimes would seem to be in violation of this provision.

While no authoritative human rights body has issued a definitive interpretation of such construction, the Human Rights Committee has adopted a General Comment on article 27 of the ICCPR,[30] providing that states are under an obligation to protect the cultural, linguistic, and religious rights of minorities. It said, in part:

Although the rights protected under Article 27 are individual rights, they depend in turn on the ability of the minority group to maintain its culture, language or religion. Accordingly, positive measures by States may also be necessary to protect the identity of a minority and the rights of its members to enjoy and develop their culture and language and to practice their religion, in community with other members of the group.[31]

In its 1981 Declaration on the Elimination of all Forms of Intolerance and of Discrimination Based on Religion or Belief,[32] the United Nations did not even address the subject of indigenous religions. The Declaration was little more than an elaboration of article 18 of the ICCPR.

Some more recent developments, however, indicate a willingness to recognize indigenous religions within the ambit of the United Nations. Through the relentless and focused advocacy of indigenous peoples and their supporters, the General Assembly in 1992 instructed the Working Group on Indigenous Populations to draft a Declaration on the Rights of Indigenous Peoples for consideration by the Commission on Human Rights.[33] The Draft Declaration explicitly recognized indigenous religions and went further than any other United Nations document in recognizing the rights of indigenous peoples and protecting their indigenous religions.[34]

The Draft Declaration, in dramatic and definitive language, affirmed in the preamble that "all doctrines, policies and practices based on or advocating superiority of peoples or individuals on the basis of national origin, racial, religious, ethnic or cultural differences are racist, scientifically false, legally invalid, morally condemnable and socially unjust."

The Draft Declaration would find unacceptable the philosophical and theological assumptions propagated by missionaries in Africa; the demonization of African religions as backward and inferior would violate the letter and spirit of the document. Elsewhere, the Draft Declaration protected indigenous peoples from any "adverse discrimination, in particular based on their indigenous origin and identity" (art. 2). More important, the Draft Declaration prohibited "cultural genocide" and disallowed "any form of assimilation or integration by other cultures or ways of life imposed on them" (art 7[d]). In a sweeping assertion of sovereignty, the Draft Declaration appeared to prohibit all forms of advocacy or proselytization by agents external to the indigenous culture when it called for the "prevention of and redress for," among other things, "any form of propaganda directed at them [indigenous peoples]" (art. 7[e]). The objective of this reasoning is to create space in which indigenous peoples and their cultures are left alone by external agents including imperial religions. If adopted, the Draft Declaration would provide guidance for the human rights movement in understanding indigenous religions and creating processes to protect them.

While the protection of indigenous cultures appears to be gaining international currency, African states remain uninterested in reclaiming the precolonial past and restoring those aspects of traditional norms and values, including elements of spirituality, which were discredited during the colonial era. The lack of interest in the past is partially due to its thorough demonization and the shame and backwardness with which the Westernized and Christianized or Islamized ruling African elites associate it. Good culture in Africa today is defined by its distance from traditional cultures and proximity to Western values. In many instances, African states continue to carry out "modernization" campaigns against "backward peoples" such as the Maasai of Kenya and Tanzania. So-called African customary laws, for example, are ordinarily overridden by received colonial laws in most legal systems and jurisdictions in Africa. In many African countries, there have been no national debates to evaluate and contextualize African customs and laws within the modern state. Many traditional practices, from polygamy to traditional healing and worship, which were discredited by the colonial state, are actively prohibited and punished by the new African-led governments. In this process of continued acculturation, African religions have been one of the major casualties of the culture of imitation.

The exception to the general disregard of the African past is the African Charter on Human and Peoples' Rights, the continental human rights instrument adopted by the Organization of African Unity in 1981.[35] In its preamble, the African Charter recognizes the "virtues" of Africa's traditions and its civilization. Elsewhere, it imposes upon individual Africans the "duty to preserve and strengthen positive African cultural values" (art. 29[7]), although it neither spells out those values nor mentions African religions. But its use of the word "positive" betrays a Eurocentric bias and implies that there is much that is negative in African culture. The only reference to religion is a boilerplate provision (art. 8), taken mainly from the ICCPR, that protects religious freedom.

Predictably, African constitutions and laws have since independence from colonial rule been of little help in addressing the problem. A survey of the constitutions of several African states shows that they make no mention of indigenous religions, choosing instead to provide the generic protection of religious freedom contained in international human rights instruments.[36] The wording of several other constitutions suggests that some forms of evangelization may be restricted.[37] The constitution of Zambia, for example, guarantees the freedom of religion except that limitations could be placed to "ensure that the enjoyment of the said rights and freedoms of any one individual does not prejudice the rights and freedoms of others."[38] The constitution of Mauritius seems to limit attempts at proselytization by protecting "the right to observe and practice any religion or belief without the unsolicited intervention of persons professing any other religion or belief."[39] Although the laws respecting indigenous religions are quite thin if not lacking, the general orientation of the policies of most African states has been hostile to precolonial, pre-Islamic, or pre-Christian values but very protective of one or both of the messianic faiths. In many cases, states continue to actively prosecute campaigns to root out "unenlightened" customs and traditions.

Ideals Versus Realities

The two basic human rights documents—the Universal Declaration of Human Rights and the International Covenant on Civil and Political Rights—seek to entrench and encourage the free exchange of ideas and the respect for difference and diversity.[40] The emphasis placed on the importance of creating and maintaining a diverse society is one of the most striking characteristics of human rights law. Diversity is encouraged, though not required, by the rights corpus in cultural, religious, political, and other endeavors and pursuits. Through this emphasis, human rights law "evidences throughout its hostility to imposed uniformity."[41] According to Henry Steiner,

The ideal of encouraging and protecting diversity informs many human rights provisions. No other norm in the human rights corpus plays as vital a role in the struggle to realize that ideal as the principle of equal protection, perhaps the preeminent human rights norm. Its premise of the equal worth of individuals and their right to equal respect necessarily applies to the ethnic groups with which individuals are associated, for discrimination has the same systemic character whether it is directed against a group or selectively against a member.[42]

Indeed, article 26 of the ICCPR prohibits discrimination on the basis of race, color, sex, language, religion, political or other opinion, national or social origin, property, birth, or other status. Article 27 affirms the same philosophy by requiring states to make sure that minorities are not denied the right to enjoy their own culture and to profess and practice their own religion. Elsewhere, the ICCPR repeatedly confirms its adherence to difference by protecting the rights of persons to assemble peacefully and to associate freely with others (arts. 21 and 22). Lawful restrictions, however, could be imposed on the basis of national security, the protection of public health or morals, or the protection of the rights and freedoms of others (art. 22[2]). Although it is clear that human rights law is obsessed with the creation, protection, and preservation of diversity, it is also clear that rights advancing this ideal—which is central to the movement—could also be curtailed to protect the rights of others.

This propagation of diversity through the freedom to exchange ideas and to associate across divides and traditional cleavages such as race, religion, culture, national origin, and gender by human rights law assumes—an assumption that is still being tested—that there is inherent benefit in cross-fertilization or contact with "otherness." When the ICCPR declares, for example, the "freedom to seek, receive, and impart information and ideas of all kinds, regardless of frontiers" (art. 19[2]), it presupposes, without final proof, an ultimate good in the exercise of that right. There are presumed "goods"—growth, vitality, search for truth, and new challenges—that would benefit humanity from interaction, difference, and diversity. Ethnic separation—whether voluntary or enforced—is not preferred; instead, openness and transparency toward the "other" might nurture respect for difference and reduce bigotry and demonization. These assumptions raise certain difficulties that I will return to later.

With regard to the right to religious belief, the ICCPR grants a wide latitude:

Everyone shall have the right to freedom of thought, conscience and religion. This right shall include freedom to have or to adopt a religion or belief of his choice, and freedom, either individually or in community with others and in public or private, to manifest his religion or belief in worship, observance, practice and teaching. (art. 18[1])

Significantly, the covenant also provides that no one shall "be subject to coercion which would impair his freedom to have or to adopt a religion or belief of his choice" (art. 18[2]). Additionally, the freedom to "manifest one's religion or beliefs," could be lawfully limited on the grounds of public safety, order, health, or morals or "the fundamental rights and freedoms of others" (art. 18[3]). Article 18 of the UDHR also provides for the "right to freedom of thought, conscience and religion."

Taken together, the provisions advocating difference and diversity and those providing explicitly for religious rights, would seem to allow proselytization by the messianic religions, although they also provide for certain limitations which might be read as possibly excluding certain modes of evangelization. For example, proselytization through force, coercion, or in the context of colonization would appear to be excluded.

Although human rights law amply protects the right to proselytize through the principles of free speech, assembly, and association, the pecking order of rights problematizes the right to evangelize where the result is the destruction of other cultures or the closure of avenues for other religions. It is my argument that the most fundamental of all human rights is that of self-determination and that no other right overrides it.[43] Without this fundamental group or individual right, no other human right could be secured, since the group would be unable to determine for its individual members under what political, social, cultural, economic, and legal order they would live. Any right which directly conflicts with this right ought to be void to the extent of that conflict.

Traditionally, the self-determination principle has been employed to advance the cause of decolonization or to overcome other forms of external occupation. The principle was indispensable to the decolonization process. This usage of the principle—as a tool for advancing demands for external self-determination—could be expanded to disallow cultural and religious imperialism or imposition by external agencies through acculturation, especially where the express intent of the invading culture or religion, as was the case in Africa, is to destroy its indigenous counterparts and seal off the entry or growth of other traditions. Furthermore, the principle could also be read to empower internal self-determination, that is, the right of a people to "cultural survival."[44] This usage of self-determination is advanced by the Draft Declaration on the Rights of Indigenous Peoples. It is also an argument against cultural genocide. It is one of the ideas advanced by advocates of autonomy regimes for minorities: unless groups are given protection against invasion and control by others, their cultural and ethnic identities could be quashed by more powerful cultures and political systems. The violent advocacy of the messianic religions in Africa could be seen as a negation of this right particularly because religion is often the first point of attack in the process of acculturation.

Christianity and Islam forcibly entered Africa not as guests but as masters.[45] The two traditions came either as conquerors or on the backs of conquerors. As they had done elsewhere, they were driven by the belief and conviction of their own innate superiority—and what they saw as barbaric African religions and cultures. This belief was not a function of an objective assessment and reflection about African religions and cultures. It was born of the contempt and ignorance of that which was different and the exaggerated importance of the messianic faiths. The messianic religions—

Christianity to be precise—came to Africa at a time of great technological and scientific imbalance between the West and the continent. Already the beneficiaries of the industrial revolution, the colonial church and state commanded superior resources in the areas of the military, economic organization and finance, the media, and other social and political spheres. Africa was no match, and the successful imposition of colonialism is proof of that fact. The West was able through coercion, intimidation, trickery, and force to impose a new political, social, cultural and, thanks to the missionaries, religious order in Africa. African political, social, and religious traditions were delegitimized virtually overnight.

Thus began the process of de-Africanization through large-scale cash-crop farming for European industries, industrialization, urbanization, and the wholesale subversion of traditional values and structures. Africa—from top to bottom—was remade in the image of Europe complete with Euro-centric modern states. Christianity played a crucial role in this process: weaning Africans from their roots and pacifying them for the new order. Utilizing superior resources, it occupied most political space and practically killed local religious traditions and then closed off society from other persuasions. It is in this sense that the practice of colonial Christian advocacy constituted a violation of the fundamental freedoms of Africans. Islam, which had invaded Africa at an earlier date, was equally insidious and destructive of local religions. Its forceful conversions and wars of conquest together with its prohibition of its repudiation, were violative of the rights of Africans as well.

The Moral Equivalency of Cultures

Individuals do not exist in the atomized language prevalent in the human rights movement. Usually, individuals, even in the industrial democracies of the West, are members of an ethnic, social, religious, or political group. Quite often, a single individual will fall under several classifications. Although many of the rights enumerated in human rights law attach to individuals, they only make sense in a collective, social perspective. This is the case because the creation or development of a culture or a religion are societal, not individual, endeavors. I make this point to underline the importance of culture or religion to individuals and groups. An individual's morals, attitudes toward life and death, and identity come from this collective construction of reality through history.

No one culture or religion is sovereign in relationship to any other culture or religion. Proper human rights ought to assume that all cultures are equal. This view rejects the notion that there is a hierarchy of cultures or religions; that some cultures are superior to others even though they may be more technologically advanced. Belief in the contrary has led to military invasions to "civilize," colonize, and enslave, as was the case with Christianity in Africa. Cultures, however, have always interacted throughout history; there are no pure cultures, as such, although many traditions retain their distinctive personality. In many cases, the voluntary, unforced commingling of cultures has led to a more vital and creative existence. Several lessons can be drawn from this premise. The human rights movement should encourage the cross-breeding of cultures and tolerance for diversity. But it should frown upon homogenization and the imposition of uniformity.

As I mentioned at the beginning, the human rights movement is premised on societies being open to new ideas and challenges; even when a creed seeks homogenization, it must be open to persuasion from other traditions. Although I agree with and share this basic ideal of the human rights corpus, I am deeply concerned that the movement's central tenets may support forms of advocacy that negate certain rights and give legitimacy to abusive conduct. In the case of Africa, the arrival of Christianity, for example, was so violent toward indigenous traditions that the possibility of the free exchange of values and a voluntary commingling was nonexistent. The missionaries and the colonial authorities defined local cultures as demonic; one had to choose between the old and the new. The new ways were promoted as the salvation from a satanic past. Progress, culture, and humanity were identified entirely in Islamic or Christian terms, never with reference to indigenous traditions. But the new converts could not become fully "Christian" or "European"; many, to this day, remain suspended between a dim African past and a distorted, Westernized existence. Most have been robbed of their humanity.

It was not the intention of this chapter to circumscribe religious human rights. I share with other scholars and activists in the human rights movement the importance of protecting religious human rights and enjoining governments from unduly burdening or prohibiting the free exercise of religion. But I am concerned by those dimensions of messianic religions that claim a right not merely to persuade individuals or groups of peoples of the "truth" as they see it but rather actively demonize, systematically discredit, and forcibly destroy and eventually replace nonuniversalist, noncompetitive indigenous religions. Quite often, indigenous religions anchor a total worldview and their destruction usually entails a fundamental distortion of ethnic identities and history.

Perhaps there is nothing that can be done today to reverse the negative effects of forced or coerced religious proselytization during the era of colonialism in Africa. Nor is it possible to reclaim wholly the African past as though history has stood still. This does not mean, however, that we should simply forget the past and go on as if nothing happened. The anguish and deprivation caused by that historical experience is with me and millions of other Africans today. We bear the marks of that terrible period. For those

Africans who choose not to be Christians or Muslims, the past is not really an option: it was so effectively destroyed and delegitimized that it is practically impossible to retrieve as a coherent scheme of values. It is this loss that I mourn and for which I blame Christianity and Islam. The human rights corpus should outlaw those forms of proselytization used in Africa, because their purpose and effect have been the dehumanization of an entire race of people. It could do so by elaborating a treaty that addresses religious human rights but provides for the protection and mechanisms of redress for forms of proselytization that seek to unfairly assimilate or impose dominant cultures on indigenous religions.

Chapter 5
The African State, Human Rights, and Religion

Religion and African Statehood

Four decades after physical decolonization, the African state is today mired in crises of identity.[1] Multidimensional and complexly dynamic, these crises primarily feed from the traditional troughs of culture and religion, ethnicity and race, history and mythology, and politics and economics.[2] In the quicksand known as the modern African state, this potent and volatile alchemical mix has all too frequently either been cataclysmic or fostered political dysfunction.[3] The realm of religion, together with its essential linkage to philosophy and culture, has been one of the pivotal variables in the construction of the identity of the modern African state.[4] Religion has been one of the critical seams of social and political rupture in several African states.[5]

Due to the centrality of religion in the construction of social reality, this critical examination of the treatment of African religions within the African state will necessarily probe the intersection of Islam, African religion, and Christianity—the three dominant religious traditions in Africa— and the role of the state in the establishment or disestablishment of one or another tradition.[6] Thus, the favor or prejudice of the state toward these traditions lies at the heart of this inquiry. Within the crucible of the African state, this chapter primarily argues that the modern African state, right from its inception, has relentlessly engaged in a campaign of the marginalization, at best, or eradication, at worst, of African religion.[7] Further, it argues that the destruction and delegitimation of African religion have been actively effected at the urging, or with the collusion and for the benefit of, either or both Islam and Christianity, the two dominant messianic traditions.

It is my contention that the conscious, willful, and planned displacement of African religion goes beyond any legitimate bounds of religious advocacy and violates the religious human rights of Africans. This orchestrated process of the vilification and demonization of African religion represents more than an attack on the religious freedom of Africans; it is in fact, on the one hand, a repudiation of the humanity of African culture and, on the other, a denial of the essence of the humanity of the African people themselves.[8] In other words, at the core of the attempts to subjugate Africans to the messianic traditions is a belief not only in the superiority of the missionary and his or her messianic dogma but also in the subhumanity of the missionary's subjects and their cosmology. Finally, the chapter explores, through the case of the Republic of Benin, the raison d'être, pressures, and tensions that attend the state-directed attempt at protecting and returning to the African past.

This inquiry does not rigidly draw an "us" and "them" dichotomy because cross-cultural penetration and counter-penetration will occur regardless of the insular impulses of cultural guardians. In fact, contact with "otherness" can be a spur for positive social change and progressive development. Societies that prevent the entry of "foreign" values or the export of their values into other cultures deny themselves the benefits of cross-fertilization. Closing off avenues for intercultural exchanges may preserve negative aspects of tradition to the detriment of the group. "Insiders" or those who map the margins of culture need continually to interrogate themselves about the effects of intercourse with "outsiders" and whether, how, or at what pace the exchange should occur. But the strategies employed in creating or managing that contact, as well as its form and content, require constant vigilance to avoid, as much as possible, dehumanizing, degrading, or destroying the "other." Culture should not be essentialized because people, time, and place conspire to construct it. But it represents the accumulation of a people's wisdom and thus their identity; it is real and without it a people is without a name, rudderless, and torn from its moorings.

It is not the argument of this chapter, therefore, that there is a purity to African religion. The genesis of ideas and cultures is always difficult to establish. What a culture has borrowed and the extent to which dynamics internal to it are the engines of change must largely remain fluid questions. At least one respected scholar, John Mbiti, has argued that even Islam and Christianity can be seen as indigenous African religions.[9] This point is only interesting because even Mbiti distinguishes Islam and Christianity from African religion.[10] Each religious tradition has its own signature, a religious DNA or genetic fingerprint, so to speak. Semitic religions, such as Islam, Judaism, and Christianity, share certain core characteristics such as belief in the afterlife and conceptions of heaven and hell.[11] Thus, one can identify, as Mbiti does, the distinguishing characteristics of African religions, although some scholars have questioned the normative framework he has employed to construct them.[12] The important point here is the recognition of the existence of an African religious universe, a spiritual space, separate and distinct from either Islam or Christianity, and the role of the state in contracting or eradicating that sphere and promoting the messianic faiths in its stead. This chapter is therefore an attempt to unmask the perverted role of the state and to argue for its reorientation in addressing African religions. This chapter does not pretend to be what it is not. Its scope is very narrow in that it only seeks to underline the denigration of African religions in the context of modernity. In addition to pleading for the better understanding of African religions, it asks that political space be created to allow the expression of that cosmology.

Identity Disorientation

No African country has officially allocated a national holiday in honor of the gods of indigenous religions. All African countries, on the other hand, have a national holiday that either favors Christian festivals (especially Christmas), Muslim festivals (such as Idd el Fitr), or both categories of imported festivals. The Semitic religions (Christianity and Islam) are nationally honored in much of Africa; the indigenous religions are at best ethnic rather than national occasions.[13]

The official suppression of African religions from public visibility throughout Africa, with the more recent exception of the Republic of Benin, speaks volumes about identity reconstruction in Africa.[14] Indeed, the status of indigenous religions within African states cannot be understood without resort to the nature and purposes of the colonial state. More specifically, the relationship between religion and the state has hinged on the ideological, cultural, and philosophical outlooks of the African intellectual, political, and civil service classes germinated during colonial rule.

There is no doubt that colonization was primarily motivated by economic reasons.[15] As a process, colonization deployed racist dogma, religious penetration, military force, and commerce to subject Africa to Europe.[16] The role of mission Christianity, with its near exclusive delivery of services in formal Western education and health, was central in coercing conversion from African religions.[17] Missionaries saw themselves as agents for Westernization and made little distinction between the church and the colonial state. According to one European author whose mission was in Africa, the entire colonial project had to involve all those responsible for the "development of a primitive people."[18] He used the term *primitive* to define "all peoples who, in the main, are in the barbaric and preliterary stage of sociological and cultural development." He likened the Bantu child (the name given to most African peoples inhabiting eastern, central, and southern Africa) to a marsupial cub, the species of "lowly" mammals like the kangaroo.

These racist misconceptions and attitudes toward Africans and their religions found fertile ground in the interpretations, dogma, and philosophy of Christianity and other Semitic religions. The view, held by many adherents of these traditions, that monotheism is the critical difference "between advanced (Western) religion and primitive paganism" has long been a basis for the treatment of other beliefs as satanic or devilish.[19] Monotheistic religions thus sit at the top of the hierarchy while *polytheism* and *animism*, the terms used to describe African religions, dwell at the bottom of the evolutionary process.[20] This theory of religious evolution, which asserts the upward, single-directional track of development from so-called animism to monotheism allows the missionary to believe in the superiority of his or her faith.[21] These exclusive claims of a final, inflexible truth provide the foundation for proselytization and spur zealotry and missionary activity.

In contrast, African religions are communal and nonuniversalist; unlike Christianity or Islam, they do not seek to convert or remake the "other" in their image.[22] The notion of converting the "other" is alien because the religion of the people is their identity and being; as one author has put it, it is redundant and tautological to talk of the religion of the Yoruba, for instance, because their identity is their religion, their way of life.[23] Mbiti has written that in traditional society there was no dichotomy between the secular and the religious, no distinction between the religious and the irreligious, and no separation between the material and the spiritual.[24] He writes, further, that "Although many African languages do not have a word for religion as such, it nevertheless accompanies the individual from long before his birth to long after his physical death."

That is why the degradation of African religions should be seen as the negation of the humanity of the African people. In the internationally acclaimed novel *Things Fall Apart*, Nigerian writer Chinua Achebe tells the story of this civilizational clash and the simultaneous deconstruction and reconstruction of the African identity by mission Christianity and the agency of the colonial state.[25] This meeting of cultures is captured through the tragic life of Okonkwo, a precolonial Igbo man whose world literally disintegrates before his eyes. A man of status and a guardian of Igbo culture and religion, Okonkwo and other Igbos resist the new faith and the authority of the colonial state; but when the resistance is almost certainly crushed, Okonkwo kills a meddling local collaborator of the colonial regime and then hangs himself rather than accept physical and spiritual surrender to the church and the colonial state.

Okonkwo had watched with bitterness as the missionaries mocked the Igbo religion, converted some of his people, including his son, to Christianity, and then used them against the Igbo opposed to the new dispensation.[26] In one telling moment, an Igbo who had become a missionary himself congratulates Okonkwo's son for running away to study at a mission school. The missionary tells him: "Blessed is he who forsakes his mother and father for my sake."[27] When Okonkwo and his Igbo resisters burn down a church, they are arrested and physically beaten on orders of the local colonial administrator. Here the church fuses with the state. According to an elder, the white man "has put a knife on the things that held us together and we have fallen apart."[28] In *Things Fall Apart*, the colonial administrator decides to write *The Pacification of the Primitive Tribes of the Lower Niger*, a book based on Okonkwo's life and death, which he sees as symbolic of Europe's victory over the Igbo.[29]

In history, Achebe's fiction was played out repeatedly throughout Africa. The encounter between Christianity and the Igbo religion has been characterized as a four-part process by Elizabeth Isichei: the establishment of a mission; recruitment of converts, usually from among the social "rejects"; attack or "persecution" of the mission by elders and guardians of Igbo religion; and the imposition of colonial rule and its protection and promotion of the mission.[30] As she puts it clearly,

Towns [African] felt an urgent need for allies and advocates in the face of the violence with which it [colonial rule] was established. They had to learn the language of the invader, to communicate with their new rulers. Large numbers of employment opportunities existed, and there was an obvious benefit to be gained from education.

Education in missionary schools was perhaps the most decisive weapon in the reconstruction of African identity. The mission usually preyed on the youth, capturing them and tearing them from their cultural moorings. The colonial state financially supported the mission schools, thus enhancing the capacity to transform social reality.[31] Isichei writes:

The missionaries succeeded in maintaining their virtual monopoly of education, and obtained adherents, not through dialogue with adults, but by cutting children off from their traditional culture and placing them in the artificially unanimous environment of the school. Today most Igbo have been baptized, and traditional religion is the preserve of a small aging minority.[32]

Without regard to which agency was the first to penetrate an African community, colonial state and church worked hand in glove in the civilizing mission. In Ghana, for example, the colonial state paternalized African rulers for their "good relations" with missionaries but attacked what it called "fetishism" and "fetish priests."[33] The colonial government's disapproval and attack on African religions and customs further encouraged new converts to reject the ways of their forebears.[34] Female circumcision, which Christians denounced as satanic, was one such custom.[35] Most significantly, the colonial state passed laws and implemented policies designed to purge the continent of African religions.[36] In Nigeria, for instance, African religions, dances, education, and art were banned.[37] "The early missionaries came to introduce a new religion; all the former religious rites and manifestations (including the dance and music) were banned, and new converts were encouraged to dispose of any art works which had been used in religious rites."

The processes of social transformation and identity reconstruction set in motion by the invasion of Africa by both Christianity and Islam, and particularly the former, dislocated and distorted the African worldview almost in its entirety. The colonial state buttressed that process through the delegitimation of African religious beliefs, and the legitimation, at the political and social levels, of the spiritual and religious cosmologies of the invaders. In the span of several decades, the peoples of Africa were largely reconstructed, never to be the same again.

The Culture of Silence and Postcolonialism

In most of Africa, the current states do not predate colonialism but were created by European imperial powers. The governing classes in Africa—both intellectual and political—are the products of the colonial state or its uncritical successor, the postcolonial state.[38] Though formally independent, the postcolonial state is conceptually much like its predecessor. The uncritical acceptance by many African leaders of the postcolonial state is not surprising considering the conceptual aspirations of the African elite. Many of the new rulers were forged in the mission and colonial schools, a process that almost certainly entailed the ideological renunciation of African religions, traditions, and beliefs and the embrace of Christianity and the traditions of the Europeans. Even as the new converts straddled the fence, as many inevitably did, and mixed the "old" with the "new," there was little doubt that the new was expected, as a matter of course, to overcome the old. The new religious, cultural, and educational structures were designed to create local servants of colonialism.

The West European educational system was introduced, replacing the informal traditional system; it was geared to the needs of the colonial administration. This objective was stated in a 1921 speech by the first [British] Governor of Nigeria: "The chief function of Government Primary and Secondary Schools . . . is to train the more promising boys from the village schools as teachers for those schools, as clerks for the native courts, and as interpreters."[39]

The new curriculum was usually conceived in the metropole, either in England or France, and required the study of political, cultural, and literary forms which were alien to Africa. The British Empire, its language, and the English themselves were presented as the agents of civilization, replacing African worldviews.[40] It was these "products" who would lead their countries to formal independence and become its rulers. In Ghana,

Kwame Nkrumah, who led the country into formal independence from Britain, invoked his Christian and Western educational background when he proclaimed, "Seek ye first the political kingdom and all other things shall be added to you".[41] Little wonder that Ghana was one of the earliest conquests of the church on the continent.[42]

Elsewhere on the African continent, mission-educated men took power as Africa emerged from direct European colonial rule. The list is long. Léopold Senghor, the first president of Senegal, now a member of the Académie Francaise,[43] is a former seminarian and a leading Catholic intellectual.[44] The late Félix Houphouët-Boigny, the Ivorian president who constructed the world's largest Catholic basilica in the country's interior, was obviously another devout Catholic. Others have similar backgrounds: Julius Nyerere of Tanzania was Catholic, Kenneth Kaunda of Zambia was Presbyterian, and General Ignatius Acheampong of Ghana had been born into a Catholic family.[45] With the possible exception of the king of Swaziland, the head of one of the few African states that predates colonialism, to my knowledge there is no African leader who openly professes African traditional religions. Note, however, that 77 percent of the population of Swaziland are Christian but only 20.9 percent adhere to African religions.[46] Virtually all African heads of state or government are Christian or Muslim. The religious affiliation of the leadership greatly influenced the character of the nascent black-governed African state and provided a smooth conceptual continuum between itself and its predecessor, the colonial state.

There is little doubt that over the last century Christianity has expanded enormously in Africa. It was estimated that the number of African Christians would rise from 10 million in 1910 to 393 million in 2000, making one in every five Christians an African.[47] Although European colonial powers saw Islam as a threat to their cultural hegemony, many writers now agree that Islam prospered during the colonial period.[48] Once colonial conquest was established, the British, for example, instituted indirect rule, using or inventing local rulers to act as the agents of the new state. A good example of indirect rule was the governance of the northern Nigerian emirates for the British by the emirs.[49] Both the French and the British supported Qur'anic schools throughout most of Africa, and used them to train civil servants and teachers to serve the colonial state.[50] Needless to say, Islam was favored over African religions. "In situations where Muslim towns supplied the local government services for a countryside that was still in practice pagan [African religions], colonial support for the Islamic authorities helped greatly to consolidate Muslim observance among the country people."

While both messianic religions grew, there was a corresponding decline in African religions.[51] The position of African religions and cultures has not differed, either substantially or qualitatively, under the postcolonial state. The combination of colonial norms and structures-which were deliberately conceived as hostile to African heritage-survived intact into the independent, African-ruled states and continued to be the conceptual basis for those new states. In essence, the new elites took over the civilizing mission of the departing colonial power and have generally sought the re-creation of Africa in the image of Europe, even in those states which were ruled by Islamic elites. The constitutional and legal norms adopted on the eve of independence, as well as subsequent laws and policies, continued to suppress African cultures and religions, in spite of demagogic overtures by some rulers to the contrary.[52]

African constitutions and laws are generally either openly hostile to African religions and culture or they pretend that such religions do not exist. Such pretense is a tacit hope that African religions have either been eliminated or marginalized and so fundamentally delegitimized that they warrant no attention. The independence constitutions, which were largely written by Europeans for Africans on the eve of independence, sought to transplant a formal liberal state to the continent, an entity whose continued survival would be guaranteed by the metropolitan power and would therefore be subservient to it.[53] None of the independence constitutions, as far as I know, make any mention of indigenous African religions.[54] Instead, they offer liberal generic protection of religious freedoms. The language used strongly suggests that "received" and not indigenous religions are the target for such protection.

A survey of several independence constitutions will suffice. Kenya's 1963 independence constitution, for example, guaranteed to each person freedom of religion, including the "freedom to change his religion or belief, and freedom, either alone or in community with others, and both in public and private, to manifest and propagate his religion or belief in worship, teaching, practice and observance."[55] It defined religion as inclusive of a "religious denomination, and cognate expressions" (sec. 22[6]). Further, it limited religious freedom to the interests of public morality and health, and guaranteed individuals the right to observe and practice any religion without the "unsolicited intervention of members of any other religion" (sec. 22[5]).

The limitations placed on religion for reasons of "public morality" and "public health" were most likely aimed at elements of indigenous African religions which many colonial states regarded as abominable.[56] Significantly, these provisions protect the right to proselytize, a feature common to Christianity and Islam. The constitutions of Malawi, Nigeria, Zambia, and Congo (Leopoldville) offer similar, if not identical, rights and protections to those granted by the constitution of Kenya.[57] None attempt to protect or reclaim African religions. Interestingly, the constitution of Guinea tersely and barely protects religious freedom while the Ivory Coast and Mali only mention religion with reference to the nondiscrimination clause.[58]

In the four decades since independence, African constitutions have not assumed a different posture toward African religions. The constitutional silence and the absolute refusal to acknowledge the existence of African religions or cultures has continued to this day. For instance, no changes have been made to the religious clause of the constitution of Kenya.[59] Similarly, no substantial changes have been made to the constitutions of Nigeria, Zaire (now the Democratic Republic of Congo), and Zambia.[60] They do not even make vague references to African religions or cultures. This silence has, additionally, been given negative meaning by government policies and laws in a number of states.

The current regime in Sudan is perhaps one of the clearest examples of the active use of the state and its resources to destroy non-Islamic religions, including African religion.[61] Attempts by the state to impose Islam on Christians and adherents of African religions in the south of the country have escalated the civil war, leading to the killing of an estimated 1.3 million southern, non-Islamic civilians. There have been widespread reports of enslavement and forced conversions of black African southerners and their indoctrination to Islam.[62] A report by a right-wing Christian group terms the process "cultural cleansing," which "seeks to eliminate a cultural group by forcibly stripping these children [adherents of Christianity and African religions] of their names, language, freedom, families, and religion."[63]

There are numerous examples of other African states that favor or promote the Semitic religions. President Frederick Chiluba declared Zambia a Christian nation, although there are substantial numbers of believers in African religions, Hinduism, and Islam.[64] In Zaire (now the Democratic Republic of Congo) a state decree in 1971 declared the Catholic Church, some Protestants, and the Kimbanguists (an independent Congolese church) the only legally recognized churches.[65] Elsewhere, African postcolonial states have banned elements of African religions.[66] The colonial state and church and later the postcolonial state banned important elements of African culture and religion. Among the Akamba of Kenya, for example, the colonial rulers abolished the recognition of Kamba shrines, the consultation of medicine men, work on Sundays, beer and tobacco consumption, dancing, polygamy, bridewealth, and use of the oath. A number of African states, including Algeria, the Comoros, Egypt, Libya, Mauritania, Morocco, and Tunisia are either constitutionally Islamic or proclaim Islam to be the religion of the state.[67]

Other states substantiate their commitment to Islam by providing for certain religious institutions or requiring that senior officials be Muslims.[68] But in an unusual turn the 1996 South African Constitution expressly recognized the "institution, status, and role of traditional leadership, according to customary law" subject to the constitution.[69] While there is no explicit mention of African religions, this provision openly recognizes

African values in the governance of the state. What most of these examples point to, however, is the delegitimation of African religions and that spiritual universe, through the implementation by the state of norms and policies in education and other arenas of public life that are based on European, American, or Arab conceptions of society or modernization.

Counterpenetration as a Farce

There can be no doubt that over the last century Africa has undergone one of the most dramatic and fundamental transformations ever witnessed in human history. Crawford Young has written that the indelible imprint of Europe on Africa is unique among world regions.[70] The fact of the displacement, transformation, and reorientation of African norms by European values has been documented and is not a source of much controversy. What is contested is the qualitative effect of those processes on the African universe. At the extremes, some cast the encounter as completely detrimental to Africa, while other apologists of colonial rule see it as the unquestioned redemption of the "dark" continent. In the middle there is a multiplicity of "moderate" characterizations of the encounter, a kind of a sliding judgmental scale which sees the benefits as well as the costs of the culture clash. This section explores these dichotomous views and probes the claim of counterpenetration.

Although the delegitimation of African cultures and religions has proceeded apace over the last century, there are still substantial numbers of Africans who adhere to them or use some of their conceptions to construct new identities. The process of incorporating European normative frameworks in addressing the changing reality started at the outset of the encounter with the West. Among the Akamba of Kenya, for example, politico-religious movements which have been termed a worldwide phenomenon at the revitalization and reorganization of indigenous societies arose in the wake of colonial expansion.[71] Many of the movements utilized African religious thought although they combined it with elements of Islamic and Christian theology.

In the early years of colonial penetration, resistance was widespread. For example, Syokimau, the Kamba priestess, prophesied the detrimental effects of the culture clash.[72] Others in Kamba society, such as Siotune Kathuke and Kiamba Mutuavio in 1911 used Kamba religious conceptions to mobilize resistance to the missions and colonial rule, actions for which they were deported to distant parts of the territory by the colonial authorities.[73] But frustration with colonial rule among the Akamba was heightened because of the economic pressures of taxation, forcible conscription into the colonial armed forces, and the imposition of new justice and religious orders.

Once the earlier, more indigenous protest movements were crushed, others arose in their stead, this time identifying themselves more explicitly with Christian theology. In 1921, Ndonye Kauti led one such movement, with the promise of delivering the Akamba to a Golden Age after expelling the missions and the "evil" Europeans.[74] Like his predecessors, Kauti was arrested and deported. The successful establishment of colonial rule vanquished these protest movements but left space for more "benign" and less "political" African Christian sects. Among the Agikuyu of Kenya, for example, Watu wa Mngu (Kiswahili for People of God) arose as a response to the opposition of clitoridectomy by Christian missions.[75] Christianity, which was now the establishment religion, selectively allowed the incorporation into its liturgy and ritual only those African conceptions which legitimized the church within Africa. The Zaire Rite, which "Africanized" worship in the Zairian Catholic church, and the use of African names for African Christians where previously missionaries insisted on European names are two examples of the "Africanization" of the church.[76] However, this model of counterpenetration is superficial and symbolic; it does not exert meaningful normative or conceptual African influence on the church.

Between 1880 and 1920, more serious attempts to "Africanize" Christianity took place in the movement called Ethiopianism.[77] Although based largely on Christian theology, these churches born of Ethiopianism have been described as utilizing explicitly African conceptions of African traditional religions. According to E. Bolaji Idowu, the Nigerian scholar of African religions, elements of Ethiopianism sought to recover Africa's "enslaved soul." He writes:

"Ethiopianism" has taken various forms, ranging from attempts at the indigenization of the Christian Church, the founding of churches by charismatic, Christian African leaders, and the establishment of splinters from European-dominated churches as separatist churches which are completely free from any form of foreign interference.

Idowu regards some aspects of the "Ethiopian" churches as "positive repudiations of Christianity" because they only used the "scaffolding of the Christian church to erect new structures for the self-expression of the traditional religion."[78] But another scholar downplays the "Africanity" of such churches; she notes that, although the new religious organizations were established by Africans, they "differed only in detail from the mission churches from which they had separated themselves."[79] Whatever the case, there has been a complex process of innovation and interaction between African churches—both European and African separatist churches—and forms and conceptions of African religions.[80] Many of the "Ethiopian" churches appear to have been more interested in political and financial autonomy, with lesser degrees of conceptual independence from Christian theology and philosophy. This is not to say that the Christian church in Africa has not been concerned with the vexing questions of enculturation and identity. These are important issues because of the European origin of the church and the inherent white racism within it.[81] Even the most devout African Christians or Muslims at best remain either as "insider-outsiders" or "outsider-insiders," because the religions they profess are anchored and mediated through other cultures, in this case either European or Arab. Africans remain the bearers of a suspended and distorted identity, because the adopted religions cannot fully express their history, culture, and being.

In any event, it is my contention in this chapter that, whatever "spin" is given to Christian penetration and its conquest or delegitimation of the African spiritual world, the process of Christianization cannot be isolated from Westernization and the consequent devaluation of the cultural identity of Africans and their humanity. It is not possible, as Lamin Sanneh contends, to legitimately consider the Christian penetration of Africa as not being part of the imperial cultural package of the West and its ideological and conceptual repudiation of Africa.[82] Sanneh asks for the transcendence of the view that

Converts [African] have capitulated to Western cultural imperialism, and that their sins have been visited on their children who are condemned to an ambiguous identity, being born, as it were, with a foreign foot in their native mouth. Converts may, for that reason, be considered cultural orphans and traitors at the same time.

Sanneh further contends that there was a "vital compatibility" between African cultures and Christianity, although he admits to the distortion of that relationship.[83] Moreover, he emphasizes the "assimilation" of Christianity into local idioms and cultures, and suggests a "benign" encounter with the West. This characterization of the meeting of the two cultures decontextualizes Christianity from the entire colonial project and the violence with which it was accomplished. Such violence was not always physical; it was also the psychological, emotional, and cultural denigration of African peoples and cultural norms.

The fact that Christianity emerged victorious in this cultural contest and has been "embraced" by the majority of Africans today does not make the process less violent or more humane. Others say that Christianity has been "translated" through African languages and cultures, as if to suggest that such a process authenticates or humanizes the encounter. It is clear that conversion, for example, was one-dimensional: the African converted to either Christianity or Islam, never the reverse. I need not abstract my views about the encounter with the West; I witnessed the schism between my parents and my grandparents as the encounter played itself out in their lives. On the one hand, my parents converted, thereby forsaking their religious identity and cutting themselves off from my grandparents. My parents presented their "choice" as "enlightened" and "progressive." To them, my grandparents represented a past without a future in the new society. But that "choice" had a lot to do with managing the new colonial dispensation. Based partially on my family history, I have concluded that the peoples of Africa have been spiritually enslaved, as it has become impossible for them to carry their cultures forward in the new global normative order. Later in life, my parents could not articulate to my inquiring mind why they had forsaken the past so completely. In my view, the programmatic agenda of the African postcolonial state demands an immersion into Eurocentric norms and forms of culture and society.

Benin Returns to Its Roots

On January 10, 1996, the Republic of Benin became the first African state officially to recognize a traditional religion when it declared a National Voodoo Day.[84] Unlike many Africans in other states, the majority of Beninese are open adherents of the African religion known as voodoo, a fact that made it easier for the government to recognize the religion:[85] 62 percent of Beninese practice voodoo as opposed to only 23 percent and 12 percent respectively who profess Christianity and Islam.[86] These numbers, together with the history and politics of Benin, were instrumental in the state's official recognition of voodoo.

The territory now constituting the Republic of Benin, known at other times as the Kingdom of Dahomey, was a firmly established state five centuries ago, before the advent of colonialism. Benin was conquered and declared a French colony in the late nineteenth century. One of the country's earlier independence constitutions made no mention of voodoo, although it protected religious beliefs in its nondiscrimination clause.[87] In a departure from earlier constitutional jurisprudence, the 1990 constitution of the Republic of Benin creates a secular state, but protects the "right to culture" and puts the duty on the state to "safeguard and promote the national values of civilization, as much material as spiritual, as well as the cultural traditions."[88] Elsewhere, the constitution allows religious institutions to operate parochial schools (art. 14) and protects the freedom of religion (art. 23). The 1990 constitution, the most democratic in the country's history, resulted from the popular defeat of the repressive Marxist regime of Mathieu Kérékou, the dictator who had ruled the Republic of Benin since the 1972 coup d'état.

Benin has been viewed by many as the birthplace of voodoo although until recently the religion was suppressed by the state.[89] The colonial state equated voodoo with witchcraft and banned it. The first indication that the state would rehabilitate voodoo and remove the stigma associated with it came in 1993 when the first festival of voodoo culture and arts was held in Ouidah, only forty-five miles outside Cotonou, Benin's capital. At the festival, also attended by invitees from Haiti, Trinidad and Tobago, and other West African states, President Nicephore Soglo, the former World Bank economist and the first democratically elected leader in two decades, underscored the importance of voodoo to the majority of Beninese and to descendants of Africans in the diaspora captured into slavery in the Americas.[90] Critics called Soglo's recognition of voodoo a ploy to pander to the electorate in the 1996 presidential elections, which he lost to Kérékou, the former dictator.[91]

There is little significance to whatever political motivations lay behind the official recognition of voodoo in Benin. What is important is the acknowledgment by the state of the religion of the overwhelming majority of its citizens. The Republic of Benin recognized facts on the ground and started the process of restoring dignity to the identity and humanity of voodoo and the human beings who practice it. Benin's example should be emulated elsewhere in Africa to end the culture of silence and repression of the identity of millions of Africans.

At the continental level, African states took an important step in reclaiming part of the past when in 1981 they adopted the African Charter on Human and Peoples' Rights, the basis for the regional human rights system.[92] Although critics have pointed out numerous problems with the Charter,[93] the instrument in its preamble claims to be inspired by the "virtues" of African "historical tradition" and the "values of African civilization." It prohibits discrimination based on religion (art. 2) and guarantees the freedom of religion (art 8). Most significantly, it burdens the state with the "promotion and protection of morals and traditional values recognized by the community" (art. 17). It also requires the state to assist the "family which is the custodian of morals and traditional values" (art. 18[2]) and enlists the state in popular struggles against foreign cultural domination (art. 20[3]). Although these provisions raise questions about the states' understanding of tradition and culture, the African Charter makes a radical statement: African traditions, civilization, and cultural values must be part of the fabric of a human rights corpus for the region.

The African Charter officially rehabilitates African philosophy and norms and may very well contribute to the reclamation of Africa's spiritual universe. This could be an essential part of the solution to the crises of identity wracking Africans and the states they claim as theirs. A return, a recognition, and a coming to terms with the African past—both cultural and religious—would help heal the spirit and lead to the creation of more stable and humane societies. I believe that this is one of the essential means through which the humanity stolen from Africa by the imperial religions can be restored.

Chapter 6
The Limits of Rights Discourse

South Africa: The Human Rights State

The post-World War II period has been characterized as the Age of Rights, an era during which the human rights movement has come of age.[1] Post-apartheid South Africa is the first state that is the virtual product of that age and the norms it represents. Indeed, the dramatic rebirth of the South African state, marked by the 1994 democratic elections, is arguably the most historic event in the human rights movement since its emergence some fifty years ago. Never has the recreation of a state been so singularly the product of such focused and relentless advocacy of human rights norms. Opponents of other overtly repressive political systems also deployed human rights discourse and imagery, but unlike their South African counterparts, they primarily emphasized a narrower conception of political participation rights.[2] In 1990, when Nelson Mandela was released after almost three decades in prison, the push for political change in South Africa had become an international human rights project. This occurred despite some Western governments' previous support for the apartheid regime and opposition to the African National Congress (ANC), the predominantly black anti-apartheid political organization.[3]

The construction of the post-apartheid state represents the first deliberate and calculated effort in history to craft a human rights state—a polity that is primarily animated by human rights norms.[4] South Africa was the first state to be reborn after the universal acceptance, at least rhetorically, of human rights ideals by states of all the major cultural and political traditions.

Numerous Western donor agencies, governments, foundations, international nongovernmental organizations (INGOs), including human rights groups and development organizations, have flocked to South Africa to assist the state's democratic experiment.[5] Internally, human rights have dominated virtually every aspect of the re-creation of the state, as evidenced by the panoply of rights enumerated in the new constitution adopted by the Constitutional Assembly in May 1996,[6] and signed by President Nelson Mandela into law on December 10, 1996.[7] In addition to the traditional structures that protect human rights—such as the separation of powers, judicial independence, and an accountable executive—the constitution establishes multiple overlapping human rights bodies under the title "state institutions supporting constitutional democracy."[8]

The new constitutional order draws extensively from international law, including human rights law. It provides that international agreements, which include human rights treaties, and international customary law are binding law unless they contradict the constitution or other laws passed by Parliament.[9] The new state also immediately ratified two major international human rights instruments, the Convention on the Elimination of All Forms of Discrimination Against Women (CEDAW) and the Convention on the Rights of the Child.[10] In 1998, the government ratified several important and major human rights treaties: the ICCPR, the International Convention on the Elimination of All Forms of Racial Discrimination, the Convention Against Torture and Other Cruel, Inhuman, or Degrading Treatment or Punishment, and the Convention on the Prevention and Punishment of the Crime of Genocide. This reliance by the new state on human rights norms is well put in a United Nations report:

The Constitution, itself, consciously and explicitly draws from international human rights law. The Bill of Rights resulted from careful analysis of international and comparative law, in light of specific South African needs. International human rights norms are frequently referred to. Courts are required by the Constitution to consider international law in the interpretation of the Bill of Rights. Moreover, the overall importance of human rights and the rule of law within the new Constitutional system is demonstrated by provisions for Constitutional review and the important reliance which the Constitution places on powerful, independent "human rights" commissions, all of which is new in South Africa.[11]

The modern state is the primary guarantor of human rights, while it is simultaneously the target of the international human rights law prescribing the standard of treatment of individuals by their governments.[12] In fact, the state is the raison d'être for the development of human rights law. In this sense, the state is the antithesis of human rights; the one exists to combat the other in a struggle for the supremacy over society. Paradoxically, human rights norms are codified by states although they are meant to contain and control state power. The "good" state controls its despotic proclivities by internalizing human rights norms and submitting to their moral preeminence.[13] The "bad" state rejects the authority of human rights norms and jealously guards its sovereignty from popular control. While tension between the state and human rights discourse can be mitigated, it cannot be eliminated.

This chapter critically explores several significant interrelated tensions manifested in the reconstruction of the South African state. This inquiry questions the viability of deploying the human rights idiom as the catalyst for a new state, one that is animated by, and has respect for, human rights norms. In particular, the chapter evaluates the use of human rights ideals as a tool for the transformation of the abysmal legacy of apartheid. In reaction to the policies of its predecessor, the new South African state explicitly recognizes equal protection norms as its foundation. Thus, the most important feature of the post-apartheid state is its virtually exclusive reliance on rights discourse as the engine of change. Without a doubt, the creators of the new South African state have also relied on other discourses such as international diplomacy, negotiation, and a variety of other secondary approaches. But it is the contention here that the rights discourse has been the predominant medium for change. Although it is still too early to say with total certainty what the exact difficulties of employing the rights discourse in South Africa are, many of the pitfalls of that medium are identified and explored here. Time will only further underscore these limitations.

While the rights discourse had the power to galvanize the oppressed and garner the sympathy of some segments of the middle and upper classes during the struggle against official apartheid, the near total dependence by the governments of Nelson Mandela and Thabo Mbeki, the man who succeeded Mandela in 1999 as president, on rights discourse as the tool for the transformation of the legacy of apartheid is a mistake. First, the double-edged nature of rights language has already become evident in South Africa. The new constitutional rights framework has frozen the hierarchies of apartheid by preserving the social and economic status quo. As aptly put by Ibrahim Gassama:

Disenchantment echoes the critique of rights discourse's double-edged quality: rights can be deployed to protect the powerful and the status quo just as easily as they can be wielded to advance the interests of the weak and excluded. The power of this observation should be increasingly apparent to rights activists in South Africa. It is not altogether surprising that even as the attainment of political participation rights by blacks in South Africa is celebrated, rights-rhetoric is being successfully deployed to protect the economic status quo—the private property rights—of the white minority in the country.[14]

If the experience of the United States, one of the "models" on which the new South Africa drew, is any guide, rights language has more often than not protected the property interests of the wealthy and the powerful.[15] The rights framework adopted by the Mandela government, and continued under Mbeki, protects existing social arrangements because it is traditional and conservative. Except for largely cosmetic effects, there is little possibility that the particular conceptualization of rights in the new South Africa will alter the patterns of power, wealth, and privilege established under apartheid. Unfortunately, South Africa has fallen victim to all the pitfalls of rights discourse.[16]

Analyses of the new South Africa support this pessimistic outlook. For instance, the Reconstruction and Development Programme (RDP)—the ANC's blueprint for reform—decried the rights abuses under apartheid and vowed that racial, gender, and other inequalities fostered under apartheid would be eliminated under an ANC democratic government.[17] However, except for high rights rhetoric, the RDP never identified concrete measures and policies to correct the legacy of apartheid, and in April 1996, the Mandela government virtually terminated the RDP when it dropped the program from cabinet status. Moreover, the apartheid bureaucracy was left intact through the guarantee of tenure for judges and magistrates, civil servants, law enforcement officials, and defense. Even more disturbing, the government has failed to institute a meaningful land reform program; virtually all land remains in white hands although the few blacks with access to funds can now purchase land on the free market. Finally, the position of women, especially black women, remains marginal. Although a predominantly black government is ostensibly in power, and blacks have been granted abstract legal entitlements, many blacks remain in the same station they occupied under apartheid: excluded and at the margins.

The chapter closely examines the evolution of the rights framework that has dominated the foundation and creation of the new state. It explores the content and formulation of the rights that predominate the construction of the new constitutional order and points to some of the tensions inherent in that project. It probes the prospects for the success of transformation using the rights discourse in several critical sectors of the South African society and questions the long-term prospects for the transformation of apartheid's economic and social norms and structures. It concludes by questioning the assumption, which seems to be widely shared among South Africans and foreigners alike and underlies the entire reconstructionist project, that South Africa cannot only be transformed into a state that respects human rights, but that it can also become a human rights state.

The success of this reconstructionist project is an essential precondition—not a guarantee by any means—for the realization of a human rights state. I distinguish between a state that formally respects human rights,[18] as do most political democracies, and a human rights state.[19] The former were initially constructed primarily as sovereign political structures whose main purpose was the exercise of authority and the maintenance of law and order for the benefit of limited segments of the population.[20] Over the last two centuries, many of these states have progressively embraced political democracy and with it the formal obligation to respect many civil and political rights.[21] A human rights state, by contrast, is a term coined here to describe an aspiration—an ideal state that would be constructed from close adherence to the prescriptions of the human rights corpus. Although a human rights state is theoretically possible given the framework of human rights law, it remains a fiction at present, not having been accomplished anywhere.

If realized, a South African human rights state would be the first of its kind. Unlike other states that have progressively assimilated a subset of human rights norms, the South African state is deliberately being constructed into a political edifice of human rights norms and structures. But is it possible to construct a state that defies the essence of statism and statehood, a polity that abandons the protection of entrenched economic and political interests and transforms social and economic arrangements for the excluded, through the rights medium? Is it feasible to re-create a deeply distorted society primarily by employing the human rights framework that is fundamentally anti-statist in its mission to curb arbitrary or excessive state power? Is it possible to do this without a cataclysmic social and political revolution in which the norms and classes of the ancien régime are categorically defeated? Or, is the South African experiment doomed to fail with the realization that at best a state can only assimilate human rights norms and ratify existing inequities? I discuss this dilemma and some of the limitations of the human rights project.

The Rights Framework as an ANC Strategy: A Snapshot of Apartheid

South Africa, Africa's fourth largest country in area, occupies a large portion of the southern tip of the continent with a population estimated in 1996 at 43,421,021.[22] Of this number, according to the notorious apartheid racial categories, black Africans made up 75.2 percent, whites 13.6 percent, Coloreds 8.6 percent, and Asians 2.6 percent. Although white domination of what is today South Africa goes back several centuries, it was not until 1948 that apartheid became the official ideology of the state. In that year, the Nationalist Party (NP), the Afrikaner political flagship, won the primarily white election and thereafter used state institutions to give preferential treatment to whites, primarily Afrikaners, in virtually all areas of political, social, and economic life.[23] Conversely, most nonwhite races, particularly blacks, were progressively stripped of whatever basic rights they retained.[24]

Apartheid, which literally "apartness" in Afrikaans, was animated completely by racial biases and classifications. Leonard Thompson has identified four ideas that composed its core:

First, the population of South Africa comprised four "racial groups"—White, Colored, Indian, and Africans—each with its own inherent culture. Second, Whites, as the civilized race, were entitled to have absolute control over the state. Third, White interests should prevail over black interests; the state was not obliged to provide equal facilities for the subordinate races. Fourth, the white racial group formed a single nation, with Afrikaans- and English-speaking components, while Africans belonged to several (eventually ten) distinct nations or potential nations—a formula that made the white nation the largest in the country.[25]

A plethora of laws, regulations, and policies were instrumental in the realization of the apartheid state. In the post-1948 period, the most important of these were the Population Registration Act of 1950, under which everyone was classified according to a "race"; the Immorality Act and the Prohibition of Mixed Marriages Act, which proscribed interracial sex, marriage, and other forms of intimate contact;[26] the Group Areas Act, which segregated racial groups in different areas, and the Promotion of the Bantu Self-Government Act, which solidified the basis for black homelands or bantustans;[27] and the Separate Amenities Act, under which the segregation of public facilities—parks, beaches, schools, and public transportation, among others—was cloaked in the color of law.

The "official" and systematic dispossession of Africans of their lands dates back to the Native Land Act of 1913 and the Development Native Trust and Land Act of 1936.[28] By 1992, 87 percent of all land had been alienated for the exclusive occupation of, and ownership by, whites.[29]

African resistance to white oppression and domination goes back several centuries. In this century, the resistance has been spearheaded by the ANC, which was founded by Africans in 1912 to fight for equality.[30] From the Defiance Campaign of the early 1950s[31] to the proclamation of the Freedom Charter in 1955[32] and the 1961 formation of the Umkhonto we Sizwe (Spear of the Nation), the military wing of the ANC, the apartheid regime was on notice that resistance would not only increase but become violent.[33]

In order to preserve the status quo in the face of determined and mounting challenge, the apartheid state enacted security laws designed to close off all remaining avenues of dissent.[34] This arsenal of legislation eliminated all due process principles and made it possible for the state to arrest, detain, torture, imprison, ban, and kill its opponents with impunity. Some of the more notorious laws included the Prohibition of Interdicts Act of 1956, which denied blacks access to courts to challenge the implementation of apartheid policies;[35] the Suppression of Communism Act of 1950; the Terrorism Act;[36] and the General Law Amendment Act. States of emergency and forced removals heightened the trauma of the black community.[37]

The devastating consequences of these policies have been manifested in virtually every statistical category on blacks and other nonwhite communities. In 1991, for example, incomes for a black household averaged a meager U.S.$3,614, as compared with $21,707 for a white household.[38] Fifty percent of blacks were unemployed, and the life expectancy for blacks was eleven years less than for whites.[39] Fifty percent of all blacks, but only 2 percent of whites, lived below the poverty line.[40] Prior to 1990, the state in its education budget spent eleven times more money on each white pupil than on each black pupil; by 1994, the state still spent four times as much for the education of a white as for a black child.[41] Only 11 percent of blacks graduated from high school as compared with 70 percent of whites. The pass rate for matriculation in 1994 was 97 percent for white students and less than 50 percent for black students. These lopsided figures were reproduced in every sector of the society: in the economy, administration of justice, land ownership, infant mortality, civil service, private sector, media, defense, police and security services, and professions. In effect, South Africa is deeply divided by the two nations within its borders: one developed and white, the other underdeveloped and mostly black.

Such is the legacy that the new South African state, under the direction of the African National Congress, undertook to transform after handily winning the first democratic all-race elections in April 1994.[42] This enormous challenge requires the state to use its resources, power, and prestige to raise the standard of living of black South Africans and other nonwhites. Such change cannot be accomplished without major economic reforms and dramatic policy shifts to stimulate further economic growth and the development of physical and human resources. The bureaucracy will have to be transformed to serve the community that it was created to repress and subjugate. Above all, mechanisms for the redistribution of South Africa's resources—particularly land—will have to be devised. So far, the South African state has opted for the rights idiom to mediate between the violent and savage apartheid past, the tenuous present, and an uncertain future.

The Evolution of a Rights Approach

The ANC, despite being banned by the apartheid regime in 1960, has been guided for most of its life by a commitment to peaceful change.[43] However, in 1961 the ANC decided to resort to armed struggle,[44] because of the legacy of the apartheid regime.

The ANC's commitment, since its foundation, to the language of rights as a strategy for change was reiterated by the explicit focus on human rights in the Freedom Charter in 1955. After its formation in 1912, the ANC initially made deputations to authorities but later escalated its protest to peaceful civil disobedience campaigns.[45] In any event, the ANC pursued nonviolent, "constitutional" avenues to reform until the 1960s. Mandela's own words underscore the ANC's commitment to the ideals of liberalism:

The Atlantic Charter of 1941, signed by Roosevelt and Churchill, reaffirmed faith in the dignity of each human being and propagated a host of democratic princi-ples. Some in the West saw the Charter as empty promises, but not those of us in Africa. Inspired by the Atlantic Charter and the fight of the Allies against tyranny and oppression, the ANC created its own Charter, called the African Claims, which called for full citizenship for all Africans, the right to buy land, and the repeal of discriminatory legislation.[46]

As the apartheid state became more repressive and unresponsive to peaceful protest, this commitment to nonviolence and multiracialism came under increasing attack within the ANC. In 1959, Robert Sobukwe and a number of other ANC members who considered the ANC too pas-sive broke away and formed the Pan Africanist Congress.[47] The resistance methods promoted by the militant PAC, which included confrontation with the police, resulted in the 1960 Sharpeville massacre.

Eventually, Mandela and other leading figures in the ANC were either imprisoned or exiled.[48] The ANC then established its principal offices in the black-ruled neighboring states of Zambia and Tanzania, from where it directed its diplomatic and military campaigns against apartheid South Africa.[49] Thereafter, the ANC pursued the dual track of mass protests sup-plemented by occasional military attacks on the symbols of the apartheid state. Nevertheless, more of the organization's energies and resources were spent on diplomacy, peaceful mass protests by its proxies inside the country, and other nonviolent methods of resistance than on military ef-forts. It was during this period—the 1960s to the 1980s—that the ANC ma-tured into a sophisticated political organization capable of capturing state power. From its bases in several African capitals and Western cities, as well as the United Nations and the Organization of African Unity, the ANC de-veloped into the single most important voice for democracy in South Africa. Within South Africa itself, it was a synonym for majority rule.

Toward the end of the 1980s, as the possibility for majority rule in South Africa seemed less remote, the ANC further clarified its commitment to a democratic, rule-of-law state by outlining its vision of a constitution for a new South Africa.[50] The outline emphasized the indispensability of a bill of rights and called for equal protection and nondiscrimination on a broad range of grounds such as gender, race, and creed.[51] It also provided for af-firmative action to remedy the wrongs of apartheid.[52]

The ANC further concretized these guidelines in a 1990 document de-voted exclusively to a bill of rights for South Africa. In 1992, the ANC pro-duced a revised draft bill of rights based on the 1990 preliminary document.[53] While the bill did not substantially depart from either the guidelines or the 1990 document, it did protect the right to own private property[54] and prohibit discrimination on the basis of sexual orientation. Significantly, the bill skirted the issue of land ownership: it proscribed forced removals without a court order, to which blacks had been routinely subject under apartheid, and also reassured whites who feared similar treatment from administrative action under an ANC government.[55] It provided for a lands claim tribunal to decide on questions of restoration for those blacks who had suffered forced removals and compensation for white beneficiaries of the removals. Only 2 percent of the land, however, was affected by forced removals. The status of more than 80 percent of all land reserved for whites was left unresolved in spite of the repeal of certain racist laws as domestic and international pressure brought the apartheid state to its knees.[56] These developments underscored the commitment of the ANC to a rights approach in negotiations for ostensible solutions to the South African crisis. Absent the military defeat of the apartheid regime and the ability to dictate the terms of the transformation, an approach that respected the rights of whites appeared to be the only viable option.

The Compromise of the Interim Constitution

Two ANC documents outlined a comprehensive constitutional philosophy and formed the basis for the organization's positions at the Convention for a Democratic South Africa (CODESA).[57] This multiparty forum, convened by the government in 1991 to negotiate the nature and character of a new South African state,[58] was dominated by the two dominant political organizations, the ANC and the NP, both of which sought to advance and protect the interests of their constituencies.[59] The ANC, confident that it would win the imminent democratic elections, wanted a strong unitary state to reverse the injustices of apartheid; the NP, on the other hand, sought to "protect white minority rights, and to ensure that the future black government will have less power than the previous white regime."[60] Because the ANC did not militarily defeat the apartheid state and instead had to negotiate with a formidable adversary in control of vast economic resources and deadly military and security apparatuses, it was forced to strike debilitating compromises in a number of key areas. The resulting Interim Constitution, approved by the all-white Parliament in December 1993, bears the marks of those historic compromises.

The Interim Constitution was a transitional document, aspects of which were designed to last until April 30, 1999, the adoption of a permanent constitution notwithstanding.[61] Perhaps the most important compromise of the Interim Constitution was the provision of a power-sharing arrangement to "mitigate" the power of the black majority in the democratic state during the transitional period.[62] Under this arrangement, the Government of National Unity (GNU), formed after the 1994 elections, was composed of the ANC, the NP, and the Inkatha Freedom Party (IFP).[63] The GNU acted as a restraint against the ANC and "reassured" whites, who mainly voted for the NP, and IFP supporters that their interests would be safeguarded. Its practical effect was to constrain the ANC from pushing through some important measures.[64]

The Interim Constitution attempted to guarantee the entire gamut of human rights within the unitary state. The most significant of these measures was the Bill of Rights[65]—which also guaranteed the right to own property[66]—and the creation of a Constitutional Court.[67] The Constitutional Court, which was proposed by the ANC, had jurisdiction as the court of final instance in all questions of interpretation of the Interim Constitution, violations of the Bill of Rights, and the constitutionality of national and provincial laws, as well as administrative and executive acts.[68] It could exercise judicial review, a power that the previous Supreme Court lacked under the parliamentary supremacy model of apartheid, whereby the courts had no right to pronounce on the constitutionality of acts of Parliament.[69] The Constitutional Court alone had the power to certify that the permanent Constitution, adopted by the Constitutional Assembly on May 8, 1996, complied with the thirty-four Constitutional Principles laid down in the Interim Constitution. Without this certification the new Constitution could not become law.[70]

The Constitutional Principles lay at the heart of the constitution-making process because they represented the core of the "solemn pact," the covenant reached primarily between the ANC and the NP on the powers and functions of the new democratic state. The principles put the ANC-dominated future government in an iron box, taking away its ability to transform South Africa according to its vision. For the NP, the principles constituted a shield for the protection of the white minority and its privilege from the possible redistributive inclinations of a black-led government. In other words, the principles were the essential link between the past and the present; through them the old order would ensure its survival. For the ANC, which ascended to power through persuasion as opposed to the defeat of its adversary, rejection of the principles would likely have delayed the transition or compounded the crisis of governance then destabilizing South Africa. The establishment was willing to transfer some powers to an ANC government so long as the resulting state would have substantially inferior powers compared with those of its predecessors.

While constitutional certification has no precedent, it is not difficult to see why both the ANC and the NP agreed to it. For the ANC, the certifying authority would be the Constitutional Court, which it had created and which would be sympathetic to it. For the NP, the certification made sure that an ANC-dominated Constitutional Assembly could not write the constitution it desired. Consequently, the final constitution would reflect the compromise reached in 1993, effectively curbing the power of the ANC to create a completely new political and constitutional dispensation. It seems that the NP got the better of the deal as it was protected against the will of the majority to substantially transform the state. What is more disturbing, however, is that CODESA, the unelected multiparty forum that produced the Interim Constitution, crafted a document that the Constitutional Assembly, the first national democratically elected body in South Africa, could not substantially alter. In a sense, the validity of the 1996 Constitution rested on the all-white Parliament that approved the Interim Constitution, and the Constitutional Court, which is an appointed body. The Constitutional Assembly, the body actually representing the will of all South Africans, essentially rubber-stamped prior political choices, despite projecting the perception that it was making a new constitution.

The Interim Constitution created watchdog institutions with broad mandates to promote and protect rights and to exercise oversight and scrutiny over state institutions, public officials, and society at large.[71] These independent commissions are the Human Rights Commission (HRC), given the broadest mandate and intended to be the leading human rights body;[72] the Public Protector, or Ombud;[73] the Commission for Gender Equality, designed to promote equality between the sexes and to advise the legislature on laws that affect the status of women;[74] and the Commission on the Restitution of Land Rights, a central organ in the government's land reform process.[75] Both the Constitutional Court and the Appellate Division of the Supreme Court have important human rights functions in that they determine the constitutionality of government acts, policies, and omissions.[76] Other commissions of import to human rights issues were: the Truth and Reconciliation Commission (TRC),[77] which was mandated to investigate and publish the abuses of the apartheid era; the Independent Electoral Commission (IEC),[78] which organized, administered, and monitored the 1994 elections; the Commission on the Restitution of Land Rights; and the Auditor-General.[79] In the 1996 Constitution, the ANC bowed to pressure from right-wing Afrikaners and permitted a provision for the establishment of the Commission for the Promotion and Protection of the Rights of Cultural, Religious and Linguistic Communities, a body intended to "protect" minority rights.[80] The 1996 Constitution also established an Independent Authority to Regulate Broadcasting.[81] The 1996 Constitution broadened the mandates of most of these commissions and further clarified their roles and functions.

In general, the Interim Constitution attempted to strike a delicate balance among all the tensions in South Africa as it sought to create an inclusive but fair state. But on many key issues, the Interim Constitution's positions danced precariously on the political precipice. For example, the Constitution glossed over the contradiction between federalism and a unitary state, and, as a result, failed to satisfy the IFP's autonomy demands. The Interim Constitution's protection of group rights through the protection of language rights, for instance, did not translate into political power by entrenched regional interests such as the IFP. Elsewhere, in its push to "reconcile" and "reconstruct" South African society,[82] the Interim Constitution treaded water on the explosive issues of land reform and security of tenure for the largely Afrikaner bureaucracy.[83]

Were it not for the legacy of apartheid, the Interim Constitution's rights orientation would have been largely beneficial to individuals and communities. Under the circumstances, however, the rights approach gave no more than formal and abstract rights to blacks and other nonwhites. For white beneficiaries of apartheid, by contrast, the rights-based state, with its independent courts and multiple rights commissions and watchdogs, provides a golden opportunity to protect most of their privileges and legitimize the results of apartheid.

The 1996 Constitution as a Normative Continuum

The permanent constitution, which was adopted by the Constitutional Assembly on May 8, 1996,[84] could only come into force after it was certified by the Constitutional Court,[85] assented to by the president, and then promulgated.[86] Some provisions of the 1996 Constitution came into effect on February 4, 1997, a date set by the president by proclamation.[87] Once in force, the new constitution repealed most of the Interim Constitution unless otherwise provided for in either the Interim or the permanent constitution. The provisions of the Interim Constitution relating to a government of national unity remained in force until April 30, 1999.[88] The focus on a rights approach to resolving South Africa's problems did not change.

The 1996 Constitution elaborated and added certain rights, such as the right to property, and broadened the mandates of human rights institutions. Of the "State Institutions Supporting Constitutional Democracy,"[89] the HRC was given the broadest mandate. Unlike other commissions that were created to address particular human rights issues, the HRC's powers are wide-ranging and subsume those of other commissions. It has broad powers to promote respect for human rights through educational campaigns and the monitoring of human rights conditions,[90] and to protect human rights through investigations,[91] reports, and suits that it may initiate. More important, the 1996 Constitution gives the HRC the power to monitor the state's compliance with particular economic and social rights contained in the Bill of Rights.[92]

The HRC's broad mandate, the vastness of South Africa, and its complex and deep-rooted human rights problems pose serious challenges to the institution. Since it opened its Johannesburg offices in March 1996, the HRC has attempted to concretely define the Commission's place in the democratization process and determine its priorities and principal areas of focus.[93] The HRC has faced a tension between emphasizing its promotional functions or actively investigating abuses, exposing violations, and seeking redress for them. The Commission appears to realize that its educational role is best served by an activist and confrontational posture.

More challenging, however, is the HRC's constitutional mandate to monitor the state's realization of social and economic rights. The problems in this area are compounded by the government's lack of adequate resources and an absence of clear normative standards in the human rights corpus.[94] Like the ICESCR, the principal human rights treaty in the field of economic and social rights, the South African Constitution gives little guidance on the content of such rights or the speed with which they must be respected. The Constitution opts for the language of gradualism, of "progressive realization."[95] The Commission will need to harness whatever jurisprudence exists internationally, contextualize it for South Africa, and develop normative criteria with which to assess the progress made by the state. In an important case, *Soobramoney v. Minister of Health* [KwaZulu-Natal],[96] the Constitutional Court has provided some useful directions for developing a jurisprudence of economic, social and cultural rights. These developments may ultimately provide some valuable lessons for the international community in this field.

The Human Rights Commission must also sort out its relationship with the other commissions focused on discrete areas of human rights to avoid redundancy. While there is little overlap with the Public Protector who is essentially concerned with official maladministration, potential conflict and tension between the HRC and the Commission for Gender Equality, and the Commission for the Promotion and Protection of the Rights of Cultural, Religious, and Linguistic Communities (CRLCC) may materialize in the future.

In September 1996, the Constitutional Court refused to certify the draft text of the 1996 Constitution, holding that it failed to meet the requirements of a number of the Constitutional Principles of the Interim Constitution. In particular, according to the Constitutional Court, the 1996 Constitution did not guarantee the right of employees to collective bargaining; impermissibly shielded a number of statutes from constitutional review; failed to require "special procedures involving special majorities" for constitutional amendments; did not entrench the Bill of Rights; did not provide adequately for the independence and impartiality of the Public Protector, the Public Service Commission, and the Auditor-General; failed to specify that the powers and functions of the Public Service Commission could impinge on legitimate provincial autonomy; did not provide a framework for the structures, and the fiscal powers and functions for local government and the formal legislative procedures that they should follow; and provided the provinces with "substantially less and inferior" powers and functions than those required by the Interim Constitution.[97]

The grounds for noncertification were important in that they indicated attempts by the ANC to alter or modify the Interim Constitution and, more specifically, the Constitutional Principles. In other words, the Constitutional Court objected to those provisions that it perceived as a departure from the 1993 settlement. A number of its objections addressed the contentious issue of the division of powers between the center and the provinces, a key question on the nature of the post-apartheid state. More importantly, those objections were an early indication of the policy choices and directions that the ANC government may push for in the future to consolidate power and attempt to reverse some of the legacies of apartheid. But the Constitutional Court emphasized that the 1996 Constitution did not contain substantial flaws. To the contrary, the Court found that the Constitution complied with most of the Constitutional Principles. It said:

We wish to conclude this judgment with two observations. The first is to reiterate that the CA [Constitutional Assembly] has drafted a constitutional text which complies with the overwhelming majority of the requirements of the CPs [Constitutional Principles]. The second is that the instances of non-compliance (sic) which we have listed in the preceding paragraph, although singly and collectively important, should present no significant obstacle to the formulation of a text which complies fully with those requirements.[98]

President Mandela welcomed the Court's opinion, noting that the Court had clarified some issues that were vaguely formulated by the Constitutional Principles.[99] He expressed confidence that the Constitutional Assembly would quickly finalize the Constitution and bring it into full conformity with the Constitutional Principles. Although most political parties welcomed the judgment, an impression was created that the Court wanted a different balance of power between the provinces and the center.[100] Some reports suggested that the Court's rejection of the draft 1996 Constitution played into the hands of Inkatha Freedom Party leader Mangosuthu Buthelezi and his demands for more provincial autonomy.[101]

On October 11, 1996, the Constitutional Assembly voted overwhelmingly to adopt a revised draft of the 1996 Constitution. The Constitutional Assembly adopted the new text by a vote of 369-1, with only eight abstentions.[102] Buthelezi's Inkatha Freedom Party boycotted the vote (it had also boycotted the initial drafting process), claiming that its wishes for more provincial autonomy and international mediation had not been accepted. The white separatist Freedom Front abstained because it could not accept all the provisions of the new text. The final text of the 1996 Constitution was certified by the Constitutional Court on December 4, 1996, and signed into law by President Mandela on December 10, 1996.

The 1996 Constitution consolidates and further clarifies the rights enumerated in, and required by, the Interim Constitution. The rights-oriented rhetoric of the Interim Constitution is affirmed and enhanced in a number of areas in the permanent Constitution. The 1996 Constitution, building on the Interim Constitution, does not permit limitations to the Bill of Rights except those permissible in an "open and democratic society" and provides a list of nonderogable rights during a state of emergency.[103] The rights and powers of certain institutions are enhanced in the new Constitution. While the National Assembly and its powers remain substantially the same as before, the Senate is transformed into the National Council of Provinces (NCP).[104] Although the National Assembly remains the main legislative body, the NCP is given almost equal legislative power: it can amend and reject most proposed laws, and this includes laws pertinent to provincial jurisdiction.[105] Regarding the right to self-determination by communities, the Constitution rejects secession and only allows the exercise of self-determination within the framework of the unitary state.[106] The 1996 Constitution relies, like its predecessor, on the grant of formal guarantees and expressions of rights by the state and its institutions to form the basic foundation for the transformation of the legacies of apartheid.

The ANC's Gradualist Rights Approach

The ANC, South Africa's premier reformist organization during apartheid, sought political reform and majority rule with a view to transforming the political and economic structures of apartheid. From its earliest days, the ANC emphasized a rights-based approach to reform, a strategy that in all likelihood is incapable of transforming the abysmal legacy of apartheid. But the struggle for equality and the right to political participation, the two prominent pillars that supported resistance to apartheid South Africa, were not pursued by the ANC and other reform-minded groups as ends in themselves. Rather, emphasis on these preeminent norms of the human rights movement was a strategy to affect the foundations of a state that excluded blacks from the economic mainstream. The struggle against apartheid was not waged so that blacks could boast of abstract political rights. It was waged so that blacks could have equal access to economic resources. Majoritarian democratic rule constrained by particular notions of property rights does not necessarily lead to the economic empowerment of the majority.[107] The challenge of the ANC-dominated government is to achieve economic empowerment of the black majority within a human rights state that protects economic rights.[108]

Economic transformation is a daunting challenge because international support for the anti-apartheid movement, especially in the West, was not driven by the desire to combat economic inequality; its main focus was extending the right of political participation to black South Africans.[109] Indeed, the economic programs of the ANC that emphasized black economic empowerment in a democratic post-apartheid state through the nationalization of key economic sectors drew hostility from most Western countries as well as the apartheid regime.[110] The ANC's economic rhetoric softened over the years as the possibility of capturing state power increased.[111] In fact, Nelson Mandela himself assured the government in secret talks in 1988 that the ANC supported a more even distribution of resources rather than wholesale nationalization, although he cautioned nationalization might be necessary in certain sectors of the economy.[112]

Just prior to the 1994 elections, the ANC issued the Reconstruction and Development Programme (RDP), the key platform and vision for the society that the ANC intended to create. After the elections and the triumph of the ANC, the RDP became the official policy under which each government ministry was to create a strategy for reform.[113] As a result, White Papers discussing and analyzing proposals for reform were produced for most sectors. Briefly, the RDP reformation had to adhere to six basic principles: an integrated and sustainable program; a people-driven process; peace and security for all; nation-building; the link between reconstruction and development; and the democratization of South Africa.[114] The five programs of the RDP were: meeting basic needs; developing human resources; building the economy; democratizing the state and society; and implementing the RDP.[115]

On the face of it, and as a broad statement of intent, the RDP's prose was seductive. The devil, however, was in more than just the details. Although the RDP decried the legacy of apartheid—racial and gender inequalities, the exclusion of blacks and other nonwhites from most sectors of society, the total control of the economy by the white minority, and incredible poverty among blacks—it had few practical measures by which to restore the humanity of the victims of apartheid. For example, in the section on building the economy, the RDP stated the obvious—that the ANC is committed to democracy, participation, and development and that the ANC was

convinced that neither a commandist central planning system nor an unfettered free market system can provide adequate solutions to the problems confronting us. Reconstruction and development will be achieved through the leading and enabling role of the state, a thriving sector, and active involvement by all sectors of civil society which in combination will lead to sustainable growth.[116]

The RDP listed among the goals of the reconstruction of the economy the following: the elimination of poverty and discrimination, the reduction of economic imbalances between regions, and the development of human resources.[117] Even though the RDP mentioned the transfer of resources from the central government to the rural areas as one possible method for alleviating rural powerlessness among blacks, there were no concrete suggestions about where such funding should come from.[118] This romantic approach—stating egalitarian goals and vague objectives—without directly and concretely identifying how industries or sectors would be transformed, from where the resources for that transformation would be seized, and how white privilege would be curtailed, permeated the RDP and undermined its credibility.

In April 1996, in a move that could be read as a sign of the ANC's retreat from this minimalist program of reform, the RDP ministerial office was dissolved and transferred to the offices of the deputy president and the Ministry of Finance.[119] Whatever the initial intent of the authors of the RDP, the actual document appears to have been sharply understated to reassure foreign investors, creditor nations and agencies, and the powerful white minority, as part of the ANC strategy to capture state power through the elections.[120] What Gassama calls the "conservative, pro-business, anti-redistributive direction"[121] of the government still enjoys the support of most white captains of industry in South Africa, the one group whose privileges have been not only protected but increased.[122] It is ironic that a democratic South African state would have considerably less power than the apartheid state ever had to transform society, even though the new state seeks to create a fair and just society, whereas its predecessor used its power to do precisely the opposite.[123]

Land Reform as a Central Plank of the Struggle

Just before the end of official apartheid, whites own 87 percent of the country's total surface area,[124] even though they constituted only 15 percent of the population of South Africa.[125] Blacks were prohibited from owning land until 1991 when the Land Act of 1936, which reserved most land for whites, was repealed.[126] Millions of Africans were divested of South African citizenship and many more were confined in the homelands.[127] It is important to remember that blacks did not fight for democracy so that whites could continue to own 87 percent of the land. These statistics, together with the politics of exclusion and discrimination, were the reasons for the anti-apartheid struggle. It is not possible to address the demands of the black majority and create a state that respects the gamut of human rights without correcting the gross imbalances and injustices related to land.

Recognizing this fact, the RDP noted that "Apartheid pushed millions of black South Africans into overcrowded and impoverished reserves, homelands and townships" and called for a land reform program to be the central plank of rural development.[128] The RDP emphasized that the abolition of apartheid laws denying blacks rights to land accomplished little since only a minuscule number of blacks could afford land on the open market.[129] Thus the RDP advocated a land reform program with two components: land restitution and land redistribution. This philosophy was the basis for the measures and programs outlined in the government's policy proposals on land reform.

These proposals and policies must, however, be construed subject to the property clause in the Bill of Rights of the 1996 Constitution.[130] The inclusion of the right to property in the Bill of Rights makes it sacrosanct and virtually inviolable. However, the right primarily serves to protect the interests of white property and landowners, the authors and beneficiaries of apartheid.

Land redistribution is supposed to benefit the rural and urban poor by providing them with an array of tenure arrangements.[131] As clearly stated in the RDP and restated in ANC-government policy, however, no radical land reform program is contemplated. The land redistribution component is based on the principle of "willing-buyer-willing-seller" without direct government involvement except as a facilitator to provide financial assistance.[132] Households with an income of less than R1,500 were eligible for a government grant of up to R15,000 to purchase rights in land.[133] The government hoped that these voluntary transactions would suffice. It did not contemplate expropriation, which it regarded as "an instrument of last resort where urgent land needs cannot be met for various reasons, through voluntary market transactions."[134] In any case, the Constitution severely restricts expropriation, which could only be done for public purposes and in the public interest and must be justly and adequately compensated.[135]

Land restitution aimed to restore land and provide other remedies to individuals who were dispossessed of their lands through past racially discriminatory laws and practices.[136] Restitution covers cases of forced removals since June 19, 1913, when the Natives Land Act was passed,[137] but it affects only about 2 percent of the land. Under the scheme, individuals with claims can apply to the Commission on the Restitution of Land Rights, which investigates claims and mediates between the parties.[138] If an agreement does not result from mediation, the commission refers claims to the Land Claims Court for adjudication.[139] The state bears the burden of compensating the land owners against whom a successful restitution claim has been lodged. By March 31, 1996, 7,095 claims had been lodged with the commission throughout South Africa.[140] It is difficult to gauge the success of the restitution scheme, although a handful of claims had been settled by 1996.[141]

Land tenure reform aims to clarify, strengthen, and secure the land rights of individuals, families, and groups who live at the margins of society.[142] Those affected would include labor tenants, squatters, and black farm workers on "white" land who live at the mercy of landowners. This scheme, by ratifying marginal "land rights," gives legal sanction and legitimates historically repressive, abusive, and exploitative relationships under which blacks have toiled for whites.

In sum, the land reform program is a far cry from a device for the empowerment of blacks. Except for tinkering at the margins, it leaves most of the land in the hands of whites and the few blacks able to purchase land on the free market.[143] The one scheme that seems promising is the restitution program, although it affects only a small number of people.

Even the government has tabulated a long list of constraints limiting land reform: limited resources and other budgetary priorities; constraints imposed by the Constitution; and organizational, institutional, and resource limitations of the state.[144] The government's exclusive reliance on the rights idiom and legal and bureaucratic processes is too slow, conservative, and unlikely to yield any major changes even in the long term. Many in the black community are too poor or unfamiliar with complex legal processes to take advantage of them. Finally, the ANC government is either stretched too thin or wholly reliant on an untrustworthy bureaucracy—the authors and enforcers of apartheid—who are loath to unravel their handiwork. These variables have made the land reform program a disappointment.

Women in Post-Apartheid South Africa

The transformation of South African society must include the implementation of women's rights and the substantial liberation of women. Black African women, who comprise 36.3 percent of the entire population, have historically occupied the most vulnerable position in society.[145] As articulated by Adrien Wing and Eunice de Carvalho,

South Africa needs a vision of equality that gives particularized attention to the needs of black women, who have endured unequal treatment because of their race and gender. Black women are in the unique position of being the least equal of all groups in South Africa. They have been oppressed by whites on the basis of race, and they have been oppressed by men, both black and white, on the basis of gender.

Under apartheid, that is until 1994, the negative consequences of all the discriminatory and exclusionary laws and policies that governed all blacks, male and female, were more acute for black women in all sectors of society. Black women were usually employed in the least skilled and lowest paid jobs of the agricultural and service areas, and women were also the least educated, generally lacked health care, and were subjected to rapes and domestic violence in large numbers.[146]

In addition to the dehumanizing policies and practices of the apartheid state, the apartheid legal system ratified many of the discriminatory norms of African law—referred to generally as customary law—and legitimized the patriarchy prevalent in many African societies. Even before the formal institution of apartheid, the state had created a dual legal system under which Africans were governed by special courts bound by customary law.[147] The status of customary courts took on a more ominous posture in 1970 when the state required that all blacks live in a homeland of their culture and language.[148] Under the homelands ploy, the apartheid state would use black puppets to preserve and perpetuate apartheid on behalf of Pretoria.

Repressive pro-apartheid homeland leaders ruled abusively and perverted many positive aspects of customary law in their zealotry to retain power.[149] Although custom is an inherently dynamic phenomenon, these political arrangements favored the conservatism of customary law and tended to freeze its gender biases.[150] In some African communities, the worst of the patriarchy of customary law was manifested in its treatment of women as minors or at least as possessing claims inferior to those of men in matters related to marriage, guardianship, succession, contractual power, and property rights.[151]

This is a legacy that the ANC has long vowed to change.[152] The ANC recognized women's rights as early as 1943 when it granted them full membership and voting rights and established the ANC Women's League.[153] In 1955, the Freedom Charter, which became the organization's guiding document, required equal protection and rights without regard to sex.[154] The Interim Constitution's equal protection clause prohibited discrimination on the basis of gender, sex, and sexual orientation.[155] Although the clause bound all state organs, it was silent on its effect on private parties.[156] The Interim Constitution allowed discrimination with reason, or fair discrimination, that is, affirmative action measures to alleviate the effects of past discrimination.[157] The Interim and 1996 Constitutions provided for the establishment for a Commission on Gender Equality to advance the status of women.[158] In 1995, the government ratified the Convention on the Elimination of All Forms of Discrimination Against Women.

These positive steps, while an admirable starting point, are complicated by several problems. First, for the constitutional provisions to be meaningful, the approach of state organs and officials who have traditionally discriminated against women must be transformed. This attitudinal paradigm shift must be widespread—in employment, education, health care, and law enforcement. The expenditure of enormous government resources to create programs targeted specifically at women will also be necessary.[159] Secondly, the constitutional provisions, which were a result of bargaining between various parties, including traditional leaders and the ANC, leave open some questions regarding customary law. Customary law is recognized by the 1996 Constitution subject to its provision. The Constitution does not, however, explicitly clarify the fate of customs that conflict with the equal protection clause. This may delay the reform of customary law to bring it into conformity with constitutional norms.[160]

The Status and Orientation of Post-Apartheid Courts

A peculiarity of South African bureaucracy is the bifurcation of key state sectorial organs into the "ministry," the political arm of government, and the "department," the executing or implementing arm.[161] This distinction is tailor-made for bipolarity and resistance to reform. The ministry is headed by a member of the cabinet who is supported by a small cast of advisors, while the department is run by a director-general and is made up of civil servants who are supposed to carry out the policies of the ministry. A further geographic division complicates the situation: the ministry literally shuttles between Cape Town, the legislative seat of government, and Pretoria, the political capital, where the departments are based. Furthermore, in South Africa today, the ministries are mostly headed by ANC members, while the departments are staffed by appointees of the apartheid era, mostly Afrikaner bureaucrats who were responsible for implementing apartheid policies. Nowhere has this tension been more poignant than in efforts to reform the administration of justice.

South Africa has inherited from apartheid a judiciary organized into two tiers: magistrate and high courts.[162] The high courts were composed of judges and comprised the Supreme Court of Appeal and the Supreme Courts. Judges were appointed by the State President from the ranks of qualified and experienced lawyers,[163] while magistrates were appointed by the director-general of the Department of Justice through his delegated power by the minister of justice.[164] To qualify for appointment as a judge, one had to have practiced law as an advocate before the Supreme Court for at least ten years,[165] a requirement that raises the "pool problem" and excludes many blacks.[166] Magistrates, who need not have law degrees, have primarily been appointed from the ranks of public prosecutors.[167]

These arrangements, structures, and requirements produced a judiciary that was overwhelmingly white and pro-apartheid in a country where most of the defendants are black. A majority of the judges and most of the magistrates are white.[168] In 1993, for example, 99 percent of all judges were white and male.[169] The figures for magistrates were not much better.[170] The numbers for women, who were virtually all white, were better at 15 percent, or 176 women of a total of 1,173 magistrates in 1992.[171] By 1994, the numbers of blacks had risen somewhat following the incorporation of the homelands back into South Africa, but over 90 percent of all regional magistrates remained white, and only 4 percent were women.[172] The importance of the magistrate courts cannot be overestimated: they handle over 95 percent of all criminal and civil matters.[173]

Under the previous regime, the structure, rules, and organization of the judiciary—including appointment, retirement, dismissals, discharge, and discipline—were designed to serve the executive and its apartheid policies. This hierarchy was fortified by the doctrine of parliamentary supremacy under which the judiciary could not question the constitutionality of laws passed by the rubber-stamp apartheid Parliament. Magistrates enjoyed less latitude than judges. As civil servants they could not question administrative orders, as that could have been construed as misconduct, and were subject to administrative discipline.[174]

In 1993, as its days drew to a close, the apartheid regime sought to protect the magistracy from reformulation by an ANC government. The apartheid Parliament passed the Magistrates Act to govern the appointment and the administration of the magistracy. The Act governs the welfare of the magistracy including appointment, promotion, training, and discharge. Under the Act, magistrates are now appointed by the minister for justice on the recommendation of the Magistrates Commission appointed by the state president. The commission has eleven members who are appointed for renewable five-year terms; five of the members are drawn from the magistracy, one from the Department of Justice, and the rest from various law-related institutions, a ratio that gives the old guard a majority.[175] More important, however, is the removal and insulation of the magistracy from the civil service and the Ministry of Justice by this law.[176] According to Lovell Fernandez, the law was a desperate attempt by the apartheid regime to preserve its values:

The trouble with this new law, as indeed with the host of other enactments passed through Parliament at record speed over the past three years, is that it reflects a desperate bid by the National Party to preserve the status quo in the administration of justice. It forms part of the panoply of laws that the Government has been sneaking in through the back door.[177]

Phineas Mojapelo, then president of the Black Lawyers' Association, called the Magistrates Act an attempt by the apartheid regime "to privatize the magistracy."[178] In effect, since the apartheid regime knew that it would no longer be there to ensure the enforcement of apartheid laws and policies, it cleverly sought to guarantee the survival of its norms by granting the apartheid magistracy judicial independence, something it had never allowed in its heyday. That guarantee was sealed by the affirmation of the security of tenure for all magistrates who were employed when the law came into force. According to the new law, magistrates can only be removed with the approval of the Parliament.[179]

The organization and administration of the magistracy under the Magistrates Act preserves almost intact the apartheid system of the administration of justice—since 95 percent of all legal matters are handled in the magistrate courts—and made it extremely difficult for Dullah Omar, the first post-apartheid minister for justice, and an internationally acclaimed human rights lawyer, to implement his policies to transform the magistracy.[180] First, he could not dismiss apartheid magistrates and replace them with more progressive and representative personnel. In any case, even when slots opened up for the appointment of new magistrates, the old guard outnumbered the reformist members of the Magistrates Commission. Most significant, the transformative posture of Omar and his key advisors in the Ministry of Justice was at loggerheads with the apartheid culture, ethos, and personnel of the Department of Justice, the agency responsible for implementing the Ministry's policies. It is difficult to see how many of the reforms envisioned by the Ministry of Justice will materialize without the repeal of the Magistrates Act.

Another peculiarity of the new South Africa, which has affected the attention paid to the reform of the magistracy, is the focus of public debate on the high courts although they handle only a mere 5 percent of all legal matters. Presumably, the high courts are more "important" than the magistrate courts because they are the guardians of the new constitutional order.[181] Effectively, the 1996 Constitution retains the historically bifurcated judiciary, paying little attention to the magistracy, which it basically leaves to Parliament to regulate. In contrast, it provides in some detail for the functions and powers of high courts and terms of service of judges. It also establishes and spells out the composition and powers of the Judicial Service Commission (JSC), the body responsible for the welfare of the high courts. Judges are appointed by the president in consultation with or at the recommendation of the JSC, whose seventeen members are drawn from a wide cross section of the legal profession.[182]

Except for the Constitutional Court, whose creation at the insistence of the ANC should be seen as a deliberate attempt to set the agenda for legal reform at the top, the high courts are dominated by apartheid era judges.[183] The security of tenure for these judges, together with the criteria and tradition of appointing judges from among senior advocates, are a major impediment to the transformation of the courts and the inclusion of women, blacks, and other nonwhites in the judiciary.[184] Furthermore, the bifurcated judiciary—governed by two different commissions and different laws, rules, and expectations—only perpetuates the mediocrity of the magistracy and indefinitely postpones the reform of the judiciary as a whole. These structures and rules have the potential to reduce to ashes the RDP's central hopes: a legal system that is accessible, affordable, and legitimate; legal processes and institutions that employ simplified language and court procedure; and the recognition and harmonization of community[185] and customary (tribunals governed by African law) courts.

Humanizing the Instruments of Coercion

The South African security forces, in particular the South African Police (SAP) and the South African Defense Forces (SADF), were the central organs that protected, defended, sustained, and secured the apartheid state.[186] In the 1980s, as the international isolation of South Africa hardened and domestic opposition shook the state to its foundations, the civilian leadership virtually turned over the control of the country to the security forces.[187] As a United Nations report politely put it:

Their [the security forces] reason for being was Apartheid and their brutality is a matter of public record. More than 800 people were killed by police during the emergency years of the mid-1980s. Torture was rampant and deaths in police custody remain a problem even today. In addition, the security forces—both police and military—developed a culture of deception in which claims of respect for the rule of law masked torture, covert action, and forces of destabilization.[188]

In the apartheid era, the SADF took on repressive policing functions in black townships and the homelands, where it was responsible for orchestrating, among other things, the so-called "black-on-black" violence, as was prevalent in KwaZulu-Natal. Yet it is these very instruments of coercion, which have been reared on the most virulent forms of racism and a culture of death and destruction, secrecy, and unaccountability, that the democratically elected, civilian, ANC-led government has relied on to govern the country and to create a human rights state. Their transformation is critical because they can easily either end the democratic experiment or effectively stymie it by their numbers and the weapons at their disposal.

The process of reforming the security forces and unifying has been under way. As a priority, the RDP called for all the security forces to be placed "firmly under civilian control" through ministries "answerable to Parliament."[189] It required that the security forces "[u]phold the democratic constitution, they must be non-partisan, and they must be bound by clear codes of conduct." It called for the South African Police Service to be "transformed, with special attention to representivity, and gender and human rights sensitivity." It stated that "The defense and the police and intelligence services must be transformed from being agents of oppression into effective servants of the community." The 1996 Constitution, echoing the letter and the spirit of the Interim Constitution, establishes civilian control over the defense and police forces and defines their primary missions.[190] The cabinet member responsible heads a constitutionally mandated civilian secretariat for each of the forces.[191] The security forces retain their positions of power and influence, but are "answerable to civilian leadership to a far greater degree than under the former government."[192]

The slightly renamed South African Police Service (SAPS) is an amalgam of some eleven different police forces, many of them from the former homelands. As of 1996, the total police force had a strength of 140,000 officers.[193] The renamed South African National Defense Force (SANDF) had a total of 100,000 members: 65,000 from the old SADF; 20,000 from Umkhonto We Sizwe, the ANC's military wing; 6,000 from the Azanian People's Liberation Army (APLA), the military wing of the PAC; and 9,000 from the forces of the former homelands.[194] While the process of creating single forces from these different groups is challenging, it has helped broaden the demographic composition and political outlook of security forces. To increase community participation and enhance local oversight over the police, the Interim Constitution provided for community policing forums attached to police stations across the country.[195] These measures may serve to broaden and democratize the views of security forces, although the mentality and training for repression are deeply ingrained. It remains to be seen whether the forces of repression can be transformed—without massive layoffs and compulsory early retirements to clean house and infuse new blood—to support the construction of a human rights state.

Rights Discourse—Not a Panacea

Theoretically, the norms being deployed for the construction of the post-apartheid South African state are the exact opposite of the founding principles of the apartheid state. The latter was explicitly based on the superiority of the peoples of European descent over those of African and other nonwhite ancestries, while the former deliberately has rejected outright these doctrines. The reborn state declared that only the human rights idiom will be the principal framework for its construction. In many respects, the new South Africa is living proof of Henkin's assertion of the preeminence of human rights over other contradictory philosophies and traditions.[196] The Interim and 1996 Constitutions are human rights manifestos that seek to assure individuals, primarily, and groups secondarily, that the new state is a radical departure from its predatory predecessor.[197] It is no wonder that a state born in the late twentieth century out of the struggle for equality would adopt the rights framework as its dominant organizing principle. What is doubtful, however, is the ability of the South African state, and the possibility for any state, to overcome such a dreadful legacy of human rights abuses primarily through the rights idiom.

In virtually all their provisions, both the Interim and the 1996 Constitutions created space between the individual and groups, on the one hand, and the state, on the other. Great care was taken where institutions of the state were provided for to make sure that their powers to invade the individual or groups and the so-called private sphere were limited, account-able, and transparent. The Constitution in this case is not only an attempt to reduce the power of the sovereign but to make its exercise a matter of conscience for the individual official and the government agency in question.[198]

Does this use of, reliance on, and faith in human rights ideals and norms give the new state the ability to transform the legacy of apartheid, and therefore create a human rights culture in a human rights state? Are rights a sufficient medium for transforming deeply rooted social, economic, and especially racial inequalities? Does the strategy by the ANC— the negotiated settlement that left intact white control of the economy—of first accepting the political kingdom as a prelude to economic empowerment for blacks make sense in the long run? Or did the ANC capture the government and lose the power?

This chapter has sought to demonstrate that the ANC reconstructionist project's assumption that rights will transform the state and society is fraught with theoretical and practical difficulties. The major difficulties relate to the nature of that post-apartheid settlement. First, while it was absolutely necessary to employ rights discourse to energize the anti-apartheid movement, it is important for the ANC to realize that the rhetoric of rights is a double-edged sword—a weapon but also a shield. Since 1994, all groups in South Africa—the wealthy and the powerful, the poor and the excluded, and even those who in the past blatantly violated the rights of others—have found either refuge or empowerment in the language of rights. As contradictory as their motives and intentions are, all these groups seek to protect or advance their interests through the medium of rights. It is a testament to the indeterminacy of this discourse that all these competing interests feel that the new constitutional order will protect them against each other and help them vindicate their goals.[199]

Nowhere is the use of the rights language more poignant than in the protection of property interests in the Constitution, in the preservation of rights and privileges of the apartheid security forces, judiciary, and bureaucracy, and in the various so-called reform programs relating to land and other resources. The protection of these interests through the new constitutional order in effect binds the ANC and robs it of any ability to carry out major reforms. In the case of South Africa, the democratic, rule-of-law, rights-based state has ironically turned out to be an instrument for the preservation of the privileges and the ill-gotten gains of the white minority. The state has become a stamp of approval for an unjust and unfair society. It is clear that a state that is unable, in the first place, to overcome these basic problems cannot become a human rights institution.

There is no question that the ANC government's commitment to the creation of a just and fair society is genuine. For the first time ever, it has introduced to South Africa freedoms that many of the country's citizens could only dream about. That accomplishment is historical, and it has not been the intention here to trivialize it or the enormous sacrifices that were made in its pursuit. Nevertheless, the goals of the ANC are not served by analyses that pretend not to see the conundrum of the rights idiom. Without doubt, rights discourse was indispensable as a strategy for energizing the anti-apartheid movement. But rights rhetoric cannot and should not be the primary, and in this the case the only, instrument for the transformation of apartheid's legacies. At the very least, rights discourse must be one of several tools, policies, and approaches deployed to alter the institutional features of the apartheid state. As Karl Klare aptly notes:

Rights discourse does not and probably cannot provide us with the criteria for deciding between conflicting claims of right. In order to resolve rights conflicts, it is necessary to step outside the discourse. One must appeal to more concrete and therefore more controversial analyses of the relevant social and institutional contexts than rights discourse offers; and one must develop and elaborate conceptions of and intuitions about human freedom and self-determination by reference to which one seeks to assess rights claims and resolve rights conflicts.[200]

This malleability of the rights discourse has cut against the interests of those excluded by apartheid. In the current unabashedly pro-capitalist and anti-redistributive international climate, rights language in South Africa has taken on the color of oppression in that it primarily has left undisturbed the economic hierarchies of apartheid. Blacks are being asked to embrace the promise of the new "color-blind" market arrangements in the hope that trickles at the edges will someday turn into rivulets. That is what is wrong with the ANC blueprint. Instead, the ANC government could pursue other policy options and measures, the limiting injunctions of the new constitutional order notwithstanding, to start the meaningful rectification of social and economic distortions. Thus, the ANC government may want to explore approaches that limit the property rights of the beneficiaries of apartheid and fashion policies whose thrust is the alleviation of the most egregious disparities in South Africa. Resort to people-centered conceptions of development, as opposed to the current rights-oriented, market-driven approach, may have a better chance of reaching those who have been completely excluded. It seems obvious that substantial land reform, the reconstruction of the bureaucracy, and the reorganization of the economy are three key areas where the ANC government will have to carry out reform if it hopes to meet the expectations of blacks and other excluded groups.

Thabo Mbeki, who in 1999 was elevated from deputy president to president upon the retirement of Nelson Mandela, the country's first democratically elected and post-apartheid leader, faces enormous challenges as he attempts to reverse the tyrannies of apartheid. It appears highly unlikely, however, that the new South Africa, which was ushered in with great fanfare and overwhelming international goodwill, will anytime soon meet the reasonable expectations of the long excluded black majority. The deployment of the rights idiom as the principle medium for transformation will in all likelihood fail to reverse the deep-seated legacies of apartheid. Blacks must continue to wait—although it is not clear for how much longer—before they can genuinely capture state power and use it in addition to the rights language to better their lot.

Conclusion

The adoption in 1948 by the United Nations of the Universal Declaration of Human Rights—the foundational document of the human rights movement—sought to give universal legitimacy to a doctrine that is fundamentally Eurocentric in its construction. Sanctimonious to a fault, the Universal Declaration underscored its arrogance by proclaiming itself the "common standard of achievement for all peoples and nations." The fact that half a century later human rights have become a central norm of global civilization does not vindicate their universality. It is rather a telling testament to the conceptual, cultural, economic, military, and philosophical domination of the European West over non-European peoples and traditions.

The fundamental texts of international human rights law are derived from bodies of domestic jurisprudence developed over several centuries in Western Europe and the United States. The dominant influence of Western liberal thought and philosophies is unmistakable. No one familiar with Western liberal traditions of political democracy and free market capitalism would find international human rights law unusual. Its emphasis on the individual egoist as the center of the moral universe underlines its European orientation. The basic human rights texts drew heavily from the American Bill of Rights and the French Declaration of the Rights of Man. There is virtually no evidence to suggest that they drew inspiration from Asian, Islamic, Buddhist, Hindu, African, or any other non-European traditions.

Many fair-minded observers have acknowledged that the West was able to impose its philosophy of human rights on the rest of the world because in 1948 it dominated the United Nations. Non-Western philosophies and traditions—particularly on the nature of man and the purposes for political society—were either unrepresented or marginalized during the early formulation of human rights. Most Asian and African societies were European colonies and not participants in the making of human rights law. Professor Mary Ann Glendon of Harvard Law School has emphasized in a recent book the important role played by Charles Malik of Lebanon and Peng-chun Chang of China in the drafting of the Universal Declaration.[1] Although non-Westerners, both Malik and Chang were educated in the

United States and were firmly rooted in the European intellectual traditions of the day. The contributions of these two prominent non- Westerners were not steeped in the philosophies or the intellectual and cultural
traditions from which they hailed.

There is no doubt that the current human rights corpus is well meaning.
But that is beside the point. Human rights suffer from several basic and interdependent flaws. International human rights fall within the historical
continuum of the European colonial project in which whites pose as the
saviors of a benighted and savage non-European world. The white human
rights zealot joins the unbroken chain that connects him to the colonial
administrator, the Bible-wielding missionary, and the merchant of free enterprise. Salvation in the modern world is presented as only possible
through the holy trinity of human rights, political democracy, and free
markets.

Thus human rights reject the cross-fertilization of cultures and instead
seek the transformation of non-Western cultures by Western cultures. To
the official guardians and custodians of human rights—the United Nations, Western governments, and senior Western scholars and human
rights activists—calls by non-Westerners for the multicultural reconstruction of human rights are blasphemous. Such calls are demonized as the
hypocritical cries of cultural relativists, an evil species of humans who are
apologists for savage cultures. What the guardians and custodians seek is
the remaking of non-Europeans into little dark, brown, and yellow Europeans—in effect dumb copies of the original. This view of human rights re-
entrenches and revitalizes the international hierarchy of race and color in
which whites, who are privileged globally as a race, are the models and saviors of nonwhites, who are victims and savages.

Perhaps in no other area than in human rights advocacy over the practice labeled in the West as female genital mutilation (FGM) is the cultural
arrogance of the European West more poignant. "Mutilation" implies the
willful, savage, and sadistic infliction of pain on a hapless victim. It is language that stigmatizes as barbaric cultures that condone the practice and
dehumanizes the women who are subjected to it. This formulation decontextualizes the cultural foundation of the practice and promotes the
stereotype of barbaric machete-wielding natives only too eager to inflict
pain on women in their own societies. It is a view that is racist.

There is an urgent need for the human rights movement to step back
from this arrogant approach. It should respect cultural pluralism as a basis
for finding common universality on some issues. In the FGM example, a
new approach would first excavate the social meaning and purposes of the
practice, as well as its effects, and then investigate the conflicting positions
over the practice in that society. Rather than demonizing and finger-pointing under the tutelage of outsiders and their local collaborators, solutions
to the issue could be found through intracultural dialogue and introspec-

tion. Such solutions might range from modifying the practice to discarding it.

In the area of political governance—and in particular on the rights to political participation and religious freedom—the practices of Western states are used as the yardstick. Political democracy may be inevitable but non-Western political traditions must be allowed to evolve their own distinctive systems conducive to their demographic, historical, and cultural traditions. On religious freedom, it is wrongheaded to simply protect the right of missionary Christianity to proselytize and decimate non-Western spiritual traditions and cultures at will. Western knee-jerk reactions to restrictions on Christians in non-Western countries such as China or India must be balanced against the duty of those societies to protect their spiritual heritages from the swarming, imperial faiths bent on the total domination of the spiritual universe.

Like earlier crusades, the human rights movement lacks the monopoly of virtue that its advocates claim. If human rights are to represent a higher human intelligence—which I believe they should—they must overcome the seemingly incurable virus to universalize Eurocentric norms and values by demonizing, repudiating, and re-creating that which is different and non-European. Human rights are not a problem per se nor is the human rights corpus irredeemable. But we must realize that the current human rights represent just one tradition, that of Europe. And even in European or Eurocentric political and philosophical universes, which include Europe, the dominant traditions in the Americas, Australia, and New Zealand, the human rights corpus is an expression of only one European tradition. It will remain incomplete and illegitimate in non-European societies unless it is reconstructed to create a truly multicultural mosaic. The universalization of human rights cannot succeed unless the corpus is moored in all the cultures of the world. Ideas do not become universal merely because powerful interests declare them to be so. Inclusion—not exclusion—is the key to legitimacy.

This book represents an attempt by a scholar from the Third World to respond—at the level of critique—to the human rights corpus. It is based partly on my long and deep commitment to the construction of decent, ethical, fair, and humane political societies. But it also springs from my resistance to a doctrine that I view as part of the colonial project in which I am a subject—not a citizen. The book therefore is not an attempt to launch a new blueprint for a competing—or even a more universal—human rights corpus. I think that the construction of a cross-culturally legitimate and genuinely universal creed of human dignity is urgently needed and that this book will in its modest way make the case and pave the way for just such a corpus.

Finally, I hope that this book serves as a footprint, a signpost for the work which must be done to reconstruct the human rights corpus by constructing normatively a more inclusive doctrine for human dignity. The is literally in a state of emergency. Ruthless, hedonistic, and relentlessly individualistic and deeply exploitative beliefs and systems have in the last decade been given "universal legitimacy" by economic and cultural globalization. The current official human rights corpus does not have the analytical or normative tools—or even the desire and gumption—to unpack the complex oppressions which globalization now wreaks on individuals and communities. Constructed primarily as the moral guardian of global capitalism and liberal internationalism, the human rights corpus is simply unable to confront structurally and in a meaningful way the deep-seated imbalances of power and privilege which bedevil our world.

The construction of a new human rights corpus must first lay a comprehensive framework for what constitutes the building blocks of an ethical, humane, and just society. In this conception, the new corpus must address in a fundamental way not only the political dimensions—with which the present official human rights doctrine preoccupies itself with—of human societies but the economic prerequisites for an ethical society. As such, the new corpus must discard the false premises of the current corpus and reject its excesses while building on those of its notions which have the potential for genuine universality. Scholars must spend less time worrying about or imagining more effective formulas for the implementation of the current human rights corpus. What is needed is groundbreaking and soul-searching work that will enable us to construct a society free of the daily avalanche of cruelties and oppressions. Such work must point us to a place that rejects colonialist and exploitative doctrines, no matter their origins. This is a project that must be pursued with urgency.

Notes

Introduction

1. Henry J. Steiner, *Ideals and Counter-Ideals in the Struggle over Autonomy Regimes for Minorities*, 66 NOTRE DAME L. REV. 1539, 1548 (1991).
2. Abdullahi Ahmed An-Na'im and Francis M. Deng, eds., HUMAN RIGHTS IN AFRICA: CROSS-CULTURAL PERSPECTIVES (Washington D.C.: Brookings Institution Press, 1990), p. 9.
3. *Id.* At 10–11. What follows is a list of several of the questions the editors ask.

Is this [cross-cultural approach to creating a universal corpus] a fanciful ideal or an achievable objective? Are we being romantic and are we unnecessarily complicating the process of universalizing the cause of human rights, or are we presenting a cultural challenge for all members of the human family and their respective cultures that can help shape the lofty ideals of universal human rights? And could such worldwide involvement in itself lead to a realization of the universality of human dignity, which is the cornerstone of international human rights? Or would it be more practical to assume that some cultures are just not blessed with these human ideals, and that the sooner they recognize this and try to adjust and live up to the challenge presented by the pioneering leadership of those more endowed with these lofty values, the better for their own good and for the good of humanity?

4. Richard D. Schwartz, *Human Rights in an Evolving Culture*, An-Na'im and Deng *supra* note 2, pp. 368–82.
5. Laura Myers, *Clinton Talk at University Prods China on Freedom*, BUFFALO NEWS, June 29, 1998, at A1.
6. Charles Babington, *Improve Rights Record, Clinton Tells Turkey*, WASHINGTON POST, November 15, 1999, at A21.
7. Nathaniel Berman, *Beyond Colonialism and Nationalism? Ethiopia, Czechoslovakia, and "Peaceful Change"*, 65 NORDIC JOURNAL OF INTERNATIONAL LAW 421, 478 (1996).
8. *See* Henry J. Steiner, *Do Human Rights Require a Particular Form of Democracy*, in Eugene Cotran and Abdel Omar Sherif, eds., DEMOCRACY, THE RULE OF LAW AND ISLAM (The Hague: Kluwer Law International, 1999), p. 193.
9. *Id.* at 200. Steiner, for example, does not dispute that the human rights text requires a political democracy. He argues that it in fact does impose just such a model. But he correctly points out that the model envisaged is not "detailed and complete." The "essential elements" of a democratic government that the human rights instruments impose do not constitute a complete blueprint but rather "leave

a great deal open for invention, for political variation, for progressive development of the very notion of democracy."

10. *Id.* at 200–201.

Chapter 1. Human Rights as a Metaphor

1. For the purposes of this chapter, the "human rights movement" refers to that collection of norms, processes, and institutions that traces its immediate ancestry to the Universal Declaration of Human Rights (UDHR), adopted by the United Nations in 1948. Universal Declaration of Human Rights, G.A. Res. 217A (III), UN GAOR, 3d Sess., 183d mtg. at 71, UN Doc. A/810 (1948).

2. This oppositional duality is central to the logic of Western philosophy and modernity. As described by David Slater, this binary logic constructs historical imperatives of the superior and the inferior, the barbarian and the civilized, and the traditional and the modern. Within this logic, history is a linear, unidirectional progression with the superior and scientific Western civilization leading and paving the way for others to follow. *See generally* David Slater, *Contesting Occidental Visions of the Global: The Geopolitics of Theory and North-South Relations*, BEYOND LAW, December 1994, pp. 100–101.

3. This chapter hereinafter refers to the "savages-victims-saviors" metaphor as "SVS." The author uses the term "metaphor" to suggest a historical figurative analogy within human rights and its rhetoric and discourse.

4. Each of the three elements of the SVS compound metaphor can operate as independent, stand-alone metaphors as well. Each of these three separate metaphors is combined within the grand narrative of human rights to compose the compound metaphor.

5. Human rights INGOs are typically "First World" nongovernmental organizations (NGOs) that concentrate on human rights monitoring of, reporting on, and advocacy in "Third World" states. *See, e.g.*, Henry J. Steiner, DIVERSE PARTNERS: NON-GOVERNMENTAL ORGANIZATIONS IN THE HUMAN RIGHTS MOVEMENT (Cambridge, Mass.: Harvard Law School Human Rights Program and Human Rights Internet, 1991). Steiner notes that these INGOs share a fundamental commitment to the proselytization of Western liberal values, particularly expressive and political participation rights.

6. In Western thought and philosophy, the state becomes savage if it suffocates or defies civil society. *See generally* John Keane, *Despotism and Democracy*, in CIVIL SOCIETY AND THE STATE (London: Verso, 1988), p. 35.

7. There has been considerable debate among scholars, activists, and others in Africa and in the West about the proper term for this practice entailing the surgical modification or the removal of some portions of the female genitalia. *See, e.g.*, Hope Lewis, *Between Irua and "Female Genital Mutilation": Feminist Human Rights Discourse and the Cultural Divide*, 8 HARV. HUM. RTS. J. 1, 4–8 (1995); *See also* Hope Lewis and Isabelle R. Gunning, *Cleaning Our Own House: "Exotic" and Familiar Human Rights Violations*, 4 BUFF. HUM. RTS. L. REV. 123, 123–24 n. 2 (1998).

8. The art and science of human rights reporting was pioneered and perfected by Amnesty International (AI), the International Commission of Jurists (ICJ), and Human Rights Watch (HRW), the three oldest and most influential INGOs. Other

INGOs as well as domestic human rights groups have mimicked this reporting. On the character, work, and mandate of NGOs and INGOs, *see generally* Nigel Rodley, *The Work of Non-Governmental Organizations in the World-Wide Promotion and Protection of Human Rights*, 90/1 UN BULL. HUM. RTS. 84, 85 (1991); Peter R. Baehr, *Amnesty International and Its Self-Imposed Limited Mandate*, 12 NETH. Q. HUM. RTS. 5 (1994).

9. Kenneth Roth, executive director of HRW, underscored the savior metaphor when he powerfully defended the human rights movement against attacks that it had failed to move the international community to stop the 1994 mass killings in Rwanda. He dismissed those attacks as misguided, arguing that they amounted to a call to close "the fire brigade because a building burned down, even if it was a big building." Kenneth Roth, Letter to the Editor, *Human Rights Abuses in Rwanda*, TIMES LITERARY SUPP., March 14, 1997, at 15. Turning to various countries in Africa as examples, he pointed to the gratitude of Africans "all of whom benefitted from the human-rights movement to throw off dictatorial regimes and inaugurate political freedom." He argued, further, that in "other countries, like Nigeria, Kenya, Liberia, Zambia, and Zaire [now Democratic Republic of the Congo], the human rights movement has helped numerous Africans avoid arbitrary detention, violent abuse and other violations."

10. Yet I contend here that the participation of non-European states and societies in the enforcement of human rights cannot in itself universalize those rights. It is important to note that the terms "European" or "Eurocentric" are used descriptively and do not necessarily connote evil or undesirability. They do, however, point to notions of cultural specificity and historical exclusivity. The simple point is that Eurocentric norms and cultures, such as human rights, have either been imposed on, or assimilated by, non-European societies. Thus the current human rights discourse is an important currency of cross-cultural exchange, domination, and valuation.

11. Margaret E. Beck and Kathryn Sikkink, ACTIVISTS BEYOND BORDERS, ADVOCACY NETWORKS IN INTERNATIONAL POLITICS (Ithaca, N.Y.: Cornell University Press, 1998), pp. 39–58.

12. *See, e.g.*, Josiah Mwangi Kariuki, "MAU MAU" DETAINEE: THE ACCOUNT BY A KENYAN AFRICAN OF HIS EXPERIENCES IN DETENTION CAMPS, 1953–1960 (Baltimore: Penguin, 1964); Kwame Nkrumah, THE AUTOBIOGRAPHY OF KWAME NKRUMAH (London: Panaf, 1973); Mohandas K. Gandhi, AN AUTOBIOGRAPHY: THE STORY OF MY EXPERIENCES WITH TRUTH (Boston: Beacon Press, 1962).

13. I use the term "cross-contamination" facetiously here to refer to the idea of cross-fertilization. Many Western human rights actors see the process of multiculturalization in human rights as contaminating as opposed to cross-fertilizing in an enriching way. For example, Louis Henkin has accused those who advocate cultural pluralism or diversity of seeking to make human rights vague and ambiguous. Louis Henkin, THE AGE OF RIGHTS (Ithaca, N.Y.: Cornell University Press, 1990), p. x. In other words, he casts cross-fertilization as a negative process, one that is contaminating and harmful to the clarity of human rights.

14. Slater argues that the "Western will to expand was rooted in the desire to colonize, civilize and possess the non-Western society; to convert what was different and enframed as inferior and backward into a subordinated same." Slater, *supra* note 2, at 101.

15. Since the rhetoric is flawed, those who create and promote it wonder

whether it will resonate "out there" in the Third World. The use of the SVS rhetoric is in itself insulting and unjust because it draws from supremacist First World/Third World hierarchies and the attendant domination and subordination which are essential for those constructions.

16. For example, Serbs sympathized with former Yugoslav President Slobodan Milosevic possibly because they felt he had been stigmatized by the West. Milosevic played to locals' fears of the West and used the arrogance of the discourse to blunt the fact that he is an indicted war criminal. *See, e.g.*, Niles Lathem, *Defiant Milosevic: Hell, No, I Won't Go!*, N.Y. POST, August 7, 1999, at 10.

17. UN CHARTER pmbl.

18. The term "Third World" here refers to a geographic, political, historical, developmental, and racial paradigm. It is a term that is commonly used to refer to non-European, largely nonindustrial, capital-importing countries, most of which were colonial possessions of European powers. As a political force, the Third World traces its origins to the Bandung Conference of 1955 in which the first independent African and Asian states sought to launch a political movement to counter Western hegemony over global affairs. *See* Robert Mortimer, THE THIRD WORLD COALITION IN INTERNATIONAL POLITICS (Boulder, Colo.: Westview Press, 1984). Many Third World states formed the Group of 77, a forum that called for the New International Economic Order (NIEO). *See* Mohamed Bedjaoui, TOWARDS A NEW INTERNATIONAL ECONOMIC ORDER (New York: Holmes and Meier, 1979).

19. Diane Otto, *Subalternity and International Law: The Problems of Global Community and the Incommensurability of Difference*, 5 SOC. & LEGAL STUD. 337, 339–40 (1996).

20. But genuine reconstructionists must not be mistaken with cynical cultural manipulators who will stop at nothing to justify repressive rule and inhuman practices in the name of culture. Yash Ghai powerfully exposed the distortions by several states of Asian conceptions of community, religion, and culture to justify the use of coercive state apparatuses to crush dissent, protect particular models of economic development, and retain political power within the hands of a narrow, largely unaccountable political and bureaucratic elite. Yash Ghai, *Human Rights and Governance: The Asia Debate*, 15 AUSTL. Y.B. INT'L L. 1 (1994).

Such cultural demagoguery is clearly as unacceptable as is the insistence by some Western academics and leaders of the human rights movement that the non-West has nothing to contribute to the human rights corpus and should accept the human rights corpus as a gift of civilization from the West. *See* Aryeh Neier, *Asia's Unacceptable Standard*, 92 FOREIGN POL'Y 42 (1993). Henkin has written that the United States viewed human rights "as designed to improve the condition of human rights in countries other the United States (and a very few like-minded liberal states)." Henkin, *supra* note 13, at 74. Elsewhere, Henkin has charged advocates of multiculturalism and ideological diversity in the reconstruction of human rights with desiring a vague, broad, ambiguous, and general text of human rights, one that would be easily manipulated by regimes and cultures bent on violating human rights.

21. For examples of critical legal scholarship, *see generally* Karl E. Klare, *The Public/Private Distinction in Labor Law*, 130 U. PA. L. REV. 1358 (1982); Mark V. Tushnet, *An Essay on Rights*, 62 TEX. L. REV. 1363 (1984).

22. For examples of feminist critiques of the law, *see generally* Frances Olsen,

Statutory Rape: A Feminist Critique of Rights Analysis, 63 TEX. L. REV. 387 (1984); Elizabeth M. Schneider, *The Dialectic of Rights and Politics: Perspectives from the Women's Movement,* 61 N.Y.U. L. REV. 589 (1986).

23. For examples of critical race theory scholarship, *see generally* Kimberle Crenshaw, CRITICAL RACE THEORY: THE KEY WRITINGS THAT FORMED THE MOVEMENT (New York: New Press, 1995); Kimberle Williams Crenshaw, *Race, Reform and Retrenchment: Transformation and Legitimation in Anti-Discrimination Law,* 101 HARV. L. REV. 1331 (1988). For critical race feminism, an offshoot of critical race theory, *see generally* Adrien Katherine Wing, CRITICAL RACE FEMINISM: A READER (New York: New York University Press, 1997); Leila Hilal, *What Is Critical Race Feminism?,* 4 BUFF. HUM. RTS. L. REV. 367 (1997) (reviewing CRITICAL RACE FEMINISM: A READER).

24. For other probing critiques of the human rights movement, *see* Raimundo Panikkar, *Is the Notion of Human Rights a Western Concept?,* 120 DIOGENES 75 (1982); Bilahari Kausikan, *Asia's Different Standard,* 92 FOREIGN POL'Y 24 (1993); Josiah A. M. Cobbah, *African Values and the Human Rights Debate: An African Perspective,* 9 HUM. RTS. Q. 309 (1987).

25. UN CHARTER art. 55(c). *See also* UN CHARTER *supra* note 17, at pmbl.

26. The UDHR argues in its preamble that it is the "disregard and contempt for human rights that have resulted in barbarous acts" and that human dignity, freedom, justice, and peace can only be achieved if human rights are respected. *See* UDHR, *supra* note 1, pmbl.

27. As noted by Mary Ann Glendon, the UDHR "is already showing signs of having achieved the status of holy writ within the human rights movement." Mary Ann Glendon, *Knowing the Universal Declaration of Human Rights,* 73 NOTRE DAME L. REV. 1153, 1153 (1998). Glendon also notes that "Cults have formed around selected provisions [of the UDHR]."

28. Henkin has called this the age of rights and asserted, unequivocally, that "Human rights is the idea of our time, the only political-moral idea that has received universal acceptance." Henkin, *supra* note 13, at ix). Philip Alston has argued that the naming of a claim "as a human right elevates it above the rank and file of competing societal goals" and provides it with "an aura of timelessness, absoluteness and universal validity." Philip Alston, *Making Space for New Human Rights: The Case of the Right to Development,* 1 HARV. HUM. RTS. Y.B. 3, 3 (1988). *See also* Thomas M. Franck, *The Emerging Right to Democratic Governance,* 86 AM. J. INT'L L. 46 (1992).

29. As noted by Thomas Buergenthal, the rise and development of the human rights movement "can be attributed to the monstrous violations of human rights of the Hitler era and to the belief that these violations and possibly the war itself might have been prevented had an effective international system for the protection of human rights existed." Thomas Buergenthal, INTERNATIONAL HUMAN RIGHTS IN A NUTSHELL (St. Paul, Minn.: West Publishing Company, 1988), p. 21.

30. Agreement for the Prosecution and Punishment of the Major War Criminals of the European Axis, August 8, 1945, 59 Stat. 1544 [hereinafter London Agreement].

31. The International Military Tribunal at Nuremberg was established in 1945 by the Agreement for the Prosecution and Punishment of Major War Criminals of the European Axis, resulting from conferences held among the United States, Britain, France, and the Soviet Union to determine what policies the victorious

Allies should pursue against the defeated Germans, Italians, and their surrogates. *Id.*

32. Howard B. Tolley, Jr., THE INTERNATIONAL COMMISSION OF JURISTS: GLOBAL ADVOCATES OF HUMAN RIGHTS (Philadelphia: University of Pennsylvania Press, 1994).

33. Nuremberg has been criticized for the Allies' selective prosecution of war criminals and the inventiveness of the applicable law and has been labeled a gross demonstration of the powers of the victors over the vanquished. Kenneth Anderson, *Nuremberg Sensibility: Telford Taylor's Memoir of the Nuremberg Trials,* 7 HARV. HUM. RTS. J. 281 (1994). Also, U.S. Chief Justice Harlan Fiske Stone said the Nuremberg trials had a "false facade of legality" and were "a little too sanctimonious a fraud to meet my old-fashioned ideas." Alpheus Thomas Mason, HARLAN FISKE STONE: PILLAR OF LAW (New York: Viking Press, 1956), pp. 715–16.

34. *See* Tolley, *supra* note 32, at 25–44.

35. Dudler Bonsal, *Lawyers and the Cold War, in Cooperation with the ICJ,* Minutes of the Association of the Bar of the City of New York, May 4, 1953, quoted in Tolley, *supra* note 32, at 34.

36. Ian Martin, *The New World Order: Opportunity or Threat for Human Rights,* Edward A. Smith Lecture at the Harvard Law School Human Rights Program (April 14, 1993), available at, <www.law.harvard.edu/programs/HRP/Publication <www.law.harvard.edu/programs/HRP/Publications/martin.html> (visited September 11, 2001).

37. The European human rights system, which includes the European Commission on Human Rights and the European Court of Human Rights, is central to the European Union. The system was put in place following the atrocities of the Second World War. *See, e.g.,* Buergenthal, *supra* note 29, at 102–73; Laurence R. Helfer and Anne-Marie Slaughter, *Toward a Theory of Effective Supranational Adjudication,* 107 YALE L.J. 273 (1997).

38. Slater, *supra* note 2, at 100.

39. Basil Davidson, AFRICA IN HISTORY: THEMES AND OUTLINES (New York: Collier Books, 1991), p. xvi.

40. A description of Henry the Navigator is telling:

The heathen lands were kingdoms to be won for Christ, and the guidance of their backward races was a duty that must not be shirked. Henry shouldered this responsibility. If he had the spirit of crusader, he had that of a missionary as well. Wherever he explored, his aim was to evangelize, to civilize, and to educate the simple savages. . . . He sent out teachers and preachers to the black men of Senegal.

Elaine Sanceau, HENRY THE NAVIGATOR (New York: Hutchinson, 1945), p. 139.

41. Slater, *supra* note 2, at 100.

42. The term "Age of Europe" denotes a historical and philosophical paradigm that describes European hegemony imposed over the globe.

43. Dana G. Munro, INTERVENTION AND DOLLAR DIPLOMACY IN THE CARIBBEAN, 1900–1921 (Princeton, N.J.: Princeton University Press, 1964), p. 76. William Alford has captured well the evolution of this American sense of predestination:

The United States has a long history of endeavoring to enlighten, if not save, our foreign brethren by exporting ideas and institutions that we believe we have realized more fully. These include efforts to bring "civilization," principally in the form of Christianity, to age-old civilizations in Asia, Africa, and elsewhere; to foster "modernization," especially as manifested through economic development; and to expound a gospel of science and technology. With the ebbing of the Cold War, democracy promotion—a capacious term used to encompass efforts to nurture electoral processes, the rule of law, and civil society, all broadly defined—has become a key organizing principle of American foreign policy, if not this nation's broader interface with the world.

William P. Alford, *Exporting the "Pursuit of Happiness"*, 113 HARV. L. REV. 1677, 1678–79 (2000), reviewing Thomas Carothers, AIDING DEMOCRACY ABROAD: THE LEARNING CURVE (Washington, D.C.: Carnegie Endowment for International Peace, 1999).

44. Mohamed Bedjaoui of the International Court of Justice has written "This classic international law thus consisted of a set of rules with a geographical bias (it was a European law), a religious-ethical inspiration (it was a Christian law), an economic motivation (it was a mercantilist law) and political aims (it was an imperialist law)." Mohamed Bedjaoui, *Poverty of the International Order*, in Richard Faulk, Friedrich Kratochwil, and Saul H. Mendlovitz, eds., INTERNATIONAL LAW: A CONTEMPORARY PERSPECTIVE (Boulder, Colo.: Westview Press, 1985), pp. 153–54.

45. Otto, *supra* note 19, at 339–40.

46. *See* Jack Donnelly, *Human Rights and Western Liberalism*, in Abdullahi A. An-Na'im and Francis M. Deng, eds., HUMAN RIGHTS IN AFRICA: CROSS-CULTURAL PERSPECTIVES (Washington, D.C.: Brookings Institution Press, 1990), p. 31; Virginia Leary, *The Effect of Western Perspectives on International Human Rights* in An-Na'im and Deng, eds., *supra* note 46, p. 15.

47. Antonio Cassese, *The General Assembly: Historical Perspective 1945–1989*, in Philip Alston, ed., THE UNITED NATIONS AND HUMAN RIGHTS: A CRITICAL APPRAISAL (Oxford: Clarendon Press, 1992), pp. 31–32.

48. UDHR, *supra* note 1, pmbl. *See also* Makau Mutua, *A Noble Cause Wrapped in Arrogance*, BOSTON SUNDAY GLOBE, April 29, 2001, p. D8.

49. *See* Franck, *supra* note 28, at 47; *see also* Gregory H. Fox, *The Right to Political Participation in International Law*, 17 YALE J. INT'L L. 539 (1992).

50. Franck, *supra note 28*, at 49.

51. In a substantial body of work, Glendon takes the view that the construction of the UDHR was more "universal" than its critics admit. *See* Mary Ann Glendon, A WORLD MADE NEW: ELEANOR ROOSEVELT AND THE UNIVERSAL DECLARATION OF HUMAN RIGHTS (New York: Random House, 2001). Other writers have tended to emphasize the role of "small" states in the writing of the UDHR. *See* Susan Waltz, *Universalizing Human Rights: The Role of Small States in the Construction of the Universal Declaration of Human Rights*, 23 HUM. RTS. Q. 44 (2001). But Virginia Leary, another prominent Western academic, has noted that:

Western influence, dominant in the origin of the development of international human rights norms, is now only one of a number of cultural influences on the development of international human rights standards. Its contribution to the development of human rights has been great, but it has not been unique, and other cultures have made and are making significant contributions to our collective conception of human dignity.

Leary, *supra* note 46, at 30.

52. *See* Amnesty International, UNITED STATES OF AMERICA: RACE, RIGHTS, AND POLICE BRUTALITY (London: Amnesty International, 1999); Human Rights Watch

and American Civil Liberties Union, HUMAN RIGHTS VIOLATIONS IN THE UNITED STATES (New York: Human Rights Watch and American Civil Liberties Union, 1993).

53. For example, Human Rights Watch recently declined to copublish a study on trade and human rights, although it had jointly commissioned it with the Montreal-based International Centre for Human Rights and Democratic Development (ICHRDD). *See* Makau Mutua and Robert Howse, PROTECTING HUMAN RIGHTS IN A GLOBAL ECONOMY: CHALLENGES FOR THE WORLD TRADE ORGANIZATION (Montreal: ICHRDD, 2000).

54. For a history of South Africa, and in particular the struggle against apartheid, *see* Nelson Mandela, LONG WALK TO FREEDOM: THE AUTOBIOGRAPHY OF NELSON MANDELA (Boston: Little, Brown, 1994).

55. For a discussion of the abolitionist impulse in human rights, *see* Makau wa Mutua, *The Politics of Human Rights: Beyond the Abolitionist Paradigm in Africa*, 17 MICH. J. INT'L L. 591 (1996), reviewing Claude E. Welch, PROTECTING HUMAN RIGHTS IN AFRICA: ROLES AND STRATEGIES OF NONGOVERNMENTAL ORGANIZATIONS (Philadelphia: University of Pennsylvania Press, 1995).

56. For example, the Legal Resources Centre (LRC), one of the best known anti-apartheid human rights organizations, was established by white lawyers in 1979 as a public interest law firm. Among the more famous white liberals to lead the LRC was Arthur Chaskalson, who in 1994 became the first president of the Constitutional Court, South Africa's highest court. For a brief history of the LRC, *see* Julius L. Chambers et al., eds., PUBLIC INTEREST LAW AROUND THE WORLD (New York: Columbia Human Rights Law Review, 1992), pp. 159–63.

57. Among the more famous whites to participate in South Africa's liberation struggle were the late Joe Slovo, the leader of the South African Communist Party, a key ally of the African National Congress, and Albie Sachs, the renowned jurist-activist who in 1994 became a justice of South Africa's Constitutional Court. Mandela recalled with fondness the lifelong political relationships he formed with whites, including Slovo, whom he had met while a law student at the University of the Witwatersrand. Mandela, *supra* note 54, at 84.

58. For example, in 1961, Jack Greenberg, a white man, was hand-picked by Thurgood Marshall to succeed him as the director-counsel of the NAACP Legal Defense and Educational Fund. Jack Greenberg, CRUSADERS IN THE COURTS: HOW A DEDICATED BAND OF LAWYERS FOUGHT FOR THE CIVIL RIGHTS REVOLUTION (New York: Basic Books, 1994), pp. 294–95. He was also instrumental in the establishment of the Legal Resources Centre in South Africa. Chambers, ed., PUBLIC INTEREST LAW AROUND THE WORLD, *supra* note 56, at 159.

59. The Iranian Constitution provides for the supremacy of the Islamic Consultative Assembly and the Guardian Council over many areas including legislation and the adoption of international agreements. IRAN CONST. arts. 71–99.

60. Elvin Hatch, CULTURE AND MORALITY: THE RELATIVITY OF VALUES IN ANTHROPOLOGY (New York: Columbia University Press, 1983), p. 8.

61. Burns H. Weston, *Human Rights*, NEW ENCYCLOPEDIA BRITANNICA , 20: 656 (15th ed., Chicago: University of Chicago Press, 1992); Henry J. Steiner, *Political Participation as a Human Right*, 1 HARV. HUM. RTS. Y.B. 77 (1988); Henkin, *supra* note 13, at x.

62. Steiner has stated that "observers from different regions and cultures can

agree that the human rights movement, with respect to its language of rights and the civil and political rights that it declares, stems primarily from the liberal tradition of Western thought." Henry J. Steiner and Philip Alston, INTERNATIONAL HUMAN RIGHTS IN CONTEXT: LAW, POLITICS, MORALS (New York: Oxford University Press, 1996), p. 187.

63. Convention on the Elimination of All Forms of Discrimination Against Women, 1249 UNTS 14 at pt. 1, art 5(a) (entered into force September 3, 1981).

64. *Id.*

65. Women's Rights Project, BRAZIL: CRIMINAL INJUSTICE: VIOLENCE AGAINST WOMEN IN BRAZIL (New York: Human Rights Watch/Women's Right's Project, 1991).

66. Women's Rights Project, RUSSIA—TOO LITTLE, TOO LATE: STATE RESPONSE TO VIOLENCE AGAINST WOMEN (New York: Human Rights Watch/Women's Rights Project, 1997); INDONESIA: THE DAMAGING DEBATE ON RAPES OF ETHNIC CHINESE WOMEN (New York: Human Rights Watch/Women's Rights Project, 1998); SECOND CLASS CITIZENS: DISCRIMINATION AGAINST WOMEN UNDER BOTSWANA'S CITIZENSHIP ACT (New York: Human Rights Watch/Women's Rights Project, 1994); RAPE IN HAITI: A WEAPON OF TERROR (New York: Human Rights Watch/Women's Rights Project, 1994); A MATTER OF POWER: STATE CONTROL OF WOMEN'S VIRGINITY IN TURKEY (New York: Human Rights Watch/Women's Rights Project, 1994). In an encouraging move, however, HRW also produced a report on the violations of women's human rights in Michigan state prisons. *See* Women's Rights Project, UNITED STATES—NOWHERE TO HIDE: RETALIATION AGAINST WOMEN IN MICHIGAN STATE PRISONS (New York: Human Rights Watch/Women's Rights Project, 1998).

67. UN ESCOR, 50th Sess., agenda item 11(a), at para. 67, UN Doc. E/CN.4/1995/42 (1994).

68. The following provisions are illustrative: arts. 21 and 22 on the rights to assembly, art. 25 on political participation, art. 19 on expression, and art. 18 on free speech (ICCPR). *See also* art. 21 on political participation, art. 20 on assembly, and art. 19 on expression (UDHR). UDHR, *supra* note 1.

69. Henry J. Steiner, *The Youth of Rights*, HARV. L. REV. 917, 930–31 (1991).

70. *See* Carothers, *supra* note 43; Stephen B. Cohen, *Conditioning U.S. Security Assistance on Human Rights Practices*, 76 AM. J. INT'L L. 246 (1982).

71. Henkin notes the extensive U.S. efforts in human rights abroad, a phenomenon attributable to conceptions of individual rights that "dominate [America's] constitutional jurisprudence, and are the pride of its people, their banner to the world." Henkin, *supra* note 13, at 65.

72. *Contemporary Forms of Slavery: Working Paper on the Situation of Systematic Rape, Sexual Slavery and Slavery-like Practices During Wartime, Including Internal Armed Conflict, Submitted by Ms. Linda Chavez in Accordance with Subcommission Decision 1994/109*, UN ESCOR, 47th Sess., agenda item 16, at 2–3, UN Doc. E/CN.4/Sub.2/1995/38 (1995). *See also* M. Cherif Bassiouni and Marcia McCormick, SEXUAL VIOLENCE: AN INVISIBLE WEAPON OF WAR IN THE FORMER YUGOSLAVIA (Chicago: International Human Rights Institute, 1996).

73. Todd A. Salzman, *Rape Camps as a Means of Ethnic Cleansing: Religious, Cultural and Ethnic Responses to Rape Victims in the Former Yugoslavia*, 20 HUM. RTS. Q. 348, 349–52 (1998).

74. For a helpful overview of the investigative process of INGOs, *see* Diane F.

Orentlicher, *Bearing Witness: The Art and Science of Human Rights Fact-Finding*, 3 HARV. HUM. RTS. J. 83 (1990).

75. Some of the major INGOs are AI, headquartered in London; Human Rights Watch (HRW), based in New York City; International Commission of Jurists (ICJ), based in Geneva; the Lawyers Committee for Human Rights (LCHR), based in New York City; and the International Human Rights Law Group (IHRLG), based in Washington, D.C. None of the major INGOs have located their headquarters in the Third World. *See, e.g.*, Mutua, *supra* note 55, at 610–12; Issa G. Shivji, THE CONCEPT OF HUMAN RIGHTS IN AFRICA (London: Codesria Book Series, 1989), pp. 34–35.

76. Steiner, DIVERSE PARTNERS, *supra* note 5, at 22–25.

77. *See, e.g.*, Africa Watch, KENYA: TAKING LIBERTIES (New York: Africa Watch, 1991), pp. 362–82 (calling on the British and American governments to push Kenya proactively toward democracy and more respect for human rights); Alice Jay, PERSECUTION BY PROXY: THE CIVIL PATROLS IN GUATEMALA (Washington D.C.: Robert F. Kennedy Memorial Center for Human Rights, 1993), pp. 69–71 (urging the United States to press Guatemala to abolish and disarm abusive civil patrols).

78. Of the three forms of female circumcision practiced, two are often described in particularly graphic and cruel language. The mildest form is "circumcision proper" in which only the clitoral prepuce is removed. Excision involves the amputation of the clitoris and all or part of the labia minora. Infibulation, also known as Pharaonic circumcision, involves the amputation of the clitoris, the whole of the labia minora, and at least the anterior two-thirds and often the whole of the medial part of the labia majora. The two sides of the vulva are then stitched together with silk, catgut, or thorns, and a tiny sliver of wood or a reed is inserted to preserve an opening for urine and menstrual blood. The girl's legs are usually bound together from ankle to knee until the wound has healed, which may take anything up to forty days. World Health Organization, *A Traditional Practice That Threatens Health—Female Circumcision*, 40 WORLD HEALTH CHRON. 31–32 (1986).

79. Images of African savagery, for example, are standard fare in the American press. Reporting on the killings of eight Western tourists in Uganda in March 1999, a journalist characterized the suspected killers as "100 Rwandan Hutus, screaming and brandishing machetes and guns," and expressed surprise that there were not more fatalities "given the killers' barbarism." Romesh Ratnesar, *In Uganda, Vacation Dreams Turn to Nightmares*, TIME, March 15, 1999, 64.

80. Philip Gourevitch, WE WISH TO INFORM YOU THAT TOMORROW WE WILL BE KILLED WITH OUR FAMILIES (New York: Farrar, Straus, and Giroux, 1998), p. 3 (emphasis added).

81. *See generally* Lewis and Gunning, *supra* note 5; Jomo Kenyatta, FACING MOUNT KENYA: THE TRIBAL LIFE OF THE GIKUYU (London: Secker and Warburg, 1953), pp. 130–54.

82. AAWORD, *A Statement on Genital Mutilation*, in Miranda Davies, ed., THIRD WORLD—SECOND SEX: WOMEN'S STRUGGLES AND NATIONAL LIBERATION (London: Zed Books, 1983), pp. 217–18.

83. *Id.* at 218 (emphasis added). As further expressed by Lewis:

A primary concern in African feminist texts is the tendency among Western human rights activists to essentialize the motivations for practicing FGS [Female Genital Surgery] as rooted in either superstition or in the passive acceptance of patriarchal domination. In rejecting these characterizations, African feminists seek to recapture and control the representation of their own cultural heritage.

Lewis, *supra* note 7, at 31.

84. UN CHARTER pmbl.

85. Henry Shue, BASIC RIGHTS: SUBSISTENCE, AFFLUENCE AND U.S. POLICY (Princeton, N.J.: Princeton University Press, 1996), p. 52.

86. Images of the victim painted by a recent AI report on refugees are standard fare. In addition to the gloomy descriptions in the report, accompanying pictures show Rwandese refugees in the wild with their worldly belongings on their heads, Afghan and Sri Lankan "boat people" arriving in Denmark, and Sudanese youths caught between government and rebel forces fleeing on a raft. The images of despair and defeat are overwhelming. Amnesty International, AMNESTY INTERNATIONAL REPORT 1997 (London: Amnesty International, 1997), pp. 3, 11, 17.

87. For a recent survey of human rights victims, *see* Human Rights Watch, HUMAN RIGHTS WATCH WORLD REPORT 2000 (New York: Human Rights Watch, 2000).

88. Andrew Whitley, ed., THE ANFAL CAMPAIGN IN IRAQI KURDISTAN: THE DESTRUCTION OF KOREME (New York: Middle East Watch, 1993), pp. 46–47.

89. *See* AMNESTY INTERNATIONAL REPORT 1997, *supra* note 86.

90. *See* Salzman, *supra* note 73, for descriptions of the female gender as the victim.

91. Amnesty International, RAPE AND SEXUAL ABUSE: TORTURE AND ILL TREATMENT OF WOMEN IN DETENTION (London: Amnesty International, 1992), p. 4.

92. A 2000 poll of Kosovo Albanians found that 52 percent thought that the 1999 American-led NATO intervention, ostensibly to create an autonomous Kosovo, was the most important event for Kosovo in the second half of the twentieth century. *NATO Intervention Was the Biggest Event, Say Kosovar Albanians*, DEUTSCHE PRESSE-AGENTUR, January 7, 2000, available in LEXIS, News Library, CURNWS File.

93. Incidentally, Bernstein claimed the mantle of savior without equivocation: "When you meet [a victim] . . . you really personalize it. It is not just some person being beat up. You think, *She could be my daughter.*" Meryl Gordon, *Freedom Fighter*, N.Y. TIMES, November 16, 1998, p. 42.

94. Other factors may, of course, enter the decision-making calculus and drive public opinion and determine whether Western states will intervene. It is unlikely, for example, that the West would rush to intervene in a domestic conflict involving a nuclear power such as Russia. For a discussion of the calculus of intervention, *see* Editorial, *The Intervention Debate*, THE DETROIT NEWS, January 10, 2000, p. A8 (discussing the rationale for intervention in Kosovo and Rwanda).

95. For a discussion of the "good" versus the "bad" Serb, *see* Thomas Goltz, *An Anti-Ethnic Diatribe*, 22 WASH. Q. 113, 118–21 (1999).

96. *Chechnya Reveals Western Hypocrisy*, TORONTO SUN, November 25, 1999, at 15.

97. This perception is often grounded in reality. Even in the United States the typical victim of human rights violations is more likely to be African American or Hispanic. A rare report by human rights groups on human rights violations in the United States focused on the death penalty, immigrants' rights, race discrimination, prison conditions, police brutality, and language rights—all areas in which the victims predominantly are African American, Hispanic, or another nonwhite minority, such as Asian Americans. Only three areas—religious liberty, freedom of

expression, and sex discrimination—did not focus on persons of color. Human Rights Watch and American Civil Liberties Union, *supra* note 52; Amnesty International, UNITED STATES OF AMERICA: RACE, RIGHTS AND POLICE BRUTALITY, *supra* note 52.

98. The intense media coverage of the tragic cases of Abner Louima and Amadou Diallo, two black immigrants in New York City who were subjects of police violence, has dramatically reinforced the perception of nonwhites as "victims" to the American public. For examples of the media coverage of these cases, see Helen Peterson, *600 Respond to 2nd Louima Jury Trial Call*, N.Y. DAILY NEWS, January 4, 2000, at 12; Alan Feuer, *Jury Selection Begins for Trial in Louima Case*, N.Y. TIMES, January 4, 2000, at B3; Kevin Flynn, *Officers in Diallo Trial Want Experts to Testify*, N.Y. TIMES, January 8, 2000, at B5; Kathleen Kenna, *New York Police Dogged by Cruelty Charges*, TORONTO STAR, January 3, 2000; Leonard Levitt, *Newspapers: Keep Diallo Court Open*, NEWSDAY, January 6, 2000, at A37. For a detailed report on the relationship between law enforcement agencies, the criminal justice system, and the victimization of persons of color in the United States, *see* Amnesty International, AMNESTY INTERNATIONAL REPORT 1999 (London: Amnesty International, 1999).

99. Susan D. Moeller, COMPASSION FATIGUE: HOW THE MEDIA SELL DISEASE, FAMINE, WAR AND DEATH (New York: Routledge, 1999).

100. Denys W. T. Shropshire, THE CHURCH AND THE PRIMITIVE PEOPLES (London: SPCK, 1938), p. xix. Or consider, for example, the repugnant views of Lord Asquith, an arbitrator in the dispute between the Sheikh of Abu Dhabi and Petroleum Development Ltd. In his view, Qur'anic law was primitive at best:

no such law can reasonably be said to exist. The Sheikh administers a purely discretionary justice with the assistance of the Koran; and it would be fanciful to suggest that in this very primitive region there is any settled body of legal principles applicable to the construction of modern commercial instruments.

Petroleum Dev. Ltd. v. Sheikh of Abu Dhabi, 18 I.L.R. 144, 149 (1951).

101. International Labour Organization, CONDITIONS OF LIFE AND WORK OF INDIGENOUS POPULATIONS OF LATIN AMERICAN COUNTRIES, Fourth Conference of American States Members of the International Labour Organization, Report II (Geneva: International Labour Organization, 1949).

102. *See* Ruth Gordon, *Growing Constitutions*, 1 U. PA. J. CONST. L. 528 (1999).

103. *See* Christopher Weeramantry and Nathaniel Berman, *The Grotious Lecture Series*, 14 AM. U. INT'L L. REV. 1515 (1999).

104. *See* Antony Anghie, *Francisco de Vitoria and the Colonial Origins of International Law*, 5 SOC. AND LEGAL STUD. 321 (1996). For example, not only does the world use the Gregorian calendar, time is universally calibrated from Greenwich Mean Time. It is the "centrality" of England in the social and political construction of the world that gave rise to designations of places as the "Middle East," "Far East," "remote," and so on.

105. Makau Mutua, *Critical Race Theory and International Law: The View of an Insider-Outsider*, 45 VILL. L. REV. 841 (2000) (Keynote Address); Makau Mutua, *What Is Twail?* PROCEEDINGS OF THE 94TH ANNUAL MEETING OF THE AMERICAN SOCIETY OF INTERNATIONAL LAW (Washington, D.C.: American Society of International Law,

2000), p. 31. *See also* James Thuo Gathii, *International Law and Eurocentricity*, 9 EUR. J. INT'L L. 154 (1998); Nathaniel Berman, *Beyond Colonialism and Nationalism? Ethiopia, Czechoslovakia, and "Peaceful Change"*, 65 NORDIC J. INT'L L. 421 (1996).

106. S. Prakash Sinha, LEGAL POLYCENTRICITY AND INTERNATIONAL LAW (Durham, N.C.: Carolina Academic Press, 1996), p. 15.

107. For a very insightful and groundbreaking discussion of the ethnocentricity of international law, *see* Antony Anghie, *Finding the Peripheries: Sovereignty and Colonialism in Nineteenth-Century International Law*, 40 HARV. INT'L L.J. 1 (1999). Anghie writes that:

The association between international law and universality is so ingrained that pointing to this connection appears tautological. And yet, the universality of international law is a relatively recent development. It was not until the end of the nineteenth century that a set of doctrines was established as applicable to all states, whether these were in Asia, Africa, or Europe. . . . The universalization of international law was principally a consequence of the imperial expansion that took place towards the end of the "long nineteenth century." The conquest of non-European peoples for economic and political advantage was the most prominent feature of this period, which was termed by one eminent historian, Eric Hobsbawm, as the "Age of Empire."

Id. at 1–2. *See also* Christopher Weeramantry, NAURU: ENVIRONMENTAL DAMAGE UNDER INTERNATIONAL TRUSTEESHIP (New York: Oxford University Press, 1992).

108. Fox, *supra* note 49, at 112.

109. Thomas Merton, CONJECTURES OF A GUILTY BYSTANDER (Garden City, N.Y.: Doubleday, 1966), p. 87.

110. *See, e.g.*, Chris Tennant, *Indigenous Peoples, International Institutions, and the International Legal Literature from 1945–1993*, 16 HUM. RTS. Q. 1 (1994), reviewing literature on indigenous peoples and concluding, among other things, that indigenous peoples have been represented as the "other" that needs saving by the West.

111. Anghie, *supra* note 107, at 7.

112. John Norton Pomeroy, LECTURES ON INTERNATIONAL LAW IN TIME OF PEACE, ed. Theodore Salisbury Woolsey (1886), p. 96. Similarly, Edward Said has identified this European predestination in the construction of Orientalism as the "corporate institution of dealing with the Orient—dealing with it by making statements about it, authorizing views of it, describing it, by teaching it, settling it, ruling over it: in short, Orientalism as a Western style for dominating, restructuring, and having authority over the Orient." Edward Said, ORIENTALISM (New York: Pantheon Books, 1978), p. 3.

113. Frederick Lugard, *Treaty-Making in Africa*, 2 GEOGRAPHICAL J. 53 (1983).

114. Alfred Henry Barrow, FIFTY YEARS IN WESTERN AFRICA (London, 1900; reprint New York: Negro Universities Press, 1969), p. 29.

115. Anghie, *supra* note 107, at 7.

116. Henkin, *supra* note 13, at ix.

117. *Id.* at x.

118. *Cf.* arts. 18 and 19, UDHR, *supra* note 1; arts. 18 and 19, ICCPR, *supra* note 1.

119. It is useful here to refer to Steiner's discussion of the connections among

liberalism, constitutionalism, and human rights. He notes that all three concepts are linked in that human rights, as it is known today, would not be possible without liberal thought and the notion of constitutionalism. *See* Steiner and Alston, *supra* note 62, at 187–92, 710–12.

120. In 1993, the United Nations established the Office of the High Commissioner for Human Rights, and mandated the High Commissioner for Human Rights to be the UN's "official with principal responsibility for United Nations human rights activities under the direction and authority of the Secretary-General," in effect a UN human rights czar. G.A. Res. 141 UN GAOR, 48th Sess., Supp. No. 49, agenda item 114(b), at para. 4, UN Doc. A/RES/48/141 (1994).

121. Steiner and Alston, *supra* note 62, at 362–63.

122. Philip Alston, *Appraising the United Nations Human Rights Regime*, in THE UNITED NATIONS AND HUMAN RIGHTS: A CRITICAL APPRAISAL, *supra* note 47, at 1.

123. *See* letter dated 99/12/15 from the Secretary-General, addressed to the President of the Security Council, UN Doc. S/1999/1257 (1999). *See generally* United Nations, THE UNITED NATIONS AND RWANDA: 1993–1996 (New York: United Nations, 1996); Peter Rosenblum, *Dodging the Challenge*, 10 HARV. HUM. RTS. J. 313 (1997), reviewing THE UNITED NATIONS AND RWANDA: 1993–1996.

124. In 1993, the UN Security Council established on an ad hoc basis the International Tribunal for the Prosecution of Persons Responsible for Serious Violations of International Humanitarian Law in the Territory of the Former Yugoslavia Since 1991. *See* S.C. Res. 808, UN SCOR, 3175th mtg. UN Doc. S/Res/808 (1993).

125. In 1994, the UN Security Council established the International Tribunal for the Prosecution of Persons Responsible for Genocide and Other Such Violations of International Humanitarian Law Committed in the Territory of Rwanda and Rwanda Citizens Responsible for Genocide and Other Such Violations Committed in the Territory of Neighboring States, Between January 1, 1994 and December 31, 1994. *See Report of the Secretary-General Pursuant to Paragraph 5 of the Security Council Resolution 955* (1994), UN Security Council, UN Doc. S/1995/134 (1995).

126. *Rome Statute of the International Criminal Court,* UN Diplomatic Conference of Plenipotentiaries on the Establishment of an International Criminal Court, UN Doc. A/Conf/183/9 (1998).

127. Benjamin B. Ferencz, Introduction to Virginia Morris and Michael P. Scharf, AN INSIDER'S GUIDE TO THE INTERNATIONAL CRIMINAL TRIBUNAL FOR THE FORMER YUGOSLAVIA (Ardsley, N.Y.: Transnational Publishers,1994) p. xxi. *See also* Makau Mutua, *Never Again: Questioning the Yugoslav and Rwanda Tribunals*, 11 TEMPLE INT'L AND COMP. L.J. 167 (1997).

128. Human Rights Watch, HUMAN RIGHTS WATCH WORLD REPORT 1995 (New York: Human Rights Watch, 1994), p. xiv.

129. The World Bank has started to consider the linkages between human rights, governance, and economic performance. *See generally* Caroline M. Robb, CAN THE POOR INFLUENCE POLICY? (Washington, D.C.: World Bank, 1998); David Gillies, *Human Rights, Democracy, and Good Governance: Stretching the World Bank's Policy Frontiers*, in Jo Marie Griesberger and Bernhard G. Gunter, eds., THE WORLD BANK: LENDING ON A GLOBAL SCALE (London: Pluto Press: 1996), p. 101; Lawyers Committee for Human Rights, THE WORLD BANK: GOVERNANCE AND HUMAN RIGHTS

(New York: Lawyers Committee, 1993).

130. The reports are called COUNTRY REPORTS ON HUMAN RIGHTS PRACTICES and catalogue violations of civil and political rights.

131. Myers, *supra* note 6, at A1.

132. Babington, *supra* note 7, at 21.

133. Although the Statute of the Council of Europe did not do so when only Western European states were members, it now requires that all Central and Eastern European states, namely the former Communist states, ratify the European Convention on Human Rights as a condition for membership in the Council of Europe. The Statute of the Council of Europe provides that "Every member of the Council of Europe must accept the principles of the rule of law and the enjoyment by all persons within its jurisdiction of human rights and fundamental freedoms." Statute of the Council of Europe, May 5, 1949, art. 3, 87 UNTS 103, 106. *See also* European Convention for the Protection of Human Rights and Fundamental Freedoms, November 4, 1950, 213 UNTS. 221; Buergenthal, *supra* note 29, at 102–3.

134. Turkey, which historically was referred to as the "sick man of Europe," is now a candidate to join the European Union, after centuries of fruitless attempts to become a full member of Europe. *See Looking West Europe, the United States and Turkey Have Much to Gain from Turkey's Joining the European Union,* FORT WORTH STAR-TELEGRAM, December 14, 1999, at 10, *available at* LEXIS, News Library, CURNWS File; *Turkey Invited to Join EU, With Conditions,* NEWSDAY, December 12, 1999, at A23.

135. Thomas Carothers, *Democracy and Human Rights: Policy Allies or Rivals?,* 17 WASH. Q. 106, 109 (1994).

136. Steiner, *supra* note 5, at 22.

Chapter 2. Human Rights as an Ideology

1. In the wake of World War II, member states of the United Nations adopted on December 10, 1948, the Universal Declaration of Human Rights, G.A. Res. 217 A(III), UN Doc. A/810, at 71 (1948) [hereinafter UDHR]. Although the UDHR was adopted without opposition by a vote of 48 to zero, it was the subject of eight abstentions: Byelorussia, Czechoslovakia, Poland, Soviet Union, Ukraine, Yugoslavia, Saudi Arabia, and South Africa. *See* Antonio Cassese, *The General Assembly: Historical Perspective 1945–1989,* in Philip Alston ed., THE UNITED NATIONS AND HUMAN RIGHTS: A CRITICAL APPRAISAL (Oxford: Clarendon Press, 1992), p. 31 n.22.

2. *Cf.* Karen Engle, *International Human Rights and Feminism: When Discourses Meet,* 13 MICH. J. INT'L L. 517, 518–19 (1992), exploring the different "affirmative" human rights approaches taken by advocates of international women's rights even as they have critiqued extant rights frameworks to better the lives of women; Karl E. Klare, *Legal Theory and Democratic Reconstruction: Reflections on 1989,* 25 U. BRIT. COLUM. L. REV. 69, 95 (1991), arguing that the "critique of rights" debate raises issues that should play a role in the democratic legal reconstruction of Eastern Europe.

3. I use the term "authors" more broadly here to describe all those individuals

and entities that have exerted discernible influence in the normative development and practical enforcement of human rights law. These include the United Nations and its various agencies, leading nongovernmental human rights organizations, based almost exclusively in Western Europe and North America, and academic and other conceptual writers. In the past several decades, thousands of organizations, activists, and scholars in Africa, Asia, Latin America, and everywhere in between, have adopted and adapted the message of the authors and added to its "universality." Regional human rights systems in Africa, the Americas, and Europe have also contributed to this phenomenon. These are anchored by the following instruments: the African Charter on Human and Peoples' Rights, June 27, 1981, OAU Doc. CAB/LEG/67/3/Rev.5 (1981), reprinted in 21 I.L.M. 59 (1982) [hereinafter African Charter]; the American Convention on Human Rights, November 22, 1969, 36 OASTS No. 36, at 1, OAS Off. Rec. OEA/Ser. L/V/II.23 Rev.2, reprinted in 9 I.L.M. 673 (1970); the [European] Convention for the Protection of Human Rights and Fundamental Freedoms, November 4, 1950, 213 UNTS 221 (1955); and the European Social Charter, October 18, 1961, 529 UNTS 89 (1965).

4. I use the term "official" to describe the mainstream and popular conceptions of the human rights movement, that is, as norms and codes of conduct developed and promoted by Westerners after the 1939–45 war for the purposes of limiting the abuse of individuals by their governments. This version of human rights has been largely authenticated and mediated through the United Nations. *See, e.g.,* UDHR; the International Covenant on Economic, Social, and Cultural Rights, G.A. Res. 2200 (XXI), UN GAOR, 21st Sess., Supp. No. 16, at 49, UN Doc. A/6316 (1966) (entered into force January 3, 1976) [hereinafter ICESCR]; the International Covenant on Civil and Political Rights, G.A. Res. 2200 A (XXI), UN GAOR, 21st Sess., Supp. No. 16, at 52, UN Doc. A/6316 (1966) (entered into force January 3, 1976) [hereinafter ICCPR]; the Optional Protocol to the International Covenant on Civil and Political Rights, G.A. Res. 2200 (XXI), UN GAOR, 21st Sess., Supp. No. 16, at 59, UN Doc. A/6316 (1966) (entered into force March 23, 1976) [hereinafter Optional Protocol].

5. *See* Jack Donnelly, *Human Rights and Western Liberalism,* in Abdullahi Ahmed An-Na'im and Francis M. Deng, eds., HUMAN RIGHTS IN AFRICA: CROSS-CULTURAL PERSPECTIVES (Washington, D.C.: Brookings Institution Press, 1990), p. 31 [hereinafter CROSS-CULTURAL PERSPECTIVES]; Virginia Leary, *The Effect of Western Perspectives on International Human Rights,* in CROSS-CULTURAL PERSPECTIVES, *supra,* at 15. A system that is comprised of human rights is comprised of the norms, processes, and institutions that protect human dignity, an ideal that is prevalent in all cultures of the world. Different cultures however have evolved different systems for protecting this human dignity. As has been argued elsewhere, the duty/rights dialectic was essential in the protection of human rights in precolonial Africa. *See generally* Makau wa Mutua, *The Banjul Charter and the African Cultural Fingerprint: An Evaluation of the Language of Duties,* 35 VA. J. INT'L L. 339 (1995).

6. The International Bill of Rights consists of the UDHR, the ICCPR, the ICESCR, and the Optional Protocol.

7. This core includes personal security rights, rights that implicate state power. In conventional jargon, they are negative, "hands off" rights that individuals enjoy in relation to the state.

8. For discussion of the norm of democratic governance in international law, *see* Gregory H. Fox, *The Right to Political Participation in International Law*, 17 YALE J. INT'L L. 539 (1992); Thomas M. Franck, *The Emerging Right to Democratic Governance*, 86 AM. J. INT'L. L. 46 (1992). The democratic project, which can be stated in explicitly human rights terms, builds on the concept that "core" rights can only be realized and protected in a political society organized through the liberal democratic framework.

9. There are, of course, other major voices, such as Martti Koskenniemi, whose work has focused on the deconstruction of human rights discourse and the unveiling of the interests, struggles, and politics that are hidden behind the rhetoric of international law and human rights. But when I speak of the paramount voices in the movement, I do not mean Koskenniemi or those with similar approaches; I speak primarily of the originators, the conceptualizers of the movement, those who are responsible for its construction. *See, e.g.*, Martti Koskenniemi, *The Politics of International Law*, 1 EUR. J. INT'L. L. 4 (1990).

10. Human rights law, like all other law, is a statist or structural construct in that it is the formulation of the package of obligatory relationships—rights as well as duties—from the state to the individual and vice versa. The dominant tradition of the human rights movement derives from that brand of Western liberalism which atomizes and alienates the singular individual from both the state and the society. *See* Donnelly, *Human Rights and Western Liberalism*, *supra* note 5, at 31. John Locke is the most prominent early Western thinker to condense this compact into a philosophy. *See* John Locke, TWO TREATISES OF GOVERNMENT (New York: Cambridge University Press, 1988).

11. *See* Henry J. Steiner and Philip Alston, INTERNATIONAL HUMAN RIGHTS IN CONTEXT: LAW, POLITICS, MORALS (New York: Oxford University Press, 1996), pp. 710–25.

12. Some academics, such as Louis Henkin, the distinguished Columbia Law School professor, should be perceived as both doctrinalist and constitutionalist; although he is primarily an academic, he is also one of the strongest and most prominent advocates of positive human rights law.

13. Although the term "negative" rights is for all intents and purposes meaningless when talking about categories of rights and the role of the state in their realization, it is the image that conventionally describes a very small collection of civil and political rights which are seen as the "core" of human rights. Such rights usually involve personal security and freedom from the state.

14. For bold universalist views and a rejection of the multiculturalist approach, *see* Jack Donnelly, UNIVERSAL HUMAN RIGHTS IN THEORY AND PRACTICE (Ithaca, N.Y.: Cornell University Press, 1989); Rhoda E. Howard, *Group Versus Individual Identity in the African Debate on Human Rights*, in CROSS-CULTURAL PERSPECTIVES, *supra* note 5, at 159.

15. Some of the world's notorious dictators have on occasion misappropriated tradition to justify repression. For example, Hastings Kamuzu Banda, formerly the absolute leader of Malawi, instituted "traditional courts" through which his political opponents were dispatched after sham trials. *See* Makau wa Mutua, CONFRONTING THE PAST: ACCOUNTABILITY FOR HUMAN RIGHTS VIOLATIONS IN MALAWI (Washington, D.C.: Robert F. Kennedy Memorial Center for Human Rights, 1994).

Similarly, some oppressive Asian states have cynically invoked tradition and culture to ward off human rights challenges. Human Rights Watch (HRW), the dominant American human rights NGO with an international mandate, has repeatedly attacked Asian governments for promoting an "Asian concept of human rights." HUMAN RIGHTS WATCH WORLD REPORT 1995: EVENTS OF 1994, (New York: Human Rights Watch, 1995), p. xiv [hereinafter World Report 1995]. HRW has argued that Asian governments falsely maintain that Asians "sought economic development before political liberty, valued communal obligations over individual rights, and supported national rather than universal human rights standards." *Id.* For a powerful critique of the positions espoused by Asian governments, *see* Yash Ghai, *Human Rights and Governance: The Asia Debate*, 15 AUSTL. Y.B. INT'L L. 1 (1994).

16. A good example of such a government is that of the United States, which, using human rights as the pretext, nevertheless applies two distinct policies to two countries with similar political systems. The United States has developed its economic and diplomatic relationships with the People's Republic of China (PRC) but has steadfastly rejected the normalization of relations with Cuba even though both countries are ruled by one-party communist regimes. According to Western human rights groups, human rights abuses in both countries are plentiful. *See* WORLD REPORT 1995, *supra* note 15, at 85–89, 142–49.

17. *See, e.g.*, Diane Bartz, *Amnesty International Scores Washington for Hypocrisy in Human Rights*, UPI, July 9, 1991, available in LEXIS, News Library, ARCNWS File (reporting that Amnesty International accused the United States of "selectively using human rights abuses as a foreign policy tool").

18. Samuel P. Huntington, THE THIRD WAVE: DEMOCRATIZATION IN THE LATE TWENTIETH CENTURY (Norman: University of Oklahoma Press, 1991), pp. 6, 7. Thus, a system is undemocratic where the following factors obtain: the opposition is not permitted to participate in elections, or is prohibited or curbed; opposition media, especially newspapers, are closed down or censored; or votes are tampered with or miscounted. Competition could be insufficient where an opposition experiences sustained failure over long periods to win elections.

19. Joseph A. Schumpeter, CAPITALISM, SOCIALISM, AND DEMOCRACY (New York: Harper, 1950). Schumpeter rejected the means and ends paradigm—which he called the "classical theory of democracy"—in which the "common good" was achieved through recourse to the "will of the people." *Id.* at 250–52.

20. Huntington, *supra* note 18, at 7. These rights are central features of the human rights corpus.

21. *Id.*

22. Although the Fifteenth Amendment to the U.S. Constitution prohibited the denial of the right to vote on the basis of race, many Southern states enacted laws designed to obstruct the exercise of that right by African Americans. For example, some laws imposed the ability to read or write as a precondition for registration, a requirement that excluded many African Americans. *See* Gerald Gunther, INDIVIDUAL RIGHTS IN CONSTITUTIONAL LAW (Westbury, N.Y.: Foundation Press, 1992), pp. 625–31.

23. Based on gender criteria alone, most states long regarded as democratic were in fact undemocratic until recently. Women were not allowed to vote on an equal footing with men in the following states until the early twentieth century:

Austria (1920); Belgium (1948); France (1944); Germany (1919); the United States (1920); and the United Kingdom (1928). *See* Fox, *supra* note 8, at 546.

24. *See* Robert A. Dahl, A PREFACE TO DEMOCRATIC THEORY (Chicago: University of Chicago Press, 1956), p. 25.

25. Henry J. Steiner, *Political Participation as a Human Right*, 1 HARV. HUM. RTS. Y.B. 77, 109 (1988) [hereinafter Steiner, *Political Participation*]. Steiner identifies some of these activities as "forming political parties, mobilizing interest groups, soliciting campaign funds, petitioning and demonstrating, campaigning for votes, establishing associations to monitor local government, lobbying." *Id.*

26. *Id.* at 109–10.

27. *See id.* at 110–11.

28. In terms of emphasis and political importance, the two most significant human rights documents are the UDHR and the ICCPR. Although the UDHR lists a number of economic, social, and cultural rights, its first twenty-one articles, which include the right to own property individually, read like a manifesto for a political democracy. *See* UDHR, *supra* note 1, arts. 1–21. The ICCPR is itself mainly a repetition and elaboration of the rights and processes that liberal democracies have evolved.

29. Although the formal body of human rights law includes economic, social, and cultural rights, the rhetoric and practice of the human rights movement, and especially its most vocal wing, the international nongovernmental organizations (INGOs), have centered on civil and political rights. The three human rights organizations most closely associated with the human rights movement, Amnesty International, the International Commission of Jurists, and Human Rights Watch, focus on state action against the individual. There is no major INGO in the West that addresses economic and social rights.

30. Sometimes writers and actors in human rights refer to "generations" of rights, a euphemism that variously describes ranking, acceptability, or even the order in which rights "ought" to be implemented or realized. Thus civil and political rights are regarded as "first generation" rights, while economic, social, and cultural rights are termed "second generation" rights. Group rights, such as the right to self-determination, and peoples' rights, such as the right to development, which are listed in the African Charter on Human and Peoples' Rights, are referred to as "third generation" rights. African Charter, *supra* note 3.

31. *See* Leary, *supra* note 5, at 15.

32. Steiner, *Political Participation, supra* note 25, at 79.

33. *See* Cassese, *supra* note 1, at 31–32.

34. For an exhaustive history and analysis of the drafting of the UDHR, *see* Johannes Morsink, THE UNIVERSAL DECLARATION OF HUMAN RIGHTS: ORIGINS, DRAFTING, AND INTENT (Philadelphia: University of Pennsylvania Press, 1999). But as Leary puts it, the drafting of the Universal Declaration of Human Rights was entrusted to the Human Rights Commission, which in turn gave the responsibility to people who were from "Western Europe or the Americas or were non-Europeans educated in the West." Leary, *supra* note 5, at 20.

35. UDHR, *supra* note 1, pmbl. Leary provides a very good summary of the origin and cultural orientation of the drafters of the UDHR. She lists the following persons as the key drafters: René Cassin of France, John P. Humphrey of Canada,

Eleanor Roosevelt of the United States, Hernan Santa Cruz of Chile, Charles Malik of Lebanon, Peng-Chun Chang of China, and Fernand Dehousse of Belgium. She notes that although this group appears culturally diverse—three from the Americas, two Europeans, and two Asians—it was in reality Eurocentric. All the drafters had received their education largely from Western institutions; Chang and Malik, the only non-Westerners, were educated at Clark College and Harvard University respectively. Malik, who had taught at Harvard, even urged the inclusion of the phrase that each person is "endowed by the Creator with unalienable rights." The phrase, which was lifted from the U.S. Declaration of Independence, was rejected. *See* Leary, *supra* note 5, at 20. Chang referred "with approval, to eighteenth-century Western philosophical theories as the source of the declaration." *Id.*

36. Although the ICESCR is included in the trilogy referred to as the International Bill of Rights, it is the least prominent of the three. It has been relegated to the backwater of human rights discourse. *See* Leary, *supra* note 5, at 32.

37. UDHR, *supra* note 1, art. 5.

38. U.S. Const. amend. 8.

39. U.S. Const. amends. 5, 6; UDHR, *supra* note 1, arts. 7–11.

40. U.S. Const. amend. 1; UDHR *supra* note 1, art. 19.

41. U.S. Const. amend. 4; UDHR, *supra* note 1, art. 12.

42. The ICCPR repeated, almost verbatim, with the exception of the right to property, many of the civil and political rights enumerated in the UDHR. The most visible demonstration of the presence of emergent states of Africa, Latin America, and Asia was the inclusion of article 1, common to both the ICCPR and the ICESCR, on the group right to self-determination. *See* ICCPR, *supra* note 4, at 28.

43. In 1986, the United Nations General Assembly adopted the Declaration on the Right to Development. G.A. Res. 128, UN GAOR, 41st Sess., Supp. No. 53, at 186–87, UN Doc. A/41/53 (1986). Leading Western states, including the United States, Germany, the United Kingdom, the Nordic countries (except Norway), and Japan, either voted against the declaration or abstained. *See* John Quinn, *The General Assembly into the 1990s*, in Alston, United Nations and Human Rights, *supra* note 1, at 55, 65.

44. Even Leary, who is more optimistic about the normative universalization of human rights, is careful not to overstate the influence of non-Western thinking on human rights. She notes that such thinking has "begun to influence Western thinking on the subject." Leary, *supra* note 5, at 29.

45. Opposition from the West to one human rights covenant covering all human rights—civil and political as well as economic, social, and cultural—led to the two instruments, the ICCPR and the ICESCR. Traditional Western thinking on rights, which used the Soviet bloc emphasis on economic, social and cultural rights as a pretext for opposing a single covenant, makes a distinction between "negative" and "positive" rights. Although this distinction has for the most part been demystified, civil and political rights have retained their prominence in the West because their implementation does not necessarily involve the redistribution of wealth or inception of programs that drastically curtail an individual's right to accumulate unlimited property. *Cf.* Donnelly, *supra* note 14, at 31, 49 (demonstrating that the positive-negative distinction fails to provide accurate labels for negative rights like the protection from torture, which requires positive governmental action, and the

right to political participation, which seems to be "more a positive than a negative right").

46. INGOs may be contrasted with the term "nongovernmental organizations" (NGOs), which, though also referring to private, nongovernmental groups, is often used to describe "domestic" or national organizations. So-called NGOs address human rights issues only in the country in which they are based.

47. Initially founded in 1920 to advocate the rights of conscientious objectors, the ACLU sees itself as the "guardian of the Bill of Rights which guarantees fundamental civil liberties to all of us." These rights include the freedoms of speech, press, and religion (First Amendment); freedom from abuses by the police, domestic spying, and other illegal intelligence activities (Fourth Amendment); equal treatment and fair play (Fifth Amendment); fair trial (Sixth Amendment); prohibition against cruel and unusual punishment (Eighth Amendment); and privacy and personal autonomy (Fourth, Fifth, and Ninth Amendments). *See* Laurie S. Wiseberg and Hazel Sirett, eds., NORTH AMERICAN HUMAN RIGHTS DIRECTORY (Washington, D.C.: Human Rights Internet, 1984), p. 19 [hereinafter NORTH AMERICAN DIRECTORY].

48. The NAACP, the United States' oldest civil rights organization, was founded in 1909 to seek equal treatment—the removal of racial discrimination in areas such as voting, employment, housing, business, courts, and transportation—for African Americans through peaceful reform. *See* NORTH AMERICAN DIRECTORY, *supra* note 47, at 161.

49. Although today the LDF and the NAACP are separate legal entities, the LDF was founded in 1939 as the legal arm of the NAACP. It has initiated legal action in courts to challenge discrimination and promote equality in schools, jobs, the electoral system, land use, and other services and areas. NORTH AMERICAN DIRECTORY, *supra* note 47, at 159.

50. *See* NORTH AMERICAN DIRECTORY, *supra* note 47, at 135.

51. *See* Rita McWilliams, *Who Watched Americas Watch?*, 19 NAT'L INTEREST 45, 53 (1990). Jerome Shestack, a prominent American lawyer who long served as the president of the ILHR and is the organization's honorary chair, was replaced in May 1996 by Scott Horton, a partner in a New York law firm. Telephone Interview with the ILHR (September 13, 1996).

52. Human Rights Watch is divided into five geographic units covering Africa, the Americas, Asia, the Middle East, and the signatories of the Helsinki Accords. It also has five thematic projects on arms transfers, children's rights, free expression, prison conditions, and women's rights. HRW asserts that it "defends freedom of thought and expression, due process and equal protection of the law; it documents and denounces murders, disappearances, torture, arbitrary imprisonment, exile, censorship, and other abuses of internationally recognized human rights." *See* WORLD REPORT 1995, *supra* note 15, at vii.

53. *See* Aryeh Neier, *Political Consequences of the United States Ratification of the International Covenant on Civil and Political Rights*, 42 DEPAUL L. REV. 1233, n. 47 (1993).

54. *See* NORTH AMERICAN DIRECTORY, *supra* note 47, at 133. PAIL itself was established in 1965 and has devoted considerable resources to the promotion of the idea of human rights. Richard Lillich, its former president, is a professor of law at

the University of Virginia School of Law, and one of the leading writers on human rights.

55. At a 1992 LDF symposium of public interest law NGOs from around the world, Julius Chambers, then director-counsel of the LDF, recalled how Thurgood Marshall, his most celebrated predecessor, had in 1959 helped write the Kenya Constitution, and had helped to endow it with doctrines of due process, equality, and justice. Chambers also remembered how Jack Greenberg, another predecessor, had laid the groundwork for the Legal Resources Centre of South Africa, one of that country's leading public interest law firms under apartheid. Instructively, he noted that he did not view the symposium "primarily as an occasion for the LDF to teach others." *See* Julius I. Chambers, et al., NAACP LEGAL DEFENSE AND EDUCATIONAL FUND, PUBLIC INTEREST LAW AROUND THE WORLD (New York: Columbia Human Rights Law Review, 1992), p. 1.

56. Laurie S. Wiseberg and Hazel Sirett, eds., HUMAN RIGHTS DIRECTORY: WESTERN EUROPE (Cambridge, Mass.: Harvard Law School Human Rights Program and Human Rights Internet, 1982), p. 216 [hereinafter WESTERN EUROPE DIRECTORY]. The term "rule of law" is commonly understood to describe a state that is accountable to the governed through the application of fair and just laws enforced by an independent and impartial judiciary. *See, e.g.*, Andrea J. Hanneman, *Independence and Group Rights in the Baltics: A Double Minority Problem*, 35 VA. J. INT'L L. 485, 523 (1995): "The extent to which a society protects human rights in general and minority rights in particular has been called the 'litmus test of liberty and the rule of law,'" citing Ralf Dahrendor, *Minority Rights and Minority Rule*, in Ben Whitaker ed., MINORITIES: A QUESTION OF HUMAN RIGHTS (New York: Pergamon Press, 1984), p. 79.

57. *See* Issa G. Shivji, THE CONCEPT OF HUMAN RIGHTS IN AFRICA (London: Codesria Book Series, 1984), p. 34. At its inception, the ICJ was funded in part by covert CIA funds. "It followed an essentially American set of priorities in its early years, then expanded and became less politically partial." Claude E. Welch, Jr., PROTECTING HUMAN RIGHTS IN AFRICA: ROLES AND STRATEGIES OF NONGOVERNMENTAL ORGANIZATIONS (Philadelphia: University of Pennsylvania Press, 1995), p. 163.

58. *See* WESTERN EUROPE DIRECTORY, *supra* note 56, at 265.

59. *See* Ian Martin, THE NEW WORLD ORDER: OPPORTUNITY OR THREAT FOR HUMAN RIGHTS?, Lecture by the Edward A. Smith Visiting Fellow presented by the Harvard Law School Human Rights Program (Cambridge, Mass.: Harvard University, April 14, 1993), pp. 4–5 [hereinafter NEW WORLD ORDER]. From 1986 to 1992, Martin was the secretary-general of Amnesty International. Benenson's article accompanied photos of six political prisoners: three were imprisoned in Romania, Hungary, and Czechoslovakia; the other three were a Greek communist and unionist imprisoned in Greece, an Angolan doctor and poet incarcerated by the Portuguese colonial rulers in Angola, and the Rev. Ashton Jones, an American who had repeatedly been beaten and jailed in Louisiana and Texas for advocating the civil rights of black Americans. Although AI now focuses most of its attention on Africa, Central America, and South America, the trigger for its creation was, ironically, the official conduct of Soviet bloc and Western governments, including the United States.

60. Statute of Amnesty International arts. 1 and 2, reprinted in Amnesty International, AMNESTY INTERNATIONAL REPORT (London: Amnesty International,

1994), app. II, p. 332 [hereinafter AI REPORT]. Prisoners of conscience are individuals detained anywhere for their beliefs or because of their ethnic origin, sex, color or language who have not used or advocated violence. *Id.* at 333. It is interesting to note that Nelson Mandela and many political prisoners in the African National Congress were not regarded as prisoners of conscience by this standard. *See* Peter Worthington, *Dancing to Castro's Tune*, TORONTO SUN, August 16, 1994, at 11, available in LEXIS, News Library, ARCNWS File; Sousa Jamba, *An Ex-Convict Runs out of Convictions*, TIMES, December 9, 1993, available in LEXIS, News Library, ARCNWS File.

61. AI REPORT, *supra* note 60, at 21. In addition, AI attacks the "arbitrary and irrevocable nature of the death penalty," its use as a "tool of political repression," and its disproportionate imposition on "the poor and the powerless." It disagrees with the argument that the death penalty has a deterrent effect on crime. *Id.*

62. *See* Henry J. Steiner, DIVERSE PARTNERS: NON-GOVERNMENTAL ORGANIZATIONS IN THE HUMAN RIGHTS MOVEMENT (Cambridge, Mass.: Harvard Law School Human Rights Program and Human Rights Internet, 1991), pp. 61–64 [hereinafter Steiner, DIVERSE PARTNERS].

63. *Id.* Pierre Sane, a Senegalese, became AI's first non-European secretary-general in October 1992. Amnesty International, press release, *Amnesty International Announces Appointment of New Secretary-General*, October 1, 1992. Adama Dieng, also a Senegalese, became secretary-general of ICJ in 1991; he left ICJ in 2000.

64. When INGOs engage Southerners, it is ordinarily for area-specific responsibilities, usually their native region. For example, Africa Watch, the division of Human Rights Watch that addresses sub-Saharan African human rights problems, has been headed by Africans since its founding in 1988. Similarly, Americas Watch has been headed by Latin Americans virtually since its inception in 1981. This author, an African, was in 1989–91 the director of the Africa Project at the Lawyers Committee for Human Rights, having succeeded Rakiya Omaar, another African. This "ghettoization"—conscious or not—seeks to legitimize the organization in the particular region while retaining its commitment to Western liberal values. It also pigeonholes non-Westerners as capable of addressing issues in only their native region and incapable of dealing with questions from other regions. In effect, these hiring patterns leave the impression that only Westerners have the ability to develop a "universal" outlook.

65. AI categorically states that "no money is sought or accepted from governments." AI REPORT, *supra* note 60, app. 8, at 352. HRW states that it "accepts no government funds, directly or indirectly." *See* WORLD REPORT 1995, *supra* note 15, at vii.

66. In 1993 I led a USAID-funded "rule of law" study mission to Ethiopia for the International Human Rights Law Group and wrote a report on the mission's findings. *See* International Human Rights Law Group, ETHIOPIA IN TRANSITION: A REPORT ON THE JUDICIARY AND THE LEGAL PROFESSION (Washington, D.C.: International Human Rights Law Group, 1994) [hereinafter ETHIOPIA IN TRANSITION]. To "broaden" its international credibility the Law Group has constituted an International Advisory Council which includes noted activists, scholars, and pro-establishment figures from Asia, Africa and Latin America. *Id.*

67. In 1986, for example, the Lawyers Committee for Human Rights honored President Corazon Aquino of the Philippines for "her achievement in leading the

people of her nation to peacefully reclaim democracy." *See* Lawyers Committee for Human Rights, 10TH ANNIVERSARY ANNUAL REPORT (1988). In 1987, it honored Robert Bernstein, the senior executive at Random House and the founder of Human Rights Watch. NBC news anchor Tom Brokaw was the master of ceremonies at the 600-guest event that attracted prominent businessmen and lawyers. *Id.*

68. *See* Aryeh Neier, *Human Rights*, in Joel Krieger et al., eds., THE OXFORD COMPANION TO POLITICS OF THE WORLD (London: Oxford University Press, 1993), p. 403.

69. Of all American INGOs, the International League for Human Rights (ILHR) has until recently taken the most favorable position toward economic and social rights. Testifying before the U.S. Congress in 1988, Jerome Shestack, ILHR president, attacked American foreign policy as deeply flawed because of its omission of economic and social rights. *See Recent Developments in U.S. Human Rights Policy: Hearings Before the Subcommittee on Human Rights and International Organizations of the House Comm. on Foreign Affairs*, 100th Cong., 2d Sess. 64–65 (1988) (statement of Jerome Shestack, President, ILHR).

70. *See* Human Rights Watch, INDIVISIBLE RIGHTS: THE RELATIONSHIP OF POLITICAL AND CIVIL RIGHTS TO SURVIVAL, SUBSISTENCE, AND POVERTY (New York: Human Rights Watch,1992) [hereinafter HRW, INDIVISIBLE RIGHTS].

71. *See id.* at vi–vii. One of the most coherent rationalizations of the opposition to economic and social rights was expressed in a meeting of American NGOs:

One participant felt strongly that it would be detrimental for U.S. human rights NGOs to espouse the idea of economic, social and cultural rights. Although they refer to important issues, they concern distributive justice rather than corrective justice, like civil and political rights. But distributive justice is a matter of policy, rather than principles; and human rights NGOs must deal with principles, not policies. Otherwise, their credibility will be damaged. Supporting economic demands will only undermine the ability of NGOs to promote civil and political rights, which are indispensable.

M. Rodriguez Bustelo and Philip Alston, *Report of a Conference held at Arden House* (1986), quoted in Philip Alston, *U.S. Ratification of the Covenant on Economic, Social, and Cultural Rights: The Need for an Entirely New Strategy*, 84 AM. J. INT'L L. 365, 390 n.107 (1990).

72. INDIVISIBLE RIGHTS, *supra* note 70, at vi–vii.

73. Human Rights Watch, *Human Rights Watch's Proposed Interim Policy on Economic, Social and Cultural Rights* (New York, September 30, 1996).

74. HRW is unlikely to expand this mandate to cover more ICESCR rights for a number of reasons, including the lack of adequate human resources. Telephone interview with Kenneth Roth, Executive Director, Human Rights Watch (October 8, 1996).

75. Steiner, DIVERSE PARTNERS, *supra* note 62, at 19 (emphasis added). The ACLU and the LDF are typical domestic "First World" NGOs. HRW, AI, and other INGOs fit Steiner's categorization.

76. An investigation, known as a human rights fact-finding mission, is conducted by the staffs of INGOs who typically spend anywhere from several days to a number of weeks in a "Third World" country interviewing victims of repression, gov-

ernment officials, local activists, local media, and academics. *See generally* Diane F. Orentlicher, *Bearing Witness: The Art and Science of Human Rights Fact-Finding*, 3 HARV. HUM. RTS. J. 83 (1990).

77. Reporting involves compiling data and information from the fact-finding mission and correlating it to human rights standards to bring out discrepancies and disseminating it through reports or other media. This method is also called "shaming" because it spotlights the offending state to the international community. *See, e.g.*, Lawyers Committee for Human Rights, ZIMBABWE: WAGES OF WAR—A REPORT ON HUMAN RIGHTS (New York: Lawyers Committee for Human Rights,1986).

78. This includes lobbying governments and international institutions to use their leverage to alleviate violations.

79. For example, according to its statute, Amnesty International works to "promote as appears appropriate the adoption of constitutions, conventions, treaties and other measures which guarantee the rights contained in the provisions referred to in Article 1 hereof." AI REPORT, *supra* note 60, app. 2 at 333. The International Human Rights Law Group undertakes rule of law assessments which aim at identifying institutional weaknesses and proposing structural reforms. *See generally* ETHIOPIA IN TRANSITION, *supra* note 74.

80. Steiner, DIVERSE PARTNERS, *supra* note 62, at 19.

81. *See* WORLD REPORT 1995, *supra* note 15, at vii.

82. Steiner, DIVERSE PARTNERS, *supra* note 62, at 19.

83. For a comprehensive journalistic account of the differences between the two communities, see Thomas Carothers, *Democracy and Human Rights: Policy Allies or Rivals?* 17 WASH. Q., 106 (1994), at 109.

84. These include governmental agencies such as USAID or their European and Canadian equivalents, quasi-governmental and nongovernmental organizations, programs at major Western universities, policy institutes, foundations, and academic and policy specialists. *Id.* at 110.

85. Although INGOs constitute the core of this group, the community also draws from government agencies—especially in the state departments or foreign ministries—universities, development institutes, and law firms. *Id.*

86. *Id.* at 111.

87. INGOs charged the Reagan administration with the perversion of Carter's human rights policy by applying it almost exclusively to communist states. By the end of his second term, however, INGOs started to admit that Reagan's policy had evolved to institutionalize human rights as a fixed concern of U.S. policy. *See* Human Rights Watch and Lawyers Committee for Human Rights, THE REAGAN ADMINISTRATION'S RECORD ON HUMAN RIGHTS IN 1988 (New York: Human Rights Watch and Lawyers Committee for Human Rights, 1989), p. 1.

88. *See id.* at 11–12.

89. Meetings at the request of INGOs with State Department officials responsible for policies in particular countries are indispensable to INGOs, whose clout often comes from their association with rich and powerful Western states. Ordinarily, INGO fact-finding missions also meet with Western diplomats to raise "concerns" and seek "inside information" about political issues in the country.

90. The Robert F. Kennedy Memorial Center for Human Rights, for example, has often given its annual award to pro-democracy activists, including Gibson

Kamau Kuria of Kenya, a leading figure in the struggle to end repressive one-party rule by introducing multiparty democracy in Kenya. *See* Robert F. Kennedy Memorial Center for Human Rights, JUSTICE ENJOINED: THE STATE OF THE JUDICIARY IN KENYA (Washington, D.C.: Robert Kennedy Memorial Center for Human Rights, 1992); Mutua, CONFRONTING THE PAST, *supra*, note 15.

91. NEW WORLD ORDER, *supra* note 59, at 6.

92. *See* Lawyers Committee for Human Rights, THE WORLD BANK: GOVERNANCE AND HUMAN RIGHTS (New York: Lawyers Committee for Human Rights, 1993), pp. 2–3 [hereinafter GOVERNANCE AND HUMAN RIGHTS].

93. Examples include Professor Louis Henkin, who serves on the board of directors of the Lawyers Committee for Human Rights, and Professor Norman Dorsen, who chaired the Lawyers Committee board of directors.

94. Louis Henkin, THE AGE OF RIGHTS (New York: Columbia University Press, 1990), pp. xvii–ix. [hereinafter Henkin, AGE OF RIGHTS].

95. Henkin acknowledges that although the universal consensus on human rights may be formal, even hypocritical and cynical in some societies, it is important that it is the idea that

[h]as commanded universal nominal acceptance, not (as in the past) the divine right of kings or the omnipotent state, not the inferiority of races or women, not even socialism. Even if it be hypocrisy, it is significant—since hypocrisy, we know, is the homage that vice pays to virtue—that human rights is today the single, paramount virtue to which vice pays homage, that governments today do not feel free to preach what they may persist in practicing. *Id.* at ix–x.

96. *Id.* at x.

97. The UDHR, Henkin says, reflects a "general commitment to ideas . . . that have become part of our zeitgeist." *Id.* The framers of the international human rights texts, Henkin writes, did not seek to build an "umbrella large enough to encompass everyone, but rather to respond to a sensed common moral intuition and to identify a small core of common values." *Id.*

98. *Id.* at 6.

99. Henkin writes that the human rights expressions "claim no philosophical foundation, nor do they reflect any clear philosophical assumptions; they articulate no particular moral principles or any single, comprehensive theory of the relation of the individual to society." *Id.* Henkin has suggested that the diversity of cultures and political traditions has caused the human rights movement to eschew inquiries into the philosophical origins and justifications for the human rights corpus, fearing that such inquiry would prove "disruptive and unhelpful." Henry J. Steiner, *The Youth of Rights*, 104 HARV. L. REV. 917 (1991), reviewing Henkin, AGE OF RIGHTS.

100. Henkin, AGE OF RIGHTS, *supra* note 94, at 6.

101. *Id.* Note, though, Henkin's acknowledgment that at the start the United States saw the human rights movement as an instrument to "improve the condition of human rights in countries other than the United States (and a very few like-minded liberal states)." *Id.* at 74.

102. *Id.*

103. *Id.* at 7 (footnote omitted), quoting UDHR, *supra* note 1, art. 21(3)).

Henkin notes that Western-style presidential and parliamentary regimes as well as communist "democratic centralism" could presumably meet this standard, provided that the governed can control how they are governed and by what policies they are governed, and that they can replace their governors at frequent and regular intervals. *Id.*

104. Steiner, *Youth of Rights, supra* note 99, at 930–31. Steiner allows that some one-party states may meet "generous interpretations" of pluralist participation if they have "extensive intraparty democracy." But the human rights corpus requires more than pluralist participation; it imposes the respect and recognition for diversity and difference, judicial independence, and a private sector, conditions which are unlikely to be met in societal typologies found in the one-party state. *Id.*

105. Henkin, AGE OF RIGHTS, *supra* note 94, at 145.

106. For a discussion of the positive-negative distinction and the ends of government, *see generally* Donnelly, *supra* note 5; on Donnelly's views on the welfare state, *see* pp. 54–55.

107. Henkin, AGE OF RIGHTS, *supra* note 94, at 153.

108. *See, e.g.*, Steiner and Alston, INTERNATIONAL HUMAN RIGHTS IN CONTEXT, *supra* note 11. This substantial work presents the inquiry into human rights as the contradiction between authoritarian, oppressive, nondemocratic, non-Western societies on the one hand, and Western liberal core values such as the rights of association, speech, due process, and the ideals of equal protection on the other. In my view, the text is the most comprehensive and provocative human rights coursebook to date.

109. Steiner, *Political Participation, supra* note 25, at 77.

110. *Id.* at 79. Steiner calls the UDHR the "spiritual parent" of many human rights treaties; the ICCPR's importance hinges on its acceptance by most of the world's states in all regions and ideological blocs. These facts give the two instruments "universal scope." *Id.* Elsewhere, Steiner writes:

To this day, it [the UDHR] retains its symbolism, rhetorical force and significance in the human rights movement. It is the parent document, the initial burst of idealism and enthusiasm, terser, more general and grander than the treaties, in some sense the constitution of the entire movement. It remains the single most invoked human rights instrument.

Steiner and Alston, INTERNATIONAL HUMAN RIGHTS IN CONTEXT, *supra* note 11, at 120.

111. Continuing the theme of universality, Steiner notes, however, that the "rights may be understood to be rooted in natural law or positive enactment. They may be justified by liberal postulates or by the imperative of socialist construction." Steiner, *Political Participation, supra* note 25, at 82–83.

112. *Id.* at 81–84.

113. *Id.* at 84.

114. UDHR, *supra* note 1, art. 21, provides:

1. Everyone has the right to take part in the government of his country, directly or through freely chosen representatives.

2. Everyone has the right of equal access to public service in his country.

3. The will of the people shall be the basis of the authority of government; this will shall be expressed in periodic and genuine elections which shall be by universal and equal suffrage and shall be held by secret vote or by equivalent free voting procedures.

ICCPR, *supra* note 4, art. 25 provides:

Every citizen shall have the right and the opportunity, without any of the distinctions mentioned in article 2 and without unreasonable restrictions:
(a) To take part in the conduct of public affairs, directly or through freely chosen representatives;
(b) To vote and to be elected at genuine periodic elections which shall be by universal and equal suffrage and shall be held by secret ballot, guaranteeing the free expression of the will of the electors;
(c) To have access, on general terms of equality, to public service in his country.

115. During the drafting of the UDHR, for example, the Belgian delegate to the Third Committee argued that the "very essence of the democratic system was the electoral competition between different political parties," otherwise the "whole democratic character of free, equal, periodical and secret elections might be distorted." UN GAOR 3d Comm., 3d Sess., 133d mtg. at 464, UN Doc. A/C.3/SR.133 (1948). But the Soviet delegate countered that such language would be "absolutely irreconcilable with the social structure of certain Member States." *Id.* at 471.

116. Steiner, *Political Participation, supra* note 25, at 93.

117. *Id.* at 134.

118. Henry J. Steiner, *Ideals and Counter-Ideals in the Struggle over Autonomy Regimes for Minorities*, 66 NOTRE DAME L. REV. 1539 (1991).

119. *Id.* at 1546–48.

120. *Id.* at 1548.

121. Steiner, *Youth of Rights, supra* note 99, at 931.

122. Alston, an Australian, is a former chair of the pivotal Committee on Economic, Social, and Cultural Rights, the body that has overseen the implementation of the ICESCR since 1991. Between 1978 and 1984, he was an official of the United Nations Centre for Human Rights in Geneva. He has taught at Harvard Law School and the Fletcher School of Law and Diplomacy at Tufts University and has been professor of law and director of the Australian National University's Centre for International and Public Law. Currently, he is a professor of international law at the European Law Institute in Florence, Italy. He has undertaken numerous high-level activities for the United Nations and its specialized agencies.

123. Philip Alston, *Making Space for New Human Rights: The Case of the Right to Development*, 1 HARV. HUM. RTS. Y.B. 3, 3 (1988).

124. *See* Statement to the World Conference on Human Rights on Behalf of the Committee on Economic, Social and Cultural Rights, UN ESCOR, 7th Sess., Supp. No. 2, Annex 3, at 83, UN Doc. E/1993/22 (1993).

125. Franck uses the term "democratic governance" to describe a legal and practical commitment to "open, multiparty, secret-ballot elections with a universal franchise." Franck, *The Emerging Right, supra* note 8, at 47. I use only this one article by Franck because among all his numerous writings, it best expresses the views relevant to my argument. Franck traces the notion of "democratic entitlement" to the

U.S. Declaration of Independence, with its assertion that governments are instituted to secure the "'unalienable rights' of their citizens . . . [and] derive their just
powers from the consent of the governed." *Id.* at 46. He also traces the international legitimacy of governments to their demonstration of "a decent respect to the
opinions of mankind," hence through their recognition and legitimization by
other nations. *Id.*

126. *Id.* at 46–49. He notes that "Very few argue that parliamentary democracy is
a western illusion and a neocolonialist trap for unwary Third World peoples."

127. This includes the UN Charter; UDHR; ICCPR; the Declaration on the
Elimination of all Forms of Intolerance and of Discrimination Based on Religion
or Belief, G.A. Res. 55, UN GAOR, 36th Sess., Supp. No. 51, at 171, UN Doc.
A/36/51 (1981), reprinted in 21 I.L.M. 205 (1982); the Convention on the
Elimination of all Forms of Discrimination Against Women, G.A. Res. 180, UN
GAOR, 34th Sess., Supp. No. 46, at 193, UN Doc. A/34/46 (1979), reprinted in 19
I.L.M. 33 (1980) (entered into force September 3, 1981) [hereinafter CEDAW];
the International Covenant on the Suppression and Punishment of the Crime of
Apartheid, G.A. Res. 3068, UN GAOR, 28th Sess., Supp. No. 30, at 75, UN Doc.
A/9030 (1973), reprinted in 13 I.L.M. 56 (1974) (entered into force July 18, 1976);
and the International Convention on the Elimination of All Forms of Racial
Discrimination, opened for signature March 7, 1966, 660 UNTS 195, reprinted in
5 I.L.M. 352 (1966) (entered into force January 4, 1969) [hereinafter CERD].

128. I use the term "outsider-insiders" to bunch together Africans, Asians, Latin
Americans, non-mainstream Western scholars, and certain members of racial and
cultural minorities in the West, such as African Americans and Asian Americans.
The latter have historically been part of the struggle to vindicate non-European
cultural viewpoints in the West. In feminist jurisprudence, for example, some
African American scholars have advocated the recognition of views other than
those of mainline white feminists. *See e.g.*, Hope Lewis, *Between Irua and "Female
Genital Mutilation": Feminist Rights Discourse and the Cultural Divide*, 8 HARV. HUM.
RTS. J. 1 (1995), distinguishing black feminist human rights approaches from mainstream perspectives and calling for a cross-cultural discussion to improve the quality of debate.

129. I have argued elsewhere that the state in Africa was organized for the purposes of colonial exploitation, it was decolonized as a tool of the international state
system and the Cold War, and it has survived without internal legitimacy or coher-
ence because of external support. See Makau wa Mutua, *Why Redraw the Map of
Africa: A Moral and Legal Inquiry*, 16 MICH. J. INT'L L. 1113 (1995); Makau wa Mutua,
*Putting Humpty Dumpty Back Together Again: The Dilemmas of the Post-Colonial African
State*, 21 BROOK. J. INT'L L. 505 (1995), book review.

130. *See* Makau wa Mutua and Peter Rosenblum, ZAIRE: REPRESSION AS POLICY
(New York: Lawyers Committee for Human Rights, 1990), documenting the abuses of the Zairian state against its own citizens.

131. B. Obinna Okere, *The Protection of Human Rights in Africa and the African
Charter on Human and Peoples' Rights: A Comparative Analysis with the European and
American Systems*, 6 HUM. RTS. Q. 141, 148 (1984) John Mbiti has argued that in
Africa the individual's rights, needs, sorrows, and duties are woven in a tapestry
that denies runaway individualism. "I am because we are; and since we are, therefore I am." John S. Mbiti, AFRICAN RELIGIONS AND PHILOSOPHY (New York: Praeger,
1970), p. 141.

132. Richard N. Kiwanuka, *The Meaning of "People" in the African Charter on Human and Peoples' Rights*, 82 AM. J. INT'L L. 80, 82 (1988).

133. Dunstan Wai argues that African conceptions of human rights guaranteed a "modicum of social justice and values concerned with individual and collective rights." Dunstan Wai, *Human Rights in Sub-Saharan Africa*, in Adamantia Pollis and Peter Schwab, eds., HUMAN RIGHTS: CULTURAL AND IDEOLOGICAL PERSPECTIVES (New York: Praeger, 1979), p. 116. Asmarom Legesse notes the importance of this balance between the individual and the society so that "individuals do not deviate so far from the norm that they can overwhelm the society." Asmarom Legesse, *Human Rights in African Political Culture*, in Kenneth W. Thompson, ed., THE MORAL IMPERATIVES OF HUMAN RIGHTS: A WORLD SURVEY (Lanham, Md.: University Press of America,1980), p. 125.

134. A vocal advocate of the Asian conception of human rights has argued, for instance, that

> many East and Southeast Asians tend to look askance at the starkly individualistic ethos of the West in which authority tends to be seen as oppressive and rights are an individual's "trump" over the state. Most people of the region prefer a situation in which distinctions between the individual, society, and state are less clear-cut, or at least less adversarial. It will be far more difficult to deepen and expand the international consensus on human rights if East and Southeast Asian countries believe that the Western promotion of human rights is aimed at what they regard as the foundation of their economic success.

Bilahari Kausikan, *Asia's Different Standard*, 92 FOREIGN POL'Y 24 (1993).

135. Human Rights Watch in particular has been very vocal in its rejection of the so-called Asian concept of human rights, which emphasizes economic development over respect for civil and political rights. *See* WORLD REPORT 1995, *supra* note 15, at xiv.

136. *See* Ghai, *Human Rights and Governance*, *supra* note 15, at 20. Ghai attacks the notion of a unique or singular Asian perspective on human rights because of the religious, political and economic diversities prevalent in the region. *Id.* at 5.

137. Kwasi Wiredu, for example, contends that the principle of innocent until proven guilty was an essential part of Akan (West African peoples') consciousness: "it was an absolute principle of Akan justice that no human being could be punished without a trial." Kwasi Wiredu, *An Akan Perspective on Human Rights*, in CROSS-CULTURAL PERSPECTIVES, *supra* note 5, at 252. Timothy Fernyhough notes that Africa's preoccupation with the right to life was manifested in the power to hand down the death penalty, which was reserved for a few elders "only after elaborate judicial procedure, with appeals from one court to another, and often only in cases of murder or manslaughter." Timothy Fernyhough, *Human Rights and Precolonial Africa*, in Ronald Cohen et al. eds., HUMAN RIGHTS AND GOVERNANCE IN AFRICA (Gainesville: University Press of Florida, 1993), p. 56. He notes, further, that "in the Tio kingdom north of modern Brazzaville . . . as elsewhere in Africa, a strong tradition of jurisprudence existed, with specific rulings for penalties cited as precedents, such as levels of fines for adultery." *Id.* at 62.

138. *See* Wiredu, *supra* note 137, at 248–49.

139. Wiredu further writes:

Akan thought recognized the right of a newborn to be nursed and educated, the right of an adult to a plot of land from the ancestral holdings, the right of any well-defined unit of political organization to self-government, the right of all to have a say in the enstoolment or destoolment of their chiefs or their elders and to participate in the shaping of governmental policies, the right of all to freedom of thought and expression in all matters, political, religious, and metaphysical, the right of everybody to trial before punishment, the right of a person to remain at any locality or to leave, and so on. *Id.* at 257.

140. Kausikan, *supra* note 134, at 38. Kausikan suggests that the collapse of communism, which many in the West saw as the triumph of its liberal democratic values and systems, has been used as a "lens through which [Western media, NGOs, and human rights activists] view developments in other regions." *Id.* at 33. Kausikan warns that an approach which gauges states by the progress of democracy is ideological because democracy is "a value-laden term, itself susceptible to multiple interpretations, but usually understood by Western human rights activists and the media as the establishment of political institutions and practices akin to those existing in the United States and Europe." *Id.*

141. Henkin, AGE OF RIGHTS, *supra* note 94, at 74. This view, according to Henkin, results from the fact that the United States is "a principal ancestor of the contemporary idea of rights." *Id.* at 65.

142. *Id.*

143. For an eloquent exploration of Western European (European Union, formerly European Community) policies linking human rights and democracy to aid and trade in their relationship with non-Western countries, *see* Demetrios James Marantis, *Human Rights, Democracy and Development: The European Community Model,* 7 HARV. HUM. RTS. J. 1 (1994).

144. *See* F. L. Osunsade, IMF SUPPORT FOR AFRICAN ADJUSTMENT PROGRAMS: QUESTIONS AND ANSWERS (Washington, D.C.: International Monetary Fund, 1993), p. 8.

145. The United States has only recently ratified two important human rights instruments: the Convention on the Prevention and Punishment of Genocide of December 9, 1948, ratified by the United States in 1988; and the ICCPR, ratified by the United States in 1992. Among others, the United States has still not ratified the ICESCR, the Convention on the Elimination of All Forms of Racial Discrimination, the Convention for the Elimination of All Forms of Discrimination Against Women, and the American Convention on Human Rights. *See* Henkin, AGE OF RIGHTS, *supra* note 94, at 74–75.

146. *See* American Association for the International Commission of Jurists, HUMAN RIGHTS AND U.S. FOREIGN POLICY: THE FIRST DECADE, 1973–1983 (New York: American Association for the International Commission of Jurists, 1984), p. 6 [hereinafter U.S. FOREIGN POLICY].

147. *Id.* at 9. As a result of these upheavals, in 1973 the U.S. Congress launched hearings to determine the type and level of recognition that human rights should receive in foreign policy considerations. *Id. See also* Makau wa Mutua, *The African Human Rights System in a Comparative Perspective,* 3 REV. AFR. COMM'N HUM. AND PEOPLES' RTS. 5, 6 (1993).

148. *See* Foreign Assistance Act, Pub. L. No. 93-559, sec. 46, 88 Stat. 1795, 1815 (1974), creating sec. 502B, codified at 22 U.S.C. sec. 2304 (1994); International Development and Food Assistance Act, Pub. L. No. 94–161, title 3, sec. 310, 89 Stat. 849, 860 (1975), creating Foreign Assistance Act, sec. 116, codified at 22 U.S.C., sec. 2151n (1994). The amendments made human rights a "principal goal" of U.S. foreign policy.

149. Congress mandated the establishment of this office and instructed it to report annually on the human rights conditions in every country in the world. International Security Assistance and Arms Export Control Act, Pub. L. No. 94-329, sec. 301(b), 90 Stat. 729, 750 (1976), amending Foreign Assistance Act of 1961, sec. 624(f), codified as amended at 22 U.S.C., secs. 2151n, 2304, 2384 (1994).

150. U.S. FOREIGN POLICY, *supra* note 146, at 17.

151. *Id.* at 21, quoting Secretary of State Cyrus Vance: "'In each case,' the Secretary explained, 'we must balance a political concern for human rights against economic and security goals.'".

152. *Id.*, quoting Lincoln P. Bloomfield, *From Ideology to Program to Policy: Tracking the Carter Human Rights Policy*, 2 J. POL'Y ANALYSIS MGMT. 1, 8 (1982).

153. Henkin, AGE OF RIGHTS, *supra* note 94, at 71.

154 U.S. Department of State, COUNTRY REPORTS ON HUMAN RIGHTS PRACTICES FOR 1985 (1986), p. 3, Report submitted to House Committee on Foreign Affairs and Senate Committee on Foreign Relations, 99th Cong., 2d Sess.

155. Henkin, AGE OF RIGHTS, *supra* note 94, at 72.

156. *See, e.g.*, Mutua and Rosenblum, REPRESSION AS POLICY, *supra* note 130.

157. *See* Jane Perlez, *On Eve of Talks with Aid Donors, Kenya is Under Pressure to Democratize*, N.Y. TIMES, November 25 1991, at A9. In May 1992, the World Bank-led groups of Malawi donors also suspended aid pending moves toward political pluralism by the Banda regime. *See* Lawyers Committee for Human Rights, MALAWI: IGNORING CALLS FOR CHANGE (New York: Lawyers Committee for Human Rights, 1992), p. 10.

158. *See generally* Human Rights Watch, HUMAN RIGHTS WATCH WORLD REPORT 1992: EVENTS OF 1991, (New York: Human Rights Watch, 1991), pp. 1-2, lamenting the Bush administration's "downgrading the significance of human rights in the formulation of U.S. foreign policy".

159. In October 1994, for example, the Clinton administration forced the restoration to power of the democratically elected Haitian government of President Aristide. *See* WORLD REPORT 1995, *supra* note 15, at 99. But in May of the same year, it also ended the linkage of China's Most Favored Nation status to human rights conditions. *Id.* at 146–47.

160. As a demonstration of the view that human rights, democracy, and free markets are intrinsically linked, the Assistant Secretary of State for Human Rights and Humanitarian Affairs has been renamed the "Assistant Secretary of State for Democracy, Human Rights, and Labor." 22 U.S.C., sec. 2151n(c) (1994).

161. World Bank, SUB-SAHARAN AFRICA: FROM CRISIS TO SUSTAINABLE GROWTH, A LONG-TERM PROSPECTIVE STUDY (Washington, D.C.: World Bank, 1989), p. 60.

162. *Id.* at 60–61.

163. *See* GOVERNANCE AND HUMAN RIGHTS, *supra* note 92, at 37–42

164. *Id.* This report by the Lawyers Committee for Human Rights is a prime example of the enlistment of donors by INGOs in the human rights crusade.

INGOs now work with donors to exploit this willingness to include human rights concerns in their relations with recipient countries.

165. The Bank's 1991 WORLD DEVELOPMENT REPORT read, in part,

Few authoritarian regimes, in fact, have been economically enlightened. Some of the East Asian [newly industrialized economies] are the exceptions, not the rule. Dictatorships have proven disastrous for development in many countries—in Eastern Europe, Argentina, Central African Republic, Haiti, Myanmar, Nicaragua, Peru, Uganda, and Zaire, to name only a few. Democracies, conversely, could make reform more feasible in several ways. Political checks and balances, a free press, and open debate on the costs and benefits of government policy could give a wider public a stake in reform.

World Bank, *The Challenge for Development*, in WORLD DEVELOPMENT REPORT 1991, at 133 (1991), cited in GOVERNANCE AND HUMAN RIGHTS, *supra* note 92, at 41–42.

166. *See* Report of the Regional Meeting for Asia of the World Conference on Human Rights, UN Doc. A/CONF.157/ASRM/8-A/CONF.157//PC/59 (1993); Kausikan, *supra* note 134, at 33–34; Ali Alatas, Minister for Foreign Affairs and Head of the Delegation of the Republic of Indonesia, statement before the Second World Conference on Human Rights at Vienna, 9 UN Doc. A/48/214 (June 14, 1993). *See also* Information Office of the State Council of the People's Republic of China, *Human Rights in China*, November 1, 1991, available in LEXIS, News Library, ARCNWS File. For more on China's positions on human rights, *see* Information Office of the State Council of the People's Republic of China, *The Progress of Human Rights in China* (1996), January 31, 1996, available in LEXIS, News Library, CURNWS File.

Chapter 3. Human Rights and the African Fingerprint

1. The African Charter on Human and Peoples' Rights, June 27, 1981, OAU Doc. CAB/LEG/67/3/Rev.5 (1981), reprinted in 21 I.L.M. 59 (1982) [hereinafter African Charter].

2. The African Charter, also referred to as the Banjul Charter, was adopted in 1981 by the 18th Assembly of Heads of State and Government of the Organization of African Unity (OAU), the official body of African states. It is known as the Banjul Charter because the final draft was produced in Banjul, the capital of the Gambia. One of the Charter's implementing organs, the African Commission on Human and Peoples' Rights (African Commission), was established in 1987. The African Commission's eleven members, known as commissioners, are elected by the OAU by secret ballot for a six-year term and serve in their own personal capacities. *See* African Charter, *supra* note 1, arts. 31, 33, 36, 45, 21 I.L.M. at 64–65.

3. The major human rights instruments include the trilogy of documents commonly referred to as the International Bill of Rights: the 1948 Universal Declaration of Human Rights, G.A. Res. 217 A(III), UN Doc. A/810, at 71 (1948) [hereinafter UDHR]; the 1966 International Covenant on Civil and Political Rights, G.A. Res. 2200 A(XXI), UN GAOR, 21st Sess., Supp. No. 16, at 52, UN Doc. A/6316 (1966) [hereinafter ICCPR], what many call the bible of the human rights movement; and (iii) the 1966 International Covenant on Economic, Social and

Cultural Rights, G.A. Res. 2200 A(XXI), UN GAOR, 21st Sess., Supp. No. 16, at 49, UN Doc. A/6316 (1966) [hereinafter ICESCR]. The last two instruments entered into force in 1976.

Apart from the African Charter, the other major regional human rights instruments include the American Convention on Human Rights, November 22, 1969, 36 OASTS No. 36, at 1, OAS Off. Rec. OEA/Ser. L/V/II.23 Rev.2, reprinted in 9 I.L.M. 673 (1970), the document that anchors the inter-American human rights system; the [European] Convention for the Protection of Human Rights and Fundamental Freedoms, November 4, 1950, 213 UNTS 221 (1955); and the European Social Charter, October 18, 1961, 529 UNTS 89 (1965), which forms the basis for the European human rights system. *See generally* Thomas Buergenthal, INTERNATIONAL HUMAN RIGHTS IN A NUTSHELL (St. Paul, Minn.: West Publishing Co.,1988); Hurst Hannum, ed., GUIDE TO INTERNATIONAL HUMAN RIGHTS PRACTICE (Philadelphia: University of Pennsylvania Press, 1992) [hereinafter HUMAN RIGHTS PRACTICE GUIDE]; United Nations, HUMAN RIGHTS: A COMPILATION OF INTERNATIONAL INSTRUMENTS, UN Doc. ST/HR/1/Rev.4 (New York: United Nations, 1993).

4. Civil and political rights, the staple of the human rights movement, have been commonly referred to as "first generation" rights, while economic, cultural, and social rights are called "second generation" rights. In addition to these, the African Charter provides for "peoples' rights," known also as collective or group rights, which include the right of peoples to self-determination, political sovereignty over their natural resources, and development. Buergenthal, *supra* note 3, at 176–77. One group right, the right to self-determination, is widely recognized and enshrined in article 1 common to both the ICCPR and the ICESCR. ICCPR, *supra* note 3, at 176–77; ICESCR, *supra* note 3, art. 1, para. 1. Chapter 2 of the African Charter, which imposes various duties on individuals, is that document's most radical contribution to human rights law. *See* African Charter, *supra* note 1, arts. 27–29, 21 I.L.M. at 63.

5. For detailed discussions and analyses of the relationships between peoples and human rights in the African Charter, *see generally* Richard Gittleman, *The African Charter on Human and Peoples' Rights: A Legal Analysis*, 22 VA. J. INT'L L. 667 (1982); U. Oji Umozurike, *The African Charter on Human and Peoples' Rights*, 77 AM. J. INT'L L. 902 (1983); Theo van Boven, *The Relations Between Peoples' Rights and Human Rights in the African Charter*, 7 HUM. RTS. L. J. 183 (1986); Jean-Bernard Marie, *Relations Between Peoples' Rights and Human Rights: Semantic and Methodological Distinctions*, 7 HUM. RTS. L. J. 195 (1986); Burns H. Weston et al., *Regional Human Rights Regimes: A Comparison and Appraisal*, 20 VAND. J. TRANSNAT'L L. 585 (1987); Richard Kiwanuka, *The Meaning of "People" in the African Charter on Human and Peoples' Rights*, 82 AM. J. INT'L L. 80 (1988).

6. There seems little doubt that private duties, implied and direct, are contemplated by most human rights instruments. Examples abound. Article 5 of the ICCPR provides, in part, that nothing contained therein can imply "for any state, group or person" any right to limit the rights of others. ICCPR, *supra* note 3, art. 5. Moreover, individuals can be punished for violations of human rights, as was the case in Nuremberg, given that the Geneva Conventions impose duties on private individuals. *See generally* Jordan Paust, *The Other Side of Right: Private Duties Under Human Rights Law*, 5 HARV. HUM. RTS. J. 51 (1992).

7. *See generally* Robert M. Cover, *Obligation: A Jewish Jurisprudence of the Social Order*, 5 J. L. & RELIGION 65 (1987). Cover argues that the myth, the jurisprudence of rights, is essential to counterbalance the omnipotent state. This myth "(a) establishes the State as legitimate only in so far as it can be derived from the autonomous creatures who trade in their rights for security—i.e., one must tell a story about the States' utility or service to us, and (b) potentially justifies individual and communal resistance to the Behemoth." *Id.* at 69. It is not surprising that Western individuals and movements employ the language of rights in their claims against society or the state. Examples range from civil rights groups to women's organizations and gay and lesbian individuals and groups.

8. John Locke, TWO TREATISES OF GOVERNMENT (New York: Cambridge University Press, 1988).

9. Jack Donnelly, *Human Rights and Western Liberalism*, in Abdullahi A. An-Na'im and Francis M. Deng, eds., HUMAN RIGHTS IN AFRICA: CROSS-CULTURAL PERSPECTIVES (Washington, D.C.: Brookings Institution Press, 1990), p. 34 [hereinafter CROSS-CULTURAL PERSPECTIVES].

10. In 1885 at the Berlin Conference, European powers carved up the map of Africa and created dozens of entirely new countries without regard to existing political entities, ethnic boundaries, economic considerations, historical alliances, or geographic and demographic variables. *See* Crawford Young, *The Heritage of Colonialism*, in John W. Harbeson and Donald Rothchild, eds., AFRICA IN WORLD POLITICS (Boulder, Colo.: Westview Press, 1991), p. 19.

11. Only Morocco, Tunisia, Ethiopia, Burundi, Rwanda, Madagascar, Swaziland, Lesotho, and Botswana have any meaningful precolonial territorial identities. *Id.*

12. For more detailed views of the concept of cultural relativism in human rights, *see generally* Jack Donnelly, UNIVERSAL HUMAN RIGHTS IN THEORY AND PRACTICE (Ithaca, N.Y.: Cornell University Press, 1989) [hereinafter Donnelly, UNIVERSAL HUMAN RIGHTS]; Raimundo Panikkar, *Is the Notion of Human Rights a Western Concept?* 120 DIOGENES 75 (1982); Adamantia Pollis and Peter Schwab, *Human Rights: A Western Construct with Limited Applicability*, in Adamantia Pollis and Peter Schwab, eds., HUMAN RIGHTS: CULTURAL AND IDEOLOGICAL PERSPECTIVES (New York: Praeger, 1979) [hereinafter HUMAN RIGHTS PERSPECTIVES].

13. Rhoda Howard, a well-known Canadian Africanist, refuses to acknowledge that precolonial African societies knew human rights as a concept. She emphasizes that "traditional Africa protected a system of obligations and privileges based on ascribed statuses, not a system of human rights to which one was entitled merely by virtue of being human." Rhoda Howard, *Group Versus Individual Identity in the African Debate on Human Rights* [hereinafter Howard, *Group Versus Individual*], in CROSS CULTURAL PERSPECTIVES, *supra* note 9, at 159, 167. Howard is so fixated with the Western notion of rights attaching only to the atomized individual that she summarily dismisses arguments by African scholars, some of whom could be classified as cultural relativists, that individual rights were held in a social, collective context.

14. Francis Deng disagrees with the view "widely held in the West and accepted or exploited in developing countries, that the concept of human rights is peculiarly Western." Francis M. Deng, *A Cultural Approach to Human Rights Among the Dinka*, in CROSS-CULTURAL PERSPECTIVES, *supra* note 9, at 261. "[T]o arrogate the concept," writes Deng, "to only certain groups, cultures, or civilizations is to aggravate divi-

siveness on the issue, to encourage defensiveness or unwarranted self-justification on the part of the excluded, and to impede progress toward a universal consensus on human rights." *Id.*

15. Donnelly, for example, dismisses cultural relativists and then declares, rather hastily, that "human rights are foreign to such communities [African, Native American, traditional Islamic social systems], which employed other mechanisms to protect and realize human dignity." Donnelly, UNIVERSAL HUMAN RIGHTS, *supra* note 12, at 118.

16. Timothy Fernyhough, *Human Rights and Precolonial Africa,* in Ronald Cohen et al., eds., HUMAN RIGHTS AND GOVERNANCE IN AFRICA (Gainesville: University Press of Florida, 1993), p. 39 [hereinafter HUMAN RIGHTS AND GOVERNANCE]. Fernyhough notes that this division is ironic because "both groups take as their starting point a precolonial Africa that they agree was precapitalist and predominantly agrarian, relatively decentralized politically, and characterized by communal social relations." *Id.*

17. Although the majority of precolonial authorities in Africa were not rigidly stratified, a number of highly centralized states such Buganda and the Nigerian emirates divided society into the repressive categories of nobles, freemen, and slaves. *See* Rhoda Howard, *Evaluating Human Rights in Africa: Some Problems of Implicit Comparisons,* 6 HUM. RTS. Q. 160, 175–76 (1984) [hereinafter Howard, *Evaluating Human Rights*]. Howard errs, however, when she asserts that the "picture of precolonial African social relations on which the communal model is based is inaccurate even regarding the past. *Id.* at 175. She deliberately fails to admit that highly centralized societies were the exception, not the norm; most were governed by ideals of communitarianism.

18. An examination of precolonial societies yields two basic models. A majority of societies, many of which were agricultural, pastoralist, or both, were relatively free of rigid social stratification, although age and gender played significant roles in determining both social and political status. A number of others had developed coercive state structures. *See generally* Eric O. Ayisi, AN INTRODUCTION TO THE STUDY OF AFRICAN CULTURE (London: Heinemann Educational, 1972); Myer Fortes and Edward Evans-Pritchard, AFRICAN POLITICAL SYSTEMS (London: Oxford University Press, 1940).

19. A basic contradiction between the European nation-state and precolonial Africa societies lies in the constitution of political society. In distinguishing what he calls "African cultural-nations" from the modern state, Mojekwu argues that

While the European impersonal governments were able to accommodate and control peoples from several ethnic, racial, and cultural origins within the nation-state, African cultural-nations controlled kinship groups within their cultural boundaries. A cultural-nation governed through familial chiefs and elders who shared authority with the community at large.

Chris Mojekwu, *International Human Rights: An African Perspective,* in Jack L. Nelson and Vera M. Green, eds., INTERNATIONAL HUMAN RIGHTS: CONTEMPORARY ISSUES (Stanfordville, N.Y.: Human Rights Publishing Group, 1980), p. 87. Few precolonial African societies were multi-ethnic.

20. Howard, *Group Versus Individual, supra* note 13, at 165–66. Howard sees no

middle ground between individual and group consciousness. She writes, incredibly, that for Africans to "assert their human rights as individuals would be unthinkable and would undercut their dignity as group members."

21. Ronald Cohen, *Endless Teardrops: Prolegomena to the Study of Human Rights in Africa*, in HUMAN RIGHTS AND GOVERNANCE, *supra* note 16, at 3–4. Wiredu defines a right as a "claim that people are entitled to make on others or on society at large by virtue of their status." Kwasi Wiredu, *An Akan Perspective on Human Rights*, in CROSS-CULTURAL PERSPECTIVES, *supra* note 9, at 243.

22. Wiredu, *supra* note 21, at 243. Akans believed that each individual had intrinsic value and was entitled to a measure of basic respect. But individuals were also members of matrilineal kinship lineages which generated duties and obligations. A person could enhance his or her "individuality" or "personhood" by executing duties such as participating in public works and sustaining a prosperous household. Conversely, if one failed to make these contributions, his or her personhood diminished. This "normative layer" in the conception of an individual bears obligations, but it is also "matched by a whole series of rights that accrue to the individual simply because he lives in a society in which everyone has those obligations." *Id.* at 247.

23. Joseph Muthiani, AKAMBA FROM WITHIN: EGALITARIANISM IN SOCIAL RELATIONS (New York: Exposition Publishers, 1973), p. 84. While all "people were considered equal in status as human beings" everyone was expected to show strangers "special generosity." *Id.* at 18. The age gradation on which the Akamba were organized was a functional structure based on the level of physical maturity. Equality and democracy were required within each age grade. Women had their own comparable but separate prestige structure which, however, was rarely consulted by the council of elders in matters of public concern. *Id.* at 80–82.

24. Wiredu, *supra* note 21, at 248–49. On occasion, an election was necessary to determine who in the royal lineage was the rightful heir. The town was the basic unit of government among the Akans. Several Akan towns could group together to form larger governmental units.

25. *Id.* at 251. "The stool was the symbol of chiefly status, and so the installation of a chief was called enstoolment and his dismissal destoolment." *Id.* The "destooling" of a chief was governed by certain processes and rules. Charges would be filed and investigations conducted before a decision could be reached. *Id.*. On rules governing a chieftainship, *see* Ayisi, *supra* note 18, at 48. Further evidence of democratic governance in traditional African society is offered by Kobia's description of the political organization among the Meru of Kenya. Members of the *njuri ncheke*, the supreme council of elders, were "very carefully elected and had to be individuals of unquestionable integrity and in good standing with the society." Samuel Kobia, THE QUEST FOR DEMOCRACY IN AFRICA (Nairobi: National Council of Churches of Kenya, 1993), p. 12. The chair of the *njuri ncheke*, which held legislative and judicial powers, "rotated among the *agwe*," leaders of the six subgroups of the Meru nation. *Id.*

26. Muthiani, *supra* note 23, at 83.

27. *Id.* at 85; *see also* Charles W. Hobley, ETHNOLOGY OF THE A-KAMBA AND OTHER EAST AFRICAN TRIBES (London: Cass, 1971), p. 78.

28. Hobley, *supra* note 27, at 78–79. Cattle were highly valued as a measurement

of wealth. Among the Maasai, another East African people, the murder of a man was compensated by the fixed fine of forty-nine head of cattle. It is interesting to note that no fine was set for the murder of women because the Maasai almost never murdered women, due to the belief that ill-luck would strike the murderer. *See* S. S. Ole Sankan, THE MAASAI (Nairobi: East African Literature Bureau, 1971), p. 14.

29. Wiredu, *supra* note 21, at 252. He further notes that neither at the "lineage level nor at any other level of Akan society could a citizen be subjected to any sort of sanctions without proof of wrongdoing." *Id.* Even dead bodies were tried posthumously before a symbolic sentence could be imposed.

30. *See generally* Ayisi, *supra* note 18, at 64–70.

31. Fernyhough, *supra* note 16, at 56.

32. *Id.* at 61. *See generally* Max Gluckman, IDEAS AND PROCEDURES IN AFRICAN CUSTOMARY LAW (London: Oxford University Press for International African Institute by the Oxford University Press 1969).

33. Fernyhough, *supra* note 16, at 62. For example, in the Tio kingdom in present-day Brazzaville, the Congo, "as elsewhere in Africa, a strong tradition of jurisprudence existed, with specific rulings for penalties cited as precedents, such as levels of fines for adultery." *Id.* Among the Akamba, for instance, the offense of assault carried numerous fines, which varied depending on the degree of assault and whether it resulted in the loss of a limb or limbs. *See* Hobley, *supra* note 27, at 79.

34. *See generally* Joseph Ki-Zerbo, *African Personality and the New African Society*, in William J. Hanna, ed., INDEPENDENT BLACK AFRICA: THE POLITICS OF FREEDOM (Chicago: Rand McNally, 1964), pp. 46–59..

35. Léopold S. Senghor, *Problématique de la négritude*, in LIBERTÉ 3: NÉGRITUDE ET CIVILISATION DE L'UNIVERSEL (Paris: Editions du Seuil, 1970), pp. 269–70, *quoted in* Janet G. Vaillant, BLACK, FRENCH, AND AFRICAN: A LIFE OF LÉOPOLD SÉDAR SENGHOR (Cambridge, Mass.: Harvard University Press, 1990), p. 244. The concept of "negritude" was initially coined by Aimé Césaire and Léopold Sédar Senghor as a reaction to white racism of the French variety. Under the philosophy of negritude, "collective organizations enfold the individual in Africa. Yet he is not crushed. What the African knows, Senghor points out, is that the realization of the human personality lies less in the search for singularity than in the development of his potential through participation in a community." *Id.* at 257. It emphasizes the importance of the family, nuclear and extended, the role of democratic, consensual decision-making with the community through the council of elders, and respect for nature.

36. The concept of *ujamaa*, the Kiswahili concept for kinship, was based on three prongs: respect, where each family member recognized the place and rights of others within the family; common ownership of property, that all must have the same basic necessities; and obligation to work, that every family member has the right to eat and to shelter but also the obligation to work. *See* Goran Hyden, BEYOND UJAMAA IN TANZANIA: UNDERDEVELOPMENT AND AN UNCAPTURED PEASANTRY (Berkeley: University of California Press, 1980), p. 98..

37. Ki-Zerbo, *supra* note 34. In her work on family structures, Sudarkasa groups the cultural factors that account for the cohesion of the African family into four principles: respect, restraint, responsibility, and reciprocity. These principles cre-

ate a complex balance of rights and duties within the family structure. *See* Niara Sudarkasa, *African and Afro-American Family Structure: A Comparison*, 11 BLACK SCHOLAR 37, 50 (November/December 1980); *see also* Josiah Cobbah, *African Values and the Human Rights Debate: An African Perspective*, 9 HUM. RTS. Q. 309–31 (1987). Special mention must be made of the importance of generosity in traditional society. As noted by Kobia, there was a "mutual caring for one another, especially strangers and travellers." Kobia, *supra* note 25, at 13. It was, for example, a "cardinal custom" in every household to prepare enough food for the unexpected stranger. *Id.* Even in today's economic difficulties, Africans—rural and urban— generally offer food to strangers and visitors.

38. Cohen, *supra* note 21, at 14. For precolonial human rights conceptions in Africa, *see also* Tunji Abayomi, *Continuities and Changes in the Development for Civil Liberties in Nigeria*, 22 U. TOL. REV. 1035, 1037–41 (1991); Fasil Nahum, *African Contribution to Human Rights*, Paper presented at the Seminar on Law and Human Rights in Development, Gaborone, Botswana, May 24–28, 1982 (on file with author); Nana Kusi Appea Busia, Jr., *The Statues of Human Rights in Pre-Colonial Africa: Implications for Contemporary Practices*, in Eileen McCarthy-Arnold, David R. Penna, and Debra Joy Couz Sobregena, AFRICA, HUMAN RIGHTS, AND THE GLOBAL SYSTEM: THE POLITICAL ECONOMY OF HUMAN RIGHTS IN A CHANGING WORLD (Westport, Conn.: Greenwood Press, 1994), pp. 225–50 [hereinafter POLITICAL ECONOMY].

39. *See generally* Dunstan M. Wai, *Human Rights in Sub-Saharan Africa*, in CULTURAL AND IDEOLOGICAL PERSPECTIVES, *supra* note 13, at 115–44; Julius Nyerere, UJAMAA— ESSAYS ON SOCIALISM (Dar es Salaam: Oxford University Press, 1968).

40. Wai, *supra* note 39, at 116. Wai further notes that channels for political participation existed in which "Discussion was open and those who dissented from the majority opinion were not punished. . . . There was a clear conception of freedom of expression and association." *Id.* at 117.

41. Asmaron Legesse, *Human Rights in African Political Culture*, in Kenneth W. Thompson ed., THE MORAL IMPERATIVES OF HUMAN RIGHTS: A WORLD SURVEY (Lanham. Md.: University Press of America, 1980), pp. 123, 125.

42. *See generally* Wiredu, *supra* note 21.

43. *See generally* Fernyhough, *supra* note 16; Lakshman Marasinghe, *Traditional Conceptions of Human Rights in Africa*, in Claude Welch and Ronald Meltzer, eds., HUMAN RIGHTS AND DEVELOPMENT IN AFRICA (Albany: State University of New York Press, 1984), p. 32.

44. In the fire ordeal, the suspect would be asked to lick a red hot sword to prove his innocence. Hobley, *supra* note 27, at 81.

45. Wiredu, *supra* note 23, at 258.

46. *Id.* at 259.

47. Generally, in precolonial Africa, women were primarily responsible for housework including child care. Men generally handled "public" affairs such as security and governance of the community.

48. Howard, *Evaluating Human Rights*, *supra* note 18, at 176.

49. *Id.* Howard attempts to explain away the index or the African notions of rights and duties by analogizing the simplicity of feudal Europe to precolonial Africa. In "closed-village societies of premodern Europe, we would also discover

that people thought of themselves more as members of their own local groups than as individuals, finding a sense of identity by fulfilling their assigned roles rather than by fulfilling 'themselves.'" *Id.* To her, what some writers "view as essentially different African and Western social structures and ways of thinking are actually differences between relatively simple and relatively complex societies." *Id.* In other words, Howard believes that preindustrial African societies could not generate the complex concept of human rights.

50. Howard, *Group Versus Individual,* *supra* note 13, at 170. Howard believes that the "African" worldview, which is "peasant" and "traditional," must give way to the "Western" worldview, which is "urban" and "modern" and anchored around the individual. She cites Kenya and Nigeria, the "more developed economies of contemporary Africa" as examples of societies where the "traditional concept of solidarity is giving way to individualism." *Id.*

51. Donnelly, UNIVERSAL HUMAN RIGHTS, *supra* note 12, at 170. He adds that "In the Third World today we see most often not the persistence of traditional culture in the face of modern intrusions, or even the development of syncretic cultures and values, but rather a disruptive 'Westernization,' cultural confusion, or the enthusiastic embrace of 'modern' practices and values." *Id.*

52. Fernyhough, *supra* note 16, at 49.

53. *Id.* at 40 (citations omitted).

54. *Id.* at 40–41. To argue, as Donnelly and Howard do, that the individual in precolonial African societies was not entitled, in certain circumstances, to be left alone—for that is what the concept of human rights is partially about—betrays gross and surprising ignorance about African societies.

55. *Id.* at 39.

56. Abdullahi A. An-Na'im, *Problems of Universal Cultural Legitimacy for Human Rights, in* CROSS-CULTURAL PERSPECTIVES, *supra* note 9, at 331, 332.

57. Clawback clauses qualify rights and permit a state to restrict them to the extent permitted by domestic law. Their purpose, apparently, is to place vague constraints on government action against the individual. For an example, article 6 of the African Charter provides, in part, that "Every individual shall have the right to liberty and to the security of his person. No one may be deprived of his freedom except for reasons and conditions previously laid down by law." African Charter, *supra* note 1, art. 6, 21 I.L.M. at 60. The Charter has also been criticized for the weaknesses inherent in its enforcement mechanisms. *See* Cees Flinterman and Evelyn Ankumah, *The African Charter on Human and Peoples' Rights, in* HUMAN RIGHTS PRACTICE, *supra* note 3, at 159, 167–69. *See generally* N. R. L Haysom, *The African Charter: Inspirational Document or False Start,* paper presented at the Bill of Rights Conference, Victoria Falls, Zimbabwe, December 10–14, 1994; Olosula Ojo and Amadu Sessay, *The OAU and Human Rights: Prospects for the 1980s and Beyond,* 8 HUM. RTS. Q. 89 (1994).

58. *See, e.g.,* Flinterman and Akumah, *supra* note 60, at 166–67; Makau wa Mutua, *The African Human Rights System in a Comparative Perspective: The Need for Urgent Reformulation,* 5 LEG. F. 31, 33 (1993) [hereinafter *African Human Rights System*]; Amnesty International, AMNESTY INTERNATIONAL'S OBSERVATIONS ON POSSIBLE REFORM OF THE AFRICAN CHARTER ON HUMAN AND PEOPLES' RIGHTS (London: Amnesty International, 1993).

59. Mutua, *African Human Rights System, supra* note 61, at 32. For duties imposed on individuals, *see* African Charter, *supra* note 1, arts. 27–29, 21 I.L.M. at 63.

60. B. Obinna Okere, *The Protection of Human Rights in Africa and the African Charter on Human and Peoples' Rights: A Comparative Analysis with the European and American Systems*, 6 HUM. RTS. Q. 141, 148 (1984).

61. International Commission of Jurists, Human and Peoples' Rights in Africa and the African Charter 27 (Geneva: International Commission of Jurists, 1986).

62. The individual's needs, rights, joys, and sorrows are woven into a social tapestry that denies singular individuality. John S. Mbiti, AFRICAN RELIGIONS AND PHILOSOPHY (New York: Praeger, 1970), p. 141.

63. Kiwanuka, *supra* note 5, at 82.

64. Deng, *supra* note 14, at 266

65. *Id.*

66. The word Bantu consists of *ntu*, a root, which means humanness. Quite often, speakers of Kikamba or Kiswahili will rhetorically ask of an abusive person as if he is or has become an animal. An individual is not a *mundu* or a *mtu*, and loses his humanness if he abuses or mistreats fellow community members.

67. Address of President Léopold Sédar Senghor of Senegal to the Meeting of Experts for the Preparation of the Draft African Charter on Human and Peoples' Rights, Dakar, Senegal (November 28–December 8, 1979), OAU Doc. CAB/-LEG/67/3/Rev.1, at 6; reprinted in Philip Kunig et al., eds., REGIONAL PROTECTION OF HUMAN RIGHTS BY INTERNATIONAL LAW: THE EMERGING AFRICAN SYSTEM (1985), p. 123 [hereinafter EMERGING AFRICAN SYSTEM].

68. Jomo Kenyatta, FACING MOUNT KENYA: THE TRIBAL LIFE OF THE GIKUYU (London: Secker and Warburg, 1953), pp. 1–2; *see also* H. E. Lambert, KIKUYU SOCIAL AND POLITICAL INSTITUTIONS (New York: Oxford University Press for International African Institute, 1956).

69. Kenyatta, *supra* note 68, at 200.

70. Muthiani, *supra* note 23, at 80–85.

71. *See generally* Wiredu, *supra* note 21.

72. Muthiani, *supra* note 23, at 82.

73. Wiredu, *supra* note 21, at 249.

74. In Africa, "the extended family unit, like family units in nearly all societies, assigns each member a social role that permits the family to operate as a reproductive, economic and socialization unit." Cobbah, *supra* note 37, at 320. But unlike the West, kinship terminologies in Africa relate to actual duties and obligations borne by members. Furthermore, the terminologies are more encompassing: aunts and mothers, for example, have similar roles within the kinship unit, regardless of biological parentage. The same is true of uncles and older cousins. *Id.*

75. Most precolonial African villages were inhabited by people related through blood or marriage.

76. Cobbah, *supra* note 37, at 321.

77. *Id.*

78. This matrix of group solidarity revolves around respect, based on seniority in age; restraint or the balancing of individual rights with the requirements of the group; responsibility, which requires commitment to work with and help others in return for security; and reciprocity through which generous acts are returned. *Id.*

at 322; *see also* Sudarkasa, *supra* note 37, at 50.

79. Cobbah, *supra* note 37, at 322.

80. Kenyatta, *supra* note 68, at 115. Kenyatta writes that "early and late, by rules of conduct in individual instances, by the sentiment of the group in which he lives, by rewards and punishments and fears of ceremonial uncleanliness, the younger generation learns the respect and obedience due to parents. The older generation do likewise." *Id.*

81. *Id.* at 116–17.

82. *See id.* at 130–54.

83. Cobbah, *supra* note 37, at 323.

84. UDHR, *supra* note 3, art. 29. The American Declaration of the Rights and Duties of Man, OAS Res. 30, Ninth International Conference of American States (1948), OAS Doc. OEA/Ser. L/V/1.4 Rev. 20 (1965), also proclaimed a list of 27 human rights and ten duties. Buergenthal, *supra* note 3, at 128. The American Convention on Human Rights, *supra* note 3, did not follow the same course.

85. Buergenthal, *supra* note 3, at 178. Others, such as Haysom, have made blanket condemnations of the concept of duties. Fearing that the concept of duties could be used to suppress rights guaranteed by the African Charter, Haysom has written that the "interpretation of a duty towards the community as to mean duty towards the state, lends itself to an autocratic style of Government." Haysom, *supra* note 57, at 6.

86. For a commanding history of the continent, spanning the precolonial era to the present, *see* Basil Davidson, AFRICA IN HISTORY: THEMES AND OUTLINES (New York: Collier Books, 1991); *see also* Ali A. Mazrui, THE AFRICANS: A TRIPLE HERITAGE (Boston: Little, Brown, 1986).

87. K. A. Busia, AFRICA IN SEARCH OF DEMOCRACY (New York: Praeger, 1967), p. 31. Hansen defines a nation as "a group that shares a common history and identity and is aware of that; they are a people, not just a population." Art Hansen, *African Refugees: Defining and Defending Their Human Rights*, in HUMAN RIGHTS AND GOVERNANCE, *supra* note 17, at 139, 161.

88. Hansen, *supra* note 91, at 161.

89. According to Busia, the

New African States are composed of many different tribes. A state can claim to be a common territory for all the tribes within it, but common descent, real or fictitious, cannot be maintained among tribes, some of which have a history of different origins and migrations, such as the Buale, Senufo, Guro of the Ivory Coast; the Yoruba, Hausa, Ibo of Nigeria; Ewe, Fanti, Dagomba of Ghana. . . . Instead of the bond of a common culture and language, there are language and cultural differences which tend to divide rather unite.

Busia, *supra* note 87, at 33; Makau wa Mutua, *Redrawing the Map Along African Lines*, BOSTON GLOBE, September 22, 1994, at 17.

90. Although, before the arrival of the Belgians, the Tutsi minority ruled over the Hutu majority and the Twa in a feudal-client relationship, the colonial state "transformed communal relations and sharpened ethnic tensions by ruling through a narrow Tutsi royalty. The access to resources and power that the Tutsi collaborators enjoyed under the colonial state irreversibly polarized Hutu-Tutsi

relations." Makau wa Mutua, *UN Must Make Rwanda a Priority*, OAKLAND TRIBUNE, May 25, 1994, at A13.

91. "One need not go into the history of colonisation of Africa, but that colonisation had one significant result. A sentiment was created on the African continent—a sentiment of oneness." Mazrui, *supra* note 86, at 108, quoting Julius Nyerere, *Africa's Place in the World*, Wellesley College Symposium, at 149 (1960).

92. Busia, *supra* note 87, at 30.

93. Hansen, *supra* note 87, at 161–62.

94. Hansen notes that the "most obvious and powerful expressions of the continued African conceptual reliance on European political forms are the African states themselves. *The states are direct and uncritical successors of the colonies.*" *Id.* (emphasis added).

95. *Id.*

96. In his discussion of the absence of the requirements of empirical statehood in postcolonial Africa, Jackson has written that, in these "ramshackle" regimes, "Citizenship means little and carries few substantial rights or duties compared with membership in a family, clan, religious sect or ethnic community. Often the 'government' cannot govern itself, and its officials may in fact be freelancers, charging what amounts to a private fee for their services." Robert H. Jackson, *Juridical Statehood in Sub-Saharan Africa*, 46 INT'L AFF. 1 (1992).

97. *See* African Charter, *supra* note 1, art. 45, 21 I.L.M. at 65.

98. *See* OAU Doc. CAB/LEG/67/3/Rev.1, *supra* note 67, at 2.

99. African Charter, *supra* note 1, art. 29, para. 4, 21 I.L.M. at 63.

100. *Id.*, art. 27, para. 2, 21 I.L.M. at 63.

101. Article 29 of the African Charter provides that the individual shall have the duty to "preserve the harmonious development of the family and to work for the cohesion and respect of the family; to respect his parents at all times, to maintain them in case of need." *Id.*, art. 29, para. 1, 21 I.L.M. at 63. The state, however, does not shirk responsibility for the aged and disabled. The Charter gives them "the right to special measures of protection in keeping with their physical or moral needs." *Id.*, art. 18, para. 4, 21 I.L.M. at 62.

102. In defense of the duty of the individual to parents, the aged, and the needy, Isaac Nguema, the first chair of the African Commission, has rhetorically asked: "How can society be so ungrateful to people who once helped to build it, on the grounds that they have become a burden, maybe no more than waste?" Isaac Nguema, *Universality and Specificity in Human Rights in Africa*, COURIER, November/December 1989, at 16, 17. He pleads for Africa to "foster the cult and the veneration of the aged." *Id.*

103. Article 27(1) of the African Charter provides, inter alia, that "Every individual shall have duties towards his family." African Charter, *supra* note 1, art. 27, para. 1, 21 I.L.M. at 63.

104. *Id.* art. 29, para. 4, 3, 2, 6, and 5, 21 I.L.M. at 63.

105. It would be surprising if the first Africa-wide human rights document did not show sensitivity to the subjugation of African peoples, a condition that has largely defined what the continent is today. Beginning with the invasion, enslavement, and colonization by Arabs and later the Europeans, Africans have been keenly aware of the traumatic consequences of the loss of sovereignty over their politi-

cal and social life. As a general rule, they have not exercised domination over others; that ledger is heavily weighted against them.

106. Although the "brain drain" is partially a result of the abusive state, the cost of education is so high that a state is entitled to ask its educated elites to contribute to national welfare.

107. Every African is required to "contribute to the best of his abilities, at all times and at all levels, to the promotion and achievement of African unity." African Charter, *supra* note 1, art. 29, para. 8, 21 I.L.M. at 63. "[A]ll levels" here implies, inter alia, unity between different ethnic groups within the same state. This provision reflects a recognition by the Charter of the destructive power of ethnic hatred or tribalism, the term Westerners prefer when referring to ethnic tensions in Africa.

108. African Charter, *supra* note 1, art. 18, paras. 1 and 2, 21 I.L.M. at 61.

109. The Charter's reference to "traditional values" cannot in good faith be interpreted as a call for the continued oppression of women. The Charter requires the individual to "preserve and strengthen *positive African cultural values in his relations with other members of the society, in the spirit of tolerance, dialogue and consultation* and, in general, to contribute to the promotion of the moral well-being of society." African Charter *supra* note 1, art. 29, para. 7, 21 I.L.M. at 63 (emphasis added).

110. "The state shall ensure the elimination of every discrimination against women and also ensure the protection of the rights of the woman and the child as stipulated in international declarations and conventions." *Id.*, art. 18, para. 3, 21 I.L.M. at 62. Note, however, that the pairing of women and children in this instance is not merely a function of sloppy draftsmanship, it most probably betrays the sexist perception of the drafters.

111. Donnelly, for example, thinks that the Soviet or socialist conception of human rights, reflected in practice and official doctrine, is "strikingly similar" to African and Chinese conceptions. Donnelly, UNIVERSAL HUMAN RIGHTS, *supra* note 13 at 55.

112. *See* Vladimir Kartashkin, *The Socialist Countries and Human Rights*, in Karel Vasak and Philip Alston, eds., THE INTERNATIONAL DIMENSIONS OF HUMAN RIGHTS (Westport, Conn.: Greenwood Press,1982), pp. 644–45.

113. Roman Wieruszewski, *National Implementation of Human Rights*, in Allan Rosas and Jan Helgesen, eds., HUMAN RIGHTS IN A CHANGING EAST-WEST PERSPECTIVE (London: Pinter, 1990), p. 270.

114. Articles 39, 50, 51, and 59 of the 1977 Constitution of the Union of Soviet Socialist Republics link individual duties to the state with the enjoyment of individual rights. Konst. SSSR, arts. 39, 50, 51, 59 (1977).

115. V. Chkhidvadze, *Constitution of True Human Rights and Freedoms*, 18 INT'L AFF. 1 (1980), cited in Donnelly, UNIVERSAL HUMAN RIGHTS, *supra* note 12, at 55.

116. Individual duties owed to intermediate groups—groups falling between the family and the state such as ethnic, professional, and other associational entities—would seem to be implied by article 27 which refers to "society" and "other legally recognized communities." African Charter, *supra* note 1, art. 27, para. 1, 21 I.L.M. at 63. Such a reading could also be attached to article 10 which refers to the "obligation of solidarity" in associational life. *Id.* art. 10, para. 2, 21 I.L.M. at 61. "Solidarity" is both "social" and "national." *Id.* art. 29, 21 I.L.M. at 63.

117. Article 18(1) compels the state to protect the family, the "natural unit" of society. *Id.* art. 18, para. 1, 21 I.L.M. at 61.

118. According to Benedek, "The human rights approach to be found in traditional African societies is characterized by a permanent dialectical relationship between the individual and the group, which fits neither the individualistic nor the collectivistic concept of human rights." Wolfgang Benedek, *Peoples' Rights and Individuals' Duties as Special Features of the African Charter on Human and Peoples' Rights*, in EMERGING AFRICAN SYSTEM, *supra* note 67, at 59, 63.

119. H. W. O. Okoth-Ogendo, *Human and Peoples' Rights: What Point Is Africa Trying to Make?*, in HUMAN RIGHTS AND GOVERNANCE, *supra* note 17, at 74, 78–79; *see* Okere, *supra* note 63, at 148–49; Amnesty International, PROTECTING HUMAN RIGHTS: INTERNATIONAL PROCEDURES AND HOW TO USE THEM (London: Amnesty International, 1991), p. 15. *See generally* Issa G. Shivji, THE CONCEPT OF HUMAN RIGHTS IN AFRICA (London: Codesria Book Series, 1989).

120. *See supra* note 57 and accompanying text; Okoth-Ogendo, *supra* note 119, at 79.

121. *See* Cohen, *supra* note 21, at 15. Cohen adds that "More importantly, the dangers of supporting state power as a fundamental 'right' are obvious. Indeed, the African record to date on that score provides serious grounds for concern." *Id.* Donnelly points to the perversion of the ordinary correlation between duties and rights in the former Soviet Union where a totalitarian, undemocratic state manipulated the concept to abrogate individual rights. Donnelly, UNIVERSAL HUMAN RIGHTS, *supra* note 12, at 55–57. However, I disagree with Donnelly when he states that rights are completely independent of duties. The link between right and duties is a social dialectic; one implies the other.

122. For exhaustive catalogs of human rights abuses by the Kenyan government, *see* Africa Watch, KENYA: TAKING LIBERTIES (New York: Africa Watch, 1991); Joel A. Solomon, FAILING THE DEMOCRATIC CHALLENGE: FREEDOM OF EXPRESSION IN MULTI-PARTY KENYA (Washington, D.C.: Robert F. Kennedy Memorial Center for Human Rights, 1993); Maina Kiai, INDEPENDENCE WITHOUT FREEDOM: THE LEGITIMIZATION OF REPRESSIVE LAWS AND PRACTICES IN KENYA (Nairobi: Kenya Human Rights Commission 1994).

123. For a comprehensive report on human rights abuses in Zaire, *see* Makau wa Mutua and Peter Rosenblum, ZAIRE: REPRESSION AS POLICY (New York: Lawyers Committee for Human Rights, 1990); Africa Watch, ZAIRE: TWO YEARS WITHOUT TRANSITION (New York: Africa Watch, 1992).

124. During its first two decades after achieving independence in 1961, Tanzania, under the leadership of the late Julius Nyerere and the Tanzania African National Union (TANU) and later Chama Cha Mapinduzi (CCM), the ruling party, appeared to be an exception to the kleptocratic oligarchies then prevalent in Africa. The state seemed genuinely committed to the realization of *ujamaa*, the policy of socialism and self-reliance. *See generally* Makau wa Mutua, *Tanzania's Recent Economic Reform: An Analysis*, 1988 TRANSAFRICA FORUM 69 (discussing Tanzania's progression toward self-reliance and socialism under Nyerere); Hyden, *supra* note 36 (discussing the implementation of *ujamaa* policies and politics in Tanzania from a political economy perspective with particular focus on the role of the peasants).

125. Okoth-Ogendo, *supra* note 119, at 79. The misappropriation of tradition by

some of Africa's despots and political charlatans to justify coercive measures against individuals should not be reason for the emotional denunciation of the duty/rights conception. Hastings Kamuzu Banda, the former president of Malawi, used "traditional courts" to silence his critics, and Mobutu Sese Seko, the long term Zairian ruler, at one point instituted *salongo*, a thinly disguised colonial practice of forced labor. Both practices, which had nothing to do with precolonial values, were cynically designed to increase the state's power over the people. *See* Makau wa Mutua, CONFRONTING THE PAST: ACCOUNTABILITY FOR HUMAN RIGHTS VIOLATIONS IN MALAWI (Washington, D.C.: Robert F. Kennedy Memorial Center for Human Rights, 1994); Donnelly, UNIVERSAL HUMAN RIGHTS, *supra* note 12, at 130.

126. Okoth-Ogendo, *supra* note 119, at 79.

127. Article 45 of the African Charter outlines the mandate of the African Commission, which includes the interpretation of the Charter and the formulation of principles and rules relating to human rights. African Charter, *supra* note 1, art. 45., 21 I.L.M. at 65.

128. *Id.* , art. 29, 21 I.L.M. at 63.

129. Umozurike, *supra* note 5, at 907. The African Charter also imposes similar obligations on states, "States parties to the present Charter shall have the duty to promote and ensure through teaching, education and publication, the respect of the rights and freedoms contained in the present Charter and to see to it that these freedoms and rights as well as corresponding obligations and duties are understood." African Charter, *supra* note 1, art. 25, 21 I.L.M. at 63.

130. Benedek observes further, that in traditional African societies "the human being could not survive apart from his people, the community, who in turn was dependent on the participation of all its constituent parts." Benedek, *supra* note 118, at 63. This relationship was one of duality, "not one of subordination but of complementary, participation, and dialogue." *Id.* The "support and allegiance" of these relationships "are still a predominant factor of the life of most Africans." *Id.*

131. Rapporteur's Report, OAU Doc. CM/1149 (XXXVII), Ann. 1, at 3, para. 10, *quoted in* Kiwanuka, *supra* note 5, at 82.

132. Article 1 of both the ICESCR and ICCPR provides: "All peoples have the right of self-determination. By virtue of that right they freely determine their political status and freely pursue their economic, social and cultural development." ICESCR, *supra* note 3, art. 1; ICCPR, *supra* note 3, art. 1. During the drafting of the ICESCR and the ICCPR, Western governments stiffly opposed common article 1 because it put at risk the continued domination of the colonies.

133.Louis B. Sohn, *The New International Law: Protection of the Rights of Individuals Rather than States*, 32 AM. U. L. REV. 1, 48 (1982). *See generally*, Kiwanuka, *supra* note 5.

134. African Charter, *supra* note 1, pmbl., 21 I.L.M. at 59.

135. Van Boven, *supra* note 5, at 188–89. In its usage of "peoples," the African Charter neither contemplates internal self-determination, the right of a people to overthrow an oppressive, undemocratic, and illegitimate regime, nor the claims of a minority or group within an independent state to its own self-determination or secession. Self-determination in the context of the OAU without a doubt refers to situations of foreign, colonial-type domination (previously the case in Namibia), or to minority-ruled regimes (formerly the case in South Africa). Ethnic groups or

communities within an independent state, such as the Luo or Luhyia of Kenya, are not envisaged by the Charter in this regard. The individual rights guaranteed in the Charter, particularly the rights to political participation, speech, association, and assembly, imply the right of citizens to a rule-of-law, democratic state.

136. Kiwanuka has identified at least four interpretations or usages of a "people" or "peoples" in the Charter: all persons within the territorial limits of a colonial state or minority-ruled regime; all groups of people with certain common characteristics who live within a colonial territory or a minority-ruled state, or minorities within an independent state (external self-determination would not be permitted under the OAU in this case); the people and the state as interchangeable; and all persons within the state. *See generally* Kiwanuka, *supra* note 5. These are the bearers of collective rights against the state which it has the duty to realize.

137. *See* Michael Chege, *Between Africa's Extremes*, 6 J. DEMOCRACY 44, 45 (1995). Chege notes the minimum conditions for the institutionalization of free and popular government which include shared democratic principles, an engaged middle class, and democratic leadership in a reasonably viable state. *Id.*

138. *Harambee* has been used in contemporary Kenya as a philosophy to drive domestic development groups. For an example, *harambee* self-help projects in rural communities account for the construction of 70 percent of Kenya's secondary schools. David Gillies and Makau wa Mutua, A LONG ROAD TO UHURU: HUMAN RIGHTS AND POLITICAL PARTICIPATION IN KENYA (Montreal: International Centre for Human Rights and Democratic Development, 1993), p. 2. *Harambee* projects have been undertaken with little or no state assistance. Conceived originally as "the social glue binding the state to society," it forced the state to be "accountable in the realm of social services" because under Kenyatta, the country's first president, it worked as "an extra-parliamentary bargaining system" for elected politicians to negotiate alliances and attract additional private resources to their constituencies. *Id.* It acted, in effect, as a redistributive mechanism where the influential politician would assemble prosperous friends to make personal monetary contributions or material to self-help projects. *Id.* However, as the state became more repressive and the political elites more cynical, *harambee* was turned into a "forced tax and an instrument of patronage" through which senior politicians would extort funds from businesses or frighten away contributors for particular causes or institutions. *Id.* at 3; *see also* Jennifer A. Widner, THE RISE OF A PARTY STATE IN KENYA: FROM "HARAMBEE!" TO "NYAYO!" (Berkeley: University of California Press, 1992).

139. *See* Cobbah, *supra* note 37, at 322.

140. Marie, *supra* note 5, at 199. This was the vision of precolonial societies.

Chapter 4. Human Rights, Religion, and Proselytism

1. The case of the Akamba, a Kenyan community targeted by European missionaries for conversion and colonization, was typical. As told by a European writer, for

Most Africans the turn to education (formal European education) brought a new involvement with the Christian religion. School and church were closely intertwined because almost everywhere missionary organizations had a monopoly on educational facilities and expertise. Problems of educational mobilization, therefore, could not be separated from the problem of adjustment to a new faith and values. School and church affairs were of vital concern to Africans seeking to come to terms with the colonial situation.

J. Forbes Munro, COLONIAL RULE AMONG THE KAMBA: SOCIAL CHANGE IN THE KENYA HIGHLANDS, 1889–1939 (Oxford: Clarendon Press, 1975), pp.147–48.

2. The movement's emphasis on respect for diversity and tolerance of difference implies that societies remain permanently open to inquiry, change, and challenge; it could be argued that this philosophy betrays the bias of the human rights corpus for a liberal, democratic society, a favoritism that could diminish the movement's claim of universality. But scholars of the movement argue that, with the possible exception of itself, "That movement institutionalizes no one ideal of social order. To the contrary, it explicitly allows for many faiths and ideologies while denying to any one among them the right or power to impose itself by force. It expresses a humanistic commitment to ongoing inquiry and diversity, as well as a deep skepticism about any final truth. It denies governments the right to close avenues of reflection, criticism, advocacy, and innovation in order to impose an orthodoxy." Henry J. Steiner, *Ideals and Counter-Ideals in the Struggle over Autonomy Regimes for Minorities*, 66 NOTRE DAME L. REV. 1552 (1991).

3. The designation of nonbelievers—individuals who do not profess the trinity of Judaism, Islam, or Christianity—by both Muslims and Christians as either pagans or infidels is one manifestation of belief in their own superiority over other religions. Christian missionaries and Islamists evidence this zeal and drive to universalize through the conversion or salvation of unbelievers from what they regard as eternal damnation. For a more detailed analysis of the attitude of Shari'a, or Islamic jurisprudence, toward nonbelievers *see* Abdullahi A. An-Na'im, *Human Rights in the Muslim World: Socio-Political Conditions and Scriptural Imperatives*, 3 HARV. HUM. RTS. J. 13 (1990) [hereinafter *Human Rights in the Muslim World*].

4. The wars between the Christian Portuguese and Muslim North Africans are well documented. In the fifteenth century, the Portuguese under the command of Prince Henry carried the crusades to Africa as part of the campaign to win back the continent from Muslims. An admiring portrait of Prince Henry said that the "flame that lit the Soldier of the Cross was kindled in his heart in early youth, and to win back Morocco from the Moors was the ambition of his life. He never drew his sword in any other cause." *See* Hans W. Debrunner, A HISTORY OF CHRISTIANITY IN GHANA (Accra: Waterville Pub. House, 1967), p. 15. Elsewhere he is called the "commander of the Portuguese Crusaders' Order of the Knight of Christ." *Id.* Even among different Christian denominations, competition for souls often turned violent as evidenced by the conflict in 1637 between the Dutch and the Catholic Portuguese at historic Elmina, part of what is today Ghana. A Catholic account of the conflict said that the "new conquerors, the Dutch, were then bitter enemies of Catholicism. Wherever they came, they burnt and destroyed the churches and would not allow a Catholic priest to preach to the people." *See* Hélè. Pfann, A SHORT HISTORY OF THE CATHOLIC CHURCH IN GHANA (Accra: Catholic Mission Press, 1965), p. 8.

5. Denys W. T. Shropshire, THE CHURCH AND THE PRIMITIVE PEOPLES (London: SPCK, 1938), p. xix. Shropshire goes on to write that, "Though he [the Native]

relies a good deal on what he has observed, he will always seek the true cause in the world of unseen powers above and beyond what we call 'Nature'—in the metaphysical realm in the literal sense, and his peculiar mental activity is largely due to his lack of distinction between what is actually present to sense and what is beyond."

6. Alfred Henry Barrow, FIFTY YEARS IN WESTERN AFRICA (London, 1900; reprint New York: Negro Universities Press, 1969), p. 29.

7. Matthew Fox, A SPIRITUALITY NAMED COMPASSION (San Francisco: Harper and Row, 1990), p. 112. "Crusades, inquisitions, witch burnings—which invariably meant the burnings of heretics and gay people, of fellow Christians and of infidels—all in the name of the cross. It is almost as if Constantine, and his empire's conversion to Christianity in the fourth century, uttered prophecy when he declared "'in the name of this cross we shall conquer'. The cross has played the role of weapon time and time again in Christian history and empire building."

8. Christian armies, much in the same way that Muslim crusaders saw themselves, considered it an honor to die for Christianity. According to many, "the supreme sacrifice was to die fighting under the Christian emperor. The supreme self-immolation was to fall in battle under the standard of the cross. . . . But by the time Christianity was ready to meet Asia and the New World, the Cross and the sword were so identified with one another that the sword itself was a cross. It was the only kind of cross some conquistadors understood." *Id.*

9. Shari'a, the legal and ethical regime of Islam, is derived from both the Qur'an and the Sunna, the Prophet's collaboration of the Qur'an through his statements and actions.

10. *See* An-Na'im, *Human Rights in the Muslim World, supra* note 3, at 22.

11. Not surprisingly, the revealed scriptures are only the Bible, Qur'an, and Torah (or the Old Testament), the holy books of Christianity, Islam, and Judaism respectively. It is inexplicable that Shari'a would disregard all other religious persuasions such as Hinduism and indigenous African or native American religions, among others, as illegitimate.

12. An-Na'im, *Human Rights in the Muslim World, supra* note 3, at 22-23.

13. *Id.* at 24. An-Na'im adds that "non-Muslim subjects of an Islamic state can aspire only to the status of dhimna, under which they would suffer serious violations of their human rights. Dhimmis are not entitled to equality with Muslims. Their lives are evaluated as inferior in monetary terms as well: they are not entitled to the same amount of *diya* or financial compensation for homicide or bodily harm as Muslims."

14. The crime of apostasy, which disallows individuals from freely changing their faith, violates human rights standards by preventing the freedom of choice.

15. Many African communities did not see any functional distinctions between the colonial administrators and the missionaries. "The political factor [colonialism] worked to the disadvantage of the missionaries in that the Kamba [an ethnic community in Kenya] like all other Africans, viewed the newcomers in terms of their local political situation. They identified the missionaries, arriving with the colonial power which gave them its support and approval, as part of the colonial authority system, barely distinguishable from administrative officers. In 1913, for example, elders in the Mwala area of Kenya inhabited by the Akamba I went to the

mission at Kabaa to obtain licenses for sugar-mills." Munro, *supra* note 1, at 104.

16. *Quoted in* K. Kiteme, WE, THE PAN-AFRICANS: ESSAYS ON THE GLOBAL BLACK EXPERIENCE (New York: Blyden Press, 1992), p. 94.

17. Shropshire, *supra* note 5, at xiii–xiv. Shropshire develops a methodology for evangelization in "primitive" cultures and pleads for the careful discrimination, preservation, transmutation and transformation of the religious and cultural institutions of the Southern Bantu [the African peoples of southern Africa], by and within a full-orbed presentation of the Christian religion." *Id.* at xix.

18. *Id.* at xxiv.

19. *Id.* at xii, 425.

20. Eric O. Ayisi, AN INTRODUCTION TO THE STUDY OF AFRICAN CULTURE (London: Heinemann, 1972), p. 57. "It has been said that they [African religions] lack any theological ideas and all the elements which make Judaism, Islam or Christianity sublime are lacking in African religion. People who should have known better, especially missionaries, were completely misguided about African religion, and by their muddled thinking propagated erroneous ideas about African religious beliefs."

21. Shropshire, *supra* note 5, at 425.

22. *Id.* A more forceful method was favored by others as this description of Henry the Navigator reveals, "The heathen lands were kingdoms to be won for Christ, and the guidance of their backward races was a duty that must not be shirked. Henry shouldered this responsibility. If he had the spirit of a crusader, he had that of a missionary as well. Wherever he explored, his aim was to evangelise, to civilise, and to educate the simple natives. . . . He sent out teachers and preachers to the black men on the Senegal [river]." Debrunner, *supra* note 4, at 15.

23. In most African cultures, the private/public distinction appears to have been absent or insignificant in the construction of social and political reality. Earthly existence constituted one whole: life was at once social, political, religious, cultural, and economic. The state (or the sociopolitical organism for the orderly running of the community, such as the council of elders) among many of the Bantu peoples of East Africa, was not apart from the community or contradictory to it. Life was one continuum, neither wholly private nor completely public. Religion has permeated every aspect of life.

24. Leon E. Clark, ed., THROUGH AFRICAN EYES: THE COLONIAL EXPERIENCE (New York: Praeger, 1970), p. 81. Mazrui thinks that Africa probably did not experience religious wars before the arrival of Christianity and Islam. He attributes the lack of religious wars in pre-Islamic, pre-Christian Africa to the nonproselytizing nature of indigenous religions and traditions. Ali A. Mazrui, *Africa and Other Civilizations: Conquest and Counterconquest*, in John W. Harbeson and Donald Rothchild, eds., AFRICA IN WORLD POLITICS (Boulder, Colo.: Westview Press, 1991), pp. 77–78.

25. According to a leading African scholar, religion is an essential element of African culture. "Africans are notoriously religious, and each people has its own religious system with a set of beliefs and practices. Religion permeates into all the departments of life so fully that it is not easy to isolate it." John S. Mbiti, AFRICAN RELIGIONS AND PHILOSOPHY (New York: Praeger, 1969), p. 1.

26. Since independence, successive Sudanese governments—which have been dominated exclusively by Sudanese Arabs—have sought to force Islam on black

Africans who are adherents of African traditional religions and Christianity in the south. In Nigeria, political instability—and the resultant inability to create a viable, economically prosperous society in spite of enormous material and human resources—must be attributed, at least partially, to the religious animosities between Muslims in the north and Christians in the south, a cleavage that also corresponds with ethnicity.

27. Basil Davidson, AFRICAN CIVILIZATION REVISITED: FROM ANTIQUITY TO MODERN TIMES (Trenton, N.J.: Africa World Press, 1991), pp. 3–4.

28. Simply put, I define as indigenous all African traditional religions which predated Islamization and Christianization. Similarly, the term could also be used to denote the religious beliefs of native, nonsettler peoples in the Americas and parts of Asia.

29. The 1966 International Covenant on Civil and Political Rights, G.A. Res. 2200 A(XXI), UN GAOR, 21st Sess., Supp. No. 16, at 52, UN Doc. A/6316 (1966) [hereinafter ICCPR], art. 18.

30. The ICCPR, the principal civil and political rights human rights treaty, establishes the Human Rights Committee, the body responsible for the elaboration, interpretation, and the encouragement of the implementation of the treaty. *Id.* art. 28. Article 40(4) of the ICCPR directs the Human Rights Committee to "study" state reports and to "transmit its reports, and such general comments as it may consider appropriate." The general comments are meant to be authoritative interpretations of the ICCPR's provisions. Article 27 of the ICCPR provides that "in those States in which ethnic, religious or linguistic minorities exist, persons belonging to such minorities shall not be denied the right, in community with others members of the group, to enjoy their own culture, to profess and practice their own religion, or to use their language."

31. General Comment No. 23, para. 6.2, UN Doc. CCPR/C/21/Rev.1/Add.5 (1994).

32. Proclaimed by General Assembly Resolution 36/55 of November 25, 1981. United Nations, HUMAN RIGHTS: A COMPILATION OF INTERNATIONAL INSTRUMENTS (New York: United Nations, 1993), pp. 122–25.

33. The Working Group on Indigenous Populations was established in 1982 by the United Nations as a subsidiary body of the UN Sub-Commission on Prevention of Discrimination and Protection of Minorities, itself an expert body of the UN Commission on Human Rights.

34. *See* Draft Declaration on the Rights of Indigenous Peoples, UN ESCOR, Commission on Human Rights, Sub-Commission on Prevention of Discrimination and Protection of Minorities, 46th Sess., Agenda Item 15, UN Doc. E/CN.4/Sub.2/1994/Add.1 (1994) [hereinafter Draft Declaration].

35. African Charter on Human and Peoples' Rights, OAU Doc. CAB/LEG/67/REV.5 (1981), reprinted in 21 I.L.M. 59 (1982).

36. *See, e.g.,* Constitution of the Republic of Ghana, sec. 27(1) (1979); Constitution of Mozambique, art. 33 (1975); Constitution of the Republic of Mali, art. 1 (1960).

37. *See* Constitution of Mauritius, sec. 11(5)(b) (1971); Constitution of Zimbabwe, sec.19(5)(b) (1980).

38. Constitution of Zambia, sec. 13 (1964).

39. Constitution of Mauritius, sec. 11(5)(b).

40. Article 19 of the UDHR provides: "Everyone has the right to freedom of opinion and expression; this right includes the freedom to hold opinions without interference and to seek, receive and impart information and ideas through any media and regardless of frontiers." Article 19 of the ICCPR is the equivalent provision although it warns that these rights carry "special duties and responsibilities" and are therefore subject to "certain restrictions" for the "respect of the rights . . . of others" and for the protection of "national security or of public order (*ordre public*), or public health and morals."

41. Steiner, *supra* note 2, at 1548.

42. *Id.*

43. The ICCPR states that "All peoples have the right of self-determination, By virtue of that right they freely determine their political status and freely pursue their economic, social and cultural development" (ICCPR, art. 1). Article 1 of the International Covenant on Economic, Social and Cultural Rights, the other treaty which together with the ICCPR and the UDHR makes the so-called International Bill of Human Rights, is identically worded.

44. *See* Steiner, *supra* note 2, at 1545–47.

45. Christians and Muslims came to Africa to wage holy war, as it were, and to subjugate and eradicate indigenous religions and cultures. They did not come to persuade; they came to conquer and did indeed conquer. This is a contradiction of the right to self-determination.

Chapter 5. The African State, Human Rights, and Religion

1. *Introduction: Posing the Problem of State Collapse,* in I. William I. Zartman, ed., COLLAPSED STATES: THE DISINTEGRATION AND RESTORATION OF LEGITIMATE AUTHORITY (Boulder, Colo.: Lynne Reinner, 1995) [hereinafter COLLAPSED STATES]; Makau wa Mutua, *Why Redraw the Map of Africa: A Moral and Legal Inquiry,* 16 MICH. J. INT'L L. 1113 (1995) [hereinafter *Why Redraw*]; Peter Anyang' Nyong'o, THIRTY YEARS OF INDEPENDENCE IN AFRICA: THE LOST DECADES (Nairobi: Academy Science Publishers, 1992); Robert H. Jackson and Carl C. Rosberg, PERSONAL RULE IN BLACK AFRICA: PRINCE, AUTOCRAT, PROPHET, TYRANT (Berkeley: University of California Press, 1982); Michael G. Schatzberg, THE DIALECTICS OF OPPRESSION IN ZAIRE (Bloomington: Indiana University Press, 1988); Ronald Cohen, Goram Hyden, and Winston P. Nagam, HUMAN RIGHTS AND GOVERNANCE IN AFRICA (Gainesville: University Press of Florida, 1993) [hereinafter HUMAN RIGHTS IN AFRICA]; Abiola Irele, *The Crisis of Legitimacy in Africa,* DISSENT (Summer 1992): 296–303.

2. Although these traditional sources of friction beset virtually all states, their centripetal and centrifugal forces have tended to lay bare the high vulnerability of the African state and on occasion to cause its implosion. *See generally* COLLAPSED STATES, *supra* note 1 (identifying and analyzing the reasons for, and process of, the collapse of a number of African states, including Chad, Uganda, Ghana, Somalia, Liberia, Mozambique, and Ethiopia). *See also* Mutua, *Why Redraw, supra* note 1; Henry J. Richardson, *"Failed States," Self-Determination, and Preventive Diplomacy: Colonialist Nostalgia and Democratic Expectations,* 10 TEMPLE INT'L & COMP. L. J. 1, 11

(1996); Aristide R. Zolberg, *The Specter of Anarchy: African States Verging on Dissolution*, DISSENT (Summer 1992): 303–11.

3. While over the last decade a number of African states have failed, many of them have been reconstructed. The collapse of the Rwandan state in 1994 has been the most dramatic to date. Another has been the Zairian state (renamed the Democratic Republic of the Congo) of the late Mobutu Sese Seko, which in May 1997 unraveled under military pressure from forces loyal to the Laurent Kabila, who overthrew Mobutu Sese Seko and was himself assassinated in January 2001 by his own bodyguard. *See* COLLAPSED STATES, *supra* note 1, at 1–11; Human Rights Watch, HUMAN RIGHTS WATCH WORLD REPORT 1995: EVENTS OF 1994 (New York: Human Rights Watch, 1995) [hereinafter WORLD REPORT 1995]; Human Rights Watch, GENOCIDE IN RWANDA: APRIL–MAY 1994 (New York: Human Rights Watch, 1995), pp. 39–48; Howard French, *In Congo, Many Chafe Under Rule of Kabila*, N.Y. TIMES, July 13, 1993, at 9.

4. J. Forbes Munro, COLONIAL RULE AMONG THE KAMBA: SOCIAL CHANGE IN THE KENYA HIGHLANDS, 1889–1939 (Oxford: Clarendon Press, 1975), pp.147–48; John S. Mbiti, AFRICAN RELIGIONS AND PHILOSOPHY (New York: Praeger, 1970), pp. 141, 300–317. The modern African state (started as the colonial enterprise known as the colonial state), the proselytization of Christianity, and the imposition of European social, economic, and political values and structures were interwoven in a continuum of cultural divestiture and alienation from precolonial African values. The church, the flag, and formal European education were all closely intertwined.

5. John S. Pobee, *Africa's Search for Religious Human Rights through Returning to the Wells of Living Water*, in Johan D. van der Vyver and John Witte, Jr., eds., RELIGIOUS HUMAN RIGHTS IN GLOBAL PERSPECTIVE: LEGAL PERSPECTIVES (The Hague: Martinus Nijhoff, 1996), pp. 402–6 [hereinafter RELIGIOUS HUMAN RIGHTS IN GLOBAL PERSPECTIVE]. Two African states, Nigeria and Sudan, have particularly been ravaged by religious conflict between Muslims and Christians in the context of the struggles for group autonomy and the control of the political state.

6. Africa's domination by Islam, Christianity, and African religions has been seductively termed its *triple heritage*, terminology which may suggest peaceful coexistence and mutual enrichment. Ali A. Mazrui, THE AFRICANS: A TRIPLE HERITAGE (Boston: Little, Brown, 1986).

7. Alfred Henry Barrow, FIFTY YEARS IN WESTERN AFRICA (London, 1900; New York: Negro Universities Press, 1969); *see also* Mbiti, *supra* note 4. Although I recognize the plurality of African religious expressions, I will often use the singular terminology of *African religion* to emphasize the near-total uniformity of assault and denigration of African religions by messianic faiths. In addition, the term also points to the similarities in cosmology and philosophy among different African religions.

8. Mbiti, *supra* note 4, at 8–13. Discussing early missionary attitudes toward Africans and their religions, and concluding that most missionaries regarded African religions as primitive and savage, Mbiti notes further that:

African religions and philosophy have been subjected to a great deal of misinterpretation, misrepresentation and misunderstanding. They have been despised, mocked and dismissed as primitive and underdeveloped. One needs only to look at earlier titles and accounts to see the derogatory language used, prejudiced descriptions given and false judgments passed upon these religions. In missionary circles they have been condemned as superstition, satanic, devilish and hellish. *Id.* at 13.

9. Mbiti has noted that "Christianity in Africa is so old that it can rightly be described as an indigenous, traditional and African religion" *Id.* at 300. But Mbiti here distinguishes between early Christianity in North Africa, Egypt, and Sudan (which he dubs indigenous) and mission Christianity beginning in the fifteenth century but particularly toward the end of the eighteenth century (according to him, this latter version is not indigenous). *Id.* at 300–303. Mbiti notes that Islam, too, is traditional, indigenous, and African in northern Africa, the Horn of the continent, and southward along the east coast. *Id.* at 317. *See also* Noel Q. King, CHRISTIAN AND MUSLIM IN AFRICA (New York: Harper and Row, 1971), pp. 1–35, describing the entry of both Christianity and Islam into Africa in premodern times.

10. According to Mbiti, Africans have their own religious ontology, which he groups into four categories: god as the supreme being responsible for humans and all things; spirits, the superhuman beings of the dead; human beings, the living as well as the unborn; and objects and phenomena without biological life. Mbiti, *supra* note 4, at 20.

11. Semitic religions often distinguish themselves from other beliefs by the emphasis they place on monotheism. *See, e.g.* Martin E. Marty and Frederick E. Greenspahn, eds., PUSHING THE FAITH: PROSELYTISM AND CIVILITY IN A PLURALISTIC WORLD (New York: Crossroad, 1988), p. ix [hereinafter PUSHING THE FAITH].

12. *See* Mbiti, *supra* note 4, at 19–20; Rosalind Shaw, *The Intervention of "African Traditional Religion*," 20 RELIGION 339 (1990); Rosalind I. J. Hackett, *African Religions and I-Glasses*, 20 RELIGION 303, 305 (1990); Rosalind I. J. Hackett, ART AND RELIGION IN AFRICA (New York: Cassell, 1996), pp. 9–12. More particularly, Mbiti paints the following picture of African religions:

For Africans, the whole of existence is a religious phenomenon; man is deeply a religious being living in a religious universe. Failure to recognize and appreciate this starting point has led missionaries, anthropologists, colonial administrators and other foreign writers on African religions to misunderstand not only the religions as such but the peoples of Africa.

Mbiti, *supra* note 4, at 20.

I define *indigenous* as all African religious expressions whose cores predate Islamization and Christianization. Such religions denote the beliefs of native, non-settler peoples and exclude Islam and Christianity.

Several scholars have charged Mbiti and other African writers with employing Judeo-Christian templates to translate African religions into a Western idiom. Some have argued that his and similar works, which they see as perpetuating a hegemonic version of African religions, are inspired by "theological" cultural nationalism. This prevalence of Western Christian discourse has remained normative within African religious studies, resulting in distortions of that universe.

13. Ali A. Mazrui, *Africa and Other Civilizations: Conquest and Counterconquest*, in John W. Harbeson and Donald Rothchild, eds., AFRICA IN WORLD POLITICS (Boulder, Colo.: Westview Press, 1991), pp. 69–70 [hereinafter AFRICA IN WORLD POLITICS].

14. On January 10, 1996, the government of the Republic of Benin inaugurated

National Voodoo Day, officially recognizing for the first time in post-independent Africa the importance of indigenous religion. All Africa Press Service, *In Benin, Government Gives Voodoo New Respect,* CHICAGO TRIBUNE, February 15, 1996, at 8.

15. Crawford Young, *The Heritage of Colonialism,* in Harbeson and Rothchild, AFRICA IN WORLD POLITICS, p. 19, describing precolonial Africa on the dawn of colonialism as a "ripe melon" with "sweet, succulent flesh" awaiting carving by European imperial powers.

16. *See* Basil Davidson, AFRICA IN HISTORY: THEMES AND OUTLINES (New York: Collier Books, 1991); Basil Davidson, AFRICAN CIVILIZATION REVISITED: FROM ANTIQUITY TO MODERN TIMES (Trenton, N.J.: Africa World Press, 1991).

17. Munro, *supra* note 4, at 148. Munro is careful to note the use of education to "attract" converts in the Machakos district of Kenya. He writes, further, that

> Christian missionaries gained an edge over their rival proselytizers. Islam, which seemed less appropriate than Christianity as a religion for those seeking to use a colonial system controlled by European Christians, made few new converts in the 1920s and the Haji [Muslim community] remained peripheral on the Kamba [Akamba, the indigenous people of Machakos district] scene. *Id.*

18. Denys W. T. Shropshire, THE CHURCH AND THE PRIMITIVE PEOPLES (London: SPCK, 1938), p. xiii, 67. Shropshire asserts that, like marsupial cubs, the children of the Bantu are more dependent on their mothers than children of "civilized" [European] parents.

19. Marty and Greenspahn, PUSHING THE FAITH, *supra* note 11, at ix.

20. Mbiti, *supra* note 4, at 9–12.

21. *Id.* at 8–9. According to Mbiti, *animism* was coined by Europeans to describe the beliefs of "primitive" peoples who consider all objects to have a soul, hence the presence in their cosmology of countless spirits.

22. Mazrui *supra* note 6, at 77.

23. Charles H. Long, *Religions, Worlds and Order: The Search for Utopian Unities,* in PUSHING THE FAITH, *supra* note 11, pp. 3–4.

24. Mbiti, *supra* note 4, at 2–3.

25. Chinua Achebe, THINGS FALL APART (New York: Anchor, 1959).

26. *Id.* at 146. In one particular incident, a missionary tells a crowd of Igbos: "All the gods you have named [Igbo gods] are not gods at all. They are gods of deceit who tell you to kill your fellows and destroy your children. There is only one true God and He has the Earth, the sky, you and me and all of us."

27. *Id.* at 152.

28. *See id.* at 176.

29. *Id.* at 208–9.

30. Elizabeth Isichei, *Seven Varieties of Ambiguity: Some Patterns of Igbo Response to Christian Missions,* 3 J. RELIGION IN AFRICA 212 (1970), p. 212.

31.Shropshire, *supra* note 18, at 431. Shropshire writes: "The education of the Bantu is largely in the hands of the missionaries whom the Government support with special grants." *Id.*

32. Isichei, *supra* note 30, at 212. This view was captured by another Christian imperialist who wrote: "Let the Missionaries and the schoolmasters, the plough and the spade, go together. It is the Bible and the plough that must regenerate Africa." *See* THE MEMOIRS OF SIR T. F. BUXTON, quoted in Hans Debrunner, A HISTORY OF

CHRISTIANITY IN GHANA (Accra: Waterville, 1967), p. 103. In Tanzania, mission schools were recognized as the "most important means by which the mission attracts converts and promotes its message." Thomas O. Beidelman, COLONIAL EVANGELISM: A SOCIO-HISTORICAL STUDY OF AN EAST AFRICAN MISSION AT THE GRASSROOTS (Bloomington: Indiana University Press, 1982), p. 198.

33. Debrunner, *supra* note 32, at 175.

34. *Id.* at 189. Emboldened by the government's rejection of African customs, Christian schoolgirls, for example, refused to undergo the "dipo" custom, which culminated in initiation into womanhood.

35. For a description and analysis of female circumcision, or *irua*, and its role in the construction of an individual's social identity within the Agikuyu, one of the African nations in modern-day Kenya, *see generally* Jomo Kenyatta, FACING MOUNT KENYA (New York: Knopf, 1965). For a thoughtful exploration of feminist debates on the practice, *see* Hope Lewis, *Between "Irua" and "Female Genital Mutilation" Feminist Human Rights Discourse and the Cultural Divide*, 8 HARV HUM. RTS. J. 1 (1995).

36. *See, e.g.*, T. A. Fasuyi, CULTURAL POLICY IN NIGERIA (Paris: UNESCO, 1973).

37. *Id.* at 21. *See also* Young, *supra* note 15, at 31. Young has written:

African culture was for the most part regarded as having little value, and its religious aspect—outside the zones in which Islam was well implanted—was subject to uprooting through intensive Christian evangelical efforts, which were often state-supported. European languages supplanted indigenous ones for most state purposes; for the colonial subject, social mobility required mastering the idiom of the colonizer. In innumerable ways, colonial subjugation in Africa brought not only political oppression and economic exploitation but also profound psychological humiliation.

38. Art Hansen, *African Refugees: Defining and Defending Their Human Rights*, in HUMAN RIGHTS AND GOVERNANCE, *supra* note 1, at 160–62.

39. Fasuyi, *supra* note 43, at 21; Otonti Nduka, WESTERN EDUCATION AND THE NIGERIAN CULTURAL BACKGROUND (Ibadan: Oxford University Press, 1965).

40. Fasuyi, *supra* note 39, at 21. Fasuyi also notes:

Students [African] had to learn things which had little bearing on their own way of life, e.g., the geography and the political, social and economic history of Britain and the British Empire. Foreign literature was studied. English became the official language, in which all transactions were affected. Indigenous languages were neglected; oral poetry gave way to Shakespeare and English literature. Those who managed to study abroad frequently came back alienated from their own society.

41. Isichei, *supra* note 30, at 339.

42. Debrunner, *supra* note 32. Christianity was brought to Ghana as early as the fifteenth century.

43. Janet G. Vaillant, BLACK, FRENCH AND AFRICAN: A LIFE OF LEOPOLD SEDAR SENGHOR (Cambridge, Mass.: Harvard University Press, 1990), p. 244. The pinnacle of French culture, the Académie Française, has forty "immortals," persons whose contribution to French culture and statecraft is unparalleled. Senghor was the first African to achieve the honor.

44. Isichei, *supra* note 30, at 339–40. Pope John Paul II opened the basilica in person, even though it was attacked as unconscionable and wasteful spending in

the midst of human poverty and suffering in a country that is only 10 percent Catholic.

45. *Id.* at 338–40.

46. 1996 BRITANNICA BOOK OF THE YEAR (Chicago: Encyclopedia Britannica, 1996), p. 721.

47. Isichei, *supra* note 30 at 1; Pedro C. Moreno, ed., HANDBOOK ON RELIGIOUS LIBERTY AROUND THE WORLD (Charlottesville, Va.: Rutherford Institute, 1996), p. 13. According to another count, in 1993 Africa was 57.3 percent Christian, 26.7 percent Muslim, and 15.4 percent African religions. For more comprehensive statistics on religious affiliations by country, *see* 1996 BRITANNICA BOOK OF THE YEAR, pp. 783–85.

48. Mervyn Hiskett, THE DEVELOPMENT OF ISLAM IN WEST AFRICA (New York: Longman, 1984); King, *supra* note 9.

49 Hiskett, *supra* note 48, at 276–301.

50 *See* Roland Oliver, THE AFRICAN EXPERIENCE (London: Weidenfeld and Nicolson, 1991), p. 202.

51 Isichei, *supra* note 30, at 324.

52 *See* Makau wa Mutua and Peter Rosenblum, ZAIRE: REPRESSION AS POLICY (New York: Lawyers Committee for Human Rights, 1990), documenting the abuses of the Zairian state against its own citizens. An example of such cynicism and manipulation of African culture as a veil for a despotic regime is that of Mobutu Sese Seko, the later Zairian president, and his "authenticity" campaign through which he forbade the use of European names and dress while running one of the most corrupt and abusive regimes with the support of France, Belgium, and the United States.

53. Kwame Nkrumah, NEO-COLONIALISM: THE LAST STAGE OF IMPERIALISM (New York: International Publishers, 1965); Robert H. Jackson, *Juridical Statehood in Sub-Saharan Africa*, 46 J. INT'L AFF. 1 (1992).

54. Makau wa Mutua, *Limitations on Religious Rights: Problematizing Religious Freedom in the African Context*, in RELIGIOUS HUMAN RIGHTS IN GLOBAL PERSPECTIVE, *supra* note 5.

55. Constitution of Kenya, sec. 22(l) (1963).

56. Shropshire, *supra* note 18.

57. Constitution of Malawi, sec. 19 (1964); Constitution of Nigeria, sec. 24 (1963); Constitution of Zambia, sec. 24 (1964); Constitution of Congo (Leopoldville) (Zaire), art. 25 (1964).

58. Constitution of the Republic of Guinea, art. 41 (1958); Constitution of the Ivory Coast, art. 6 (1960); Constitution of the Republic of Mali, art. 1 (1960).

59. Constitution of Kenya, sec. 78 (1988).

60. Constitution of the Federal Republic of Nigeria (Promulgation) Decree, sec. 37 (1989); Constitution of the Republic of Zaire, art. 17 (1990); Constitution of Zambia, sec. 20, (1991).

61.*See generally* 1996 BRITANNICA BOOK OF THE YEAR, p. 719. The National Islamic Front (NIF) government in Sudan came to power in 1989 following the overthrow of the democratically elected government of Saddiq Al-Mahdi. The NIF has sought to impose an extreme version of Shari'a or Islamic law on all citizens, including non-Muslims. It is estimated that Sudanese are 74.7 percent Islamic, 17.1 percent African religions, and 8.2 percent Christian.

62. Nat Hentoff, *Slavery and the Million Man March*, WASHINGTON POST, November 28, 1995, at A17; Moreno, *supra* note 47, at 36–37.

63. Moreno, *supra* note 47, at 36.

64. 1996 BRITANNICA BOOK OF THE YEAR, 754; Charles Mwalimu, *Police, State Security Forces and Constitutionalism of Human Rights in Zambia*, 233 GA. J. INT'L & COMP. L. (1991). Zambia is 72 percent Christian, 27 percent African religions, and 0.3 percent Muslim.

65. Moreno, *supra* note 47, at 41.

66. Munro, *supra* note 4, at 106; Kenyatta, *supra* note 35, at 261.

67. Constitution of Algeria, art. 2 (1989); Constitution of the Federal Islamic Republic of the Comoros, pmbl. (1992); Constitution of the Arab Republic of Egypt, art. 2 (1971) (as amended in 1980); Constitutional Proclamation of the Socialist People's Libyan Arab Jamahiriya, art. 2 (1969); Constitution of the Islamic Republic of Mauritania, art. 5 (1991); Constitution of the Kingdom of Morocco, art. 6 (1992); Constitution of the Tunisian Republic, art. 1 (1959).

68. *See, e.g.,* Constitution of the Kingdom of Morocco, art. 21 (1992); Constitution of the Islamic Republic of Mauritania, art. 23 (1991); Constitution of the Tunisian Republic, arts. 38, 40 (1959).

69. South African Constitution, Chapter 12, §§ 211–12 (1996).

70. Young, *supra* note 15, at 20. Crawford Young notes:

The cultural and linguistic impact [of Europe on Africa] was pervasive, especially in sub-Saharan Africa. Embedded in the institutions of the new states was the deep imprint of the mentalities and routines of their colonial predecessors. Overall, colonial legacy cast As shadow over the emergent African state system to a degree unique among major world regions.

71. Munro, *supra* note 4, at 110.

72. *Id.* at 11.

73. *Id.* at 114–17.

74. *Id.* at 100, 118–21.

75. Kenyatta, *supra* note 35, at 263.

76. Isichei, *supra* note 30, at 2–3.

77. E. Bolaji Idowu, AFRICAN TRADITIONAL RELIGION: A DEFINITION (Maryknoll, N.Y.: Orbis, 1975), p. 206.

78. *Id.*

79. Isichei, *supra* note 30, at 3. Isichei notes that in any event such churches are in a "state of relative, and sometimes absolute, decline, overtaken by the immense proliferation of 'prophetic' or Zionist churches." *Id.*

80. *See generally* Jacob K. Olupona, AFRICAN TRADITIONAL RELIGION IN CONTEMPORARY SOCIETY (New York: Paragon House, 1991).

81. Isichei, *supra* note 30, at 3.

82. Lamin Sanneh, ENCOUNTERING THE WEST: CHRISTIANITY AND THE GLOBAL CULTURAL PROCESS: THE AFRICAN DIMENSION (Maryknoll, N.Y.: Orbis Books, 1993), pp. 15–17.

83. *Id.*

84. All Africa Press Service, *In Benin, Government Gives Voodoo New Respect,* CHICAGO TRIBUNE, February 15, 1996; Associated Press, *Benin Voodoo Receives Official Nod,* AFRICA NEWS, January 1996.

85. 1996 BRITANNICA BOOK OF THE YEAR, p. 565.

86. T. O. Elias, AFRICA AND THE DEVELOPMENT OF INTERNATIONAL LAW (Boston: Martinus Nijhoff, 1988), p. 11. For example, the *Oba* (king) of Benin sent envoys to Portugal in 1514 to procure arms..

87. Constitution of Dahomey, art. 13 (1964).

88. Constitution of The Republic of Benin, art. 10, law no. 90–32 (1990).

89. Alan Cowell, *Pope Meets Rivals in the "Cradle of Voodoo"*, N.Y. TIMES, February 5, 1993, at 11.

90. AFRICA NEWS, *supra* note 84, at 108.

91. Jean-Luc Aplogan, *Benin's President's Camp Acknowledges Poll Defeat*, REUTERS, April 2, 1996.

92. African Charter on Human and Peoples' Rights (1981), OAU Doc. CAB/LEG/67/3/Rev.5 (1981), reprinted in 21 I.L.M. 59 (1982). The African Charter came into force in 1986.

93. Issa G. Shivii, THE CONCEPT OF HUMAN RIGHTS IN AFRICA (London: Codesria Book Series, 1989); H. W. O. Okoth-Ogendo, *Human and Peoples' Rights: What Point Is Africa Trying to Make?*, in HUMAN RIGHTS AND GOVERNANCE, *supra* note 1; Cees Flinterman and Evelyn Ankumah, *The African Charter on Human and Peoples' Rights*, in Hurst Hannum, ed., GUIDE TO INTERNATIONAL HUMAN RIGHTS PRACTICE (Philadelphia: University of Pennsylvania Press, 1992), p. 159.

Chapter 6. The Limits of Rights Discourse

1. Henkin triumphantly declares that "Ours is the age of rights. Human rights is the idea of our time, the only political-moral idea that has received universal acceptance." *See* Louis Henkin, THE AGE OF RIGHTS (New York: Columbia University Press, 1990), p. ix.

2. Struggles to open up one-party dictatorships in Eastern Europe, Africa, Latin America, Asia, and the former Soviet Union primarily sought political democracy, defined narrowly as the creation of governments through competitive multiparty elections. Despotic restrictions on expressive rights and the sole control of political power by a party or a political elite was seen as the evil that the exercise of political participation rights would cure. In these regions, quite often advocacy for the respect of human rights focused exclusively on political participation rights, whereas in the context of South Africa, the corpus of human rights was material for battle against the state. *See generally* Samuel P. Huntington, THE THIRD WAVE: DEMOCRATIZATION IN THE LATE TWENTIETH CENTURY (Norman: University of Oklahoma Press, 1991), discussing political transitions from repressive one-party regimes to political democracies from the 1970s to the 1990s. *See also* Gregory H. Fox, *The Right to Political Participation in International Law*, 17 YALE J. INT'L L. 539 (1992); Thomas Franck, *The Emerging Right to Democratic Governance*, 86 AM. J. INT'L L. 46 (1992); Henry J. Steiner, *Political Participation as a Human Right*, 1 HARV. HUM. RTS. Y.B. 77 (1988).

3. *See generally* Chester Crocker, HIGH NOON IN SOUTHERN AFRICA: MAKING PEACE IN A ROUGH NEIGHBORHOOD (New York: W.W. Norton, 1992); Watch Committees and Lawyers Committee for Human Rights, THE REAGAN ADMINISTRATION'S RECORD ON HUMAN RIGHTS IN 1986 (New York: Watch Committees and Lawyers Committee

for Human Rights, 1987), pp. 119-25. The U.S. Congress imposed limited sanctions on South Africa, overriding Reagan's veto and his policy of constructive engagement with South Africa. *See* Comprehensive Anti-Apartheid Act of 1986, Pub. L. No. 99-440, 100 Stat. 1086 (1986); Crocker, *supra,* at 304–32.

4. Namibia, however, provided important lessons in this regard. The Namibian independence constitution protects a wide array of human rights and reads like a human rights instrument. For the text of the Namibian Constitution, go to <www.newafrica.com/namibia/Constitution.asp>. *See also* Adrien Katherine Wing, *Communitarianism vs. Individualism: Constitutionalism in Namibia and South Africa,* 11 Wis. Int'l L.J. 295, 337–44 (1993).

5. A number of countries have committed funds and other resources to assist South Africa in its transition. Some of these are: Denmark in the establishment of the Commission for Gender Equality; the Netherlands, Sweden, Britain, and Canada in reforming the police; Britain in the integration of the various liberation armies and the South African Defense Force (SADF) into one national force; Denmark in the prevention and monitoring of violence in the prisons; Denmark, the United States, Sweden, and Canada in the reform of the administration of justice; the European Union, Denmark, and Sweden in supporting the Truth and Reconciliation Commission. In addition, some UN agencies, such as the United Nations Development Programme, and some Western philanthropies, such as the New York-based Ford Foundation, have been involved in supporting various governmental and nongovernmental efforts. *See* United Nations High Commissioner for Human Rights, Centre for Human Rights, Programme of Technical Cooperation in the Field of Human Rights, *Report of the Needs Assessment Mission to South Africa (6–25 May 1996)* (1996), pp. 51–54 [hereinafter *UN Needs Assessment Report*]. In addition, Canada assisted in the retraining of Magistrates, and Belgium funded the Legal Resources Centre (LRC), a leading nongovernmental organization, and the Center for Applied Legal Studies (CALS) at the University of Witwatersrand. Telephone interview with Shadrack Gutto, Deputy Director, Center for Applied Legal Studies (CALS) at the University of Witwatersrand, in New York (December 4, 1996).

6. The permanent Constitution replaced the Interim Constitution negotiated primarily by the ANC and the Nationalist Party (NP) and adopted by the formerly all- white Parliament in 1993. On September 6, 1996, the Constitutional Court, the authority empowered to certify the new Constitution, referred the text back to the Constitutional Assembly for reconsideration. On December 4, 1996, the Constitutional Court finally certified the text. *See* Certification of the Amended Text of the Constitution of the Republic of South Africa, 1996 (4) SA 744 (CC) (Case 37/96, December 4, 1996) (visited February. 20, 1999 www.law.wits.ac.za/judgments/ cert2.txt>. *See also Mandela Signs New South African Constitution,* Agence France Press, December 10, 1996, available in LEXIS, News Library, CURNWS File.

7. President Mandela signed the Constitution on International Human Rights Day—December 10—before a huge crowd in Sharpeville, scene of the 1960 massacre of sixty-nine blacks by the apartheid security forces. *See* Chris Erasmus, *South Africans Embrace Rights of a New Constitution,* USA Today, December 11, 1996, at A4.

8. The most important of these include the Human Rights Commission, the

Public Protector, the Commission for the Promotion and Protection of the Rights of Cultural, Religious, and Linguistic Communities, the Commission for Gender Equality, and the Electoral Commission. *See* S. Afr. Const. (1996 Constitution) chap. 9, sec. 181(1).

9. S. Afr. Const. (1996 Constitution), *supra* note 8, chap. 14, secs. 231, 232, and 233; S. Afr. Const. (Interim Constitution, Act 200 of 1993) chap. 10, sec. 181(1).

10. Convention for the Elimination of All Forms of Discrimination Against Women, opened for signature March 1, 1980, 1249 UNTS 14 (entered into force September 3, 1981); Convention on the Rights of the Child, G.A. Res. 44/25, 44 UN GAOR, 43 Sess., Supp. No. 49, at 166, UN Doc. A/44/49 (1989). South Africa ratified the Convention on the Rights of the Child on June 16, 1995. *See* Julia Sloth-Nielsen, *Ratification of the United Nations Convention on the Rights of the Child: Some Implications for South African Law,* 11 S. AFR. J. HUM. RTS. 401 (1995).

11. *See* UN Needs Assessment Report, *supra* note 5, at 11.

12. *See* Henry J. Steiner, *The Youth of Rights,* 104 HARV. L. REV. 917 (1991), reviewing Henkin, *supra* note 1.

13. In reality, of course, the state does not charitably and of its own volition choose to be "good"; the nongovernmental and private sectors, sometimes referred to as civil society, limit its power and determine the normative content of its operational philosophy and guiding principles. For a discussion on the relationship between the state and civil society, *see generally* John Keane, CIVIL SOCIETY AND THE STATE: NEW EUROPEAN PERSPECTIVES (New York: Verso, 1988).

14. *See* Ibrahim J. Gassama, *Reaffirming Faith in the Dignity of Each Human Being: The United Nations, NGOs, and Apartheid,* 19 FORDHAM INT'L L.J. 1464, 1540 (1996).

15. *See* Morton J. Horwitz, *Rights,* 23 HARV. C.R.-C.L. L. REV. 295, 404–6 (1988).

16. For analyses and critiques of the limitations of rights discourse, *see* Alan Freeman, *Racism, Rights and the Quest for Equality of Opportunity: A Critical Essay,* 23 HARV. C.R.-C.L. REV. 295, 331 (1988); Peter Gabel, *The Phenomenology of Rights Consciousness and the Pact of the Withdrawn Selves,* 62 TEX. L. REV. 1563 (1984); Patricia Williams, *Alchemical Notes: Reconstructing Ideals from Deconstructed Rights,* 22 HARV. C.R.-C.L. L. REV. 401 (1987).

17. African National Congress, THE RECONSTRUCTION AND DEVELOPMENT PROGRAMME (Johannesburg: Uhanyang Publishers, 1994), pp. 2–3 [hereinafter RECONSTRUCTION AND DEVELOPMENT PROGRAMME].

18. This particular reference indicates civil and political rights, not economic, social, and cultural rights. In most democracies, where the human rights corpus principally draws most of its philosophical roots and development, human rights were effectively narrowed to civil and political rights. Although economic, social, and cultural rights are formally part of that corpus, they belong to a "lower" rank of rights. *See* Philip Alston, *The Committee on Economic, Social and Cultural Rights,* in THE UNITED NATIONS AND HUMAN RIGHTS (Oxford: Clarendon Press, 1992), p. 490.

19. To date, South Africa has had the best opportunity to create such a state. Other states, such as Western democracies where the idea of individual rights was first born under liberalism, were not initially created as human rights states although they now embody many human rights norms in their constitutional and legal frameworks. A human rights state would not simply constitutionally guarantee civil and political rights while relegating economic and social rights to the pre-

carious welfare state. Instead, in a true human rights state, all rights would be made constitutionally effective and practically realizable and enforceable. South Africa could have attempted to erase the inequities of apartheid by collapsing this traditional dichotomy.

20. Only within the last century have European states committed themselves to formal political democracy with universal adult suffrage. *See, e.g.*, Thomas T. Mackie and Richard Rose, THE INTERNATIONAL ALMANAC OF ELECTORAL HISTORY (Washington, D.C.: Congressional Quarterly, 1991).

21. *See* Franck, *supra* note 2, at 49.

22. CIA WORLD FACTBOOK 2000—SOUTH AFRICA, available at <www.odci.gov/publications/factbook/geos/sf.html> (visited on May 9, 2001).

23. Thompson describes how the Afrikaners used the state to ram through perverted "affirmative action" programs for themselves after they captured the state in 1948. Leonard M. Thompson, A HISTORY OF SOUTH AFRICA (New Haven, Conn.: Yale University Press, 1990), p. 188.

24. *Id.* at 187–220.

25. *Id.* at 190.

26. Sexual Offenses Act (No. 23) of 1957; Prohibition of Mixed Marriages Act (No. 55) of 1949.

27. *See, e.g.*, Group Areas Act (No. 41) of 1950. Pass laws required blacks to carry passes authorizing them to be in "white" areas. Homelands were established by the Promotion of the Bantu Self-Government Act (No. 46) of 1959. The ten "ethnic" black homelands were Lebowa, Qwa-qwa, Bophuthatswana, KwaZulu, KaNagwane, Ciskei, Transkei, Gazankulu, Venda, and KwaNdebele. By 1981, four of these homelands—Bophuthatswana, Ciskei, Transkei, and Venda—accepted "independence" from Pretoria, effectively divesting their African populations of South African citizenship. No state except South Africa recognized the homelands as "independent." For more discussion of South Africa's homelands, *see* Henry J. Richardson, *Self-Determination, International Law and the South Africa Bantustan Policy*, 17 COLUM. J. TRANSNAT'L L. 185 (1978); John Dugard, *South Africa's "Independent" Homelands: An Exercise in Denationalization*, 10 DENV. J. INT'L L. & POL'Y 11 (1980); Thompson, *supra* note 23, at 191. Prior to the 1994 all-race democratic elections, all the homelands were "reincorporated" into South Africa.

28. The dispossession of Africans of their land by European settlers in South Africa goes back to the arrival of the Dutch in the seventeenth century. *See* South African Department of Land Affairs, OUR LAND: GREEN PAPER ON SOUTH AFRICAN LAND POLICY (Pretoria: Government of South Africa, 1996), p. 36 [hereinafter GREEN PAPER ON LAND] (a Green Paper is a draft policy document circulated by the government to solicit public comments before the publication of a White Paper for presentation to Parliament, *id.* at 85). *See also* Makau wa Mutua, *Why Redraw the Map of Africa: A Moral and Legal Inquiry*, 16 MICH. J. INT'L L. 1113, 1126–37 (1995), discussing the occupation and colonization of the African continent by European powers and the creation of the colonial state by war, fraudulent treaties, and conquest.

29. *See* Albie Sachs, ADVANCING HUMAN RIGHTS IN SOUTH AFRICA (Cape Town: Oxford University Press, 1992), p. 70. Furthermore, Albie Sachs has explained that under apartheid, any simple "deed of transfer has by law to contain an affirmation

that the seller and purchaser belong to the racial group permitted to own land in the area in question." *See* Albie Sachs, *A Bill of Rights for South Africa: Areas of Agreement and Disagreement,* 21 COLUM. HUM. RTS. L. REV. 13, 33 (1989) [hereinafter *Areas of Agreement and Disagreement*]. *See also* Anne Shepherd, *The Task Ahead,* AFRICA REP., July–August 1994, at 38, 39–40.

30. *See* Nelson Mandela, LONG WALK TO FREEDOM: THE AUTOBIOGRAPHY OF NELSON MANDELA (Boston: Little, Brown, 1994). The ANC was established on January 8, 1912 in Bloemfontein, Orange Free State Province. Saki Macozoma, *The ANC and the Transformation of South Africa,* BROWN J. WORLD AFF., (Winter 1994), at 241.

31. The Defiance Campaign was organized by the ANC with the intent of protesting and defying racist laws and the segregation of public facilities. Mandela, *supra* note 30, at 140–61.

32. The Freedom Charter was drafted by the ANC and adopted by a mass meeting of some three thousand delegates, named the Congress of the People, in Kliptown, several miles from Johannesburg, on June 25-26, 1955. Until the ban on the ANC was lifted and Nelson Mandela was released in 1990, the charter was the principal manifesto outlining the basic tenets of the anti-apartheid philosophy and its movement. It emphasized multiracialism, equal protection, the protection and enjoyment of economic and social rights, and the ownership of land by those who work it. For a text of the charter, *see* THE FREEDOM CHARTER, reprinted in 21 COLUM. HUM. RTS. L. REV. 249–51 (1989). *See also* Mandela, *supra* note 30, at 199–207.

33. Umkhonto we Sizwe, (MK) was formed in 1961 after the 1960 Sharpeville Massacre, in which 69 unarmed protesters were shot to death by South African forces, convinced the ANC that nonviolence and peaceful protest—an ANC philosophy since its founding in 1912—would not bring about an end to white domination and majority democratic rule. The banning of the ANC following the massacre was the central reason for abandoning nonviolence, since the ANC was thereby deprived of the right to nonviolent peaceful protest. Nelson Mandela founded MK and then recruited Joe Slovo and Walter Sisulu to the High Command with himself as chairman. *See* Mandela, *supra* note 30, at 325–27. *See also* Wing, *supra* note 4, at 351.

34. A senior American human rights scholar described apartheid as a "complex set of practices of domination and subjection, intensely hierarchized and sustained by the whole apparatus of the state, which affects the distribution of all values." *See* Myres S. McDougal et al., HUMAN RIGHTS AND WORLD PUBLIC ORDER: THE BASIC POLICIES OF AN INTERNATIONAL LAW OF HUMAN DIGNITY (New Haven, Conn.: Yale University Press, 1980), p. 523.

35. Mike Robertson, ed., HUMAN RIGHT FOR SOUTH AFRICANS (Cape Town: Oxford University Press, 1991), p. 57.

36. Suppression of Communism Act (No. 44) of 1950; Terrorism Act (No. 83) of 1967; General Law Amendment Act (No. 76) of 1962.

37. For more information on states of emergency and other human rights violations, *see* Lawyers Committee for Human Rights, THE WAR AGAINST CHILDREN (New York,: Lawyers Committee for Human Rights, 1986); Lawyers Committee for Human Rights, CRISIS IN CROSSROADS (New York, 1988); Africa Watch, THE KILLINGS IN SOUTH AFRICA: THE ROLE OF THE SECURITY FORCES AND THE RESPONSE OF THE STATE (New York: Africa Watch, 1991) [hereinafter THE KILLINGS IN SOUTH AFRICA].

38. 1996 BRITANNICA BOOK OF THE YEAR (Chicago: Encyclopedia Britannica, 1996), p. 716.. A Colored household averaged U.S.$7,455, while an Asian household brought home $11,487.

39. UN Needs Assessment Report, *supra* note 5, at 6.

40. Gail Bensinger, *Still Waiting in South Africa*, S.F. EXAMINER, April 28, 1996, available in LEXIS, News Library, CURNWS File; *Color Gap Hobbling South African Economy*, Japan Econ. Newswire, December 21, 1995, available in LEXIS, News Library, CURNWS File.

41. *See* Shepherd, *supra* note 29, at 40. *See also* UN Needs Assessment Report, *supra* note 5, at 6.

42. In the April 1994 first-ever nonracial democratic elections that ended over 300 years of white minority rule in South Africa, the ANC garnered nearly 63 percent of the total vote, barely missing a two-thirds majority. It also won 252 of the 400 seats in the National Assembly. It carried seven of South Africa's nine provinces, with the exception of Western Cape, which was won by the NP with a plurality of 53 percent, and KwaZulu-Natal, where Chief Mangosuthu Buthelezi's Inkatha Freedom Party (IFP) just managed to top 50 percent. F. W. De Klerk's NP captured a shade over 20 percent of the vote, while the IFP came in third with a little over 10 percent. Two other historically important parties, the black nationalist Pan Africanist Congress (PAC) and the Liberal Democratic Party (DP), were routed. *See* Patrick Laurence, *Election Results Analyzed*, AFRICA REP., July–August 1994, at 18–19.

43. On the ANC's nonviolent philosophy, *see* Allister H. Sparks, THE MIND OF SOUTH AFRICA (London: Heinemann, 1990), pp. 235–37.

44. *See* Mandela, *supra* note 30. Nelson Mandela, himself a lawyer, was instrumental in pushing the ANC toward armed struggle. Notwithstanding the ANC's public position before 1961, he believed that "nonviolence was a tactic that should be abandoned when it no longer worked." Mandela, *supra* note 30, at 322. He argued his view, which prevailed over the organization's tradition, thus:

the state had given us no alternative to violence. I said it was wrong and immoral to subject our people to armed attacks by the state without offering them some kind of alternative. I mentioned again that people on their own had taken up arms. Violence would begin whether we initiated it or not. Would it not be better to guide this violence ourselves, according to principles where we saved lives by attacking symbols of oppression, and not people? If we did not take the lead now, I said, we would soon be latecomers and followers to a movement that we did not control. *Id.* at 322.

45. *See* John W. Cell, THE HIGHEST STAGE OF WHITE SUPREMACY: THE ORIGINS OF SEGREGATION IN SOUTH AFRICA AND THE AMERICAN SOUTH (New York: Cambridge University Press, 1982), pp. 266–67; John M. Selby, A SHORT HISTORY OF SOUTH AFRICA (London: Allen Unwin, 1973), pp. 250–51.

46. *See* Mandela, *supra* note 30, at 110.

47. Selby, *supra* note 45, at 250–55. *See also supra* note 3.

48. *See* Roland Oliver, THE AFRICAN EXPERIENCE (London: Weidenfeld and Nicolson, 1991), p. 240.

49. *See* Commonwealth Secretariat, MISSION TO SOUTH AFRICA: THE COMMON-

WEALTH REPORT (Harmondsworth: Penguin,1986), pp. 85–89.

50. African National Congress, CONSTITUTIONAL GUIDELINES FOR A NEW SOUTH AFRICA (1989), reprinted in 21 COLUM. HUM. RTS. L. REV., 235 app. A (1989).

51. The Constitutional Guidelines provided that: "The constitution shall include a Bill of Rights based on the Freedom Charter. Such a Bill of Rights shall guarantee the fundamental human rights of all citizens irrespective of race, colour, or creed, and shall provide appropriate mechanisms for their enforcement." *Id.* at 237.

52. The affirmative action clause of the Constitutional Guidelines provided that: "The state and all social institutions shall be under a constitutional duty to take active steps to eradicate, speedily, the economic and social inequalities produced by racial discrimination." *Id.* With regard to the status of women, it provided that: "Women shall have equal rights in all spheres of public and private life and the state shall take affirmative action to eliminate inequalities and discrimination between the sexes." *Id.* at 238.

53. Constitutional Committee, African National Congress, DRAFT BILL OF RIGHTS: A PRELIMINARY REVISED DRAFT (1992), reprinted in Sachs, ADVANCING HUMAN RIGHTS IN SOUTH AFRICA, *supra* note 29, app. 1, at 215.

54. The draft bill provided, in part, that "All South Africans shall, without discrimination, have the right to undisturbed enjoyment of their personal possessions, and, individually, in association or through lawfully constituted bodies, be entitled to acquire, hold or dispose of property." *Id.* at 226. The Bill also conditioned the taking of property on the public interest and just compensation. Elsewhere, the bill stated that "Discrimination on the grounds of gender, single parenthood, legitimacy of birth or sexual orientation shall be unlawful." *Id.* at 222.

55. *Id.* at 222–25.

56. Interview with Geoff Budlender, director-general, Department of Land Affairs, in Pretoria, South Africa (May 1996). Domestic and international pressure caused the gradual collapse of the apartheid state and the repeal in 1990 by the De Klerk white government of several apartheid laws. Key examples were: the Reservation of Separate Amenities Act of 1953, the Land Act of 1913, and the Group Areas Act of 1936. *See* Johan van der Vyver, *Constitutional Options for a Post Apartheid South Africa*, 40 EMORY L.J. 745, 759–60 (1991).

57. These are ANC Constitutional Committee, WHAT IS A CONSTITUTION? (1990); ANC Constitutional Committee, CONSTITUTIONAL PRINCIPLES AND STRUCTURES FOR A DEMOCRATIC SOUTH AFRICA (Bellville, South Africa: Centre for Development Studies, University of Western Cape, 1991). *See* Wing, *supra* note 4, at 359.

58. CODESA was boycotted by the extreme right wing white group Afrikaanse Weerstand Beweging (AWB) and two left-leaning black groups, the PAC and the Azanian Peoples Organization. The PAC charged that the ANC was selling out to the NP government. Philippa Garson, *The PAC Enters the Fray*, AFRICA REP., November–December 1992, at 19.

59. Patrick Laurence, *Buthelezi's Gamble*, AFRICA REP., November–December 1992, at 13.

60. Wing, *supra* note 4, at 366.

61. *See* S. Afr. Const. (Interim Constitution, Act 200 of 1993), sched. 4, Principle 33. The Constitutional Principles enumerated in this section must be met by the

1996 Constitution, which will replace the Interim Constitution, Act 200. *See id.* chap. 5, sec. 71(a).

62. *See id.* chap. 5, sec. 71(a). In May 1996, the NP withdrew from the Government of National Unity (GNU). *South Africa: End of Honeymoon,* SWISS REVIEW OF WORLD AFFAIRS, July 1, 1996, available in LEXIS, News Library, CURNWS File.

63. The Constitution provided that any party with at least 20 seats in the National Assembly or 5 percent of the vote was entitled to one or more cabinet posts in proportion to the seats it held in the National Assembly. In addition, every party that holds at least 80 seats in the National Assembly or 20 percent of the vote is entitled to designate an executive vice president from among the members of the National Assembly. Members of the National Assembly and Senate are determined through proportional representation, a principle that allows minority parties a voice in the legislative process. *See* S. Afr. Const. (Interim Constitution, Act 200 of 1993), chap. 4, secs. 40(1) and 48(1).

64. Both the Interim Constitution and the 1996 Constitution required the president to consult with the leaders of other parties participating in the Government of National Unity before taking and executing policy decisions, making ambassadorial and other senior appointments under the Constitution, and signing international agreements, among other responsibilities. *See* S. Afr. Const. (1996), Annexure B, sec. 1; S. Afr. Const. (Interim Constitution, Act 200 of 1993), chap. 6.

65. The Bill of Rights was entitled "fundamental rights" and drew heavily from the ICCPR and the ICESCR. The rights protected include the traditional civil and political rights as well as nontraditional rights such as the rights to a healthy environment, education, and language and culture. Also protected were children's rights, labor rights, and the unqualified right to life. *See* S. Afr. Const. (1996), Annexure B, sec.1; S. Afr. Const. (Interim Constitution, Act 200 of 1993), chap. 6.

66. The property clause was hotly contested because of the exclusion of blacks from economic life by apartheid and the total control by whites of virtually all economic resources. As it stands, the clause caters to both groups, although white property owners had cause to celebrate its wording. It protected the right of every person to acquire property and to dispose of it and prohibited expropriation without compensation. This language permitted blacks to acquire property, a right Africans were generally denied during apartheid, but it also protected white property owners. In any case, the mere right to own property was of little consequence to a segment of the population that has few or no resources to acquire property in the first place. *See* S. Afr. Const. (Interim Constitution, Act 200 of 1993) chap. 3, sec. 28.

67. *Id.* chap. 7, sec. 98. The Constitutional Court is composed of a president and ten other judges who are appointed by the State president for a nonrenewable seven-year term. *Id.* chap. 7, sec. 99. Most of the judges of the current Constitutional Court have strong reputations as human rights lawyers and scholars.

68. *Id.* chap. 7, sec. 98(2).

69.Sachs, *Areas of Agreement and Disagreement, supra* note 29, at 15. *See also* L. W. H. Ackermann, *Constitutional Protection of Human Rights: Judicial Review,* 21 COLUM. HUM. RTS. L. REV. 59 (1989), discussing the need for judicial review, which was nonexistent in apartheid South Africa, in a post-apartheid state. *See* Wing, *supra* note 4, at 359.

70. *See* S. Afr. Const. (Interim Constitution, Act 200 of 1993) chap. 5, secs. 71, 73–74. The new Constitution could not have come into force unless it was certified by the Constitutional Court. *Id.* sec. 71(2).

71. *Id.* chap. 8.

72. *See id.* secs. 115-18. *See also* Human Rights Commission Act (No. 54) of 1994, further defining the powers of the Human Rights Commission and the responsibilities of its officials.

73. S. Afr. Const. (Interim Constitution, Act 200 of 1993) chap. 8, secs. 110–14. *See also* Public Protector Act (No. 23) of 1994.

74. S. Afr. Const. (Interim Constitution, Act 200 of 1993) chap. 8, secs. 119–20.

75. *Id.* secs. 122-23. *See also* Restitution of Land Rights Act (No. 22) of 1994.

76. S. Afr. Const. (Interim Constitution, Act 200 of 1993) chap. 8, secs. 98 and 101.

77. The TRC was based on the final clause of the Interim Constitution, which called for a mechanism to address human rights abuses during the apartheid era. *See also* The Promotion of National Unity and Reconciliation Act (No. 34) of 1995. For a brief description of the history, purpose, structure, and mandate of the Truth Commission, *see* Republic of South Africa, Ministry of Justice (Justice in Transition), TRUTH AND RECONCILIATION COMMISSION (Pretoria: Government of South Africa, 1995).

78. The IEC was dissolved after the 1994 elections and replaced by a permanent Electoral Commission. See Independent Electoral Commission Act (No. 150) of 1993.

79. S. Afr. Const. (Interim Constitution, Act 200 of 1993) chap. 12, secs. 191–94.

80. S. Afr. Const. (1996) chap. 11, sec. 181(1)(c) and chap. 12, secs. 185–86. It was ironic that Afrikaners, who had either denied or marginalized the cultural and linguistic rights of blacks and other nonwhite minorities, would seek protection for similar rights under the new Constitution. Although Afrikaners are a numerical minority, they still overwhelmingly command important institutions in the new state and the economic sector.

81. This body is "intended to regulate broadcasting in the public interest, and to ensure fairness and a diversity of views broadly representing South African society." *Id.* chap. 12, sec. 192.

82. The final clause of the Interim Constitution is entitled "National Unity and Reconciliation," and emphasized the need for magnanimously addressing past human rights violations to build a foundation for a secure and fair society.

83. Public officials, mostly Afrikaner, were guaranteed security of tenure, a fact that has made it difficult to restructure and transform the bureaucracy and create a representative civil service. S. Afr. Const. (Interim Constitution, Act 200 of 1993) chap. 15, secs. 229–50. Specifically, sec. 236(2) guarantees continued employment to persons employed in a public service or department of state prior to April 27, 1994, the date of entry into force of the Interim Constitution.

84 *Id.* chap. 5, sec. 73(1). The Constitutional Assembly had to pass a new constitution by May 9, 1996, two years from the first sitting of the National Assembly under the Interim Constitution, or the president would dissolve Parliament and call a new election. The new Constitution is a result of extensive negotiations, particularly between the ANC and the NP, and widespread public hearings and a

national media campaign. As a result of these thorough consultations, the more than 1.7 million submissions entered by the public were summarized and made available to the Constitutional Assembly. Similarly, the progress of the constitution-making process and analyses of issues were frequently and regularly presented to the public through the print and broadcast media and the Internet. *See* UN Needs Assessment Report, *supra* note 5, at 8.

85. In September 1996, the Constitutional Court declined to certify the 1996 Constitution, holding that it did not fully comply with a number of Constitutional Principles set out in the Interim Constitution. *See* Certification of the Constitution of the Republic of South Africa, 1996, 1996 (4) SA 744 (CC). On December 4, 1996, the Constitutional Court certified the 1996 Constitution after the Constitutional Assembly revised it to respond to the objections of the Constitutional Court. *See* Certification of the Amended Text of the Constitution of the Republic of South Africa, *supra* note 6.

86. S. Afr. Const. (Interim Constitution, Act 200 of 1993) chap. 5, sec. 73(13).

87. S. Afr. Const. (1996 Constitution) chap. 14, sec. 243(1)

88. For example, S. Afr. Const. (Interim Constitution, Act 200 of 1993) sched. 4, Principle 32 is incorporated in S. Afr. Const. (1996) Annexure B. The same arrangement of a multi-party government of unity applied to provincial governments. *See* S. Afr. Const. (1996) Annexure C.

89. This is the title (and the name given to independent human rights commissions and other watchdogs) of the chapter providing for human rights institutions in the S. Afr. Const. (1996 Constitution) chap. 9, secs. 181-94.

90. *Id.* chap. 9, sec. 184(1)

91 The HRC has the power to compel testimony, search premises, and subpoena witnesses. *See* Human Rights Commission Act (No. 54) of 1994, secs. 9, 10. *Id.* sec. 7(1)(e); S. Afr. Const. (1996) chap. 9, sec. 184(2).

92. These are the rights to housing, health care, food, water, social security, education, and the environment. S. Afr. Const. (1996) sec. 184(3).

93. The HRC was inaugurated on October 2, 1995 and opened its offices in Johannesburg in March 1996. UN Needs Assessment Report, *supra* note 5, at 35.

94. As Alston has clearly stated, both national and international human rights law have done little to give content to the norms of economic, social, and cultural rights:

By contrast [to the ICCPR], the range of rights recognized in the other Covenant [ICESCR] was, with the exception of labor-related rights, considerably in advance of most national legislation. Indeed, this is still the case today so that international lawyers seeking enlightenment as to the meaning of rights such as those pertaining to food, education, health care, clothing, and shelter will find little direct guidance in national law.

Alston, *supra* note 18, at 490.

95. For South Africa, the language of the Constitution requires, for example, that "The state must take reasonable legislative and other measures, within its available resources, to achieve the progressive realization of each of these rights [that is, rights to health care, food, water, and social security]," S. Afr. Const. (1996) chap. 2, sec. 27. This language echoes the phrasing of the ICESCR, which requires each state to take steps "to the maximum of its available resources, with a view to

achieving progressively the full realization of the rights recognized in the Covenant." International Covenant on Economic, Social and Cultural Rights, G.A. Res. 2200 A, UN GAOR, 21st Sess., Supp. No. 16, at 49, UN Doc. A/6316 (1966) [hereinafter ICESCR], at 49.

96. Constitutional Court of South Africa, Case CCT 32/97, November 27, 1997 or <www.law.wits.ac.za/judgements/soobram.html>.

97. Section 229 of the 1996 draft text of the Constitution violated Constitutional Principle 18. S. Afr. Const. (1996) chap. 7.

98. Certification of the Constitution of the Republic of South Africa, 1996, 1996 (4) SA 744 (CC), 483.

99. Office of the President, *President Mandela on the Constitutional Court Judgement* (September 9, 1996).

100. Interview with Shadrack Gutto, *supra* note 5. This view is supported by the Constitutional Court's rejection of the draft 1996 Constitution because of its strong centralizing thrust, a key objection of the IFP. *See* R.W. Johnson, *Boost for ANC After New South African Constitution Spurns Federalism*, London TIMES, December 10, 1996, *available in* LEXIS, News Library, CURNWS File.

101. *See* Gumisai Mutume, *South African Politics: IFP Returns to the Fold*, INTER PRESS SERVICE, October 1, 1996, *available in* LEXIS, News Library, CURNWS File.

102. *Id.*

103. These include human dignity and life, for which derogation is entirely prohibited, and others, including freedom and security of the person, to which some degree of derogation is permitted. S. Afr. Const. (1996) chap. 2, sec. 37 (5)(c).

104. *Id.* chap. 4, sec. 60.

105. *Id.* chap. 4, secs. 74, 75 and 76. Note that the provinces remain the same although some were renamed: Eastern Cape, Free State, Gauteng, KwaZulu-Natal, Mpumalanga, Northern Cape, Northern Province, North West, and Western Cape.

106. *Id.* chap. 14, sec. 235. The new constitution extends to provincial authorities essentially the same concurrent and exclusive legislative competencies as before. *Id.* schedules 4 and 5.

107. For example, India, the world's largest democracy, also has the largest number of illiterate citizens. *See* Myron Weiner, THE CHILD AND THE STATE IN INDIA: CHILD LABOR AND EDUCATION POLICY IN COMPARATIVE PERSPECTIVE (Princeton, N.J.: Princeton University Press, 1991), p. 3. With a population of 935,744,000, India has a per capita income of US$290. *See* 1996 BRITANNICA BOOK OF THE YEAR, at 628.

108. As put by one South African intellectual:

In the context of South Africa, the majority of whose people have inherited extreme levels of poverty, malnutrition, and political, social, and economic deprivations, democracy means much more than the right to vote in a multiparty system. It means the ability of the new government to satisfy the basic educational, social, and economic needs of the victims of oppression in a manner that will significantly narrow the gap between white affluence and mass (black) poverty.

Sipho Shezi, *South Africa: State Transformation and the Management of Collapse*, in I. William Zartman ed., COLLAPSED STATES: THE DISINTEGRATION AND RESTORATION OF LEGITIMATE AUTHORITY (Boulder, Colo.: Lynne Reinner, 1995), pp. 200–201.

109. *See* Gassama, *supra* note 14, at 1531.

110. The Freedom Charter advocated the restoration of the country's wealth to all South Africans and the transfer of mineral wealth, banks, and other industrial monopolies to ownership by the people. *See* FREEDOM CHARTER, *supra* note 32, at 250. The United States was for a long time bitterly opposed to the ANC, which it deemed communist and a surrogate of the Soviet Union during the Cold War. President Reagan commended Pretoria's repressive practices, which he saw as the regime's right to maintain law and order against "terrorists" (ANC). He harshly attacked the alliance between the ANC and the South African Communist Party (SACP) and the support of the two by the Soviet Union. *See* Michael Clough, FREE AT LAST? U.S. POLICY TOWARD AFRICA AND THE END OF THE COLD WAR (New York: Council on Foreign Relations Press, 1992), p. 106.

111. Gassama, *supra* note 14, at 1533–34.

112. Mandela, *supra* note 30, at 642.

113. UN Needs Assessment Report, *supra* note 5, at 7.

114. *See* RECONSTRUCTION AND DEVELOPMENT PROGRAMME, *supra* note 17, at 4–7.

115. *Id.* at 7-13.

116. *Id.* at 78-79.

117. *Id.* at 79.

118. *Id.* at 84.

119. UN Needs Assessment Report, *supra* note 5, at 7. A cabinet member in the government gave the RDP clout, profile, and independence, and established it as an important point of reference to which all state institutions could address their concerns. The cancellation of the cabinet post downgrades the RDP and reduces its visibility and urgency.

120. Gassama has articulated this point well:

In the course of the negotiations [CODESA] and during the electoral campaign, the ANC in fact devoted considerable energy toward reassuring South African and international investors and financial institutions about its socio-economic plans. The ANC made it clear that it would not take any radical steps to change the economic conditions it would inherit. To some extent then, economic inequalities were ratified or legitimated by the very process of negotiations and the subsequent elections. The South African civil service, the foreign service, the police, the military, and the business sector are still dominated by the very people who presided over or prospered under apartheid, their jobs and privileges protected under the new arrangement.

Gassama, *supra* note 14, at 1531–21.

121. *Id.* at 1533.

122. In the period between April 1994—when the ANC won the elections—and December 1995, South Africa's net inflows of capital totaled R30.8 billion, compared with net outflows of R51.7 billion between 1985 and April 1994, at the height of the country's isolation internationally. *See* Ben Hirschler, *Rand Rate Rise Hurt. S. African Business Confidence*, REUTER EUR. BUS. REP., May 7, 1996, available in LEXIS, News Library, CURNWS File.

123. The nature of the displacement of the apartheid state and the transitional arrangements agreed to by the ANC made sure to leave intact economic disparities between blacks and whites. According to a noted South African political analyst:

"Much of the new constitution [Interim Constitution] was devoted to assuring the white minority that the tables would not be turned on them in a regime of vengeance. It promised cabinet seats to minority parties for the first five years, and it protected the jobs and pensions of white soldiers, police, and civil servants." *See* Allister Sparks, TOMORROW IS ANOTHER COUNTRY: THE INSIDE STORY OF SOUTH AFRICA'S ROAD TO CHANGE (New York: Hill and Wang, 1995), p. 194.

124. Sachs, ADVANCING HUMAN RIGHTS IN SOUTH AFRICA, *supra* note 29, at 70, 72.

125. 1996 BRITANNICA BOOK OF THE YEAR, at 716.

126. *See* Sebastian Mallaby, AFTER APARTHEID: THE FUTURE OF SOUTH AFRICA (New York: Times Books, 1992), p. 446. *See also* Zola Skweyiya, *Toward a Solution to the Land Question in Post Apartheid South Africa: Problems and Models,* 21 COLUM. HUM. RTS. L. REV. 211 (1989).

127. GREEN PAPER, *supra* note 28, at 9.

128. RECONSTRUCTION AND DEVELOPMENT PROGRAMME, *supra* note 17, at 19–20

129. *Id.* at 20.

130. S. Afr. Const. (1996) chap. 2, sec. 25.

131. GREEN PAPER, *supra* note 28, at iii. Land redistribution is also intended to benefit "farm workers, labour tenants, women and entrepreneurs." *Id.*

132. *Id.* at 25.

133 *Id.* at 52-53.

134 *Id.* at 25. Under the Provision of Certain Land for Settlement Act (No. 126) of 1993, the government estimates that 13,500 families will obtain land for rural settlement. *Id.* at 4.

135. S. Afr. Const. (1996) chap. 2, sec. 25. Wing notes that the costs of the just compensation requirement impede redistribution. In Zimbabwe, a decade after independence, the government had managed to resettle only one-third of 160,000 families who had been promised land at independence. Wing, *supra* note 4, at 358.

136. GREEN PAPER, *supra* note 28, at iii. It is estimated that 3.5 million people, mostly black, were removed from their lands between 1960 and 1980. *Id.* at 9.

137. *Id.* at 20. Other laws used to remove blacks from their lands include the Black Administration Act of 1927, the Development Native Trust and Land Act of 1936, the Group Areas Acts of 1950, 1957, and 1966, and the Black Resettlement Act of 1954. *Id.* at 36.

138. Restitution of Land Rights Act (No. 22) of 1994 (establishing the Commission on Restitution of Land Rights); S. Afr. Const. (Interim Constitution, Act 200 of 1993) chap. 8, secs. 121–22 (providing for the establishment and powers of the Commission on Restitution of Land Rights). The Commission was established on January 18, 1995, with the Chief Land Claims Commissioner and four Regional Commissioners. Commission on Restitution of Land Rights, FIRST ANNUAL REPORT (Capetown: Commission on Restitution of Land Rights, 1996), p. 2.

139. The Land Claims Court, which was created under the Restitution of Land Rights Act of 1994, was sworn in on March 29, 1996. GREEN PAPER ON LAND, *supra* note 28, at 20; *See also* Commission on Restitution of Land Rights, *supra* note 138, at 2.

140. Commission on Restitution of Land Rights, *supra* note 138, at 10.

141. *See* Glynnis Underhill, *Square Deal for My Lady Cavendish . . .,* SATURDAY

WEEKEND ARGUS, Capetown, May 18/19, 1996; Regional Office of the Commission on Restitution of Land Rights (Northern and Western Cape), MONTHLY REPORT FOR THE MONTH OF APRIL 1996, p. 2, reporting that two claims, involving 200–600 families, had been settled and awaited court validation (on file with author).

142. GREEN PAPER, *supra* note 28, at 43.

143. Shadrack Gutto has written that the land reform program does not historically depart from other market-oriented land reform programs in Kenya and Zimbabwe, which eventually confirmed the status quo and failed to alleviate the problem of the poor and the landless. Gutto argues that the challenge for South Africa is finding a middle road between state ownership of land, as happened in Mozambique, and the market, as happened in Kenya, without surrendering to either. *See* Shadrack Gutto, PROPERTY AND LAND REFORM: CONSTITUTIONAL AND JURISPRUDENTIAL PERSPECTIVES (Durban: Butterworths, 1995), pp. 59–67.

144. GREEN PAPER, *supra* note 28, at 2.

145. Adrien K. Wing and Eunice P. de Carvalho, *Black South African Women: Toward Equal Rights,* 8 HARV. HUM. RTS. J. 57, 58 (1995). According to 1980 figures, white women made up 7.8 percent of the population, while the Colored and Indian women constituted 4.6 percent and 1.3 percent respectively.

146. *Id.* at 67–69, 70–75. For example, the estimated one million black women who worked at "domestics" in white homes were not guaranteed minimum wages, maternity benefits, maximum work hours, or job security. *Id.* at 68. *see also* U.S. Department of State, COUNTRY REPORTS ON HUMAN RIGHTS PRACTICES FOR 1991 (1992), pp. 371-72, discussing the subordinate status of women, especially black women, in South Africa.

147. The dual system was created under the Black Administration Act (No. 38) of 1927 (amended most recently in 1991). *See* T. W. Bennett, THE APPLICATION OF CUSTOMARY LAW IN SOUTHERN AFRICA: THE CONFLICT OF PERSONAL LAWS (Cape Town: Juta, 1985), p. 41. *See also* Wing and de Carvalho, *supra* note 145, at 63—64.

148. The Bantu Homelands Citizenship Act of 1970 started the process of divesting blacks of their South African citizenship. *See* Geoffrey Bindman, SOUTH AFRICA: HUMAN RIGHTS AND THE RULE OF LAW (London: Pinter, 1988), p. 25.

149. *See, e.g.,* Yvonne Mokgoro, *The Role and Place of Lay Participation, Customary and Community Courts in a Restructured Future Judiciary,* in Michelle Norton, ed., RESHAPING THE STRUCTURES OF JUSTICE FOR A DEMOCRATIC SOUTH AFRICA (Vlaeberg: National Association of Lawyers, 1994), p. 75 [hereinafter RESHAPING THE STRUCTURES OF JUSTICE].

150. *Id. See also* Wing and de Carvalho, *supra* note 145, at 63–65.

151. Wing and Carvalho, *supra* note 145, at 64. *See also* Kim Robinson, *The Minority and Subordinate Status of African Women under Customary Law,* 11 S. AFR. J. HUM. RTS. 457 (1995).

152. The RDP has boldly stated that gender equity and the elevation of the status of women must be one of the central goals of the post-apartheid state:

Ensuring gender equity is another central component in the overall democratization of our society. The RDP envisages special attention being paid to the empowerment of women in general, and of black, rural women in particular. There must be representation of women in all institutions, councils and commissions, and gender issues must be included in the terms of reference of these bodies.

RECONSTRUCTION AND DEVELOPMENT PROGRAMME, *supra* note 17, at 121–22.

153. UN Needs Assessment Report, *supra* note 5, at 10.

154. FREEDOM CHARTER, *supra* note 32, at 249.

155. S. Afr. Const. (Interim Constitution, Act 200 of 1993) chap. 3, sec. 187.

156. *Id.* sec. 7(1).

157. *Id.* sec. 8(3)(a).

158. *Id.* chap. 8, secs. 119-20; S. Afr. Const. (1996 Constitution) chap. 9, sec. 187.

159. *See* Wing and de Carvalho, *supra* note 145, at 80-85. In contrast to the apartheid regimes of the past, women are beginning to play more meaningful and visible roles in public life, although much remains to be done. The ANC promise of creating a nonsexist society received a boost from the 1994 elections. Almost one-third of all members of the National Assembly are women. Eighteen of the 90 members of the Senate (National Council of Provinces) are women, and a woman is the Speaker of the National Assembly. The ANC set a 50 percent goal for female candidates in the 1995 November local elections. In March 1996, then Deputy President Thabo Mbeki announced the creation of an Office on the Status of Women, to be located in his office. UN Needs Assessment Report, *supra* note 5, at 11.

160. Care should be taken, however, not to engage in the wholesale demonization of African (customary) law as is popular in the West, where commentators primarily highlight only those elements that conflict with equal protection norms. As Justice Mokgoro has noted:

Dispute resolution in traditional African courts gives full recognition to the idea that the public trial is only a minor phase in the progress of a dispute. The aims and procedures in these courts revolve around mediation or arbitration and reconciliation as opposed to adjudication with a win-or-lose result as in western courts.

Mokgoro, *supra* note 149, at 75.

161. UN Needs Assessment Report, *supra* note 5, at 9.

162. *Id.* at 29.

163. In the apartheid era, all judges were appointed by the state president, usually in consultation with the judge president (in the case of provincial divisions of the Supreme Courts) and the chief justice (in the case of the Supreme Court of Appeal), although the consultative element grew out of practice and was not required by the Supreme Court Act. *See* David McQuoid-Mason, *Transformation of the Personnel of the Judiciary*, in RESHAPING THE STRUCTURES OF JUSTICE, *supra* note 149, at 101, 104.

164. Lovell Fernandez, *Analysis and Critique of the Present South African Structures Administering Justice*, in RESHAPING THE STRUCTURES OF JUSTICE, *supra* note 149, at 116, 118–19. *See also* Public Service Act (No. 54) of 1957.

165. Fernandez, *supra* note 164, at 118.

166. The legal profession in South Africa is split into advocates and attorneys: only the former can appear before the Supreme Court and would be eligible for appointment as judges. Attorneys can only appear before the magistrates' courts. Only 10 percent of advocates are black; 90 percent are white. *See* McQuoid-Mason, *supra* note 163, at 106.

167. The magistracy is further divided into two classes: the regular or district

magistrates, who are at the bottom of the ladder, and regional magistrates, who unlike their colleagues must have a law degree. *See* Fernandez, *supra* note 164, at 117–18.

168. As noted by Justice Arthur Chaskalson, president of the Constitutional Court:

There are approximately (as of 1993) 150 judges appointed to the various divisions of the Supreme Court in South Africa. Apart from Judge Mahamed (Ismail) and Judge van den Heever they are all white men. If we add the judges appointed to the courts of Transkei, Bophuthatswana, Venda, and Ciskei ("independent" black homelands) another name can be added to the list of exceptions, Judge Kumalo, but the list of white men would grow even longer. There can be no doubt that the profile of the judiciary needs to be changed.

Arthur Chaskalson, *Reshaping the Structures of Justice for a Democratic South Africa, in* RESHAPING THE STRUCTURES OF JUSTICE, *supra* note 163, at 13, 14.

169. McQuoid-Mason, *supra* note 184, at 106.

170. In 1990, all 144 regional magistrates (in South Africa but excluding the four "independent" homelands) were white, while 807 of the 820 district magistrates were white. Three were Colored, 10 Indian, and not a single one was African. *Id.* at 107.

171. *Id.*

172. Of 1,511 magistrates, 987 were white; 474, most of them from the former homelands, were African; 26 were Colored; and 24 were Indian. *See* Lovell Fernandez and Tseliso Thipanyane, ADMINISTRATION OF JUSTICE IN SOUTH AFRICA: MAGISTRATES AND THEIR COURTS (South Africa: Community Peace Foundation, 1995), p. 27 (on file with the author).

173. Fernandez, *supra* note 164, at 116.

174. *Id.* at 119. As former prosecutors themselves, magistrates are inclined to side with the police or exhibit little functional independence from the executive in general. *See* UN Needs Assessment Report, *supra* note 5, at 29.

175. *See also* Fernandez, *supra* note 164, at 120; UN Needs Assessment Report, *supra* note 5, at 30.

176. Although the minister of justice makes the regulations respecting the conditions of service, functions, powers, and duties of the magistrates, most key decisions are taken by the Magistrates Commission, which initially was appointed by then President De Klerk. *See* Fernandez, *supra* note 164, at 120.

177. *Id.*

178. Phineas Mojapelo, quoted in *Id.* at 120.

179. Fernandez, *supra* note 164, at 120. The retention of the apartheid judiciary defeats one of the key requirements of reform. As noted by Masemola:

The South African revolution will be incomplete if it leaves the present judiciary in place because it is invidiously intertwined with the present state. Conversely, under the ANC Guidelines, the judiciary shall be restructured since it is seen as an instrument of apartheid. Additionally, the present practice of maintaining a largely white judiciary shall, as one point of the restructuring, be terminated.

Nathaniel M. Masemola, *Rights in a Future South African Constitution: The Controversial and the Non-Controversial,* 21 COLUM. HUM. RTS. L. REV. 45, 51 (1989).

180. Dullah Omar, an advocate, formerly directed the Community Law Centre at the University of the Western Cape, which played a leading role in the formulation of the new constitutional order in South Africa. *See* Community Law Centre, 1995 ANNUAL REPORT (1995), p. 5. As the minister of justice, Omar started a process for major reforms of the system of the administration of justice. *See* Ministry of Justice, JUSTICE VISION 2000 (1996). Justice Vision 2000, which was formulated by Omar and the newly created Planning Unit of the Ministry of Justice, was the strategic plan to transform the administration of justice. It focused on six key areas: the unification and integration of the Department of Justice; access to justice through legal representation, the use of plain language to simplify law and legal processes, and the use of alternative dispute resolutions mechanisms; addressing crime through reform of the criminal processes in concert with other government agencies; reforming the courts to make them accessible, service-oriented, fair and predictable, representative, and professional; training personnel to assimilate and advance reform; and reform of the legal profession as a whole to make it accessible, representative, and professional. *Id. See also* UN Needs Assessment Report, *supra* note 5, at 28; interview with Dullah Omar, minister of justice, in Cape Town, South Africa (May 17, 1996); interview with Enver Daniels, senior advisor to minister of justice, in Cape Town, South Africa (May 16–17, 1996); interview with Essa Moosa, director, Planning Unit, Ministry of Justice, in Cape Town, South Africa (May 19, 1996); interview with Thuli Madonsela and Medard Rwelamira, Planning Unit, Ministry of Justice, in Pretoria, South Africa (May 21, 1996). Omar was also the major force behind the conceptualization and formulation of the Truth and Reconciliation Commission. *See* Ministry of Justice, TRUTH AND RECONCILIATION COMMISSION (1995), pp. 3–4.

181. Only the high courts (High Courts, Supreme Court of Appeal, and Constitutional Court) may "enquire into or rule on the constitutionality of any legislation or any conduct of the President." S. Afr. Const. (1996) chap. 8, sec. 170. The structure of the judiciary in South Africa is as follows. The Constitutional Court sits at the pinnacle, and directly under it is the Supreme Court of Appeal (formerly the appellate division of the Supreme Court). The High Courts, formerly the Supreme Courts, come next, and at the bottom of the ladder are the magistrates courts. *Id.* sec. 166.

182. *Id.* secs. 174, 178. The JSC is sharply different from the Magistrates Commission, which is dominated by apartheid era officials connected to the Department of Justice. In contrast, the JSC, which is a creation of the ANC-led government, is regarded as progressive and committed to the reform of the judiciary. UN Needs Assessment Report, *supra* note 5, at 31.

183. True to its billing, the Constitutional Court, which is composed of many of the most prominent human rights lawyers in South Africa, is quickly earning a well-deserved reputation as a human rights court. In just its second decision, the Constitutional Court abolished the death penalty, a long term goal of the ANC, by declaring the punishment unconstitutional. State v. Makwanyane & Mchunu, 1995 (3) SALR 391 (CC). Other rulings have limited the use of coerced confessions by the police, banned corporal punishment in the criminal justice system, upheld the right to state-funded counsel, and guaranteed access to police records. U.S. Department of State, *supra* note 159, at 241-48.

184. In November 1996, the Ministry of Justice started a joint project with human rights NGOs, bar associations, and human rights programs at universities

for the further education of lawyers from historically black universities who have been traditionally excluded from major commercial practice. Telephone interview with Shadrack Gutto, CALS, *supra note 5.*

185. Community courts were unofficial tribunals that were formed in black areas—to fill the vacuum left by the illegitimacy of the apartheid courts—beginning in the 1960s to adjudicate disputes. *See* Mokgoro, *supra* note 1149, at 76-78; RECONSTRUCTION AND DEVELOPMENT PROGRAMME, *supra* note 17, at 124.

186. These forces were the "agents of oppression." RECONSTRUCTION AND DEVELOPMENT PROGRAMME, *supra* note 17, at 124. *See also* Basil Davidson, AFRICA IN HISTORY: THEMES AND OUTLINES (New York: Collier Books, 1991), pp. 341–51.

187. This reliance on the security forces is put succinctly by Shezi:

Feeling the loss of political initiative and control, the state resorted to the intensification of repression. Increasingly, the control of the state shifted to the securocrats—a tightly knit security bureaucratic infrastructure led by the top echelons of the South African Defense Force, South African Police, and the National Intelligence Service, who assumed a significant political role of the state, especially under P. W. Botha in the 1980s.

Shezi, *supra* note 108, at 193 (citations omitted).

188. UN Needs Assessment Report, *supra* note 5, at 14.

189. RECONSTRUCTION AND DEVELOPMENT PROGRAMME, *supra* note 17, at 124.

190. Compare S. Afr. Const. (Interim Constitution, Act 200 of 1993) chap. 14 with S. Afr. Const. (1996) chap. 11.

191. S. Afr. Const. (1996) chap. 11, secs. 204, 208 (defense and police civilian secretariats.)

192. U.S. Department of State, *supra* note 159, at 241.

193. UN Needs Assessment Report, *supra* note 5, at 14.

194.U.S. Department of State, *supra* note 159, at 241.

195. S. Afr. Const. (Interim Constitution, Act 200 of 1993) chap. 14, sec. 221. This could be a double-edged sword. Local property owners, working in cahoots with the police, could use this tool to privatize apartheid or entrench practices of exclusion and discrimination on any number of grounds.

196. Henkin notes that the idea of human rights has "commanded universal nominal acceptance, not (as in the past) the divine right of kings or the omnipotent state, not the inferiority of races or women, not even socialism." *See* Henkin, *supra* note 1, at ix–x.

197. As noted by Cyril Ramaphosa, former ANC secretary-general, one of the key founders of the new state, and a major force during the negotiations to end apartheid, the ANC long knew that it wanted a human rights constitution:

The Constitution must enshrine human rights. South Africa under successive National Party governments (including the present government) has a history of violations of human rights. Our long suffering tells us that we need to end the phenomenon of gross violation of human rights. The ANC does not seek to replace one kind of domination with another. We do not want reverse violation of human rights. That is why the ANC insists upon the incorporation within the context of a new constitution of a bill of rights which contains the universally and internationally recognized human rights enshrined in various United Nations documents and instruments.

M. Cyril Ramaphosa, *A Constitutional Framework for a New South Africa*, 28 Stan. J. Int'l L. 23, 28 (1991).

198. The high courts, headed by the Constitutional Court, are placed at the ready to pounce on legislation or any government conduct or action that violates human rights norms. The human rights commissions, which are independent watchdog agencies, supplement the role of the courts in supporting the new constitutional order.

199. Gassama, *supra* note 14, at 1540. *See also* Karl E. Klare, *Legal Theory and Democratic Reconstruction: Reflections on 1989*, 25 U. Brit. Colum. L. Rev. 69, 97–99 (1991), discussing the limitations of rights in bringing about social change.

200. Klare, *supra* note 199, at 101.

Conclusion

1. Mary Ann Glendon, A World Made New: Eleanor Roosevelt and the Universal Declaration of Rights (New York: Random House, 2001).

Index

Acknowledgments

It is customary for authors to thank those who have been most helpful in the research, writing, and preparation of a book. Yet I think this is a custom that cannot be fully faithful to history. So I find myself in a terrible quandary because I really do not know—and cannot tell—exactly when and where this project started. Nor can I remember all those who have educated and influenced me and are therefore ultimately implicated in this work. This is true for the distant past as well as the present. So I painfully recognize these limitations even as I directly identify some of those to whom I owe my gratitude for their help.

My scholarship and academic career have benefited greatly from many people, some of whom provided me with valuable insights for parts of this book. In this regard, I want to express my deep appreciation to Bill Alford, Antony Anghie, Abdullahi An-Na'im, Roberto Aponte Toro, Jamal Benomar, Nathaniel Berman, Guyora Binder, Marcella David, Karen Engle, Ibrahim Gassama, James Gathii, Mohan Gopal, Shadrack Gutto, David Hall, Leila Hilal, Robert Howse, Mary Ann Glendon, Joseph Kanywanyi, David Kennedy, Duncan Kennedy, Randall Kennedy, Benedict Kingsbury, Edward Kwakwa, Hope Lewis, Mahmood Mamdani, Isabel Marcus, Frank Michelman, Martha Minow, Felix Morka, Willy Mutunga, Balakrishnan Rajagopal, Henry Richardson, Peter Rosenblum, Issa Shivji, Anne-Marie Slaughter, the late Frederick Snyder, Henry J. Steiner, Charles Ogletree, Obiora Okafor, Joe Oloka-Onyango, Richard Parker, Claude E. Welch, Adrien Wing, David Wilkins, and John Witte.

It has been my good fortune to learn from my work with Evelyn Ankumah, Stephanie Kleine Ahlbrandt, Alice Brown, Margaret Burnham, Bernadette Cisse, Maina Kiai, Alamin Mazrui, Gay McDougall, and Taswell Papier. Their work and experiences have positively influenced this project.

I want to thank Thomas Haidon, Ian Lester, and Thomas Sheehan for their research assistance. I am appreciative of Dawn Fenneman, my assistant at the University at Buffalo School of Law, for her support. I am grateful to the Baldy Center for Law and Social Policy at the University at Buffalo for financially supporting my research and other costs related to the preparation of the book manuscript.

I would be remiss if I did not thank Nils Olsen, my dean, for his constant encouragement and support.

I want to acknowledge Bert Lockwood, the Series Editor, for his guidance and support. His dedication and commitment to human rights scholarship are great gifts to the field. I would also like to thank my editors at the University of Pennsylvania Press for a job well done.

Last—but certainly not least—I want to express my deep gratitude and heartfelt thanks to Athena Mutua for her unstinting support and encouragement for my career and scholarship. Her critiques and insights have made me a better writer and a more humane person.